biennial boom

biennial boom

Paloma Checa-Gismero

biennial
boom

MAKING

CONTEMPORARY

ART

GLOBAL

DUKE UNIVERSITY PRESS
Durham and London
2024

Project Editor: Lisa Lawley
Designed by A. Mattson Gallagher
Typeset in Kepler by Westchester Publishing Services

Library of Congress Cataloging-in-Publication Data
Names: Checa-Gismero, Paloma, [date] author.
Title: Biennial boom : making contemporary art global /
Paloma Checa-Gismero.
Description: Durham : Duke University Press, 2024. | Includes
bibliographical references and index.
Identifiers: LCCN 2023043182 (print)
LCCN 2023043183 (ebook)
ISBN 9781478030515 (paperback)
ISBN 9781478026280 (hardcover)
ISBN 9781478059486 (ebook)
Subjects: LCSH: Bienal de La Habana. | inSite (Exhibition) |
Manifesta. | Biennials (Art fairs)—History. | Art, Modern—
20th century—Exhibitions—History. | Art and globalization—
History—20th century. | Art—Political aspects. | BISAC: ART /
History / Contemporary (1945–) | ART / Criticism & Theory
Classification: LCC N4396 .C44 2024 (print) | LCC N4396
(ebook) | DDC 709.04—dc23/eng/20240126
LC record available at https://lccn.loc.gov/2023043182
LC ebook record available at https://lccn.loc.gov/2023043183

Cover art: Henrik Plenge Jakobsen, *Everything is Wrong*
(two details), Manifesta 1, Witte de With, Rotterdam, 1996.
Acrylics on wall, 400 × 400 cm. Courtesy of the artist.

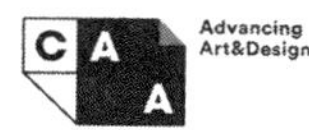

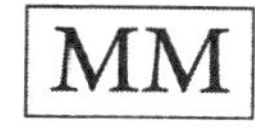

PUBLICATION OF THIS BOOK HAS BEEN AIDED BY
A GRANT FROM THE MILLARD MEISS PUBLICATION
FUND OF CAA.

For Christo

CONTENTS

Plates

ACKNOWLEDGMENTS

As I look back into the last decade, I am humbled by the many individuals whose work and vision have shaped my own. I am genuinely grateful for the imagination and commitment of all artists, curators, and arts administrators who worked to create the objects and exhibitions considered in this study, sometimes from the center but often from the uncertain margins of established cultural circuits. In order to learn about these histories, I have relied on a number of institutional archives. I am deeply grateful to the generous staff at the archives at Centro de Arte Wifredo Lam (Havana), Casa de las Américas (Havana), Casa del Historiador (Havana), the Cuba Heritage Collection at the University of Miami Libraries (Miami), el Centro de Documentación, Información e Investigación Arkheia del Museo Universitario de Arte Contemporáneo (Mexico City), Casa Lamm (Mexico City), Archivo del Museo Tamayo (Mexico City), Special Collections Library at the University of California, San Diego (San Diego), Centro de Documentación del Museo Nacional Reina Sofía (Madrid), Manifesta Foundation (Amsterdam), Witte de With Center for Contemporary Art (renamed Kunstinstituut Melly, Rotterdam), Het Nieuwe Instituut (Rotterdam), and BAD Foundation (Rotterdam). Through conversations and interviews since 2013, generous interlocutors have helped me complicate and supplement archival materials, refining the complex histories that documents pointed me to and often facilitating artwork images that were difficult to find. In no particular order, I thank Gerardo Mosquera, Lesbia Vent Dubois, José Manuel Noceda, Nélson Herrera Ysla, Margarita González, Margarita Sánchez, Dannys Montes de Oca, Jorge Fernández Torres, Llilian Llanes, Luis Camnitzer, José Manuel Valenzuela, Michael Krichman, Carmen Cuenca, Osvaldo Sánchez, Lucía Sanromán, Melanie Smith, Irmgard Emmelhainz, Merete Kjaer, Lucy Lippard, Fiamma Montezemolo, Kamiel Verschuren,

Wendy Bos, Adelheid Smit, Jeanne van Heeswijk, Marieke van Hal, Nury González, Eugenio Dittborn, Terry Allen, Louis Hock, Rubén Ortiz Torres, Janet Koenig, Gregory Sholette, Abraham Cruzvillegas, Willy Thayer, Felipe Cooper, Eduardo Abaroa, Sofía Táboas, Iosif Király, Henrik Plenge Jakobsen, Joseph Grigely, Miran Mohar, Dušan Mandič, and many others.

I am honored to have received generous support for my inquiry throughout its many stages, support that has equipped me to better respond to the many challenges that arise from contemporary, multi–case-study, transdisciplinary work. I am grateful for a Meiss Publication Support Award, College of Art Association (2022); a Constance Hungerford Faculty Development Award, Swarthmore College (2020); a Visual Arts Department Dissertation Completion Fellowship, UC San Diego (2018–2019); a University of California Humanities Research Institute (UCHRI) Dissertation Support Award (2018–2019); a University of California-Cuba Summer Research Fellowship (2017); a Russel Grant, Visual Arts Department, UC San Diego (2017); three Tinker Summer Research Grants, Center for Iberian and Latin American Studies at UC San Diego (2014, 2015, 2016); two graduate awards by the Friends of the International House, UC San Diego (2015, 2018); and research funding from the Visual Arts Department, UC San Diego (2013–2016).

In addition to these important sources of financial support, I consider myself extremely fortunate to have been mentored by caring and dedicated scholars. At UC San Diego I was lucky to receive from Mariana Botey, Norman Bryson, David Serlin, Luis Alvarez, and Rachel Weiss crucial guidance on the histories, methods, and theories that informed my analysis as well as on approaches to writing that inspired its final form. I am especially indebted to Grant Kester for his continued generosity since 2013. Unlike many leading scholars, Grant practices what he theorizes, modeling an approach to scholarly work that is dialogical and inclusive, selfless and empathy-driven. His important contribution to the field of art history matches his commitment to a more just world, both of which have transpired in our many conversations to date and shape my own work as a teacher and a researcher. At Swarthmore College I have been welcomed by an effervescent intellectual community of scholars who have continued to nourish my work. In particular, I thank my colleagues Brian Goldstein, Patricia Reilly, and Patricia White for their friendship and mentorship, and my students in the art history program for the exceptional class discussions about many of the materials included in this book.

In addition to these individuals, throughout the years this project has benefited from the feedback of friends and scholars who have helped me develop an approach of my own to the study of this thing we call art. I am indebted to Natalia Brizuela and Julia Bryan-Wilson for encouraging me over a decade ago to pursue a career in art history. I thank Claire F. Fox, Izabel Galliera, Matilde Córdoba Azcárate, Tania Islas Weinstein, and Sascha Crasnow for their notes on specific chapters of this book. In seminars and work groups I have learned from peers including Amanda Cachia, Kevan Aguilar, C. C. McKee, Osman Balkan, Ahmad Shokr, and Saúl Hernández Vargas. Conversations with Fernando Domínguez Rubio, Selina Blasco, Alberto Gamoneda, and Gonzalo Navarro informed through the years my thinking on the role that art institutions play in social life. Lesley Stern, Lucy Lippard, and Cristina Rivera Garza have been superb role models for my practice as a writer. Gracias a Tatiana Flores for her rich advice on how to improve my project and, more generally, for the many ways in which she has supported me and my work through the years. In addition, I thank my two reviewers at Duke University Press for their encouragement and prescient observations on this manuscript and members of the Duke University Press Editorial Advisory Board for their input and endorsement of this volume.

Contemporary art historians' access to our case studies often derives from our own proximity to the very industry we study, making us beneficiaries of the structures of power we critique, even as we strive for autonomy. I thank Marti Manen for inviting me to write a catalog essay for *Los Sujetos*, the exhibition he curated for the Spanish Pavilion in the 56th Venice Biennale (2015). I also thank the team behind Manifesta 8 (Murcia, 2010) for selecting my project "La sabiduría del artesano" and allowing me to experience firsthand the inner contradictions of global biennials as an artist years before I set to study them as a historian.

The multiplicity of narratives and interests that surround art informs the muddy pools of meaning in which the art historian paddles, stressing the dialogical nature of our practice—a practice that changes us, historians, as much as it affects the narratives about our present that surround us and we help craft. Many people have contributed to rendering my ideas in clear, accessible form. Cara Jordan edited early versions of these chapters. Laura Portwood-Stacer's advice clarified many questions on manuscript development. My research assistants at Swarthmore, Eva

Baron and José Valdivia, provided important help during the last stages of book preparation. More recently, the skilled team at Duke University Press has gracefully handled me and my materials through my first experience in academic book publishing. I am honored to have worked with Ken Wissoker, who since our first conversation in 2020 has believed in this project and has been a thoughtful editor and solid supporter throughout. I also thank Ryan Kendall, Lisa Lawley, A. Mattson Gallagher, David Rainey, Laura Sell, and Donald Pharr for their labor.

Friends keep reminding me that beauty can only be sensed in the messiness of life. In San Diego, Noni Brynjolson, Patrick Dunford, Alex Kershaw, Andrea Mavros, Katrin Pesch, Tim Ridlen, and Amy Reid were virtuous role models in the arts of cooking, dancing, and surfing during dark historical times. In addition to providing inspiration for my work with their own as artists and scholars, on multiple occasions they have offered very helpful feedback for sections of what is now this book. In Philadelphia, Pilar Goñalons Pons, Sarah Banet-Weiser, Mason Austin, Daniel Aldana Cohen, and Jack Bratich radiated care and comradeship during a cold pandemic writing winter. En las olas de calor de 2022, mientras terminaba revisiones del manuscrito, Carlos Crespo Alonso me sacó a dar paseos nocturnos por Madrid. Un viaje a Kassel con Teresa Solar Abboud me ayudó a tomar distancia y ver nudos en mi argumento con claridad. Ana Núñez González fue, es y será compañera modélica de vinos y confesiones. Finalmente, agradezco a mi familia. A mis hermanos, Eduardo y Andrés, por la bondad, las bromas y el cariño. A mis padres, Rosa y Eduardo, por inculcarme el amor por la lectura y el viaje y una ética de trabajo a los que debo mucho. A los cuatro agradezco su apoyo y amor, siempre.

Among the marvels that California had in store for me are my two life companions. Clio is a scruffy confidant-muse in cuddles and naps. She is the most refined accomplice in strolls through time and plants. To close, I dedicate this book to Christo, my lover and partner. For the past ten years Christo has offered patient, unwavering support. During the research and writing of this book he gave me space when I needed it, held my hand at critical times, and provided endless advice for its improvement and ultimate completion, all of which I am forever grateful for.

Biennial Conversions at the Borders of Liberalism

AN INTRODUCTION

Art biennials are now a familiar exhibition form for publics interested in contemporary art. Many readers of this book have probably heard of them or even visited a few. Others might step foot in an art biennial in the years to come. But art biennials were not always a commonplace way for art audiences to experience contemporary art. Whereas they have existed since the end of the nineteenth century, for most of the twentieth century art biennials played a relatively marginal role compared to museums and galleries in the selection, exhibition, and valuation of institutionally legitimated art. The comparatively marginal significance of the art biennial began to change during the 1980s. In 1983, when Fidel Castro created the Bienal de La Habana by state decree, approximately four art biennials happened regularly throughout the world: the Venice Biennale, the Bienal de São Paulo, the Sydney Biennial, and documenta. By the end of the twentieth century, around 150 biennials had proliferated worldwide, and an estimated 250 biennials sprouted regularly throughout the globe before the onset of the COVID-19 pandemic in 2020.[1] This explosion in art biennials has come to be known by art world insiders as the "biennial boom," and it has prompted important changes in how institutionally legitimated art worlds curate and exhibit art on the international, national, and local levels. What was once a rare and exceptional event has become perhaps the most important staging ground for contemporary art trends, bringing about a reformulation of what we understand as art, how we relate to it, and how knowledge about it is produced.

What triggered this swift proliferation of art biennials? What allowed biennials to become, in such a short period of time, the favored display form of contemporary art professionals and patrons throughout the world? What dreams and desires did early-boom biennials address and help to create? Motivated by these and related questions, this book zooms into three art biennials in the very early years of the biennial boom: the Bienal de La Habana (Havana), inSITE (San Diego and Tijuana), and Manifesta (Rotterdam). By looking closely at these three early cases, the book documents and analyzes the conditions of possibility for the consolidation of the art biennial as the period's dominant exhibition form. Placed at the borders of North Atlantic liberalism, each of the three biennials examined in this book gained prominence shortly before and immediately after the demise of the Soviet Bloc: their emergence was tightly interwoven with the seismic political and economic transformations that led to and accompanied the end of the Cold War. Significantly, each of these three biennials dealt with the end-of-the-century legacies of aesthetic programs bred in socialist revolutions. They all helped prefigure what many hoped would be a largely pacified world at the end of a tumultuous century. Early-boom biennials like these three portrayed themselves not only as exhibitions of artistic innovation and venues for knowledge production but also as mechanisms that would help mend the social, political, and cultural divisions that had accrued during the long Cold War. In the early stages of the 1990s economic and cultural globalization, these exhibits actualized two foundational hypotheses for European modern aesthetics: the possibility of a relation of causality between aesthetic experience and world peace, and art's capacity to articulate truthfully the driving spirit of a historical moment.

The term *art biennial* is applied equally to a variety of temporary exhibits that take place every two, three, or five years in different parts of the world.[2] These large-scale group exhibitions present before audiences a comprehensive selection of artworks that aim to attest to the latest trends in contemporary art. But biennials are not mere reflections of preexisting artistic fashions. Rather, they have become some of the key sites through which the global art world has been constituted and configured in the manner that it has. As this book will show, over the past thirty years, biennials have become increasingly central to the shaping of elite art worlds—including professionals, audiences, aesthetic tendencies, and bodies of knowledge. Their ambitious scope and dimensions require several days of commitment from the audience. Often installed in a variety of venues in their host cities, they invite wandering and sightseeing, blending the phenomenology of art with that of its surroundings for the art tourists who travel the world in pilgrimage chasing the biennial calendar. As Caroline A. Jones explains, the propagation of art biennials has yielded a biennial culture moved by "an appetite for art as experience," a culture that is highly influenced by the practice of tourism and that has a clear impact on the urban fabric where biennials are staged.[3] Biennials are also discursive operations, where artwork selection and installation translate curatorial authorial voices into the gallery.[4] In most cases, biennial curatorial teams change per iteration, bestowing to the biennial phenomenon the function of cyclically delivering newness and feeding an industry of qualified professionals. To their rhythm and spread, Terry Smith adds biennials' aptness to reflect the global contemporary art world's capacity to entertain, instruct, and fuel competition, as well as their role in facilitating negotiations between local and global art worlds.[5] Some biennials have at times restricted their artist selection to a particular constituency, with the purpose of advancing the artistic production of a specific community or creating new regional artistic categories; however, others embrace variably loose notions of the "global" to signal their scope. Although explicit political affiliation is not a constant, many of these events have outspokenly embraced particular political causes. Others have remained seemingly apolitical in their programmatic stances—a silence that hasn't, however, made them politically innocuous.[6]

Biennial Conversions

The fall of the Berlin Wall kindled a newfound sense of relief for many across the globe—especially through the regions on the East and the West of the Iron Curtain divide, who since 1947 had lived through the many conflicts of the long Cold War. The magic of the moment spread over the following few years, as the Soviet Union collapsed and liberal democracy stormed, hand in hand with capitalism, into the former socialist states, announcing an end to decades-old antinomies. The public was ripe for feelings of interrelation, closeness, and communion. Markets grew to incorporate products, consumers, and industries that had previously been off-limits, launching a new era of economic and cultural globalization. Books were written; songs were sung.[7]

Art also reflected this optimistic vision of a world rapidly reordering. After a difficult 1980s marked by the HIV/AIDS epidemic and hostile cultural policies in the North Atlantic art capitals, contemporary art worlds in early-1990s Western Europe and the United States experienced significant shifts.[8] Economic recession hindered contemporary art acquisitions, prompting a younger generation of contemporary artists to embrace a wide diversity of media to reflect the times' reordering of boundaries and renewed experience of connectedness. In the 1993 Whitney Biennial, for example, Allan Sekula's *Fish Story* reflected on the contradictions of the period's economic globalization by documenting scenes at four major maritime trade ports in the wake of the first Gulf War. Many artists also adopted a critical disposition toward the art institution in their work. Fred Wilson presented twinned installations at the 1993 Whitney and Cairo biennials, reclaiming Ancient Egyptian heritage to trace African-centric global histories that unveiled museums' bias toward white-centric, elite North Atlantic narratives. The art institutional complex opened itself to slowly welcome artists from regions formerly excluded from it. The Australian pavilion in the 1990 Venice Biennale featured the work of two Aboriginal artists for the first time: Trevor Nicholls and Rover Thomas. Their intrinsically political work rendered the violences shaping the contemporary Aboriginal experience before primarily US and Western European art audiences. In that same exhibition, the San Diego / Tijuana-based collective Border Art Workshop / Taller de Arte Fronterizo represented the United States with a series of installations that shed light on the forms of coloniality, past and present, shaping life at the borders of liberalism. Artists in the early 1990s also expressed an increased interest in site-specificity. In documenta 9 (1992), Nigerian artist Mo Edoga built *Signal of Hope*, a makeshift tower with driftwood from the local Fulda River that changed during the hundred days of the exhibition, and Japanese artist Tadashi Kawamata applied favela homebuilding techniques to produce *People's Garden*, an assemblage of huts alongside a canal in the biennial's gardens.

The conciliatory spirit of the moment drastically influenced the institutional conventions dominant in the contemporary art world, prompting the art biennial as a favored exhibition form to stage, via contemporary art, these widely held longings for world peace. Exhibitions promoting unification and conviviality were many, and they prefigured the time's big geopolitical changes to come. This belief in the potential of biennial art exhibitions to join historically separate stakeholders reflected the increased access of art world actors from Western Europe and the United States to territories and artistic repertoires that had until then enjoyed only a limited presence in the North Atlantic–centric international art world—such as regions under former Soviet influence but also Africa, Latin America, and Asia.

Although art biennials had been organized before to celebrate cultural alliances and signal political change, they became especially serviceable as markers of the many transformations that would reshape artistic practice in these transitional years. These exhibitions became an ideal display device: their cyclical nature conferred upon them a singular capacity to sync to the time's fast-paced changes. As well, the then-relative absence of a standard biennial organizational tool kit granted them an unmatched malleability to adapt and convert diverse locales, publics, and topics into global issues. Unlike museums, which were bound to nation-making narratives, art biennials in the early to mid-1990s promised to connect cities directly with emerging global networks of culture and commerce. During the decade, these exhibitions would multiply to become key devices shaping what has come to be known as "global contemporary art," an art shaped by the new relations of production that surrounded the making of art under global neoliberalism. Throughout this book I will use the term *biennial conversions* to designate the countless turns and exchanges between artistic genealogies that, motivated by this cosmopolitan optimism, would ultimately allow for the development of global contemporary art as we know it.[9]

These biennial conversions were historically situated in the geopolitical reorderings at place. The period's desires for cosmopolitan unity held important contradictions at their core: although for many the end of the Cold War offered a historical opportunity to put an end to decades, if not centuries, of conflict, many others knew well that forms of slow and fast violence would continue to unfold as a new world order took shape. Many victories had taken place during the Cold War that escaped large-scale narratives centering the US-versus-USSR axis; countless wars would mark the following years of presumed world peace.[10] The cultural field was not exempt from these competing views, which greatly shaped the resurgence of the art biennial as an exhibition form favored by many. On the one hand, supporters of early-boom biennials presented themselves as facilitators of an inclusive and universal art world. Curators, regional backing elites, publics, artists, and administrators endeavored to craft a form for displaying art that mirrored the wide artistic diversity of a world in rapid change. On the other hand, these actors were culturally situated, just like everyone else, which created the challenge of how to best translate and value differences across cultural frameworks while simultaneously escaping their own inherited biases.

Biennial conversions refers to these discursive and material efforts to accommodate and value difference, while simultaneously prefiguring a pacified world through the cyclical temporality of globally oriented art exhibitions. These conversions entailed the selective inclusion of cultural practices from outside elite, white-centric North Atlantic art worlds into the loci of the new global exhibitionary complex. Welcoming these cultural practices in these new frameworks prompted their adaptation to codes that were legible to and appreciated by the new global cosmopolitans—de facto audiences and patrons of the nascent global contemporary art industry. The discursive work happening within early-boom biennials facilitated these conversions. At best, they enriched artistic repertoires and widened the scope of what was institutionally distinguished as art. When successful, biennial conversions led to the creation of new art historical categories (or the revamping of existing ones under a new guise) that superseded the nation and enabled the circulation, legitimation, and valorization of artworks, artists, and experts in supranational networks that extended beyond the specific sociocultural contexts in which they had originated.

As I describe in detail in this book, some of these new artistic categories—such as "Third World avant-garde," "Border art," and "new European art"—attempted to incorporate artistic genealogies that had developed in parallel to each other as well as the dominant North Atlantic art genealogy, partly as facets of historical socialist revolutions, and now met in these new art spaces with global aspirations. Yet biennial conversions were not seamless or politically neutral. In their reframing of aesthetic value they required concessions, cuts, exclusions, and alterations of the cultural objects and genealogies that had previously been excluded from dominant North Atlantic art worlds. These filterings and adaptations often left behind not only important material and immaterial aspects of the cultural practices that were targeted for inclusion but also, most importantly, the situated values, meanings, and social purposes that originated them. As foundations for the eventual constitution of a *global* exhibitionary complex, globally oriented art biennials entailed important losses.

These biennial conversions were a post–Cold War articulation of a longer and more general process that I call "aesthetic conversions." Aesthetic conversions involve the reframing of an object under a new aesthetic paradigm. They are historically situated negotiations that reidentify, reorient, and reorder the function, meaning, and value of culture. More generally, aesthetic conversions are a common process in the production of art as experienced in North Atlantic modernity. Often shaped by structural determinations that condition how objects and actors enter new spaces of circulation in a given context, these conversions facilitate the repeated displacement of artifacts, practices, and symbols across geographical and categorical lines. A core feature of Western European and US elite art worlds throughout modernity, these displacements are likely familiar to many readers of this book. They include, for example, the incorporation of African masks into the portraits of European cubist painters and the inclusion of weaving and crocheting into the art canon by feminist artists throughout the twentieth century. Such displacements have repeatedly shaken art-world audiences, many of whom are initially unable to reconcile the newly incorporated objects and symbols with their preexisting understandings of what constitutes "art." In this way, aesthetic conversions were integral to many avant-garde movements in elite, white-centric North Atlantic art worlds during the nineteenth and twentieth centuries.

Aesthetic conversions are supported through a combination of discursive work and display maneuvers. That is, they are intrinsically tied to art's predication to exhibitionary logics—in their different formulations within diverse reception spaces through time. By distinguishing a variety of phenomena as art within socially revered exhibition frameworks, aesthetic conversions can have positive consequences, such as upholding for public appreciation cultural forms and social phenomena that had been formerly denied cultural worthiness by dominant art institutions. For instance, it is through aesthetic conversions that the art institution incorporates the work of contemporary artists with disabilities—a much-needed move resulting from the sustained advocacy and labor of practitioners, curators, and art historians.[11] But aesthetic conversions can also have negative effects, especially when framed exclusively by formalist valuation standards, a too-common misstep that tends to conceal colonial and extractivist relations.[12] By erasing and distorting the situated meanings and social practices that contributed to the creation of specific objects, aesthetic conversions can deny publics the opportunity to substantively learn about ways of experiencing the world that are different from their own and exclude the situated value of culture beyond dominant aesthetic frameworks. Moreover, this severing of objects from their social and cultural conditions of production is often unbalanced and tends to benefit the preservation of hegemonic perspectives over other ways of life—most often to the benefit of elite, white-centric, Western European and US culture. A good portion of this book examines this tendency of aesthetic conversions to erase and distort local worldviews in the context of early-boom biennials.

Like translations, aesthetic conversions transfer the meanings and values of culture. However, through their capacity to turn into art objects previously denied such status, aesthetic conversions have ontological implications. The history of modern art is ripe with examples of seemingly nonartistic objects, places, and relations that, when subject to aesthetic conversions, acquire artistic status and are welcomed into socially revered cultural frameworks. Aesthetic conversions also affect the formal and material qualities of artworks. For example, artists from a region formerly marginal to dominant art worlds may suddenly embrace the use of a specific material that was previously unavailable to them yet is popular in mainstream exhibition circuits, thus altering the practices of art production, circulation, collection, and preservation. As well, aesthetic conversions shape other important processes involved in the production of art, such as the professional practices of art-world actors, including curators, artists, administrators, handlers, and critics; forms of audience engagement; and the design of exhibition spaces. For example, the collector-driven demand for large-scale installations and photographs in the early 2000s triggered the emergence of highly specialized technicians who developed unique production processes. Importantly, as this book shows, aesthetic conversions are dialogical: they happen in relation, transforming both hegemonic and subaltern repertoires, albeit with an eschewed bias that tends to preserve the superiority of aesthetic paradigms dominant in the reception spaces that frame each conversion. As a result, an analytical focus on aesthetic conversions draws attention to the inherent power relations that are brought forward or tamed down in acts of cultural exchange and inclusion. As later chapters demonstrate, artistic genealogies that were previously excluded from hegemonic art worlds often end up losing their original emancipatory intentions, while retaining their formal attributes, when they are converted for inclusion in new exhibition spaces.

Though operating in very different locations and conditions, the biennial conversions that took place in the post–Cold War years continued a long history of aesthetic conversions in ways that were particular to the conditions of their time. If former moments in this history had helped tie initially para-institutional avant-garde artworks to nation-building projects through their eventual acquisition by national museums, biennial conversions helped articulate contemporary artworks to cultural, economic, and political supranational projects—participating in the early moments of late twentieth-century cultural globalization. The aesthetic conversions that contributed to the formation of national artistic canons through the institutional form of the museum infused a teleological temporization to the unfolding of artistic forms, from which a national art history existed in parallel to the imagined foundation, longevity, and prehistory of a nation. By contrast, biennial conversions infused the duration of two years as the unit to pace changes in artistic discourses, forms, and standards. The modern Hegelian vector was now a centrifugal spiral speeding in cycles of exponential capital growth. These biennial conversions renewed the formal and thematic qualities of art in elite, white-centric North Atlantic art worlds, upholding them as a joint sphere of meaning making that reflected the time's post–Cold War global cosmopolitanism. In so doing, biennial conversions became particularly engrained in the relations of production that surrounded the "art" category in this period of cultural globalization. Increasing numbers of art actors within the early-boom biennials practiced new forms of art labor marked by the principles of deregulation, market-driven demand, and mystified mobility prevalent within neoliberalism. As we will see in the chapters that follow, biennials in noncapitalist spaces, such as the Bienal de La Habana, offered a political counter-model to these neoliberal labor practices, whereas Manifesta and inSITE incorporated them more organically from their peripheral contexts.

These biennial conversions helped convert cultural forms practiced outside of elite North Atlantic art worlds into codes that would be legible to the new global art publics, whose understandings and appreciation of art were very much tied to aesthetic valuation standards and practices dominating in elite, white-centric North Atlantic art worlds. By displacing cultural productions outside of their original emplacement and adapting them into new paradigms of aesthetic value, these conversions facilitated the renewal of the North Atlantic modernist-formalist canon and its end-of-the-century legacies. They fed contemporary art production within the early-boom biennials with formal, thematic, and conceptual elements that had been produced in regional art genealogies until then mostly overlooked by or excluded from dominating art worlds in Western Europe and the United States. Ultimately, these conversions played an important role in the production of new parameters for the valuation of artistic merit.

Importantly, the discursive labor of artists, critics, curators, and historians played a crucial role in the conversion of cultural productions into artworks, granting them value as potential collectibles in a growing global art market. Yet it would be in art fairs, not in art biennials, where these converted objects would be exchanged not on the basis of their use value but rather according to their presumed uniqueness, discursive sophistication, and proximity to their author. Global contemporary artworks follow a market logic similar to that of luxury and heritage goods. According to Luc Boltanski and Arnaud Esquerre, buyers and sellers of these exclusive goods respond to factors such as the object's novelty in relation with a tradition; its authenticity, vis-à-vis a specific regional or national identity; and an aura of exceptionality.[13] Seldom displayed alone, these exceptional objects move within coveted spheres of circulation, such as the biennial circuit, where their closeness to reputable actors—artists, curators, collectors, and art historians—aids in their distinction. Through the production of theories that justified their curatorial selections, early biennial curators composed compelling arguments for the conversion of previously extra-artistic symbolic orders into the permeable space of the art biennial. In doing so, they delivered discursive resources that art dealers and other participants in art markets used to valorize and distinguish art objects as luxury goods.

Sustained through time, these biennial conversions would ultimately yield at the turn of the century what Caroline A. Jones has called a "platform formalism" in global art biennials.[14] For example, in Rotterdam in 1996 they helped recompose Europe's manifold modernisms as new pan-European contemporary art anchored in commonalities found in artworks from western, eastern, northern, and southern European regions. Furthermore, through these displacements biennials converted extra-artistic elements of everyday life into institutionally legitimized art phenomena. These conversions distinguished these elements as worthy of aesthetic appreciation, enriching their value and extending their capacity for circulation in the art institution. These processes of aesthetic conversion were especially important at the borders of North Atlantic liberalism.

In San Diego and Tijuana in 1994 they took place through the commissioning of site-specific artworks that would disclose to foreign audiences particular qualities of place—such as the everyday forms of interpersonal communication across the iron fence at the international border. Taken together, the three biennials studied in this book helped convert artistic genealogies that had been produced in the aftermath of three historical socialist revolutions—the Mexican Revolution, the Soviet Revolution, and the Cuban Revolution—into North Atlantic modernism's late twentieth-century formal inheritances.

By thematizing aspects of everyday life and featuring them as forms and materials in artworks, early-boom biennials aided in the selective bracketing of more and more aspects of regional sociocultural commons, rendering them legible to a global art audience in formation. As we will see, early-boom biennials often promised art-mediated encounters with local authenticity to nonlocal visitors and helped connect local histories with present concerns by facilitating opportunities to participate in the new and exciting scenarios of so-called global art. Eventually, thanks in part to processes of biennial conversion, many early-boom biennial artworks and artists were able to access an expanding global art market. In gaining this access, they were subject to processes of valorization shepherded by curators and other cultural brokers as part of their conversion into ecumenically legible codes. As the following chapters show, these processes were far from clean and linear; they often involved on-the-ground negotiations between a number of actors, negotiations that grew from diverging expectations about how to interpret widely held desires for convergence.

Biennials in Context

Early-boom biennials helped bring forth and standardize newly powerful ways of selecting and valorizing contemporary art, but they also reactivated a familiar avant-garde aspiration: the desire to merge art and life. As subsequent chapters document, curators working for early-boom biennials attempted to prefigure a world of friendship and conviviality after the Cold War by commissioning artworks that, in their majority, looked toward *everyday* symbols, relations, and materials. They also attempted to reimagine the particular geographic regions that hosted each exhibit as integral to, rather than cut off from, an emerging world order. Although each biennial pursued different reconciliatory aims, their approaches shared an inclination toward site-specificity that attempted to incorporate aspects of everyday life in their regions into the new regional art categories that the biennials themselves were helping to construct. Mirroring the more general optimism of the moment, cultural and political elites from around the world embraced art biennials as a seemingly benign and forward-looking way to help realize their hopes for a convivial and inclusive future. During its first decade, between 1984 and 1994, the Bienal de La Habana, for example, translated into the aesthetic field what had been a decades-long effort on behalf of Cuba's political elites to consolidate Cuba's leadership in Third World solidarity campaigns.[15] Its organizers, who were supported by the Cuban state, researched the contemporary art production of subaltern peoples from around the world in order to offer international audiences a distinctively Third World avant-garde that challenged the exclusionary epistemic principles of North Atlantic modernisms. Likewise, between 1994 and 2005, inSITE amplified deep-seated interests by regional elites to reimagine the US-Mexico borderlands as a region of conciliation and conviviality, despite escalating reinforcement of the geographic boundary between the nations by the Mexican and US federal governments. The exhibition was an operation of unprecedented capacity for regional art institutions that aimed to attract international audiences to a region that was frequently overshadowed by more prominent art centers, such as Los Angeles and Mexico City. In doing so, the organizers reformed the preexisting label of "Border art" so that they could bring together manifold local artistic traditions, chiefly the emancipatory artistic practices legacy of the Chicano art movement, with artistic repertoires that were imported from the North Atlantic art capitals. In 1996 in Rotterdam, Manifesta's first iteration responded to the post-Maastricht policy framework driving cultural and identity integration in the newly formed European Union. Sponsored by regional philanthropy and government officials on the municipal, national, and supranational levels, Manifesta attempted to join Europe's diverse modern art genealogies into a common project, namely of creating a distinctively European approach to contemporary art.

Unlike the museum or the gallery, which had claimed art as a rarefied and autonomous field, early-boom art biennials expressed an explicit intention to acknowledge and value their surrounding locales and to be inclusive of cultural forms and practices that had been historically excluded from canonical art institutions. They largely attempted to do so in two ways. First, they often embraced what has come to be known in the art world as site-specificity, a tendency of art making that, in Miwon Kwon's account, celebrates the cultural and physical attributes of particular places that surround the walls of supposedly esoteric spaces such as the gallery and the museum. Second, and relatedly, they sometimes promoted artists who relied on collaboration and dialogue with non-artists and nondominant groups to help orchestrate a more equal and just world—a genre of art making that Grant Kester calls "dialogical aesthetics." The three early-boom biennials chronicled in this book did in principle attempt to engage with local cultural practices and deploy dialogical methods that seemingly valued mutual recognition and empathy as a way to mend social ills. However, and as scholars such as George Yúdice have shown and I further explore in this volume, the class affiliations of influential actors within the early-boom biennials often had the effect of watering down and sometimes erasing the inclusionary intentions and liberatory drives behind the dialogical aesthetic framework. In doing so, although they sometimes expressed their heteronomous engagement with site as the practice of solidarity, early-boom biennials ultimately contributed to a nascent ecumenical multiculturalism that ironically accentuated already existing social divisions and relations of coloniality.[16]

The organic alliances that developed among biennial curators, biennial organizers, and supporting political and economic elites in the regions where the exhibitions were placed were important contributors to this unintended result that I explore in this book. I will argue that by publicly embracing a rhetoric of dialogical heteronomy and site-specificity but engaging in social selection and cultural distinction, the early-boom biennials became a highly effective and malleable operation that, on one hand, could graft itself on to the situated social complexities of a wide array of cultural practices and social scenarios across the world while, on the other hand, extending the exclusionary logics and cultural hierarchies that had long characterized elite, white-centric, North Atlantic art institutions to new areas and regions.

Early-Boom Biennials

Like their immediate precursors, the nineteenth-century international expositions, art biennials have long provided their visitors with highly particular imaginings of the world as a totality. Caroline A. Jones has traced the commonalities between these two kinds of exhibitions in detail: their "presumed universality, goals of knowledge production, ties to tourism, implications for urban infrastructure, regulation of international art-world trade routes, rehabilitation—through the cosmopolitan city—of previously restrictive or totalitarian regimes, and openings for multinational capital investment and new geopolitical ambitions, all in paradoxical conjunction with local political purposes."[17] The first of many international expositions opened in the middle of the nineteenth century in London and Paris, marking these two capitals' imperial rivalry. Art was featured in these expositions from the beginning, alongside thousands of objects of science and nature, all of them indexing their respective nation's imperial reach and domestic industrialization. In the first, London's Great Exhibition of the Works of Industry of All Nations (1851), art objects were installed throughout the exhibition's many booths and helped guide visitors through the pavilion. Four years later, at the Exposition Universelle des Produits de l'Agriculture, de l'Industrie et des Beaux-Arts in Paris (1855), art received a dedicated pavilion as a separate state-sanctioned category—famously prompting a reaction by Gustave Courbet, who in a first act of vanguardist self-determination against the exclusive criteria of the macro-exhibition inaugurated his own Pavillon du Réalisme across the street, to the great satisfaction of the curious Parisian public. Art biennials appeared soon after: 1895 was the inaugural year of the Biennale de Venezia (Italy), followed in 1896, by the first Carnegie International Exhibition (Pittsburgh, United States). In keeping with the Eurocentric worldviews of their sponsors— Venetian aristocracy for the former and North American industrialist oligarchy for the latter—these exhibitions surveyed what their organizers deemed to be state-of-the-art artistic production in Europe and the United States, thus reproducing the imperialist world visions that had scaffolded international exhibitions in these same regions.[18]

For more than fifty years, the Biennale de Venezia and the Carnegie International Exhibition were the only two recurring biennials, but the onset of the Cold War sparked what Charles Green and Anthony Gardner call "the second wave" of biennials. These new biennials included the Bienal de São Paulo (Brazil, 1951), the Biennale de la Méditerranée in Alexandria (Mediterranean Biennial, Egypt, 1955), Ljubljana's Biennale Grafike (Biennial of Graphic Arts, Slovenia 1955), and documenta (Kassel, West Germany, 1955), among others. Remarkably, documenta aspired to heal political divides, at least symbolically, by being strategically placed near the border between East Germany and West Germany, and by appealing to audiences from both sides of the Iron Curtain. Since documenta 5 (1972), curated by Harald Szeemann, art biennials also became a breeding ground for the independent biennial curator, a figure who would become the paradigmatic art actor during the 1990s biennial boom. As Green and Gardner have described, Szeemann stopped pursuing art-historical validation and asserted the curatorial as an autonomous field invested in the production of its own canon. His defiance of artists' intentions and art-historical categories turned the space of the exhibition into a field for the deployment of innovative curatorial narratives to be experienced and interpreted by audiences in phenomenological encounters with the curated art objects.[19]

Conversely, São Paulo, Ljubljana, and Alexandria hosted the first biennials outside of Western Europe and the United States, and they helped advance alternative internationalisms in the artistic field.[20] São Paulo played an important role in making Brazilian art visible abroad while simultaneously importing artistic developments from Western Europe and the United States.[21] Similarly, Ljubljana and Alexandria rejected, in their own ways, the influence of North Atlantic liberalism to mirror contemporaneous efforts at state formation that pursued international alliances with other Third World nations. If Ljubljana exemplified Yugoslavia's nonaligned socialism, Alexandria commemorated the anniversary of the 1952 Egyptian Revolution. As the Cold War progressed, more biennial exhibitions slowly emerged, such as the Biennale de Paris (Paris Biennial, 1959–1985) and the Sydney Biennial (1973), which continues to this day and from its beginning was one of the first biennials to embrace Szeemann's thematic curating, instead of Venice's national pavilion model.[22] However, the "biennial boom," the aforementioned rapid multiplication of the biennial form worldwide sometimes also referred to as "biennialization," would not occur until the last decade of the twentieth century.[23] During this period an astonishing proliferation of art biennials would bring the exhibition form to Shanghai, Gwangju, Istanbul, Johannesburg, Berlin, Liverpool, Lyon, Dakar, and many, many, many other sites.

Throughout this book I use the term *early-boom biennials* to speak of those biennial exhibitions that took place in the early years of the art biennial boom. Echoing the magic of the moment, these events articulated in the realm of curatorial practice the widely held belief that a convergence of diverse artistic forms could help heal historical wounds and prefigure social unity. Unlike their immediate predecessors, they anticipated new supranational relations that promised to surpass the Cold War geopolitical order—only incorporating terms such as *global* and *globalization* in their discursive repertoires after the mid-1990s. Reflecting the period's general cosmopolitan optimism, early-boom biennials performed a dual function: they facilitated the development of regional art scenes, and they broadened the category of art to include artistic modernisms hitherto excluded from the North Atlantic art capitals. As noted, the new biennials were both an expansion of and an alternative to the museum. The three case studies discussed in this book attest to the benefits brought about by these exhibitions, chiefly by their diversification of the global artistic archive, by helping dynamize new art scenes, and by spearheading new networks to connect formerly separate art worlds. These were important contributions that have helped to value local expertise and, at times, bring about substantial infrastructural improvements.

Embracing the revisions to curatorial practice proposed by the new museological turn of the 1980s, early-boom biennials helped expand the art institution outward toward its surrounding locales. But they also marked a transition away from the museum and its founding allegiances with the nation-state by relying on the curation of art objects to amplify the new supranational political programs. For instance, the Bienal de La Habana (1984) sought to produce a new Third World avant-garde that would support Cuba's Third World solidarity agenda; inSITE (1994) was a festival of site-specific art that hoped to showcase the changing qualities of the US-Mexico borderlands in response to the North Atlantic Free Trade Agreement (NAFTA, 1993); and Manifesta (1996), in its roving locations, aimed to showcase a new pan-European identity that dovetailed with the unification agenda of the Treaty on European Union (1992).

It would take until the turn of the century for the processes of institutional isomorphism to yield something close to a standardized art biennial model, a "global design" to use Walter Mignolo's term, that would be replicated throughout the world with adaptable variations.[24] However, it was the end of the Cold War that prompted the rearrangements of political power and institutionalized curatorial practice that triggered important transformations to the processes and constituencies involved in the production of this thing we call "art." These rearrangements accelerated flows of elite art professionals and ideas throughout the planet in ways that often mirrored the unequal distribution of power and resources that can be found in so many areas of the world today.[25] During this time of growing Western European and US influence worldwide, boom biennials often revived the tightly knit bond between imperialist aspirations and display cultures of nineteenth-century international expositions, conferring global dimensions to what Tony Bennett has termed the "exhibitionary complex."[26] They did so, chiefly, by proposing visions of artistic production that were seemingly inclusive of aesthetic diversity. In most cases, however, their efforts tacitly asserted the dominance of elite, white-centric North Atlantic modernisms and their legacies over other aesthetic paradigms. I record the details of this nuanced but important implication in the historical chapters that follow.

Biennials at the Borders of Liberalism

The three cases that I explore in this book attest to how the borders of Cold War liberalism were especially ripe terrain for early-boom biennials. Placed in strategic locations at what were then the edges of North Atlantic liberal hegemony, these exhibitions helped propel the centrifugal expansion of biennials to new lands in the incipient cycle of neoliberal globalization. The border, as a symbol and a physical entity, was often a feature of these exhibitions, which operated as a porous membrane that simultaneously blocked and enabled the selective filtering of relations, forms, and values between diverse aesthetic genealogies. In this sense, early-boom biennials echoed Étienne Balibar's characterization of the border as a polysemic and heterogeneous space that demarcates and territorializes, prompting processes of aesthetic conversion that would help North Atlantic liberalism expand to new lands.[27] Early-boom biennials supported this work of reterritorializing and expanding economic and political arrangements, but they did so by operating through a seemingly autonomous sphere: that of so-called high culture. Even an initially anticapitalist biennial, such as the Bienal de La Habana, eventually succumbed to the trends of the global contemporary art industry once the Soviet Union, Cuba's main economic ally when the exhibition was created, was no longer a player in the international field.

Thinking of the early-boom biennial as a border operation that selectively frames and filters the flows of aesthetic repertoires correlates to the heightened presence of migration as a theme in artworks and exhibitions throughout the decade. Many biennial artworks registered the time's interest in migration as a function of globalization, sometimes representing migrant subjects and at other times addressing related processes of cultural hybridity. Additionally, both early-boom biennials and their artworks often reflected the protagonism of supranational formations over modern nation-states during this stage of globalization. In addition to the exhibitions included in this study that celebrated supranational treaties such as the Non-Aligned Bloc, the European Union, or NAFTA, Terry Smith remarks that many of the artworks that circulated in these transnational networks registered, in a variety of ways, responses to processes of postcolonial state formation and decolonization.[28] Partly structural, partly arising from artists' own quasi-autonomous concerns, this responsiveness to the interruption of the modern institutionalized bond between art production and national identity turned global contemporary art into a vortex for myriad aesthetic repertoires coproduced in local, regional, national, and transnational relations.

Propelled by the cosmopolitan aspirations of their organizers, early-boom biennials both entered into and helped construct exclusive supranational networks for the circulation of objects, knowledge, professionals, and private capital during neoliberal expansion in the 1990s.[29] By successfully grafting a regional art scene into these existing networks, regional cultural and economic elites could access exclusive social networks that spanned the planet, as the nascent network itself expanded to new regions and territories. In this way the early-boom biennials helped shape the globalized art industry as we now know it, as well as the cosmopolitan habitus that predominates within it. But these outcomes were not the stated aims of many of the people who were instrumental to the production and spread of the early-boom biennials. Rather, a contagious cosmopolitan idealism that grew in the immediate aftermath of the Cold War often provided political, economic, and cultural elites in the early to mid-1990s with ideological motivation and justification for their expansionary endeavors. After all, like other cosmopolitans throughout history, these individuals believed that agreement on aesthetic matters signaled moral convergence between diverse actors. According to this framework, which through Immanuel Kant's formulation became foundational for European aesthetics, agreeing on the aesthetic value of works by canonical turn-of-the-century artists, such as El Anatsui or Candida Höfer, became more than a singular appreciation for the inherent qualities of concrete objects: it also signaled the existence of a common sense—that is, a more-or-less shared epistemic, moral, and aesthetic framework among members of an incipient community of global cosmopolitans. The artistic forms that circulated within the global biennial circuit during the 1990s and early 2000s were frequently presented in specialized media as exemplifying an aesthetic—and thus moral—universalism for a globalizing era. Some neo-Kantian promoters of cosmopolitanism, such as Thierry de Duve, reflected the enthusiasm of many global cosmopolitans for art biennials as *glocal* sites where the tacit sharing of aesthetic judgment facilitated the participation of globally oriented municipal actors into a nascent global community of biennial patrons.[30]

Yet community belonging, including to the coveted global art world, is also negotiated on the basis of individuals' dexterous expressions of aesthetic taste.[31] Aware of this tendency, artists and scholars from outside hegemonic art worlds have long problematized the dangers of aesthetic universalisms for their historically racist, sexist, and classist biases. For example, curator Okwui Enwezor understood well, and early on, the symbolic and practiced rampages concealed by the global turn in curatorial practice, yet chose to wield the term in the benefit of further diversifying the field while acknowledging the limitations of his intervention.[32] Aware of these risks, artist Luis Camnitzer has noted that practicing the aesthetic codes dominant in the so-called global art world entails incorporating its hegemonic language and its production practices. Similarly, artist Rasheed Araeen has argued that during the biennial-boom art world, actors whose journeys began outside of North Atlantic centers of power continued to wrestle with an inherently white Eurocentric aesthetic framework that was exclusionary of aesthetic difference yet welcoming of identity diversity—a tension that often reinforced historical relations of coloniality but that was cloaked behind so-called universalist programs. Araeen's analysis lends support to Craig Calhoun's point that "as a social condition, cosmopolitanism is not universalism; it is belonging to a social class able to identify itself with the universal." In my approach to the global I thus side with these views and join recent art-historical critiques of the universalist character that is often automatically conferred to the global, such as the one written by art historian Amelia Jones.[33] The following chapters depart from an understanding that all art worlds are particular and historically situated, including hegemonic ones. Further, they account for several instances where artists and artworks originated outside of North Atlantic modern aesthetic genealogies clashed with the tacit norms informing dominating approaches to late-century cosmopolitanism.

This book builds on these critiques of cosmopolitanism to show how affinities between curatorial expertise and local elites in the early-boom biennials resuscitated the contradictions already present in earlier cosmopolitan programs, thus privileging access and agency to local elites in the formation of local and global art worlds. These organic partnerships between art experts and internationally oriented regional elites were formed through the envisioning, manufacture, and staging of these exhibitions. Together, they brokered mutual access into and helped construct the emerging circuits of elite culture and economic power that we today recognize as the global contemporary art world. Further, these art exhibitions shaped turn-of-the-millennium notions of art labor, artistic autonomy, and art's relation to capital.[34] Across the world, market-oriented economic and political reforms in the 1980s and 1990s facilitated renewed alliances among regional governments, business leaders, and the cultural sector that eased the flow of capital and culture within and through their borders. These transformations helped forge a new class of art patrons and collectors that were members of (or hoped to join) a new global elite that William Robinson characterizes as regional dominant groups with aspirations to access new circuits for the global circulation of capital, culture, and political influence.[35] During the early post–Cold War years, culture was again a key sphere for reorganizing power on supranational and regional levels. Cultural institutions, including early-boom biennials, supported new regional articulations of power by helping to galvanize legitimacy and consent on the local level around the new world-peace aspirations of political and economic elites. One important outcome of these operations was the inclusion of art forms and artists from regions previously off-limits to the hegemonic art institution into a new canon in formation. As this book shows, these inclusions were never seamless, and they often involved subtle yet often coercive maneuvers of conversion into dominant frameworks for the valuation of artistic merit.

Another important consequence of early-boom biennials was their impact in the production of a common sense beyond the limits of art worlds. Art's power to reframe the meanings of identities, land, and culture afforded early-boom biennials ideological agency, involving these operations in the consolidation of hegemony at the borders of liberalism. The meanings and values that naturalize everyday experience, what we call "common sense," are organized through permanent negotiations between actors in competing social positions. Always historical and mutable, common sense is indicative of the temporary symbolic order that cements hegemony and is a key tool to understand how art biennials participated in the new regional configurations of power that set forth end-of-the-century

Western European and United States neocolonial programs.[36] I am far from the first analyst to remark on the relation between global contemporary art and hegemony. Recently, Oliver Marchart has explored biennials' entanglements with hegemony around the case of Kassel-based quinquennial documenta.[37] In the same way that Alexander Alberro and Amelia Jones articulate, from different positions, I believe that exploring the entanglements of contemporary art worlds in the production of hegemony allows us to see not only the many internal contradictions that inform contemporary art but, importantly as well, the diversity of subject positions and political agencies that contribute to its formation—some involved in the consolidation of hegemony, others invested in its dismantlement or reformation.[38]

In line with the importance of the border in the early-boom biennial, my inquiry into how these operations participated in the production of new hegemonic orders leads me to Jorge González's dialogical model of the "cultural fronts." González continues a long line of subaltern Marxist thought that takes culture as the privileged field of struggle between competing worldviews and moral orders. Building on Gramsci, he defines hegemony as the "momentum of the objective relationships of forces that exist between different social agent … situated in a determined social space which we observe from a symbolic point of view—that is, where the creation and recreation of meanings take form in the enactment of all social relations."[39] González designates as "centripetal" the symbolic frameworks put forward by institutionalized expertise and as "centrifugal" those defended from the bottom up by everyday actors. When centripetal and centrifugal forces wield a synchronous symbolic repertoire, they reflect a condition of hegemony. This opening up of the concept of hegemony from its classical macro-political focus allows accounting for everyday life experience and demonstrates that hegemony is always ultimately accomplished through symbolic negotiations of quotidian order—such as in the site-specific biennials that favored artworks concerned with everyday life experience. Amid this climate, these exhibitions played a key role in reimagining the everyday lives of subaltern groups into codes that were legible to the new global elites.

To date, most analyses of art biennials consider how the institutionalized discursive expertise of curators reshapes the symbolic orders *within* the art institution. In this book I build on those contributions to show how on-the-ground (centrifugal) dialogical practices like those carried out by members of a squat art space in Rotterdam *and* institutional (centripetal) agendas of political convergence became synchronized in their joint commitment to a better world thanks to the mediation of biennial curatorial practice. This synchronicity was achieved in diverse ways. In the Bienal de La Habana, for example, synchronicity happened through the formulation of a "Third World avant-garde" that blurred the categorical boundaries between popular art, craft, avant-garde art, and the many expressions of modern art found outside of North Atlantic elite art worlds. Through the commission of site-specific artworks, inSITE bracketed material and relational aspects of life and space at the US-Mexico borderlands for their exhibition to foreign audiences. In the Rotterdam Manifesta, the process entailed the inclusion of artistic projects started by members of the local art community to claim a place in the exhibition's program as a way to protest and reverse their initial exclusion from the curatorial selection.

Like museums and other art institutions, early-boom biennials sought to facilitate contacts between separate cultural and artistic worlds. Yet these contacts exposed the uneven power relations shaping actors' access to and aesthetic sovereignty within the exhibition space.[40] Mediating between North Atlantic modernist genealogies and cultural paradigms originated outside these regions, the early-boom biennials that I document in this book acted as liminal frontier operations that staged the crafting, partly via contemporary art, of a new common sense for a cosmopolitan class in the making. These conversions consolidated the diverse symbolic referents of differently situated groups under seemingly benign and inclusive labels such as "Border art" (in its mid-1990s refurbishing), "European art," and "Third World avant-garde." As we shall see, the production of such labels designated moments in the consolidation of Western European and US hegemony worldwide.

The Book's Structure

At the end of the Cold War, art biennials at the borders of liberalism helped imagine a new reconciled world. The time's confident embrace of this until-then marginal exhibition form propelled it to become the dominant staging ground for contemporary art by the end of the century. In their widening the scope of the "art" category, early-boom biennials visibilized artworks and artists from sites previously excluded from the North Atlantic–centric art institution. This inclusionary move often came, alas, at the expense of faithfulness to the values and intentions fueling cultural genealogies outside this region, which would be dramatically reshaped, if not lost, in their inclusion in the new global art institutional complex. In this rapidly changing world, local elites in these liminal regions grasped this exhibition form as an avenue through which to reimagine their locales and help leverage their positionality in a new world order. The renewed alliance between globally oriented local elites and artistic production contributed to the formation of a new social class of global cosmopolitans who became ideal audiences of the soon-to-be omnipresent biennial exhibition form. These aesthetic and social processes were simultaneous with the reevaluation of the centrality of the nation-state and the promotion of supranational formations as ideal polities for a new global order. Embracing the myth of free circulation for capital and culture, this revamped internationalism accentuated already existing forms of inequity and coloniality between peoples and eased the appearance of new ones. In this book I provide detailed analysis of how these big processes materialized in the situatedness of three early-boom biennials: the Bienal de La Habana, inSITE, and Manifesta.

The book has three parts. Each considers a particular dimension of the early-boom biennial, taking as case studies the germinal iterations of the Bienal de La Habana, inSITE, and Manifesta. Each chapter details different ways in which biennial conversions helped prefigure a unified world and the end of the Cold War. Chapters 1, 2, and 3 look at the anticolonial biennial conversions in place in the Bienal de La Habana, an art biennial founded to spearhead avenues for the circulation and valuation of art autonomously from the influence of North Atlantic modernisms. Although this counter-hegemonic operation ultimately succumbed to the logics driving the period's large-scale geopolitical processes, these chapters show how socialist ideology, in both its orthodox and nonorthodox versions, informed the ideals, practices, and artwork selection within the exhibition. Chapter 1 explores how the Bienal translated to the artistic field the Cuban government's doctrine of Third World solidarity, challenging the time's dominant North Atlantic–centric art world and opening avenues for the legitimation of subaltern culture worldwide. Chapter 2 expands on the centrality of collaboration for the first iterations of the Bienal to show how the exhibition put forward a practice-led understanding of socialist theory that differed from Fidel Castro's Leninist approach. The chapter shows how the organization of curatorial expertise in the Bienal mirrored the military strategy of *foquismo* and relied on dynamic alliances between local and transnational constituencies to produce situated transferable knowledge.

Chapter 3 evaluates how the category of craft anchored the proposal of an anticolonial revision to the North Atlantic–centric art canon in the early iterations of the Bienal, subverting taxonomies that historically facilitated the exclusion of artists from other world regions from the spaces of artistic legitimization. The biennial conversions at place within this effort helped redraw socialist aesthetics and show how, despite their shared efforts to group diverse artistic genealogies in regional art categories, not all early-boom biennials necessarily embraced neoliberal globalization, but some helped imagine an internationalism of the subaltern instead.

Sprouting at the frontiers of liberalism, early-boom art biennials also bore important territorial implications: they helped ground political agendas to sites. Precisely because of their placement at the borders of Western Europe and the United States, these exhibitions were able to prefigure life otherwise in regions that would soon adopt neoliberal policy frameworks. The second part of this book considers inSITE, a festival of site-specific art in San Diego and Tijuana, and its involvement in the reimagining of space and population at the US-Mexico borderlands. Chapter 4 describes inSITE as an operation that overlooked the everyday experience of most border residents, favoring instead the perspectives of beneficiaries of the new NAFTA policy framework. Facilitating the disassociation of the category of "Border art" from its origins in Chicano civil rights activism, inSITE helped reassociate this category with artistic forms that instead trended in the globally oriented art industry. Chapter 5 studies how the global aspirations of local economic elites facilitated the sprout of art biennials across the globe. It argues that inSITE's emphasis on site-specific art satisfied widespread desires to render the US-Mexico borderlands as a pacified region by subjecting the conflicted border zone to an aesthetic imperative. Chapter 6 discusses inSITE as an operation that facilitated the entrance of young Mexico City artists into the nascent global contemporary art industry, aiding the internationalization of the Mexican contemporary art scene through this new outpost in the *frontera norte*. In addition to changes to regional art categories, these biennial conversions facilitated by inSITE helped render land in forms that were legible to cosmopolitan art actors.

At times of political change, early-boom biennials responded to the dreams and interests of a new cosmopolitan class by joining broader efforts for the convergence of culturally, ethnically, and politically diverse constituencies under new shared myths of belonging. The third part of this book examines these processes by considering Manifesta's involvement in the production of a new European identity. Chapter 7 portrays Manifesta as an organization that translated the European Union's unification agenda into the spaces of so-called high art, projecting a classed project of European unity that gathered private and public interests on the municipal, national, and supranational level around the new art biennial. Furthermore, because many early-boom biennials inherited modernist defenses of the art exhibition as a bracketed conciliatory realm, they delivered images of appeasement that contrasted with ongoing conflicts outside of the art institution. Chapter 8 considers the conflicts within artworks, among professionals, and among nations that surrounded Manifesta 1 in Rotterdam (1996) and focuses on the discord between forms of curatorial practice within the biennial. It also examines the tensions that resulted from the insertion within the exhibition of artworks that relied on human relations as form. Last, in contrast with widespread art-world calls to evaluate art exhibitions as discursive productions that are detached from social life, early-boom biennials invoked—and sometimes even nourished—strong ties with their host locales, participating in their cities' everyday life. Chapter 9 centers Manifesta's investment in Rotterdam as the former industrial city worked to forge a new postindustrial identity in an era of economic globalization. The chapter shows how although the art biennial initially failed to represent Rotterdam's artistic diversity by limiting its alliances to established cultural institutions, it ultimately acknowledged cries for inclusion articulated by a faction of the local art community. The biennial conversions taking place within Manifesta 1 show how the pursuit of cultural unity often comes at the expense of silencing conflict and neutralizing critique.

This book is not a comprehensive study of the art biennial boom.[41] Nor is it an attempt to write a unified history of global contemporary art. Readers may take this book as a critique of this category, following Gayatri Chakravorty Spivak's understanding of critique as a "careful description of the structures that produce an object of knowledge."[42] In the following pages I devote my attention to the early arrangements that *preceded* the boom of art biennials at the turn of the century. Others have written about the art biennial as a global standardized form, its entanglements with the art market, and its implications for the globalization of the art industry.[43] This monograph looks at the very early days of this phenomenon, times when "biennial boom" was not even a term yet, to describe how early-boom

biennials were part of larger artistic, sociocultural, and political transformations at place in a diversity of locales grappling, in their own ways,
with a changing world. I chose to study the early iterations of these three
biennials in order to better understand how early-boom biennials came
to be, developed relations with their surrounding regions that allowed
these exhibitions to become institutions, and helped imagine a pacified
world through the curation of artworks. By analyzing these three different
mutations of an institutional form at times of historical change, I describe
only three of the many possible variations of an existing motive. Writing a
biography of a single biennial felt limiting to me, in the sense that it would
not have allowed me to see various solutions to an artistic problem of ut-
most importance at the end of the Cold War—what forms best satisfy our
desire to represent a changing world—knowing that the picturing might
always be biased. This is thus a partial history centered around the early
iterations of three art biennials at the borders of liberalism.[44] I look forward
to others supplementing this study by expanding its analytical scope to
other geographies and shedding additional light on this critical period in
recent art history.

part one

Anticolonial Collaboration in the Bienal de La Habana's Early Iterations

HAVANA, 1984–1991

one

Polyphonic Internationalism

The camera zooms in on a man. Slim and bare-chested, he bows to a long piece of wood. He paints with an air brush and wears a flat, white cap with the logo of the 1986 Bienal de La Habana. Next to him diverse workshop tools, wood pieces, and tape rest on a table. In the background, two men talk. One is young, his back to the camera; he wears a striped cotton shirt. The other, older, is Argentine kinetic artist Julio Le Parc, in a white lab coat and the same white hat. Behind them, four tall wood-cut silhouettes are propped up against the wall: a nude man in profile with wings, a crown, and a tiny trumpet; a woman with long hair, big cubist eyes, and a tiara; a figure with braided hair wearing a long leopard-print robe; and a half-horse, half-woman in profile, her big mouth open and head tilted up. The voice-over says, "With the purpose of provoking an attitude of creative experimentation, this workshop by Julio Le Parc, Argentine painter and engraver, protagonist of the optic-kinetic trend and of attempts at collective participation in the work of art, is informed by a group of Cuban artists interested in calling the attention of a new spectator in active exchange with the public."[1]

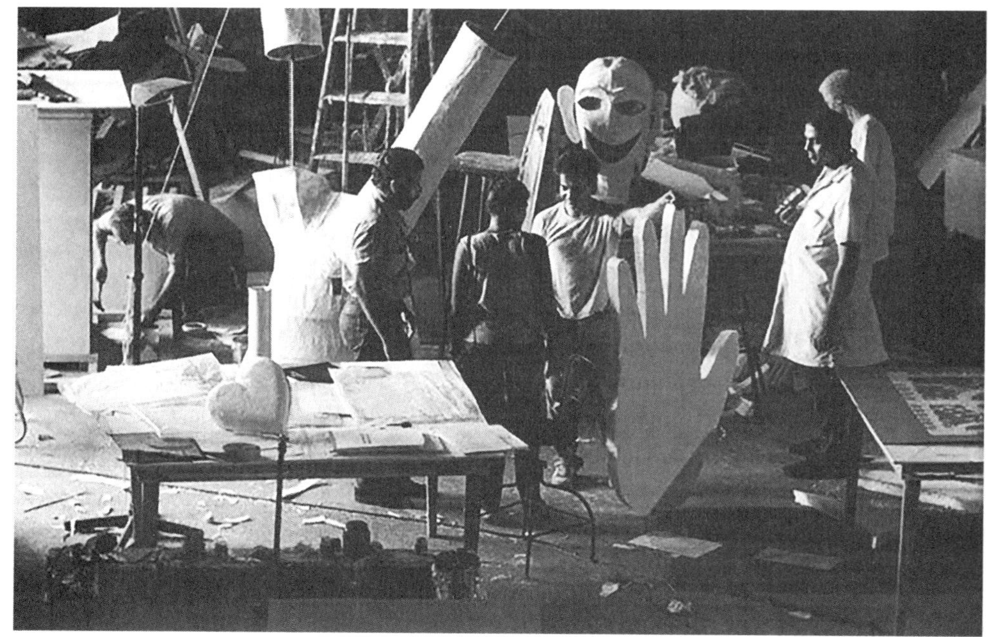

1.1   Julio Le Parc, workshop scene. Preparations for a festival of kinetic art, CODEMA park, 2 Bienal de La Habana, 1986. Source: Santiago Álvarez, *Noticiero ICAIC Latinoamericano.*

This scene opens a longer clip that was broadcast on Cuban national television documenting Le Parc's public-art intervention in CODEMA park in the Vedado district for the 1986 Bienal de La Habana. It also introduces key elements in this chapter: the gathering of an internationally acclaimed Latin American artist and art students from Havana around new symbols that referenced different art-making traditions in African, Latin American, and North Atlantic art worlds. Later scenes in this reportage will evoke *el hombre nuevo*, the ideal of a socialist new man: a reformed subject moved by the commitment to humanity's emancipation from capital. Scenes like this one illustrate the strong public-facing orientation of the early Bienal iterations in the 1980s. These first exhibitions were shaped by the effervescence of Havana's cultural scene at the time and the ongoing discussions among its members about culture's role in the socialist revolution. Like other biennials of the early boom years, the

Bienal de La Habana became a fertile space for the development of new approaches to curatorial practice as its *especialistas* (the name originally given to its curators) worked to carve spaces of autonomy in their production of a Third World avant-garde—a mission that grew from their own artistic commitments but aligned, as well, with the state's doctrine of Third World solidarity.[2]

Following a rich history of Latin American–oriented cultural events in the postrevolutionary period, art programs that joined local and international actors were not infrequent in Havana during the 1980s.[3] The city had a robust art scene that gathered artists, filmmakers, writers, musicians, dancers, and philosophers immersed in discussions about the possibilities of a renewed socialism and was more connected than ever with international developments in the arts. Since the 1960s, Havana had been an intellectual and cultural center for the Latin American artistic avant-garde. After a hiatus during the repressive period known as the *quinquenio gris* (the five Gray Years: 1971–1976), the city regained in the 1980s its reputation as the cultural capital of non-Soviet socialism, attracting cultural producers from nation members of the Non-Aligned Bloc. A variety of factors contributed to making Havana a particularly exciting cultural hotspot in the 1980s: the coming of age of the first artist generation raised in the Revolution; geopolitical developments outside of Cuba, such as reforms in the USSR and US military intervention in Central America; and the period's reevaluation of socialist doctrine in the island nation—within and beyond state institutions. These and related processes made the 1980s an especially ripe time to inaugurate an art biennial in the Cuban capital.

A Nonorthodox Marxist Cultural Policy

Testifying to this cultural effervescence were the many internationally oriented events that occurred in Havana in the 1980s, predominantly around institutions such as the Instituto Cubano de las Artes e Industrias Cinematográficas (Cuban Film Institute [ICAIC]) and Casa de las Américas. Yet the city's contemporary art scene was not exempt from this effervescence. The first generation of young artists and critics raised in socialism began curating exhibitions in smaller galleries, self-instituting themselves as an avant-garde invested in the renewal of Cuban arts. Whereas previous generations of artists worked in synchrony with developments in art throughout Latin America, Western Europe, and the United States, this younger generation looked with special interest to Africa and its diaspora. Especially invested in the rich Afro-Cuban culture was Grupo Antillano, an art collective that reclaimed African and Caribbean culture in its work and showed in a series of exhibitions, titled *Queloides*, between 1978 and 1983.[4] Similar to this approach—but with a more direct engagement with foreign neo–avant-garde forms such as conceptual art, installation, performance, and site-specific art—were the artists included in the exhibition *Volumen I* (1981), a show that positioned young Cuban artists in simultaneous dialogue with international art tendencies and the Afro-Cuban cultural legacy.[5] Originally organized at a private residence, the exhibition was eventually relocated by the Ministry of Culture to the Centro de Arte Internacional in an attempt to discourage the emergence of autonomous galleries in the capital. Gerardo Mosquera, who was already an active art critic in the local scene, wrote the exhibition essay in the small pamphlet edited for the occasion. Soon after, Mosquera would become a foundational member of the Bienal de La Habana's curatorial team, playing an important role in its theoretical program. Throughout the 1980s, other art collectives would be active in the Cuban capital, including Arte Calle, Grupo Puré, Grupo Provisional, and Grupo Imán.

This artistic effervescence mirrored changing winds within Cuban cultural policy. The creation in 1976 of the Ministry of Culture sought to appease artists' discontent and pushback against the government during the particularly repressive quinquenio gris of the early 1970s. Its founding greatly invigorated intellectual and cultural production in Havana, in large part due to the intellectual commitments of Armando Hart, the new minister of culture. A member of the original revolutionary cadre, Hart was nevertheless perceived as a so-called liberal, having distanced himself from the Soviet-oriented orthodoxy dominant in the Cuban Communist Party (CCP). Married to Haydée Santamaría, the first director of Casa de las Américas and an influential cultural strategist, Hart perceived the cultural field as a fertile terrain for the renovation of socialism. His own position as a Marxist was attuned to contemporaneous rearticulations in Western Europe, Latin America, and the United States of a culture-driven internationalism that could serve as a basis for emancipatory cultural strategy—positions closer to those held by the New Left than those of the orthodox Moscow bureaucrats and their Cuban affiliates. Though conditioned by the Central Committee's diverging positions on the culture question and Moscow's permanent hovering over national politics, reforms of the cultural-policy framework spearheaded by Hart supplemented Cuba's robust art institutions. These changes helped buttress the national art education system and exhibition venues and created new opportunities for artists to participate in international circuits. Foreign visitors to Cuba marveled at the conditions for artistic production. In the words of US art historian Dore Ashton, "The support system of the Cuban state has been exceptionally generous, allowing the young Cuban painters, sculptors, and installation artists ample latitude. With it, they have managed to absorb a striking variety of contemporary techniques."[6]

This period also coincided with what has come to be known as the *Rectificación de los errores* (The rectification of mistakes), a time of reevaluation of Cuba's historical experience of revolutionary socialism that coincided with the *perestroika* reforms started by Mikhail Gorbachev in the Soviet Union in 1984. During this time, the Cuban state distanced itself from its previous Moscow-dictated orthodoxy to implement new agendas in economic, social, and cultural policy. Partly inspired in the 1960s liberal agenda, whose main representatives included such internationally visible figures as Ernesto Guevara and Haydée Santamaría, this turn reinvigorated some of the most idealist and humanistic aspects of the Revolution. In cultural matters, the impact of Guevara's humanistic model of the hombre nuevo was felt again throughout the state. In economic policy efforts to diversify the agrarian portfolio sought to phase out the dominant monocrop sugar-plantation model.[7] The period's overall reforms of socialism primed the context for the Bienal's important reevaluation of culture's role in historical materialism.

Reflecting on his experience as an important actor in the 1959 Cuban Revolution, in 2005 Armando Hart published a retroactive evaluation of historical materialism in the twentieth century that helps explain the transformations of Havana's cultural scene in the 1980s. For the former minister of culture, socialism's biggest mistake had been Joseph Stalin's ascent to power. Hart believed that Stalin's rule had severed socialist doctrine from its necessary reliance on culture as a field for the production of subjectivity. For Hart, Stalin's economic determinism had fueled an obsessive desire to control artistic production, a position that ultimately prevented the necessary renovations to socialist doctrine that only culture could have organically delivered. Unlike other leaders of successful socialist revolutions like Vladimir Lenin, Ho Chi Min, and Fidel Castro, Stalin lacked the worldliness that life abroad had afforded to their programs and was thus illiterate in the nuanced art of articulating universalist visions from the vantage point of situated knowledge.

Part of the superstructure, art and culture participate in the transformations of consciousness that are necessary for successful, long-lasting change in the relations of production. But in order to renew socialism, culture, in its methodological and ideological repertoire, ought to speak to the specificities of life in its emplacement. Particularly concerned with the future of socialism in Latin America, Hart rooted his anti-Stalinism on the legacy of José Carlos Mariátegui, an early twentieth-century Peruvian Marxist and pioneer in articulating a socialism from the South grounded on the life and work conditions of Indigenous subjects. He also proposed a return to the foundations of Marxist theory. He cites from Marx and Engels's first critique of Ludwig Feuerbach: "The main defect of all previous materialism—including that of Feuerbach—is that they only perceive things, reality, of the senses, under the form of object or observation but not as a human sensorial activity, not as practice, not as subjective."[8] This emphasis on a theory formulated from the vantage point of sensory driven practice would shape, too, the work of curators and artists within the Bienal. The culture minister's late-life reflection on historical materialist theory conferred to culture the role of protagonist in the Cuban Revolution that helps explain the spirit of relative openness and renewal infusing Havana's cultural scenes of the 1980s.

Alongside the changes that this climate provoked in curatorial practice, the regime's practiced internationalism deeply influenced the Bienal's mission. Starting with its second iteration, the Bienal de La Habana veered toward the Third World, extending into the cultural field Cuba's military and medical solidarity campaigns throughout Africa, Southeast Asia, and the Caribbean. The Bienal also continued the regime's pan-Americanist cultural agenda, which had until then mostly relied on institutions such as Casa de las Américas and Instituto Cubano del Arte e Industrias Cinematográficas. Later sections of this chapter detail how these internationalist visions materialized in artist selection for the exhibition.

Following Fidel Castro's initiative, a 1983 state decree inaugurated the Centro de Arte Wifredo Lam, honoring the renowned Cuban surrealist painter after his death. Directed in its first iteration by a provisional team, the Bienal de La Habana was from 1985 onward organized by a stable cluster of especialistas. The group, led by Llilian Llanes, included curators Gerardo Mosquerda, Nélson Herrera Ysla, Ibis Hernández, Margarita Sánchez, and

Manuel Noceda.[9] Joining worldwide anticolonial struggles of the period, it embraced Lam's reliance on avant-garde art as a Trojan horse with which to intercept Eurocentric aesthetic paradigms. The center's main role would be to produce the Bienal de La Habana, the first art biennial of the Third World, in just one year. Its functions included promoting "internationally the artwork of artists from Asia, Africa, and Latin America, as well as of artists that struggle for cultural identity and that are related to those territories ... [and] to endorse international activities in the field of visual arts in order to develop and establish networks of cooperation."[10] The Bienal sought to decenter the North Atlantic art canon by producing and disseminating new knowledge about the state of art production in the Third World, exhibiting for the whole international community Third World artworks as theorized by Third World experts in a Third World venue.[11]

This new device drew alternative geographies of artistic production that challenged the dominating presence of Western European and US modernisms in the international art world. Although especialistas in the Bienal were mostly concerned with expanding definitions of art prevalent in elite North Atlantic art worlds, the Bienal's internationalism continued the regime's reliance on culture for the formation of a revolutionary consciousness in Cuba and abroad. Despite its openly political character, the work of especialistas within the Bienal managed to secure relative independence from state oversight—at least until the onset of the Special Period in Times of Peace (1991–2001), a time of acute economic crisis during which the cultural industries were progressively realigned with a new economic policy.[12] Heralded by many as the first truly global biennial exhibition of contemporary art, in its first four iterations the Bienal fought the worldwide advance of North Atlantic-centric aesthetic paradigms, continuing Cold War struggles for anti-imperialist resistance and excluding European and US artists from its selection. Yet since its beginning, the Bienal occupied a delicate position. While it acted as a counter-hegemonic aesthetic operation abroad, internally, the exhibition helped strengthen elites' grasp on the local contemporary art scene.

One of the Bienal's key contributions was the production of a "Third World avant-garde," an inherently polyphonic and diverse category that included the artistic repertoires of subaltern peoples around the world. This category challenged the centrality of formalism in the North Atlantic art canon, primarily through its emphasis on audience participation and multisensory engagement beyond the visual. In its early years, this exhibition realized the legacy of nonorthodox Marxism, as practiced by artists and intellectuals in the 1980s, despite contextual pressures to operate within policy tolerance and adjust to the rise of the freelance curator model in Europe and the United States. Structural conditions such as Cuba's infrastructural precarity and the impact of the US embargo on international communications drew an aura of sacrifice and shared struggle around the Bienal, uplifting its emancipatory spirit. Notably, in the words of Ecuadorian painter Oswaldo Guayasamín, overcoming these geopolitical obstacles turned the event into an "act of faith in the Cuban Revolution . . . faith in what Cuba is doing for Latin America" and Cuba's inspirational influence in the Latin American Left during the Cold War. How unlikely was it that this small Caribbean island nation, a socialist enclave far removed from its ideological and economic allies, would destabilize canonical art-historical principles, such as creative individualism and aesthetic negation, and sponsor an anti-imperialist revolution in the international art world?

A Third World Avant-Garde

In the 1960s and the years beyond, Left-oriented artists and intellectuals throughout Western Europe and Latin America were vocal advocates for the Cuban Revolution, which they perceived as fertile ground for the development of a non-Soviet socialism. Julio Le Parc was one of them, frequently visiting Havana and participating in artistic and intellectual events.[13] Recipient of a top award in the first Bienal (1984), he returned to the second Bienal (1986) to direct a workshop to design and organize a kinetic art festival in collaboration with local artists at CODEMA park. The month-long workshop began with discussions among participants on topics such as the state of Latin American arts on the international circuit and possible strategies for its improvement. Participants collaborated in the design and fabrication of a number of interactive public sculptures that would be inaugurated with a daylong festival. Among the objects were climbing structures of metal and rubber, wood carts decorated with geometric motives, and balloons resembling large-scale floral bouquets. Wooden disks rotated on an abacus-like structure, placed a few feet from the ground; swings wrapped in papier-mâché hung from trees, painted with straight geometries in primary colors. A large rope-climbing structure for children hovered in tension, tied to ground and trees; an articulated wood and thread labyrinth moved and morphed as children ran through it. Le Parc was just one of the numerous international artists who gathered in Havana during the Bienal's first four iterations. In the 1986 Bienal alone 700 artists participated with 2,500 artworks. It would be impossible to account here for the more than three thousand artists featured between the 1986 and the 1994 Bienals, yet the rich selection illustrates the diversity of participants included in the organizers' Third World-oriented vision.

In its signaling of the Third World as its organic constituency, the Bienal worked as a polyphony of subaltern peoples.[14] Widely divergent artistic styles, techniques, materials, and approaches to meaning-making gathered in the exhibitions offered divergent examples of the kinds of objects deemed worthy of cultural distinction across the Third World. This diversity problematized the tacit criteria for artistic value dominant in European aesthetics. It showed that cultural worthiness is always relative to situated worldviews. The product of this, at first glance, stylistic hodgepodge was a category whose very strength relied in defying expectations of formal coherence and hierarchies of media prevalent in elite, white-centric North Atlantic art institutions. Bienal especialistas referred to this category as "Third World avant-garde." It involved many aesthetic conversions between art genealogies that converged in a unified front in the Bienal's galleries. Wire toys, fabrics, kites, oil paintings on canvases, wood carving, photographs, and drawings from throughout the Third World reflected the many positions included in this new avant-garde. The aesthetic conversions at work in the Bienal paid little attention to the thematic and formal aspects of objects. Instead, these operations foregrounded artworks' embeddedness in the relations of coloniality, past and present, shaping their contexts of origin. As a result of these conversions, objects that spoke, for instance, of the Philippines' colonial history, Mozambique's recent independence, or racist systemic violence in the United States each reinforced the others' anticolonial positions as discrete anchors of the exhibition's broader vision.

This Third World avant-garde forged an unprecedented alliance that included artists with different degrees of visibility in the North Atlantic art capitals. A niche group of its artists had already benefited from some degree of validation by Western European and United States art institutions, in many cases following their migration to cities such as Paris, London, New York, and Madrid. In this group were Le Parc, Argentine artist Liliana Porter, Angolan painter and theorist Viteix, Pakistani painter and writer Rasheed Araeen, Uruguayan artists Antonio Frasconi and Luis Camnitzer, and Haitian painter Hervé Télémaque. Others had received international validation through pan-American cultural networks facilitated by the Visual Arts section of the US-led Pan American Union, such as those built around the Standard Oil (ESSO) and PepsiCo art awards in Bogotá, Córdoba, Cartagena, Buenos Aires, and Mexico City, or through growing private collections of Latin American art in the US (Hilton Hotels, Pan Am airlines). Participation in North Atlantic institutions such as the Paris Biennial, the Venice Biennial, and other expositions abroad had brought validation to some Bienal participants, including Ecuadorian Oswaldo Guayasamín, Brazilian Oscar Niemeyer, Venezuelans Carlos Cruz-Diez and Alejandro Otero, and Mexicans Helen Escobedo, Felipe Ehrenberg, José Luis Cuevas, and Graciela Iturbide.[15] Several of these names were included in an exhibition titled *Latin American Masters* in the second biennial. Similarly, an important contingent of US-based Left-leaning art workers visited the 1986 Bienal. Names included Juan Sánchez, Rudolf Baranick, May Stevens, Eva Cockroft, Lucy Lippard, Waldo Rasmussen, Vivian Browne, Douglas Crimp, Shifra Goldman, Josely Carvalho, Benjamin Horowitz, Pacita Abad, Carmen Vega Rivera, Liliana Porter, Henry Isaacs, Rachel Weiss, David Finn, and Honor Moore.[16] This group of internationally visible artists and writers played a key role in attracting to the Bienal visitors from Europe and the United States who joined as audiences and engaged in the peripheral events—including workshops, conferences, and roundtable discussions.

Seeking support from internationally acclaimed artists and intellectuals abroad had been a common strategy of Cuban cultural agencies since the 1960s, as a way to signal to international publics their distance from Soviet cultural doctrines and their symbolic kin with Western European socialist programs. Left-leaning Europeans had participated, for instance, in the Salón de Mayo (1967), organized in Havana by surrealist painter Wifredo Lam and Carlos Franqui, director of the magazine *Revolución*.[17] Valued by their respective national cultural fields, a large majority of Latin American Bienal artists had been trained in European-style art academies either in their countries of origin or in Paris, London, or Madrid and engaged, to varying degrees, with contemporaneous approaches to art making in the international field. They were well-versed in the genealogy of North Atlantic modernisms and frequently embraced avant-garde dispositions not dissimilar to those adopted by artists in the North Atlantic art capitals. Because of a relatively strong network of state-sponsored cultural centers on the continent (and, since the 1950s, of foreign-sponsored cultural networks as well), these artists were in dialogue with the discussions shaping European and United States art circles via exhibitions in local museums, foreign journals, travel, grants, and exchange programs. Relatively accessible for Cuban cultural agencies through the Casa de las Américas' rich directory, some of them had frequented the Cuban art scene before the Bienal and, like Le Parc and Guayasamín, generally supported the Revolution's mission.

But Cuba's allies extended beyond Latin America in the 1980s to reach other Third World nations that embraced (or were sympathetic to) socialism in their post-independence national reconstruction. The important presence of African art in the 1986 edition exemplifies this affinity. Artists Do Mesrine (Togo), Saka Acquaye (Ghana), Amir Nour (Sudan), Henry Tayali (Zambia), Worku Goshu (Ethiopia), and Helen Lieros (Zimbabwe) shared the second-floor galleries at the Museo Nacional de Bellas Artes with several Makonde carvings and paintings, and two Shona carvings. Nigerian artist F. I. Osague had a solo exhibition at Casa de África. Mozambique, a recipient of Cuban military and humanitarian support during its transition to independence from Portugal, was represented in the 1986 edition by painter Bertina Lopes; painter Malangatana Ngwenya, who was honored with a solo exhibition at the Casa de África; and Alberto Chissano, who received the first award in the category of sculpture.[18] Chissano was a self-taught artist who had exhibited internationally, albeit mostly in Lisbon and capitals of socialist nations, such as East Berlin, Moscow, and Luanda, but would later gain international exposure in Europe and the United States. His wooden sculptures reflected on the legacy of traditional culture in the postcolonial nation. In that same iteration, Angola, another Cuban ally and fellow socialist postcolonial state, was represented by Afonso Massongui, Victor Texeira, and Antonio Ole. Ole received the first award in the category of painting in the second Bienal (1986) for *Animal Herido* (Wounded animal). Younger than other biennial artists, he had spent time in the United States and would later have a strong presence in the global contemporary art world. His work featured high-value colors and influences from pop art and surrealism. Finally, Angolan Vitor Texeira (Viteix) was an artist and theorist who served as director of the National Union of Angolan Artists at the time of his participation in the second Bienal (1986). Viteix had taken part in cultural events in Havana before, and he subscribed to Ernesto Guevara's belief in art's crucial role in anti-imperial liberation. As an active member of the MPLA (Popular Movement for the Liberation of Angola) during

Angola's independence from Portugal in 1975, Viteix shared with other contemporaneous liberal Marxists concerns about the risks of top-down political leadership. His art practice blended traditional and foreign contemporary art forms. He relied on Redinha and Chokwe pictorial traditions to address Angolan social concerns, proposing *Angolinidade*, a worldview that aspired to be simultaneously local and universal, urban and rural. For Viteix, Angolinidade offered an alternative framework to the individualist models of artistic production dominant in North Atlantic art worlds.[19]

But the majority of artists featured in the exhibition had been excluded from elite North Atlantic–centric art legitimization circuits. The Bienal's counterhegemonic mission opened previously nonexistent cultural-exchange channels between Cuba and Third World nations that helped remediate the often lacking cultural infrastructures left by the former colonial powers in the young postcolonial states. The new relations established by Bienal curators provided artists throughout the Third World access to international art networks that were otherwise off-limits. In many cases, receiving validation from the Bienal facilitated their participation in art circuits within their own regions of origin. One such artist was Roberto Feleo, a Filipino sculptor whose fourteen two- and three-dimensional objects in the second Bienal (1986) narrated Filipino history by combining materials and processes from popular culture and Indigenous arts to explore national history and Filipino identity. Feleo, who frequently used in his sculptures materials such as *sawali* (woven bamboo strips), twigs, and sawed wood, would later in his career incorporate tattooing as an Indigenous practice of anticolonial resistance. In the 1986 Bienal his piece *The Blueprint of Man* joined descriptive Tagalog captions and images to envision man's essential physical, mythological, and social traits. Against dark-purple mountains and a celestial-blue sky, a white fine-line drawing dissects a human body into muscles and energy points. In a surrounding circle, eight small scenes show human and animal figurines dancing, riding, and wrestling. His stand-alone wooden sculpture *The Malay Entry to the 1976 Bicentennial Celebration* is shaped like a sea vessel, featuring two prominent extensions at each end and hundreds of tiny wood poles emerging from the center, reminiscent of a ship loaded with humans. As a local journalist reported, Feleo's pieces registered the rich cultural baggage of a country that, despite its long history of colonization, looked optimistically toward the future.[20]

Starting in 1991, the Bienal exhibited work by a small group of non-white artists from the United States and Canada as a gesture of acknowl-

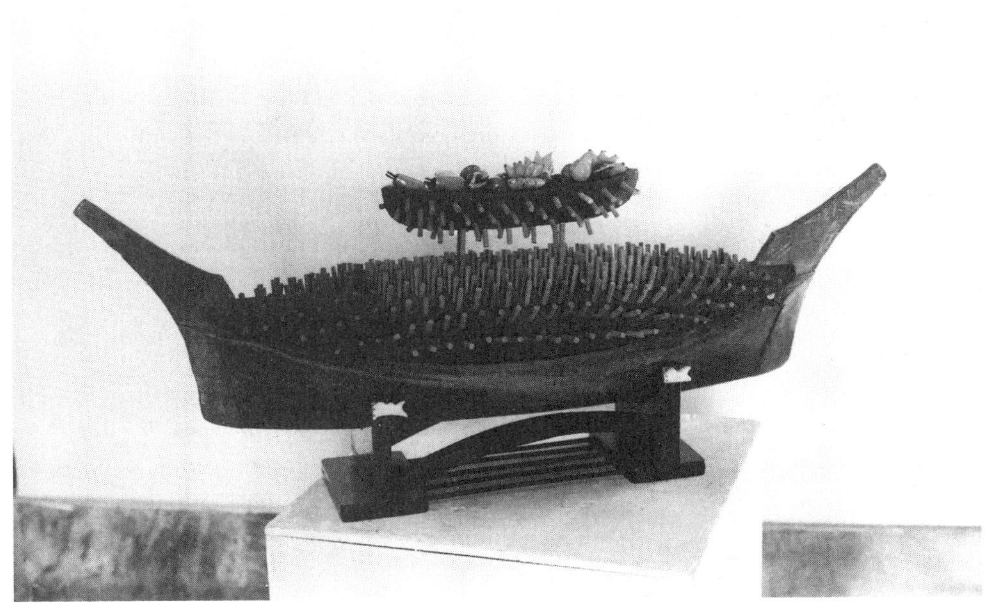

1.2 Roberto Feleo, *Malay Entry to the 1976 Bicentennial Celebration*, 2 Bienal de La Habana, 1986. Courtesy of the Luis Camnitzer and Rachel Weiss papers, Cuban Heritage Collection, University of Miami Libraries, Coral Gables, Florida.

edgment of their subjugation to colonial oppression within the North Atlantic centers of power. The main show included a large representation of Chicano artists, including Enrique Chagoya, Salvador García, Bárbara Carrasco, Francisco Pérez, and Carlos Almaras. This selection was complemented by peripheral exhibitions of art by subaltern communities from the United States and Canada. The first show included works by Puerto Rican artist Cristina Emmanuel, African American Caryl Henry, Japanese American Betty Kano, Cuban American Gloria Longval, African American Bisaj Washington, Korean American Yong Soon Min, and Filipino American Carlos Villa. Henry's piece, titled *Ancestor's Mask*, was a monotype interpreting an African mask. Emmanuel's piece, *Ella vino, vió y conquistó* (She came, saw, and conquered), was an installation of an altar with portraits of the Sacred Heart of Jesus, a vase with flowers, and four sacred-heart silver figurines. Henry's piece could be read as a commentary on the inclusion of African masks in European avant-garde painting, and Emmanuel's piece grew from a long tradition among US Latinx artists who incorporate domestic forms of image making, such as altars, into their work. One entire gallery at the Wifredo Lam Center was devoted to First Nations art in Canada, featuring work by Lance Belanger, Rebecca Belmore, Domingo Cisneros, Joseph Tehwaron David, Richard Martel, Ronald J. Noganosh, and Edward Poitras (see plate 1).

In addition to this diverse artist alliance, a third important constituency anchored the Bienal's anticolonial goals. Informed by producers of objects historically classified in the North Atlantic museum as "primitive" or "ethnic" art, this third group included as well those behind objects perceived as belonging to the realm of popular arts, crafts, and artisanship which often escaped institutionalization. Exhibitions of *adiré* fabric dyeing from Nigeria, Simon Bolívar toys from Venezuela, Mexican rag dolls, Chinese paper kites, African wire toys, and many other examples signaled the organization's intent to reach broad interest groups while simultaneously underscoring a revolt against the aura of elitism and exclusivity of the North Atlantic art institution. As Rachel Weiss states, the rich cultural and social diversity found in Third World nations "meant that each site visited by the curators presented its own set of parameters and criteria through which the ideas of 'art,' 'tradition,' 'contemporaneity,' and 'Third World' were encountered."[21] Although the idiosyncrasies of these sites complicated the logistics of curatorial research, they enriched the Bienal's theoretical apparatus with a multiplicity of aesthetic frameworks and worldviews that to date remained unacknowledged by North Atlantic attempts to curate art from the Third World. As I discuss in chapter 3, this deficiency backboned contemporaneous exhibitions such as *Magiciens de la Terre* (Centre d'Art Georges Pompidou, Paris, 1989) and *Primitivism* (Museum of Modern Art, New York, 1984–1985). This plural alliance of artists came together as a bloc in defense of their commonalities as subaltern peoples, gathering discordant constituencies in their struggle for international recognition as a "Third World avant-garde."

The Avant-Garde in Postrevolutionary Cuba

In order to understand the tactical value of this diverse international alliance, it is important to locate the Bienal in the legacy of debates about the role of art in socialism, which were as old as the Cuban Revolution itself. Although the Bienal amplified the state agenda of Third World solidarity by pursuing independence from dominant North Atlantic–centric art legitimation channels, Bienal *especialistas* realized early on that this autonomy would require a strategic reformulation of what it meant to rely on the avant-garde for historical change. This was not the first time that such a conversation happened in Cuba. Artistic production in post-1959 Cuba had been shaped by ongoing conflicts between "orthodox" and "pragmatist," and "liberal" and "extremist" factions of the government. Orthodox cadres defended Soviet-oriented bureaucratized management models, perceiving all avant-garde art as a bourgeois obstacle interrupting Soviet-style socialism. On the other side were "liberals," who aligned with the dynamic internationalism proposed by members of the original revolutionary group such as Ernesto Guevara, Armando Hart, Melba Hernández, and Haydée Santamaría. Liberals argued for a critical Marxism closer to that of its contemporaneous New Left in Europe, sectors of the civil rights movement in the US, and Latin American liberation theology, pursuing theoretical and methodological autonomy from the USSR. They defended the capacity of free culture to lead humanity into its ultimate emancipation from capital. For orthodox factions, liberals were too Left leaning and romantic, idealists enamored with utopian notions of subjectivity, whereas liberals saw the orthodox contingent as blind right-wing followers of the USSR's mechanistic approaches who prioritized rigid state control over all matters, including culture.

These differences first reached the cultural sphere during the Revolution's early days when, in 1961, the censorship of *P.M.*, a short documentary on Havana nightlife by Sabá Cabrera Infante and Orlando Jiménez Leal, prompted heated discussions between government factions and members of ICAIC. In their defense of their right to freedom of form and content in their art, the filmmakers signed a public letter stating that competing but coexisting "aesthetic ideas and tendencies live *necessarily* in *struggle*," arguing against the supposed "class character" of artistic forms.[22] The filmmakers understood that in this healthy struggle, dialectical superation, rather than externally imposed suppression, would determine the victory of certain aesthetic forms over others. In their view, it was a mistake to assume that specific art forms could be seen as direct reflections of particular class interests. However, orthodox members of the government who aligned with official USSR cultural doctrine of the time disagreed. Figures such as neo-Stalinist Edith García Buchaca, who served as president of the Consejo Nacional de Cultura from its foundation in 1961 until 1964, did not support the coexistence of diverse aesthetic tendencies within the socialist state, negating the right of artists to determine, even in speculative form, the parameters of art's development.[23] García Buchaca and similar figures called for the censoring of art forms that they deemed hermetic and dehumanized: not aligned with Soviet doctrine. Guidance and control of artistic forms ought to be, for García Buchaca, the exclusive purview of the government.[24] Attempting to silence these debates, Fidel Castro delivered the speech "Words to Intellectuals" (1961), in which he addressed the limits of creative freedom, the role of the state in promoting and guiding national culture, and the autonomy of artists in setting the conditions for their work. Castro's speech opened an ambiguous gate for freedom of form and content in art, particularly his statement that "within the Revolution, everything; without the Revolution, nothing." At first glance, Castro's double-edged wording distanced Cuba's position from the Soviet doctrine of social realism. His ambiguity also seemed to echo contemporary discussions on the nature of avant-garde art in Cuba and abroad, placing art's innovative potential in the free development of its form and entrusting to art's self-critical attitude the task of fitting its content to the revolutionary narrative framework. However, the interpretive plasticity that his phrasing invited became instrumental at times of alternate oppression and tolerance of artistic freedom for decades, most significantly during the repressive quinquenio gris.

Despite these conflicting views, Cuban culture managed to leverage its autonomy from Soviet attempts to influence cultural policy. In 1961, during Nikita Khrushchev's presidency (1953–1964), the doctrine of socialist realism was still in place in the USSR—albeit in a tamed form—putting official Soviet cultural positions in the Stalin-Pujanov-Gorki line. Socialist realism was "realistic in form, socialist in content," and it defended the use of theory to optimistically portray the role of social life in the formation of the new Soviet individual.[25] In addition to García Buchaca, a big proponent of this view was Luis Pavón Tamayo, director of the Consejo Nacional de Cultura during the quinquenio gris. Vocally opposed to it were practitioners, including visual artists, writers, and filmmakers, who had been active cultural producers since before the Revolution and had helped promote Cuban arts abroad. This roster initially included abstract surrealist painters René Portocarrero and Wifredo Lam, as well as geometric abstract painters Loló Soldevilla, Zilia Sánchez, and Raúl Martínez (an important pop-art designer, as well as author of Guevara's and Camilo Cienfuegos's mural portraits in the Plaza de la Revolución in Havana). Supporters of socialism, they defended culture's protagonism in social change, a topic that had been widely discussed in Havana's art publications of the pre-Revolution 1950s, such as *Noticias de Arte* and *Arquitectura*, which had continent-wide reach. As Weiss remarks, these artists' initial support for the Revolution did not, however, impede their later censorship and persecution by the regime, as the cases of writers Nicolás Guillén and Antonia Eiriz and artists Martínez and Chago demonstrate.[26] Even if socialist realism was never implemented as state doctrine, during these years artists and thinkers perceived to challenge official state positions were deemed *parametrados*, meaning that they didn't fit the official parameters expected of cultural production. This led to their work being silenced and excluded from distribution channels; many were sent to forced-labor camps, and many others left the island seeking exile abroad.

But despite these challenges, sympathizers of the film community and the avant-garde art scene were also present within the high cadres of government in the early Revolutionary period. For example, Ernesto Guevara criticized socialist realism as a sign of socialist bureaucratization, a "Proudhonian mistake of returning to the past" that forces man to renounce the strength of his contemporary art expressions. Remarkably, Guevara did not see freedom of expression in the arts as incompatible with single-party rule. In his words, "The probabilities that important artists will appear [within Socialism] will be greater to the degree that the field of culture and the possibilities for expression are broadened."[27] Trusting the natural development of "cultural ideological mechanisms that allow for investigation and the discarding of bad weeds, easily multiplicative under state subsidies," Guevara defended art's self-regulating capacity, making a strong argument for its relative autonomy from the state.

This position participated in broader reevaluations, outside Cuba, of the role that culture plays in emancipatory struggle. Guevara's words remind us of Peter Bürger's interpretation of the *Grundrisse*, where he places on art's self-critical faculties its capacity to identify traces of capitalism. These diagnostic capacities invalidate arguments in favor of art's autonomy, an autonomy that is never real but an illusion sustained in the alienation of artists and publics from artistic means of production. In the words of Bürger, "Like the public realm, the autonomy of art is a category of bourgeois society that both reveals and obscures an actual historical development. All discussion of this category must be judged by the extent to which it succeeds in showing and explaining logically and historically the contradictoriness inherent in the thing itself."[28] This position not only renders art's self-critical flair useful in the transition to socialism, but, like Armando Hart's critique, registered earlier in this chapter, would later convey, it portrays Soviet-style regulation of artistic form and content as a theoretical mistake. Until the fall of the USSR, the cultural field managed to leverage a certain degree of autonomy from Moscow-oriented governance models, chiefly during the 1960s and 1980s. Throughout these years, the "liberal" Marxist position survived in some cultural institutions, first at the Casa de las Américas and ICAIC, to resurface again two decades later at the Centro de Arte Wifredo Lam, despite the vigilant eye of government orthodoxy.[29]

Emancipatory Neo–Avant-Gardes

In addition to the many artworks exhibited in its several venues, since its early days the Bienal featured frequent collaborative workshops with foreign artists. These experiential formative spaces departed from the principle that collaborative artistic production was an inherently emancipatory practice. Within the biennial, this emphasis on collaboration invited reformulations of the North Atlantic–centric art canon. Beyond the biennial, it served as a metaphor for the possibilities offered by a socialism renewed through a practiced engagement with the senses, a nonorthodox Marxism that acknowledged the importance of aesthetic experience in the shaping of emancipated subjects. Workshops with foreign artists highlighted the key role that collaboration played for some art genealogies bred outside of North Atlantic liberalism. In Le Parc's workshop, for example, the will to facilitate unmediated audience engagement with the objects at CODEMA park mirrored the kinetic artist's career-long belief in the liberatory agency of active spectators. A highly visible figure in the kinetic art movement during the 1960s, Le Parc was a founding member of Groupe de Recherche d'Art Visuel (GRAV). The Argentine artist, a resident of Paris, exhibited broadly throughout the United States, Latin America, and Europe, a testament to the popularity of kinetic art in the 1960s.[30] GRAV's reliance on multimedia multiples questioned the fetishism of unique artworks, embracing the visual effects and standardized production processes of new technologies and industrial materials. In their work, kinetic artists pursued a symbolic alliance with the industrial working classes, challenging the metaphysical gesturing of US abstract expressionism and *art informel* in France, movements that the group viewed as complacent with the bourgeois status quo. GRAV exited the gallery to reclaim public urban space because artists "should tend to the collective multiple, the playroom, the public demonstration, in which every group of spectators will be simultaneously involved and each of them become actor and object of the show at the same time."[31] Kinetic art, with its popular acclaim, liberatory goals, and democratic orientation had been famously met with suspicion by canonical modernist critics like Clement Greenberg, who discounted it as a case of "novelty art," a "logical moment in the working out" of art's expungement of the "odd, the incongruous, and the socially shocking" in itself, and as "rather easy stuff," a mere transitional stage toward minimalism.[32] Against Greenberg's disembodied rationalism, Le Parc embraced instead wholesome sensual perception as a democratic emancipatory gateway, relying on optical illusions to shock audiences out of their complacency and into a better understanding of the human condition.[33] This defense of the aesthetic as a collaborative and participatory relation was not exclusive to Le Parc. It permeated throughout the first iterations of the Bienal, helping position nonorthodox Cuban socialism as a more appealing and humanist alternative to Soviet socialist rigidity.

Le Parc's embrace of playful participation as emancipatory practice echoed the Bienal's belief in the freeing potential of aesthetic education for individuals and society at large. The experience led by Le Parc partly replicated another workshop that he had led in Madrid in 1985, during which he and twenty-one young artists met for several days to discuss issues related to artistic professionalization and the potential of art to provoke social change.[34] Both workshops resulted in carnivalesque actions in urban parks aided by kinetic art objects, yet there were important differences between the two. Whereas in Madrid the intervention in Retiro park had been a collective decision reached "little by little" during workshop discussions, in Havana the installation was a prerequisite from the beginning, curtailing participants' agency and limiting the project's dialogical nature to the final interaction of the audience with the pieces. Participants in Le Parc's Havana workshop were a mix of local art students, foreign artists, and Cuban artists (some of whom exhibited in the Bienal). Almost every student, Le Parc remembers, "needed to be able to put aside their habitual work or study activities so as to have disposable time [for the workshop]. This can be

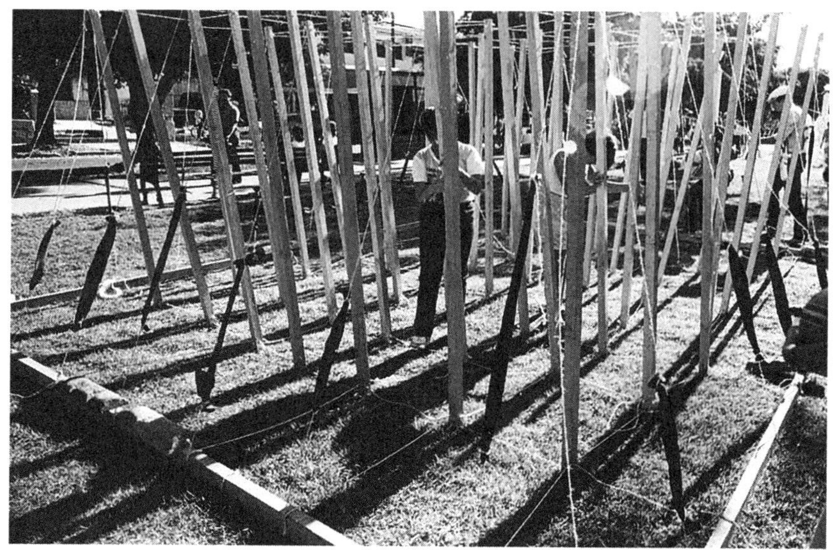

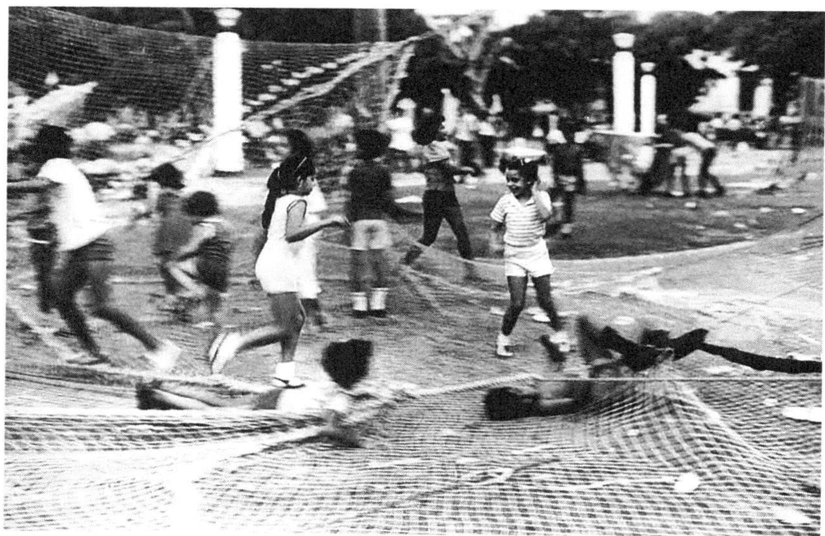

1.3   Julio Le Parc, a festival of kinetic art, CODEMA park, 2 Bienal de La Habana, 1986. Source: Santiago Álvarez, *Noticiero ICAIC Latinoamericano*.

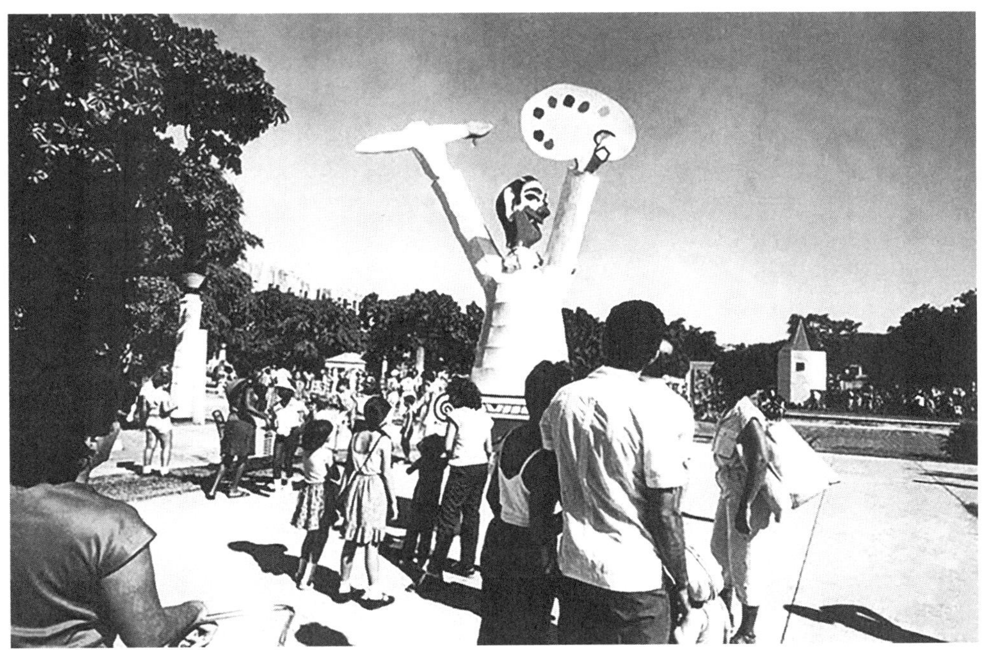

1.4   Julio Le Parc, a festival of kinetic art, CODEMA park, 2 Bienal de La Habana, 1986. Source: Santiago Álvarez, *Noticiero ICAIC Latinoamericano*.

positive, but at the same time it can be considered as a provisional change of their workplace. . . . [The] Cuban participants might have thought, at least at the beginning, that they were there to help me produce my own personal project."[35] As many foreign artists invited to the Bienal recall, it was common for art students to be recruited into the exhibition as participants in workshops or as assistants to foreign artists in order to facilitate professional-development opportunities. Further, in 1980s Cuba, members of the Brigadas José Martí were often employed as nonremunerated support personnel for cultural events, their labor framed as a contribution to nation building and the socialist project. At least ideally, the students were meant to participate in the workshop both as support personnel *and* as coauthors of the intervention at CODEMA park. In both Madrid and Havana, Le Parc's pedagogical method was based on the exchange of information among participants and the subsequent fabrication of public artworks. In his dialectical model, theses and antitheses precluded art-mediated joy in the public space.

Like many Left-leaning artists in the second half of the Cold War, Le Parc saw the public as a collective social being capable of engaging in alliance building, diagnosing social contradictions, and self-guiding toward emancipation. His views had developed during his involvement in the Atelier Populaire, a collective, anonymous press behind the now-iconic May 1968 posters. In his manifesto "Guerrilla Cultural" (1968), he called on young artists to revert traditional art's complacency to power, "questioning the prerogatives or privileges of our own situation [as artists,] ... awakening everyone's potential to participate—and decide on their own—and to arrive at the promise of coming together with others in the development of a common action, so that [everyone] plays a real role in what informs their lives. [Artists] must become aware that the scheme through which [art] touches people is the same one that upholds the systems of domination."[36] In this sense, Le Parc's intervention in CODEMA park celebrated the power of sensory-driven engagement to forge social cohesion, disrupt passive subordination, and mobilize the masses as agents of history. The interactive objects produced for the park were conceived with expectations of playfulness based on Le Parc's belief in the public as "a social being who, together with other interested parties, can establish their own criteria, see problems and propose solutions" within a social reality that required transformation.[37] Rendering Havana's social fabric in a new and playful way, Bienal works like Le Parc's portrayed everyday life in socialism as modern, fun, and free.

Toward the end of the footage of Le Parc's festival, the camera centers on one object: a bulky fabric sack filled with cut-up newspaper featuring a hand-drawn caricature of Ronald Reagan. Hanging from a tree like a piñata, kids hit the sack with a stick until it tore open, releasing loads of tiny newspaper cuttings. This celebratory attack on United States official symbols was especially relevant in 1986, during the escalation of threats to Cuba by the Reagan administration and its aggressive military interventionism in Latin America. The reportage shows how ritualized communal violence against the United States president's portrait triggered feelings of euphoria and pride in the participants, rooting this shared catharsis in Cuba's decades-long anti-imperialist resistance. The festival closed with a parade of a papier-mâché painter—an ephemeral "anti-statue" larger than human scale—meant to be left at the park. Eyes and tongue articulated in and out of the head. Arms up in the air, he wielded a brush and a palette. In place of legs, an Ionic capital.[38] Le Parc called it a *bonhomme*, a fellow, a buddy, your everyday guy, inviting readings of the figure as both a naïve, down-to-earth individual and as a ceremonial object, something like a snowman for the festival of public arts. The parade ritualized the demise of the bohemian artist—individualistic, detached from society, bound to modern art medium hierarchies, heir to classic aesthetics.[39] By emphasizing multisensorial, explorative relations between objects and humans, Le Parc's intervention provided an alternative to the delayed emancipatory promises of visually driven modernist negation. The new man, *el hombre nuevo*, was now free, joyfully embracing forms and colors alongside others in public.

As in other sites during the early biennial boom years, political and artistic interests merged around the art biennial. At times of increasing US belligerence in Central America and changing political winds in the USSR, Cuba sought to reposition itself as a leader within the Third World. In order for this situated goal to succeed, it ought to be articulated in universalist claims, highlighting Cuba's commonalities with subaltern peoples worldwide. An art biennial in Havana offered a good opportunity to advance the anticolonial goals of the Cuban state while making a significant contribution to the histories of contemporary art through the showcase of artworks from Latin America, Africa, Asia, and the Middle East. For its organizers, the Bienal and its peripheral events had the potential of bringing disparate international constituencies together under their shared commitment to countering Western European and United States dominance in the cultural field. Desires to articulate a counter-hegemonic response to the North Atlantic art canon afforded the Bienal de La Habana a temporary vantage point for the staging of a Third World avant-garde, a new artistic category achieved through manifold conversions between aesthetic paradigms and artistic genealogies. In the words of Mosquera, as an institutional alternative to the North Atlantic–centric international art world, the Bienal "represents a Third World effort—if not an entirely conscious one—at constructing a new international order of culture and a more universal perspective wherein the interests of all peoples converge, this being in opposition to the fabricated cosmopolitanism from the island of Manhattan."[40] This programmatic emphasis on featuring art from all corners of the Third World turned the exhibition space into a choral consciousness of subaltern peoples that proposed alternative models for the valuation and legitimation of culture. Bienal especialistas provided institutional support to culture from the Third World in ways unseen in North Atlantic art institutions to that date.

These internationalist longings enlivened a Marxist tradition that centered culture as the site for the unraveling of socialism's internal contradictions. Against the management-oriented Marxism-as-state-science dominant in the Soviet Bloc, Bienal curators joined their nonorthodox contemporaries in Cuba and abroad, defending the potential of an aesthetic kernel within Marxist theory. In its own way, the Bienal institutionalized Left-leaning liberal tendencies within Cuban socialism at the time, foregrounding the importance of culture as a space for the enactment of emancipated social relations. I address the implications that this perspective brought for curatorial expertise in the Bienal in the following chapters. For now, we are left with images of the exultant joy that kinetic art installations awakened in Havana residents in 1986.

two

Curating the Third World

One evening, at a cultural event in the late 1980s, the Bienal de La Habana director, Llilian Llanes, chatted casually in a corner with a small group of colleagues. Suddenly, the hall went silent: Fidel Castro was in the room. In his customary green uniform, he crossed the room walking toward her and asked, "Are you the director of the [Wifredo] Lam [Center]? I've been wanting to pay you a visit." Some months later, Castro's transport arrived at the Lam at 9:00 a.m. sharp. He and Llanes toured the facilities and galleries as she briefed him on the preparatory work for the next Bienal edition. Llanes explained that every *especialista* was involved in all parts of the curatorial process: traveling for research, discussing artist selection and planning the event, and actively participating in the production and installation of each show. As they conversed, Castro seemed to disagree with her approach, defending instead the need to secure the autonomy of experts. According to Llanes, "Fidel wanted detached scientists and artists. I wanted to train especialistas for whom theory and practice were the same thing."[1] This anecdote, as recalled by Llanes, mythologizes the Bienal's origins as framed by the clash between Castro's "orthodox" understanding of expertise and the Bienal's "liberal Marxist" version. Although Llanes indeed took a directive, protagonist role in the exhibition's early editions, the Bienal's operative model was devised as a series of ad hoc, experimental solutions to its mission taken in collaboration by the whole team of especialistas. Castro's preferred paradigm of expertise was hierarchical and autonomous from practice, but the Bienal's approach was closer to nonorthodox socialism's goal of overcoming alienation by enhancing collaborative relations between workers.

These opposing models reflected the diverse ways in which socialist strategists and thinkers had conceptualized the relationship between theory and practice since the 1850s. As I argue in chapter 1, liberal, nonorthodox Marxism was not a dominant position in the Cuban Communist Party—which, especially during the 1970s, had remained closer to Moscow's bureaucratic, top-down approach to the organization of expertise. Nonetheless, nonorthodox Marxism enjoyed wide support by members of the Cuban intellectual and cultural circles, as well as by some visible figures within the revolutionary cadres, including Casa de las Américas founder Haydée Santamaría, Minister of Culture Armando Hart, and Ernesto Guevara, outspoken defenders of this approach within Cuba and internationally. The nonorthodox Marxist framework preferred a humanist socialist culture of work that was dialectical, collaborative, and participatory. It operated on the principle of "dialectical discipline" (versus discipline as submission to management hierarchies within orthodox Marxist bureaucracy), promoted collaborative deliberation based on "collective discussion" and "democratic centralism," and sought to improve "increasing workers' participation through their organizations in the management" of workplaces.[2] As they materialized in the Bienal, these ideals shaped an essentially horizontal and collaborative approach to the production of artistic knowledge and curatorial authorship. In contrast to the model of the individual curator as author that was by then gaining traction in Western Europe and the United States, especialistas in Havana formed a polyvocal curatorial body as they engaged in research trips abroad, collective curatorial discussions, and the cumulative production of the exhibitions, mirroring the anti-hegemonic nature of the Bienal. However, this singular approach faced obstacles, such as the limitations of Cuba's diplomatic reach, the precarity of communication infrastructures and the cultural industries in some Third World nations, and, chiefly, the difficulties that Bienal experts faced in trying to eventually abandon the North Atlantic–centric art-historical framework in which they had been trained.

Art biennials are porous organizations that incorporate relational models from their extra-artistic contexts. To support its ambitious anticolonial mission, the Bienal de La Habana drew from models of ideological export and military strategy practiced by the Cuban state as much as from the everyday forms of reciprocity and collaboration informing life in the Cuban capital. The Bienal's curatorial strategy resembled *foquismo*, a dynamic form of guerrilla warfare developed by Ernesto Guevara.[3] Not unlike the exhibition's program, foquismo's dynamism pursued the convergence of rural and urban actors, who came together in cells to facilitate ideation and execution of their moves. Similarly, Bienal especialistas and their widely diverse artist selection joined in tactical alliance against dominant art paradigms, emulating the guerrilla units known as *focos*.

Literal and figurative equivalencies between art and military strategy were, however, not exclusive to Cuba. They date back to the conception of the term *avant-garde* as an analogy drawn in early nineteenth-century French Saint Simonian circles between the prefigurative power of an army's vanguard and the imaginative faculties of artists, scientists, and industrialists, capable of anticipating, and planning for, better social arrangements. In the words of French mathematician Olinde Rodrigues, "It is we, artists, that will serve as your avant-garde; the power of the arts is indeed the most immediate and fastest.... We address ourselves to the imagination and feelings of people: we are therefore supposed to achieve the most vivid and decisive kind of action."[4] Saint-Simonian social-reform circles conferred on the arts the capacity of imagining and helping popularize articulations of social life that benefited the common good. Heir to this legacy, the Bienal instituted itself as an operation of avant-garde intentions, in the classic sense, prefiguring emancipated social life while simultaneously incorporating forms of contextual collaboration into its model.

Collaborating, in Theory and Practice

Collaboration is a fundamental feature of art worlds, including those around and within the porous walls of the art biennial. Necessarily situated in their particular context, collaborative relations offer experiential, ad hoc responses to particular needs while facilitating instances of subjective identification and learning. As Howard Becker describes in his symbolic interactionist theory of art worlds, relations of cooperation inform the production and circulation of the practical conventions, professional roles, and theoretical frameworks that make art possible.[5] But these forms of symbolic reciprocity are always complemented by instances of material reciprocity that permit the production of art. The latter are necessary for the sustenance and cultivation of cultural infrastructures, labor relations among cultural workers, and the procurement of the material and immaterial elements that inform art objects in their institutional and para-institutional lives. Furthermore, art historian Grant Kester reminds us that in addition to facilitating the joining of disparate worldviews around the aesthetic experience, collaboration brings actual human bodies together, facilitating instances of empathic identification between actors.[6] Despite the growing protagonism of the independent curator-as-author in turn-of-the-century art worlds worldwide, early-boom art biennials relied heavily on contextual collaborative flows since their beginnings.[7] In the early iterations of the Bienal de La Habana, collaboration occurred through preparatory research trips, deliberative meetings among curators, the installation of artworks, artist workshops, peripheral programming, and the active participation of audiences and foreign guests in the many activities that surrounded this first biennial exhibition of art from the Third World. In all, collaboration conferred on the exhibition a marked dialogical nature that served as basis for the gathering of the multiple constituencies under the label of "Third World art."

Fueling the monumental effort of crafting a Third World avant-garde was the belief that cooperative relations can achieve great things. Actors collaborating in the Bienal as artists, workshop participants, or engaged audiences embodied the nonorthodox Marxist ideal of de-alienated workers engaged in the coproduction of socialism as a social as much as an aesthetic enterprise. This belief grounded the work of artists and especialistas in a foundational question for socialist theory: What organization of labor is better suited to support humanity's emancipation from capitalist exploitation? In part because it preceded the Industrial Revolution (and continues throughout), collaborative labor plays a central role in Marx's analysis of capitalist production, where it is sometimes idealized as a precapitalist labor form exempt from inherent exploitation. But it is the social strength and heightened vitalist excitement that occur in collaboration that make this form of labor crucial for accomplishing critical results otherwise unattainable through an equivalent amount of work hours performed by workers in isolation, thanks to the added spiritual connection among workers that is absent in isolated labor. Defined in *Capital* as the relation of production that involves many individuals working together on the same (or tightly connected) production process, cooperative labor, for Marx, lies at the core of major historical works of "magnificence and utility": grandiose, beautiful, and purposeful productions, such as monuments, colossi, and major works of art and architecture in Asia and Egypt that survived through history thanks to the unique virtues of this relation of production.[8] The Bienal de La Habana, as a monumental enterprise itself, was possible because of cooperative work throughout, from projects like Julio Le Parc's public-art workshop to the Bienal's unique curatorial research model and the joint conceptualization of a Third World avant-garde.

In late-1980s Havana, Castro's defense of the social autonomy of expertise clashed with the Bienal's dedication to nurturing especialistas embedded in the social fabric. Castro's position followed Lenin's model of scientific socialism, where experts produced theory to drive workers objectively into a logical historical direction: the communist state. Conversely, the Bienal carried out a methodological inversion of this model, in which expertise was by necessity embedded in cultural practices. This foundational discrepancy actualized important methodological debates within Marxist theory. The organization of expert labor in the Bienal emulated the dialectical method outlined by Marx in his 1857 afterword to the second edition of *Capital*. This method, which Stuart Hall called "rising to the concrete," critiques the ideological determinism behind Hegel's model of teleological history and proposes instead a knowledge driven by careful attention to detail in the analysis of particular social formations as they take form in the material world. In the words of Marx, "For Hegel, the process of thinking, which he even transforms into an independent subject, under the name of 'the Idea,' is the creator of the real world, and the real world is only the external appearance of the idea. With me the reverse is true: the ideal is nothing but the material world reflected in the mind of man and translated into forms of thought."[9] Castro's envisioning of expertise was highly influenced by Lenin's Hegelian approach, according to which detaching consciousness from practice would allow for the development of "pure theory," yielding a socialist objective science of governance—itself a motor of linear history. However, the Bienal's predication of theory to practice that was most obvious in the work of the especialistas, echoed, instead, the dynamic models of class conflict and consciousness transformation bred in the interstices of bottom-up strategy, such as foquismo. This fruitful methodological debate allowed for an on-the-ground, research-driven curatorial inquiry that delivered knowledge about the state of art production in the Third World, in its many forms, while providing situated guidance on how to present this knowledge to publics.

Well-Rounded Curatorial Labor

Collaboration can, indeed, achieve great things. Collaborative relations of production shaped the Bienal de La Habana from its early days. When the Bienal was created in 1983, there were no funds, staff, curatorial team, or venue allocated for it.[10] The project officially reported to the Ministry of Culture, and in its first iteration the director of the National Plastic Arts Council (CNAP), Marcia Leiseca, was charged with convening a team of employees from the Ministry of Culture and the Visual Arts Department at Casa de las Américas.[11] The former contributed skills such as curatorial experience and bureaucratic knowledge. In addition to their experience with Latin American culture, employees from Casa de las Américas, as some of the few local art experts with a solid network of foreign contacts, brought to the new biennial their valuable social capital.

This diverse core granted the Bienal partial autonomy from government oversight in its earliest days. As a then-curator in the Visual Arts Department at Casa de las Américas remembers, Casa curators "often traveled to research the arts in Latin America, and so we brought the invitations on behalf of the [Bienal] team. . . . We relied on friends in those countries to distribute them."[12] Those joining from Casa de las Américas also shared technical knowledge about logistics as important as artwork transportation from other Latin American nations to Cuba, a process that, because of the US embargo on the island, often happened via Madrid or Paris. Casa's spearheading of solidarity ties among cultural workers, artisans, and intellectuals throughout Cuba and Latin America had helped forge a Latin American Left-leaning intellectual class that upheld Havana as its ideological capital. The short time allowed for the preparation of the first Bienal in 1984 limited participation to Latin American artists, for the team initially relied on Casa de la Américas to invite participants (although their contact list would soon exceed Casa's).[13]

Once the final team formed in 1985 to start preparing the second iteration, Bienal especialistas embarked on a years-long investigation about the state of art production in the Third World. They now worked under the directorship of Llilian Llanes. Research travels by Bienal especialistas began to trace Cuba's Third World internationalism, surveying the extent of the nation's diplomatic network.[14] At the beginning, Nelson Herrera Ysla researched the Arab world, Gerardo Mosquera traveled across sub-Saharan Africa, Margarita Sánchez worked in South America, José Manuel Noceda studied the Caribbean, José de Ayala scouted the Philippines, and Ibis Fernández toured Southern Asia. Mirroring foquista strategy, their long research missions sought to establish relations with regions outside the North Atlantic art complex by recruiting allies for their venture and gathering situated knowledge on cultural and artistic production in these regions. In its second iteration the exhibition included artworks from sixty-one nations in Africa, Asia, and Latin America, reaching the whole of the Non-Aligned Bloc.[15] Although their assignments would sometimes change, in most cases the curators have worked on their regions of expertise for decades, developing a deep knowledge of the state of art production in these regions, sustained by cultivated reciprocal relations with local art actors. When research trips were not possible, the especialistas would ask local critics or curators to propose an artist selection from their region.

Despite this robust strategy, curatorial research was conditioned by scarce material resources. Funds allocated by the Ministry of Culture for research travel covered airfares and meals. Before each trip, every special-ist reached out to personal contacts in their areas of expertise, who pro-vided them with a place to sleep and connected them to other artists and theorists in their area. Individual-to-individual hospitality solved material limitations and, most importantly, provided legitimacy for the specialists when they were introduced into a local art scene. Noceda remembers how, in the early years, Llanes

> always reserved funds that, once a Bienal iteration was over, would allow us to start curatorial [research] travels, to start exploring and researching for the next edition. But those funds were too meager and barely allowed us to pay for plane tickets and meals for especial-istas. And so, through friends, Llilian or we looked for people who would provide us with housing. Sometimes critics, artists, friends of an artist . . . would let us have a small room with a bathroom and there we stayed fifteen, twenty days . . . there were some who traveled for even longer.[16]

Margarita González, a specialist in the art of Mexico, Chile, and Argentina, remembers one occasion when she was in Mexico City for a month, during which time she lived in the home of a Mexican artist who has since become a friend and an important trusted informant about Mexico's contemporary art scene.[17] When individual contacts were not enough, Llanes reached out to personal acquaintances in the Ministry of Foreign Relations, who would in turn connect her to Cuban ambassadors and their cultural attachés abroad. These high-level official endorsements helped sustain researchers' initial ventures into some regions and provided valuable help outside of Latin America. Cuban diplomats abroad also provided material and travel support to especialistas. During a trip through sub-Saharan Africa, officials at the Cuban embassy in Angola escorted Mosquera across the border with a neighboring nation, providing military protection at times of armed conflict and facilitating his movement through the continent when inter-African flights were not yet frequent.[18] Similarly, his introduction by a member of the Cuban diplomatic mission in a Middle Eastern nation led Herrera Ysla to visit a valuable art collection located at the guarded residence of a chief of state.[19] To most, support from the Cuban diplomatic body translated to board and shipping aid, for the big collections of catalogs, leaflets, photos, books, and other materials gathered during fieldwork were too heavy to accompany the especialistas on flights, and were instead sent to Havana via diplomatic mail. Herrera Ysla summarized the research process as follows: the artist selection "is based on already existing information, in journals, books, and catalogs, as well as on our consultations with art critics in cases of countries with an active criticism practice.... We consult with professors, historians, and researchers. Our other source is the most direct one: going to these countries. There are Cuban especialistas collecting information in Mexico, Canada, Africa. After [their trips,] we meet in Havana and engage in analysis."[20]

These trips were beneficial in several ways. First, they provided empirical grounding for the especialistas' investigations. In the words of Noceda, "Curatorial travels allowed one to confirm on the ground what one had already studied in books and catalogs ... all the information that one had been reading here, sitting in this very same chair and desk."[21] Second, they provided especialistas from the Lam Center with firsthand access to local art scenes when specialized literature on them was limited or nonexistent, such as in the Middle East and sub-Saharan Africa. Third, they helped advertise the Bienal abroad as both an opportunity for symbolic anticolonial emancipation and a new space of art legitimization. Fourth, they strengthened the especialistas' relations with their regions of expertise, informing years-long relationships with individual agents and art institutions. Finally, they often provided especialistas with the opportunity to earn supplementary incomes by participating in events in local art scenes. The Bienal, in turn, gained exclusive locally sourced data on art practices yet unseen in North Atlantic art capitals. This material was later collectively processed, upon return, by the whole group of especialistas while crafting the next Bienal iteration and later archived in the Centro de Arte Wifredo Lam. The restricted nature of international travel in Cuba made these research trips especially attractive: few Cubans had the opportunity to travel abroad. These trips were a source of symbolic, social, and material capital for the researchers and of cultural and social capital for the Bienal. Their coveted status has made them a point of particular contention between Bienal organizers, interested in protecting them, and Ministry of Culture officials, permanently lowering budgets allocated for travel. As well, the onset of the Special Period in Times of Peace in 1991 significantly impacted these research trips, reducing the especialistas' research capacity.[22]

Upon their return from research trips, the especialistas embarked on the collective processing of empirical material. During this second stage, they held weekly three-day meetings to discuss and evaluate the proposals made by each member regarding the artworks to be included in the exhibition. As Llanes remembers, "The whole group voted [on each proposal]. We held collective discussions about each candidate. Each especialista had to explain their rational choices about artists, not so much artworks, but about how each artist saw the world."[23] Several especialistas shared with me that the group valued artists' subjective interpretations of the exhibition's premise instead of discussing specific artworks. This interest in the artists' consciousness and their worldviews over particular objects resonates with conceptualizations of labor within the nonorthodox socialist framework, as discussed elsewhere in this chapter. Further, it highlights how especialistas relegated objects' stylistic and formalist commonalities to a second plane, to center artworks' expressions of their subaltern status within broader colonial relations. The group sought to reach consensus, yet when it wasn't possible, Llanes delegated decisions to the region's expert. Once the selection was finalized, the group arranged the artists in the gallery space according to their personal statements rather than the formal characteristics of their artworks.

These discussions behind closed doors provided especialistas with relative independence from the other tasks involved in the preparation of the Bienal during a bracketed period. Llanes recalls that during the discussion stage, she tried to "protect especialistas from organizational headaches," such as budgetary limitations, permit processing, and the coordination of available galleries for exhibitions.[24] However, as the next section of this chapter shows, the especialistas were thrown into organizational duties soon after the selection of artists concluded. This second stage of collective decision making produced the categories that would articulate the Bienal's iteration. Avoiding a formalist exhibition logic, they grouped artists instead by the compatibility of their subjective positions and worldviews, challenging exhibition conventions like formal affinity and technique and favoring instead the creation of a diverse choral consciousness—a set of criteria that was already present in the first biennial iteration. For example, a newsreel about the 1984 Bienal's opening shows the juxtaposition of stylistically diverse artworks: two large, realistic drawings of human figures in charcoal, an oil portrait of the profile of a child *campesino* (peasant) with heavy brushstrokes in an almost impressionist materiality, two colorful schematic frontal portraits of Black women with birds on their heads, and a large painting of a human-like creature with a serpent body in the jungle.[25]

After the conceptualization stage came the cumulative production of the exhibition. The especialistas collaborated with all members of the Lam's small staff, installed artworks in specific settings, organized peripheral events, and arranged for logistics, such as lodging and meals for guests. This last stage involved the multifaceted intervention in the institutional and spatial fabric of the city, grounding in practical technique the abstractions of art-historical expertise. It further shows the ad hoc forms of cooperation that allowed for the Bienal to exist. The shipping of artworks often posed difficulties, given the restrictions on international transport to and from Cuba by the US embargo on the island. Artwork production and installation was also a challenge, for the scarcity of materials required their importation or the improvised alteration of the artwork's specificities. Sometimes, materials were donated or loaned by other agencies in the city, found only after several personal phone calls requesting production remnants or the like. At the beginning of the Special Period in 1991, dependency on interpersonal solidarity became crucial. For his production of an installation including one of his *aeropostal* pieces at the former military building of Morro Cabaña, Chilean artist Eugenio Dittborn had requested several tons of salt to fill a gallery room in the Castillo del Morro (see plate 2). Another Chilean artist, Nury González, needed several hundred fishing weights and considerable amounts of soil for her installation *El Sur Total del Mundo* (The world's total south) at the Museo Nacional de Bellas Artes (see plate 3). Given the acute scarcity of food and goods in Cuba at the time, these materials were extremely hard to find. After several days of consulting with different agencies, a personal connection led Llanes to contact high-ranking officials in the armed forces who, in turn, connected her with a military diner and the headquarters of Havana's fishing fleet. Because of the mediation of this high-ranking official, these two organizations provided the coveted salt and fishing weights to the artists. Further, although the specialized technical skills required for the installation of some artworks were available in Havana, the Bienal's limited budget could not afford the hiring of additional labor force for installation. In some cases, voluntary labor from the Brigada José Martí arrived. Nury González remembers how workers at the shipyard cut the fishing weights to her desired length and how an art student, assigned to her as her assistant, traveled with her throughout several parks in Havana so that she could fill plastic bags with soil from the playgrounds.[26] Peripheral events, such as talks, presentations, and workshops, were organized in a similar fashion: hosted temporarily at other venues, produced with shared or repurposed resources, and put together by voluntary labor.

The Bienal was also an important formative space. In the absence of formal training opportunities on how to organize and run an international art exhibition of these dimensions, Bienal especialistas and other employees at the Lam Center developed their professional skills via ad hoc improvisation and informal apprenticeships. Senior especialistas brought inherited knowledge from their previous fields: Llanes, a professor of Cuban architecture history, contributed her savviness on Cuban bureaucracy and event organization, as well as a rich list of personal contacts in official spheres (because she was a well-positioned member of the Cuban Communist Party). Mosquera, who had previously worked in the Dirección de Artes Plásticas and was already a prolific art critic, played a key role in shaping the Bienal's sophisticated theoretical and art-historical framework. Herrera Ysla, an architect and poet, also contributed to the exhibition's theoretical and logistical apparatus. The interdisciplinary staff and the hands-on approach provided key formative opportunities for its younger staff, who learned by apprenticeship, for they usually joined the organization without formal curatorial training. Noceda, a recent art history graduate when he

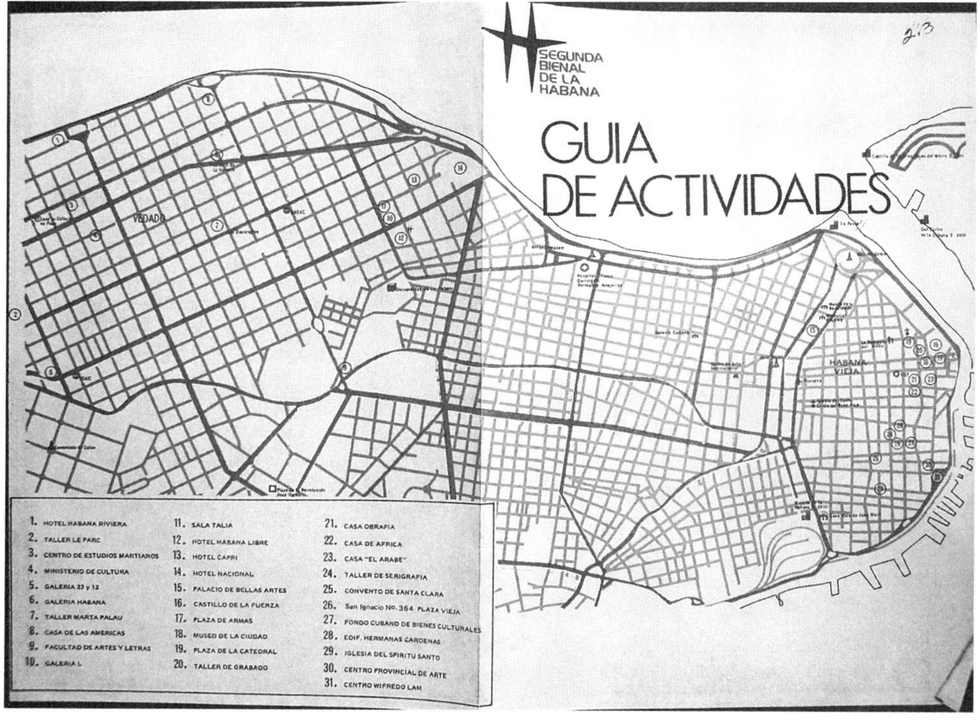

2.1   Map of 2 Bienal de La Habana, 1986. Source: Archivos Centro de Arte
       Wifredo Lam, Havana, Cuba.

started working in the Bienal, remembers that "when I joined the team, that is, in late November 1984, the center was just Llilian [Llanes], Nelson [Herrera Ysla], and [Gerardo] Mosquera. One comrade and I joined; we were the first recently graduated students who began to work in the center."[27] Thus, through years of improvisation and ad hoc learning, the Bienal developed an organizational memory of its own, hosted in the embodied expertise of its workers to this day.

Grounding in Context

The model of well-rounded expertise shaped the Bienal's projection into Havana, grounding the curatorial choral consciousness in the specificity of its context. Its popular orientation turned the Bienal into an educational space for the general public. Its rich programming facilitated young art actors' engagement in technical and theoretical learning, their access to professional opportunities abroad, and their cultivation of their social capital through the many workshops and public programs. For example, Jorge Fernández, current director of the Museo de Nacional Bellas Artes and director of the 2012 and 2015 Bienales, recalled in an interview how working as a young reporter at a local radio station had introduced him to Bienal events at a formative stage and ultimately awakened his interest in art criticism and the arts more broadly.[28] Further, for Cuban art critic Magaly Espinosa, having the opportunity to be involved in different aspects of the Bienal helped her and her peers "encounter, first, the work and thought of the most advanced Latin American artists, art critics, curators, and visual theoreticians, and, second, contrast it with our Eastern Marxist-Leninist formation."[29] This pedagogical mission continues to this day and is a valuable professionalizing platform for artists, curators, and art critics on the island.

In addition to its formative value, the Bienal embedded itself in the city of Havana through forms of interpersonal and interagency reciprocity. The cultivation of interpersonal exchanges helped ease mutual recognition between foreign and local actors. In the absence of resources to organize receptions and dinners for foreign guests, Llanes remembers how local chapters of the Committees for the Defense of the Revolution welcomed artists and theorists into their weekly community dinners with neighbors.[30] In addition to solving organizational and material needs, these community dinners connected the foreign visitors with Havana residents in encounters not directly supervised by the Lam Center, often allowing for the exchange of stories and goods from abroad while satisfying the thirst for authenticity that often shapes tourist experiences. Further, the installation of bars and small cafés in the streets surrounding the exhibition venues prompted additional opportunities for exchanges between local and foreign art actors, reinforcing the exhibition's embeddedness in everyday Havana. Albeit unscripted, these encounters provided visitors with seemingly unmediated access to the backstage of Cuban everyday life and fed years-long curiosity about life in socialism for allies in Europe and the United States attending the Bienal, years before new tourism regulations widely opened Cuba to foreign travelers in the mid-1990s. Most importantly, they helped forge robust interpersonal bonds between art actors from different parts of the Third World, reinforcing an international art world autonomous from dominating North Atlantic–centric forces.

Partnerships with multiple city agencies became vital as the scale of the exhibition grew over time. The three galleries at the Wifredo Lam Center could not hold the thousands of artworks shown in each iteration, a limitation that organizers solved by borrowing temporary exhibition space elsewhere. The first Bienal used galleries at the National Museum of Fine Arts and the Pabellón Cuba. After the second iteration, the Bienal extended to new spaces, such as Castillo del Morro, Casa de las Américas, Museo de Artes Decorativas, Casa de Obrapía, and municipal galleries. Of remarkable importance was the collaboration between the Bienal and the Asambleas Municipales del Poder Popular, municipal-level government councils in charge of administering the economy, culture, health, and social needs of their district. Asambleas from the Havana region provided support in the form of materials, space, and housing for artists during the worst years of the Special Period. Representatives connected Bienal organizers with residents in their districts who were willing to voluntarily host a foreign artist and mediated with directors of neighborhood cultural centers for extra exhibition space. They also helped in the sourcing of materials needed for the production of artworks.

Through the years, these forms of interagency collaboration have remained a constant in the Lam Center's engagement with the city. Artworks designed for the public space helped forge a symbiotic bond between the Centro de Arte Wifredo Lam and the Oficina del Historiador de la Ciudad (Office of the City Historian). The two agencies' shared commitment to the promotion of culture made the Oficina del Historiador a trusted comrade in the Bienal's permanent search for exhibition space from its early days. A document from 2000, titled "Preliminary Proposal for Project Emplacement: Historic Center, Old Havana," proves the collaboration between these entities. The seventeen-page document responds to the Bienal's requests and provides detailed legal, structural, and aesthetic recommendations to the Bienal, either authorizing or denying the installation of artworks on facades and street corners, and in public squares. For example, in response to a request to hang silk-screened banners from arches surrounding plazas for Honduran artist Regina Aguilar's piece, the report reads: "We agree with the proposal by C. W. L. [Centro de Arte Wifredo Lam]. We suggest using the Plaza Vieja so as to enhance this important public space of the Historic Center. You can only use the arches of restored buildings." This is followed by three site recommendations, complete with addresses and apartment numbers. Formal recommendations like these were part of each

Bienal's preparation: they both authorized the use and alteration of public spaces and in some cases foresaw the preservation of those interventions through time. The Office of the City Historian, autonomous from Cuba's central government, has been a key agent in the structural renovation of Havana's colonial architectural heritage since 1981.[31] Although it is often taken as a model for responsible urban development, the development of tourist facilities often resulted in the displacement of large numbers of Old Havana residents to outer neighborhoods.

In addition to the collaborative work carried out in the three stages of research, deliberation, and installation, each Bienal iteration had an allocated budget to cover expenses mostly related to fortifying its impact abroad. An internal budget for the second Bienal shows the expenses incurred in the year 1986. Of an initial allocated total of US$400,000, which ultimately translated into an expense of US$418,226, the organization spent $141,000 for travel and lodging costs for international guests, $34,474 for international shipping of artworks, $14,000 for communications, $112,701 for local transportation, $693 for customs, $45,459 for publication costs, $10,732 for catering, $14,524 for the opening and closing events, $24,794 for meals for support personnel, $1,757 for national airfares, $547 for venue rental, and $17,303 for unexpected expenses. It is important to note that none of the $8,000 allocated in the initial budget for support personnel were used: this need was met through voluntary labor. Additionally, of the initial $14,579 reserved for venue rental, only $547 was used to cover expenses derived from renting an office at hotel Habana Libre to set up a dedicated reception desk for Bienal guests. The memo accompanying this budget reads, "[We] didn't need to rent exhibition venues because we coordinated with all institutions so that their planned activities for the year aligned with the Bienal."[32]

As a porous organization, contextual labor practices permeated the Bienal's internal functioning. In particular, its all-rounded curatorial model aligned with a culture of resource redistribution and worker participation practiced in Cuba and promoted by the nonorthodox liberal socialist agenda. This approach, which posited practice-led theoretical inquiry as emancipated expertise, shaped the research, decision making, and exhibition installation involved in the production of each Bienal iteration. Anecdotes like the one involving Dittborn and González illustrate the great lengths that the curatorial team went to in order to realize the biennial's anticolonial program. What may seem like an improvisational

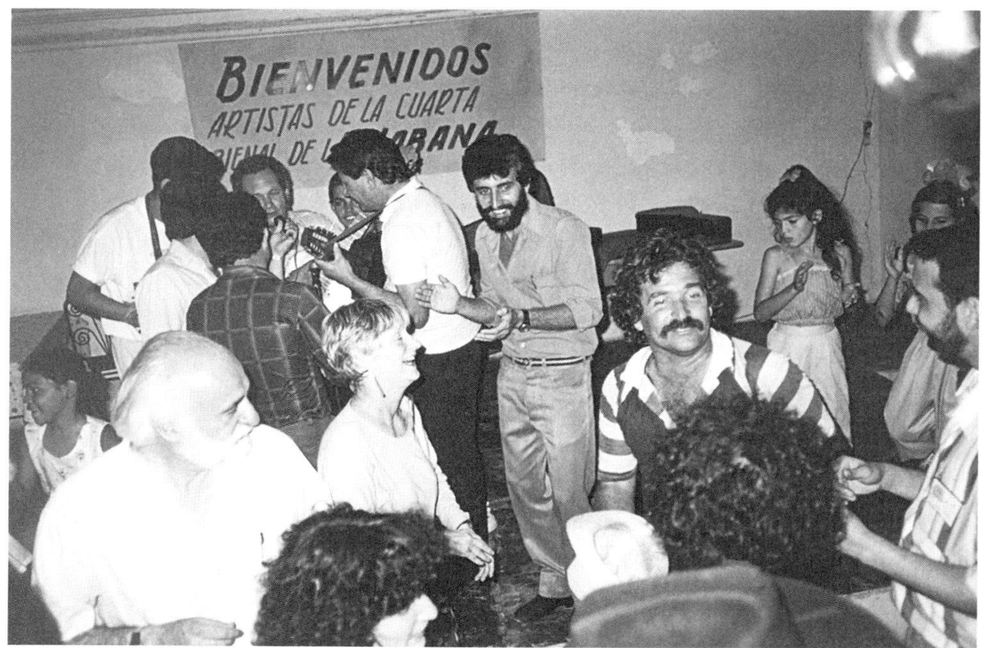

2.2   Event at agricultural cooperative in Havana, Cuba, 1991. Courtesy of
Llilian Llanes.

approach to exhibition production speaks, in fact, to a culture of resource
sharing and worker participation in the workplace where "theory and
practice unite."[33] The relations of production that allowed the Bienal de
La Habana to exist challenged top-down models of expertise dominant in
the elite North Atlantic–centric art institution.

Strategic Expertise

Against individualist models of artistic heroism prevalent at the time in the
North Atlantic art world (see chapter 8), the Bienal offered a polyphony of
voices and practices from the Third World. In words of Los Angeles–based
art critic David Pagel,

> Llanes' patchwork network of experts and amateurs, field research-
> ers, professors, students, artists and critics visits studios and con-
> ceives both elaborate and simple schemes to ensure that their

governmental organization stays in touch with the grass-roots cultures it is committed to exhibiting. More than anything else, they talk. Discussions, arguments, propositions, manifestoes and speeches are all an integral part of Cuban life, and are central to the organization of the biennial. All decisions are reached by committee, after seemingly endless sessions of seductive persuasion and implacable stubbornness.[34]

One of the collaborative models that the Bienal emulated to enact this particular organization of expert labor was the military strategy form of foquismo, which had been used by the Cuban government in its assistance of anti-imperialist revolutionary processes in Africa and Latin America. Foquismo, conceived by Guevara and popularized abroad by Régis Debray in his book *Revolution in the Revolution?* (1967), differed from Leninist scientificism in that it relied on mobile autonomous revolutionary cells where urban and rural working classes came together to act as motors for the organization of resistance against oppressive social forces. In such cells, strategists and members of the proletariat worked together toward political agency, awareness of their own subalternity, and guidance to overcome exploitation. Whereas Lenin disregarded what he perceived as the directionless spontaneity of the masses, foquismo appreciated it as an expression of the masses' situated insights about their field of action and a sign of their anger-driven insurrectionist potential.

In its practice and its theorization, foquismo envisioned the rural peasant as the ideal subject for Latin American insurgency. This dynamic model benefited from the economization of resources and time, avoiding the ideological compromises of urban politics and class alliances. Art researchers from Casa de las Américas, first, and the Bienal, later, used a similar approach to their formation of an anticolonial approach to art curation. In their research travels and their object selection they gathered artisans and artists from rural and urban areas in the same organic formation, hoping to nourish an anticolonial subjectivity. Recalling her years as a curator in Casa de las Américas, Lesbia Ves Dubois described their international research trips as follows: "It's just like the guerrilla. You first have small nuclei. Then one nucleus contacts the other, that contacts the other. In Casa it all started with literature. It was our way to establish those contacts. Some of [these writers] were already famous, although it wasn't the boom yet, but others.... In the visual arts it all began through the popular arts."[35] The Bienal inherited from Casa more than a contact list abroad. In its partial autonomy from government oversight (at least in its beginnings), the Bienal helped keep the legacy of revolutionary strategy alive.

This dynamic approach to consciousness formation was influential beyond Cuba. As art historians Grant Kester and Paula Barreiro López argue, foquismo, as a tactical organization of emancipatory action, was very influential among Left-leaning Latin American avant-garde artists during the Cold War. In his analysis of *Acción del Encierro* (1968) by Argentine artist Graciela Carnevale, Kester describes foquista action as double-faced: it is as inspirational and instrumental as it is pedagogical and martial.[36] Further, Barreiro López argues that this Cuban form of guerrilla warfare was a popular model for politically engaged artists that reached Western European intellectual spheres as well, influencing the work of semiologist Umberto Eco, art critics Alain Juffroy and Germano Celant, and artists Antonio Saura, Roberto Matta, and Julio Le Parc, among others.[37] Like foquista-inspired avant-garde artists elsewhere, Bienal especialistas pursued the participation of non-artist actors into their curation, hoping that their work with the on-the-ground, situated knowledge of their informants throughout the Third World would yield a unified resistance to the forces that they identified as responsible for their shared oppression. The resulting subaltern consciousness would burst in an act of exemplary violence that, if seemingly abstract—as was the case of the sought-after epistemic break with North Atlantic–centric art canon—would hopefully translate into the opening of important avenues for material emancipation, such as an anticolonial art exhibition.

The Bienal de La Habana was not the first exhibition to foreground cooperation among agents, agencies, and nations as a way to signal regional affinities. In the 1950s, for instance, the Biennale de la Méditerranée in Alexandria, Egypt, was based on the promise of relying on artistic collaboration to showcase a purported Mediterranean identity shared throughout the region.[38] The curatorial strategy devised by Bienal especialistas to deliver a worthy representation of art from the Third World traced the extent of Cuba's allies in the Non-Aligned Bloc and Latin America. In its first ten years, its team worked with great efforts to exhibit contemporary art from Africa, Asia, Latin America, and the Middle East. The first exhibition, in 1984, traced the cultural collaboration networks forged by Casa de las Américas since 1960, replicating the scope of anti-imperialist continental fraternity that Cuban independence leader José Martí had envisioned one century before. Yet from 1986 on, the Bienal translated to its curatorial repertoire contemporaneous emancipatory programs by postcolonial thinkers, such as Franz Fanon and Ernesto Guevara. Cuban plans to organize a biennial of art from the Third World—excluding European and US artists until the mid-1990s—mirrored efforts to consolidate a nonaligned geopolitical bloc after the Bandung Conference in 1967 and continued former attempts to forge cultural collaboration networks in the region and beyond, such as the festival CARIFESTA, an itinerant multimedia festival of Caribbean culture launched in Guyana in 1972; the Bienal de San Juan, a biyearly exhibition of graphic art that began in 1970 in San Juan, Puerto Rico; the Biennale de la Méditerranée in Alexandria in 1955; and Ljubljana's Biennale Grafike in 1961.[39]

In its first decade, the Bienal de La Habana practiced a well-rounded curatorial expertise model based on the commitment to anticolonial work that grew from diverse on-the-ground alliances. Its embeddedness in Havana, combined with its nurturing of transnational and transclass alliances, drew important parallels with the military strategic model of foquismo. Contradicting Castro's Leninist articulation of a scientificism where theory is protected from practice, expert labor, as practiced in the Bienal, continued other polyvocal strategies spearheaded by cultural institutions after the Revolution, such as Casa de las Américas and ICAIC. Although the Bienal operated with relative autonomy from the state, it took only a little time for the latter to enhance oversight of its actions. The early Bienal model weakened as the fall of the Iron Curtain left Cuba increasingly isolated from its former international partners and losing almost all financial support. The country plunged into the Special Period in Times of Peace, a decades-long economic and social crisis that had lasting impacts on the nation's population, its infrastructure, its community of experts, and its overall stamina.[40] Seeking to attract foreign capital, the Ministry of Culture would begin to welcome foreign guest curators and funding sources into the Bienal after 1997. It was these influxes of capital and expertise from the new North Atlantic–centric global art circuits imported into the Bienal artistic paradigms that caused the exhibition to deviate from its original antihegemonic mission. In turn, the globalization of the art industry throughout the 1990s would popularize collaborative approaches to curatorial labor, as practiced within the Bienal, facilitating their implementation in other global exhibitions.

three

An Aesthetics of Production

Beauty can be subversive. And it was, for some years, at the monumental exhibition of art from the Third World organized in Havana by a small group of curators. Joining objects of artistic merit from postcolonial nations all throughout Latin America, Africa, the Middle East, and Southeast Asia, Bienal de La Habana especialistas sought to offer a polyphony of voices that reflected the wide diversity of cultural forms excluded from the North Atlantic–centric art world. Amplifying artistic practices from the so-called Third World, thousands of objects and actors gathered in Havana for each iteration, together, under a new artistic category: a Third World avant-garde. Collaboration was a central tenet in the research and installation of the exhibit, as much as in its public-facing events and approaches to audience engagement. But the anti-hegemonic operation went beyond artist selection and cooperative event production. The Bienal, an exhibition that prefigured the possibility of an anticolonial art world, pursued alternative models of aesthetic value. As this chapter shows, these were based not so much on the reception-driven criteria then dominant in the North Atlantic exhibitionary complex but on foregrounding artistic production as a universal entry point into the aesthetic experience.

Exhibiting Craft

During its first editions, the Bienal de La Habana targeted the taxonomies, prevalent in North Atlantic museums, that distinguished art from craft and amateur approaches to cultural production. The fourth biennial (1991) featured five shows exclusively dedicated to objects that would traditionally have been classified as craft in other institutional settings. These included Bogolan paintings from Mali, feather art from Bolivia, indigenous textile arts from Brazil, and paper kites from Weifang (China). Two years earlier, four of the third-Bienal (1989) exhibitions were devoted to craft, including one of contemporary Latin American textile art, a show of Simón Bolivar wood figurines from Venezuela, an exhibition of Mexican fabric dolls, and an exposition of African wire toys. These were complemented with a series of craft workshops, such as *adiré* traditional fabric-dyeing from Nigeria (taught by Oyewunmi Fagbenro), ceramics (taught by Uruguayan ceramicist Gustavo Naclé), paper making (taught by Colombian Nirma Zárate), and new approaches to textile art in Latin America (taught by Luis Ernexto Aróztegui from Uruguay, Nora Aslan and Luis Negrotti from Argentina, and Marta Palau from México). The second Bienal (1986) featured production workshops by guest artists Marta Palau and Julio Le Parc, a screen-printing workshop, a workshop on mural painting restoration, and an engraving workshop. In addition, six exhibitions were devoted exclusively to craft: a retrospective show of ceramist Domingo Ravenet (in Lisa municipality), a collective show of Cuban ceramics (in Arroyo Naranjo municipality), a collective show of contemporary Cuban crafts titled *Necesidad y creación* (Necessity and Creation, in Lisa municipality), and a display of works produced in the ceramics workshop at Santiago de las Vegas (in Boyeros municipality). The first Bienal (1984), planned in a short time with an ad hoc organizational team that did not yet include Llilian Llanes, Gerardo Mosquera, and Nélson Herrera Ysla, did not actively pursue the inclusion of artisanship in the show and featured a majority of paintings in its artwork selection.

This emphasis on craft was matched with an almost equal attention to art made by groups that would have been dismissed as *amateur* or outsider in other settings. For example, the second Bienal (1986) included

POPULARTE, an exhibition of sculptures of colorful animals produced by residents of the Juanelo neighborhood under the guidance of artist Antonia Eiriz (in San Miguel de Padrón municipality). The workshop had been jointly sponsored by local agricultural communities (DESAs) and Committees for the Defense of the Revolution. Tacitly referencing the choral consciousness pursued through the Bienal's organizational model and selection of artworks, the catalog spoke of the artists as "a disciplined but bizarre army, workers, housewives, students, elderly people, teenagers," whose only connective thread was the shared technique of papier-mâché modeling.[1] Participants in *POPULARTE* were not instructed on the history of art in Western Europe and the United States, hoping that the resulting objects would be uncontaminated by this dominant art canon. Also within the second Bienal was the fourth iteration of *TELARTE*, a project that merged textile design with its large-scale production (see plate 4). In *TELARTE*, approximately 600,000 square meters of cotton canvas were printed with thirty-one motifs designed by twenty-eight artists.[2] The Ministries of Culture and Light Industries, which worked alongside national textile factories such as Desembarco del Granma (in Villa Clara province) and Textilera Ariguanabo (in Bauta, La Habana province) on the production of the fabric, coordinated *TELARTE*. The premeditated positioning of craft and the popular in equal status to art within the Bienal articulated an explicit attack against the tacit principles that distinguish these cultural categories in the elite North Atlantic–centric art institution. In this context, craft, understood as the skillful production of beauty, acted as a cultural universal practiced by colonized peoples all throughout the world. This intervention twisted dominant notions of artistic value, history, and labor bred within modern capitalism that predominantly anchored modern and contemporary art in the so-called First World. This move, which set the grounds for what I refer to as a "production aesthetics," was at the core of the Bienal's anticapitalist, anticolonial, internationalist program.

Revolutionary Textiles

Among its many events, the third Bienal de La Habana (1989) hosted an exhibition of miniature Latin American textiles. The show aimed to present a comprehensive panorama of contemporary approaches to textile work in the region, showing objects of under 25 by 25 by 25 cm created by eighty-one artists. Bi-dimensional and tri-dimensional objects were testament to the renovation of formal and material approaches to textile work since the 1970s. In his catalog essay, Bienal especialista Nelson Herrera Ysla explained this formal diversity as a process of renewal: "This *revolutionary* process within textile art reached its peak in the decade of the seventies with the detachment of tapestry from the wall and its incursions, increasingly audacious, into the three-dimensional space through the pursuit of artworks with sculptural and environmental goals."[3] Herrera Ysla framed the diversity of approaches to textile work in terms of an understanding of medium specificity not unlike those that had articulated formalist approaches to art criticism in New York circles. For him, weaving's detachment from the wall was a gesture of emancipation akin to that undertaken by other two-dimensional mediums, such as painting. Textile art's sculptural and environmental pursuits pushed objects into the gallery space in a move that some art historians and critics would retroactively qualify as a move toward site-specificity. Good examples of the medium's formal and material renovations were Argentine Ernesto Aroztegui's *La compinche del Papa. Triple retrato anamorfoseado de Teresa de Calcuta* (The Pope's accomplice: triple anamorphic portrait of Teresa of Calcutta [1989]), a two-dimensional Gobelin tapestry that featured photocopied paper and drawing; and Bolivian Gustavo Medeiros Anaya's *Ofrenda al mar, Opus 572* (Offering to the sea, opus 572 [1989]), a three-dimensional piece that used a wooden chair as loom, with wool, ceramics, and bronze as woven materials.

But textile art's formal and material diversity was for Herrera Ysla more than just a formal question. Importantly, his framing departed from textile art's capacity to place Bienal audiences before forms of cultural production that preexisted Spanish colonization of the Americas. Weaving was practiced in both America and Europe before 1492 and thus offered crucial insights into techniques of textile work that predated, per Herrera Ysla's characterization, the subsequent processes of cultural hybridization. Evoking the chronicles by Spanish colonizers who, he claimed, were surprised by the beautiful attire of the original Caribbean inhabitants, he praised weaving's transhistorical capacity to simultaneously serve artistic purposes and fulfill practical needs—such as in the making of tools, sacks, and basketry. For Herrera Ysla, "Weaving made with artistic intentions was also part of the textile abundance of our peoples, and is today considered an important source of data and knowledge about the cultural and transcultural processes of the diverse groups and societies of Latin America."[4] Displaying a bond with precolonial knowledge, the eighty-one works included in the exhibition also toyed with the "archaeological and the ethnographic" while simultaneously being framed as art by the biennial. This simultaneous recourse to artistic innovation and precolonial forms of cultural production echoed throughout the Bienal's overall operation.

Textile work's revolutionary potential was not exclusive to the Bienal's effort to undermine the historical split of the arts and the crafts. The focus on the textile as a critical turning point for the reformulation of value bore important symbolism. This form of work was also key in classical Marxist theory, where it served as the locus for Karl Marx and Fredrik Engels's analysis of capitalist political economy. In *Capital*, Marx builds from data about textile-laborer exhaustion in his diagnosis of exploitative working conditions in the factory, and he uses the transition of textile labor from domestic spaces to workrooms and industrial settings as the case to illustrate the cheapening of labor and subsequent exploitation of workers.[5] In this foundational treaty, workmen revolted against ribbon looms in the sixteenth and seventeenth centuries, and thousands of overworked children and women employed in lace schools sustained industrial capitalist expansion in eighteenth- and nineteenth century England. Concerns for their bodies, the threat of death by exhaustion, and their agency over their own time, labor power, and consciousness fueled what would become a long corpus of Marxist theory that would provoke numerous responses by artists, crafters, and designers concerned with the improvements that overall aesthetic reform could beget in social life. Some of those came as direct responses to Marx's analysis and materialized in the late romanticism of the Arts & Crafts movement in nineteenth-century England. Others appeared later throughout the twentieth century at times of renewal of socialist thinking. See, for example, the effervescence experienced by textile work in the Bauhaus in Germany of the 1910s to 1920s, during the 1920s artistic reform of post-Revolution Russia, or in the exile of Europeans to the Americas during the 1930s and 1940s. In the careers of Gunta Stölzl and Anni Albers, May and William Morris, Lyubov Popova and Varvara Stepanova, textile work became an exemplary practice for the reformulation of labor as creative and emancipated in North Atlantic modernity. Further, as chapter 2 details, the displacement of textile work from the domestic space into the factory meant for Marx the loss of the collaborative relations that had shaped the former. Collaboration was visible in the many workshops, exhibitions, and forms of expert labor that informed the Bienal—see the kinetic art festival in a Vedado park by Argentine artist Julio Le Parc or Nury

González's installation at the Museo Nacional de Bellas Artes—but it also proved to be of significant value in the Bienal *especialistas'* intervention into aesthetic theory.

An Aesthetics of Production

In all of these instances the loom propelled a deep questioning of the classic arts versus crafts split, facilitating aesthetic conversions of objects traditionally classified as craft in the museum into the category of Third World avant-garde art. These examples show how the Bienal anchored its program in an aesthetics of production that forced a reconsideration of Immanuel Kant's model for the judgment of beauty, as well as its long-lasting legacy within modern European aesthetic philosophy. Kant's model posits a valuation of beauty that derives from its reception—a disinterested engagement that, for him, is not possible with objects of artisanship. This position characterizes art as pure and superior—*free* beauty—and relegates the crafts (within and outside of Europe) to a secondary, instrumental role—*adherent* beauty. As he records in *The Critique of the Power of Judgment* (1790), free pure beauty is autonomous and "presupposes no concept about what the object ought to be." However, adherent beauty is always predicated and ought to be judged based on the ends that it helps serve. He respectively calls them "liberal art" and "remunerative art." If the first concerns self-standing activities, the latter takes a dimension of laborious, effortful action.[6] This distinction concealed the disdain for "purposeful" cultural productions, seen by the philosopher as material culture at the service of practical matters such as ritual, productive, or ornamental purposes. Against these, Kant offered purportedly disinterested objects, such as nature and artworks, that are beautiful without ulterior motive. Throughout the robust institutional legacy of this model, objects in the first group have predominantly been cataloged as craft, folkloric, or ethnographic; those closer to the latter have historically been taxonomized as art. Kant supports this hierarchy of culture with a Eurocentric account of the various human races' capacity to engage in the purposeless experience of beauty. In this ranking, white Europeans occupy the summit of historical and cultural sophistication, whereas nonwhites and non-Europeans are incapable of appreciating *free*, self-sustaining beauty.

Postcolonial thinkers, including the Bienal especialistas, disagreed with Kant's program because of its implications for the racialization of aesthetic experience. In their view, the Eurocentrism of Kant's legacy exceeded the realm of aesthetic theory to support as well the dehumanization of particular groups throughout modern history.[7] In effect, the Kantian split has scaffolded object and knowledge taxonomies of modern cultural institutions in Western Europe and the United States, and has been exported throughout their areas of influence via their colonial and neocolonial expansion. Formalized in the disciplinary programs of aesthetics and art history, this distinction still determines how cultural institutions and publics in Western Europe, the United States, and their regions of influence classify culture, producers, and publics. Such a framing has often supported nation-building processes, helping not only to amplify state ideology but also to service demographic classifications within and beyond the nation, ultimately excluding social groups from canonical institutions and historical narratives. The Bienal's subversion of the Kantian split supplemented other tactics used by the Cuban state to resist North Atlantic hegemony, expand political and cultural influence among Third World nations, and, importantly, defend the aesthetic value of objects otherwise excluded from the period's international art worlds.

A workshop led by Mexican artist Marta Palau was a good example of what I refer to as the Bienal's aesthetics of production. Celebrated at the second Bienal (1986), this weaving workshop involved twenty-four Cuban artists in the collective making of woven objects.[8] The setting was Cuba's Museo de Artes Decorativas, an institution housed at a petit-pavilion–like palace in the district of Vedado, commissioned by Cuban aristocrat María Luisa Gómez-Mena to French architects P. Virad and M. Destuque in the 1920s, following French Renaissance and Neoclassical styles. Among the museum's collections were porcelains, lacquers, ivories, and European and Chinese furniture. Under the guidance of Palau, a feminist and socialist artist, and an important name in the Mexican neo–avant-garde groups since the 1970s, participants in this month-long workshop first built a monumental loom that filled the building's central hall, accommodating itself to the space's architectural features. They then produced a series of separate small looms, where they each wove their own fabrics, experimenting with techniques and materials. To conclude, the group jointly engaged in collaborative weaving at the central loom, employing autochthonous plant-based materials such as yagua, tobacco, henequén, palm branches, vines, bejuco lianas, cotton, hemp, and loose roots. By occupying the national decorative arts museum with woven objects made of plants associated

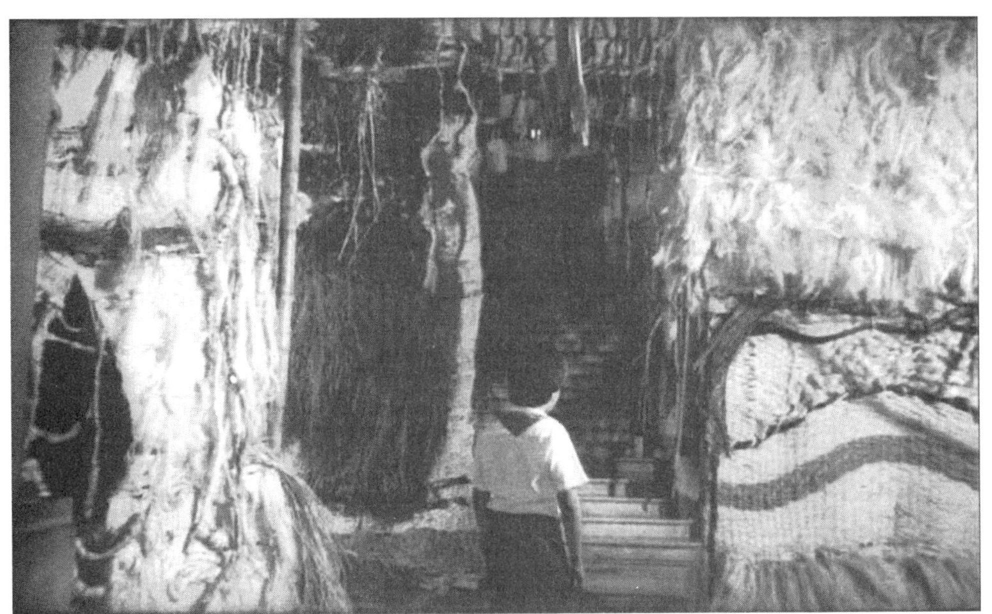

3.1   A child stands amid the large looms built during Marta Palau's weaving workshop in the central lobby of the Museo Nacional de Artes Decorativas, Havana, Cuba. Newsreel still. Source: Santiago Álvarez and Héctor Veitia, *Noticiero Latinoamericano ICAIC: Actualidades Nacionales e Internacionales* (Havana: ICAIC, 1986).

with rural agricultural labor, the artists defied traditional museographical taxonomies, such as those distinguishing art, craft, and the decorative arts.

Yet in addition to subverting how museums classify culture, this intervention posed questions related to the relations of production upholding life in Cuba. Sugar cane, tobacco, and henequén were major crops in Cuba and the Caribbean, staples in the plantation economies of the colonial and postcolonial periods. The first was planted by Spanish colonizers as early as 1523; the other two were endemic to the Caribbean region. Over the centuries, they were harvested throughout the Caribbean by enslaved labor—the large majority of which was of African origin—to be shipped back to the imperial metropoles in Western Europe for their processing and consumption. A small fragment of those refined goods were sent back to colonial capitals for their consumption by colonial elites—like the original

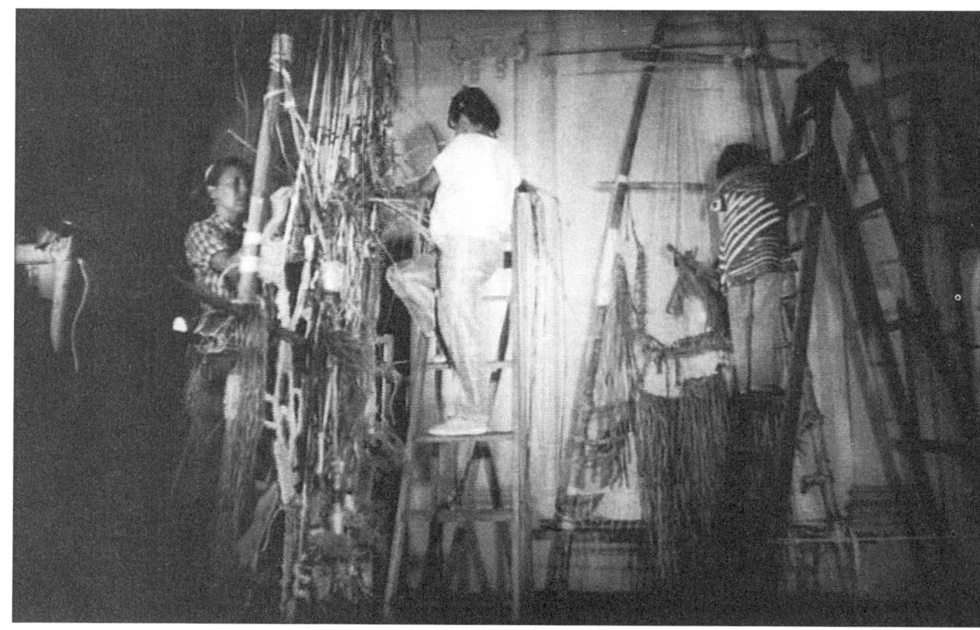

3.2   Marta Palau and workshop participants building large looms in the central lobby of the Museo Nacional de Artes Decorativas, Havana, Cuba. Newsreel still. Source: Santiago Álvarez and Héctor Veitia, *Noticiero Latinoamericano ICAIC: Actualidades Nacionales e Internacionales* (Havana: ICAIC, 1986).

owner of the building housing the museum. At the time of this workshop, sugar cane exports to the metropole still accounted for 76 percent of Cuba's exports. No longer Spain or the United States, the metropole was now Moscow, one of the two Cold War imperial powers and the one subsidizing Cuba's economy. The collaborative weaving workshop led by Palau offered participants the opportunity to learn about the raw materials sustaining Cuba's colonial dependency for centuries. The fibers offered glimpses of an important—yet often occluded—part of Cuban heritage, a fragment of the nation's foundations associated with Blackness, labor, and rural life. The workshop invited reflections on Cuba's mono-crop economy and its indebtedness to colonial relations of production. By distinguishing these fibers in a national museum devoted to the decorative arts, artists upheld them for public contemplation, visualizing them as part of the national infrastructure. Honoring them in a distinguished setting, they pushed aside lacquers, ivories, and porcelains to show, center and clear, what was really at stake in the institutional distinction of some cultural products over others as part of the national cultural canon.

The aesthetics of production practiced by the Bienal de La Habana in its first iterations prioritized collaborative labor as a sensory-driven process involved in the production of beauty. In a weaving workshop at a national museum of decorative arts, as preparation for a public art festival in a park, in a group-painting exhibition, in a theoretical discussion of Caribbean aesthetics, or an exhibition of wire toys, the Bienal made a laudable effort to center the production of beauty in the exhibition apparatus. This subversive move offered an important counterpoint to the experience of beauty in capitalist spaces. Capitalist ideology conceals labor and infrastructure, casting shade and doubt over the physical and cognitive effort involved in the production of commodities—including cultural commodities. By distinguishing technical training, skills development, and research on materials within the art institution, Bienal especialistas honored art making as a potentially universal faculty. After all, many gathered in the Bienal inherited, as members of the Third World, a colonial interpellation originally articulated on the basis of their labor power. The Bienal's aesthetics of production were supported by aesthetic conversions between categories such as art, craft, amateur art, and design—which were made to be exhibited together within an art institutional setting. The taxonomical displacements entailed in these aesthetic conversions supplemented others of geographical nature, by which culture from different parts of the world fit now under the same category of a Third World avant-garde. Objects that would not have shared rooms—or a building!—in most Western European museums were now displayed together, under the premise of offering valuable knowledge about the practices involved in the production of beauty throughout the Third World: an abstract painting, a drape doll, a wooden portrait of a revolutionary leader, a charcoal drawing, a performance, and a woven fabric.

A Socialist Aesthetics

The Bienal's aesthetics of production came to be during a rich renovation of socialist philosophy and praxis worldwide. Some of its precedents were the Sandinista Revolution in Nicaragua; Chile's socialist government in the early 1970s; liberation theology Marxisms throughout Latin America; Third World socialism in its African, Middle Eastern, and Southeast Asian manifestations; the New Left and the practiced emancipatory politics of May 68 in Western Europe; and the civil rights movement in the United States. Of remarkable importance to the Cuban process were the contributions to aesthetic theory of Adolfo Sánchez Vázquez, a Republican Spanish exile, Mexican philosopher, and frequent participant in Havana's nonorthodox Marxist circles. Sánchez Vázquez admitted being severely affected by the Cuban Revolution, a historical experience that led him to reconsider his own understanding of Marxist philosophy. The Cuban process was, for him, a praxis from which to rebuild theory. Central to his oeuvre is an inquiry into the possibility of a Marxist aesthetic philosophy that actualizes Marx's and Engel's foundational writings for the political demands of Cold War Latin America—especially Marx's discussion of alienation in the *Economic and Philosophic Manuscripts of 1844*, which had become readily available only in the late 1950s.[9] Sánchez Vázquez was a close reader of Friedrich Schiller and Immanuel Kant, but his contribution to the Marxian body was deeply rooted in the reclaiming of Latin American Marxisms, such as the Indigenous Marxist cosmopolitanism anchoring the work of early twentieth-century Peruvian José Carlos Mariátegui. Against idealist aesthetic programs, such as those of Schelling and Wincklemann, Sánchez Vázquez proposed a dialectical aesthetics that centered production as an act of creation.

For Sánchez Vázquez, aesthetics encompassed much more than art. While art was very much at the center of his approach, he felt aesthetic theory ought to concern itself with experience beyond reductive taxonomies. He defended an aesthetics that, grounded in actual practiced experience, could simultaneously guide artists in their own engagement with forms, materials, and languages and aid their emancipation from aesthetic ideologies that distorted both their perceptions of their own social position and the role of their labor and their artworks in society. However, his emphasis on production was not to be confused with a sociology of art. The latter, for him, missed aesthetic value as a legitimate object of inquiry and failed to account for the uniqueness of its experience. For Sánchez Vázquez, a dialectical aesthetics ought to equally acknowledge the subjective, immediate, and unmediated nature of aesthetic perception, as well as the objective historical configuration of society that makes it possible.[10]

Central in his program were two interventions into the North Atlantic–centric art canon. The first regarded the disinterestedness presumed to be inherent in beauty in Kantian aesthetics and the status of this disinterestedness in European modern philosophy. Kant had described disinterest as both the absence of desire toward and the absence of an ulterior end to beauty. Instead, Sánchez Vázquez proposed an essentially interested aesthetic contemplation, in which interest could be aesthetic and/or extra-aesthetic—that is, driven either by an object's beauty and/or by any other reason. He offered the example of a landscape. Interest for a landscape can be fueled by its beauty or, perhaps, by the subject's curiosity about extra-aesthetic matters such as its business potential for tourist development. His second, related intervention pertained to the concept of beauty. Originating in the celebration of classical Greco-Roman legacy as the most refined expression of pure form, the idealism inherent to modern European aesthetics neglected the historical transformations of social relations, Sánchez Vázquez argued. European aesthetics had enshrined the Greek canon as the summit of beauty, celebrating its values of harmony, symmetry, and proportion as principles applicable to the evaluation of beauty across time and space. But for him, this nostalgia for the classical canon concealed as well a nostalgia for past notions of order, harmony, and proportion that, when applied to social life, imposed an outdated Eurocentrism to experience. Sánchez Vázquez was well aware of the important service to colonial domination that calls to classical beauty standards had offered through history. He made Hegel, Winckelmann, and Marx responsible for the imbrication of European aesthetics' classicist idealism into modern political thought. Instead, he called for an appreciation of beauty that was situated in historical configurations of social relations—including those taking place within and beyond the niche spaces of art production.

Moreover, Sánchez Vázquez's philosophy paid close attention to the creative act, which he understood to be of essentially productive nature. He saw great subversive potential in the production of art. In cultivating an engagement with the senses, the creative act was for him a humanistic experience that exemplified relations free from capitalist alienation. Through artistic work, the artist "unfolds his [inner] richness on a concrete-sensible object, after an 'internal demand,' an internal need. His activity elongates and elevates the essence of human labor, always circumscribed to the material usefulness that products of labor must satisfy." Crucially the aesthetic works as an avenue for subjective *and* communal emancipation from capital. Deeply influenced by Schiller's concept of aesthetic education, this all-encompassing revolution would arrive, for Sánchez Vázquez, through a purposeful deployment of the senses in aesthetic experience—within the specific realm of art but also in many other fields of culture and life. Regarding the question of beauty and our perception of it, he offered a provocation: to consider beauty not in essentialist or metaphysical terms but to think of it instead as a social relation: "Aesthetic consciousness, the aesthetic sense, is not a given, it is not innate or biological, but only comes to be in a historical and social manner, on the basis of the material and practical activity that is labor."[11] His three-point intervention was echoed in the Bienal de La Habana's initial iterations. Objects throughout the exhibition galleries proposed a polyphony of beauties that were situated in particular and historical social relations informing life throughout the Third World. With their aesthetic qualities, they attracted viewers interested in learning more about the objects' original settings. They came together through cooperative, sensuous-driven artistic work, offering the possibility of emancipation at the personal level while simultaneously prefiguring collective, anticolonial liberation. Finally, they all acted, unapologetically, as instances of creative production, and testified to the power of unalienated labor.

Although Sánchez Vázquez's program was very popular among nonorthodox Marxists throughout Latin America at the time, including in Havana, it was not applied without context to the Bienal. One member of the initial team of especialistas, Gerardo Mosquera, was very familiar with Sánchez Vázquez's work and had himself offered a systematic account of the social relations involved in the aesthetic experience. Adopting a historically informed position, Mosquera published in 1989 his own take on the legacies of Kantian and Hegelian aesthetics, centering craft as a contested category. The book's release happened the same year as the third Bienal. His book *El diseño se definió en Octubre* (Design was defined in October [1989]) examined the impact of industrial capitalism's division of labor on the ways in which art, craft, and design are considered in social life. For Mosquera, the democratization of designed goods and the coeval formation of an autonomous sphere of distinction around the fine arts as a result of industrial capitalism had relegated craft objects to a secondary, undervalued category. As Mosquera saw it, these changes had turned craft into an especially crucial object category. Craft objects were skillful and unique. But most importantly they kept traditional knowledge and expertise alive, and allowed for the creation of a subjective and even sentimental bond between object and maker. This last facet conferred a particular kind of aura to artisanal objects that, in some way, brought them closer to artworks. Craft objects were, for Mosquera, "objects of exception." In their experiential working through them, artisans escaped (even if temporarily) capitalist relations of production and were exempt from the standardizing and efficiency mandates of mass-produced design. Artisanal work was thus an exceptional form of delineated labor that allowed for self-inquiry into workers' consciousness. In addition to the clear influence of European and Latin American Marxists, crucial to Mosquera's proposal were the writings of postcolonial thinkers like Franz Fanon and Humberto Pérez, from which he took culture's agency in processes of postcolonial emancipation. Also influenced by Néstor García Canclini's investigations on cultural production in Latin America during the late Cold War years, Mosquera posited craft as a category capable of bridging through the "scission of localities" produced with the advance of Western European and US influence in the region in order to reach into a para-industrial space where social relations can be imagined free from colonial domination.[12]

An exhibition of paintings from the Solentiname Archipelago in Nicaragua is a good example of how the categories of art, craft, and popular art often blended in the Bienal. They were painted by *campesinos*, inhabitants of a remote communal artist colony started in the late 1960s by liberation theology priest and poet Ernesto Cardenal who, during a crisis of faith, sought solace in the small archipelago to establish an egalitarian *comunidad de base* inspired by interpretations of a program of primitive communism in the Gospels.[13] Via a program jointly developed with Nicaraguan painter Róger Pérez de la Rocha, Cardenal sought to improve the life and work conditions of local fishermen via an aesthetic education program that joined primitivist themes and techniques with references to modernist painting, and elements from local crafts, such as fiber arts and gourd painting, as practiced by the Chorotega people.[14] The canvases escaped trends in elite North Atlantic art worlds and would have been described as decorative or amateurish by contemporaneous art criticism. US art critic Mike Alewitz called them "intricate representations of the jungle plant and animal life [that] reflect the unspoiled surroundings in which the untrained artists work"; in his account, the paintings "burst off the wall with color detail; the personality of each painter emerged through the thousands of tiny flowers and leaves portrayed." Cardenal's belief in the liberatory agency of creative work in the comunidad de base was a good precursor to the Bienal's challenge against the Kantian distinction and its extra-artistic implications. As a believer in the liberation theology doctrine, Cardenal sought to foster in the islands a nonorthodox Marxist laboratory inspired in the communal reading of writings by Latin American Marxists like Che Guevara alongside foundational Christian scriptures, including the Bible. The paintings from Solentiname were also a symbol of international solidarity. During the last years of the repressive Somoza regime, the National Guard ravaged the colony and its art, turning it after the Sandinista victory (1979) into a symbol of socialist and Indigenous resistance. The Solentiname paintings, shown alongside work by other Nicaraguan artists, testified to Nicaragua's slow embrace of its own Indigenous culture. As Alewitz wrote, "Today's Nicaraguan artists look to the country's black, Indian, and Spanish roots as the basis for a national artistic identity."[15]

One Hundred Thirty-One Mexican Dolls

Coded into the Bienal's proposal for an aesthetics of production was a call for solidarity of all subaltern peoples. This emphasis on solidarity was practiced through the inclusion of objects and artists from all over the world in the exhibition. It was also visible through the diversity of theories and art-historical programs amplified in the parallel events. But it was maybe articulated in a most sophisticated way in exhibitions that relied on cooperation between actors for the making of objects of artistic merit. A group of 131 cloth dolls exemplified well the Bienal's intention to foreground craft as an exceptional category in which to anchor its solidarity-driven, anticolonial aesthetics. There were two main types, *Lucha* (Struggle) and *Victoria* (Victory), of which the seamstresses produced many variations (see plate 5). The dolls represent young women and animals merging in their anatomy and attire symbolic references to urban and rural life, with some hints to canonical European artworks. These dolls came to be in the aftermath of the deadly earthquake (8.1 on the Richter scale) that ravaged Mexico on September 19, 1985. Most of the workshops in San Antonio Abad, the location of Mexico City's textile industry, collapsed. Thousands of workers, unattended by factory owners and government rescue units, were left to perish among the debris. The sector's predominantly female, Indigenous, and low-paid workforce lost coworkers, future employment opportunities, and work equipment. In the face of an inadequate state and municipal response to the crisis, textile workers organized the Sindicato 19 de Septiembre (September 19th Workers' Union). Marked by a feminist orientation, the union committed to a direct-action politics in its negotiations with factory owners and government authorities. This approach helped strengthen group identity and nourished strong internal and external solidarity ties. Diverse demographic groups in Mexico City came out in support of the Sindicato: supporting rescue operations, fund-raising for survivors and families, and helping workers organize for economic self-management.[16] As part of their strategy, the Sindicato workers created a Department of Dolls, through which they allied with prominent names of the city's artistic avant-garde to produce a large number of fabric dolls. Canonical artists like Helen Escobedo, Marta Palau, and Vicente Rojo helped lead the alliance, amplifying the campaign to other sectors of the city's cultural scene. Locally, these dolls had the double purpose of raising funds and awareness about the Sindicato's struggle within Mexico; abroad, they appealed to the solidarity of international art audiences as they toured through several exhibitions in Mexico, the United States, Germany, and Sweden.[17]

In Cuba the dolls visited the third Bienal (1989), brought by Silvia Pandolfi, director of the Museo de Arte Carrillo Gil in Mexico City, and artist Marta Palau.[18] They were shown at Casa de las Américas, alongside drawings by contemporary Mexican artists like Marta Palau and Alberto Mejías. Echoing Mosquera's characterization of craft objects as objects of exception, Mexican curator Jaime Vázquez described in the catalog that acquiring a doll resembled more an adoption than a commercial transaction, conferring upon them a degree of personhood and uniqueness, an aura shared by humans and artworks.[19] He recognized that in their capacity to build solidarity ties and help raise awareness of the Sindicato's mission, the dolls had a particular kind of agency. They were exceptional objects, bracketing trans-class alliances involving Indigenous rural working classes and white urban elites. They were living proof that craft could indeed be of appeal to a wide range of publics. This exhibition was followed by a doll-production workshop in the fourth Bienal iteration (1991), where Cuban and Mexican members of the public joined contemporary artists under the direction of two Mexican seamstresses from the original group, María Berta Morales and Mariela Franco.[20] In 1989 and 1991, the dolls carried with themselves an important symbolic load. While affirming the crucial role played by the textile workshop in the development of labor solidarity, they reminded audiences that *Capital*'s diagnosis of labor exploitation in textile production was not a thing of the past but was very much alive in contemporary capitalism too.[21]

Importantly, the dolls invited reflections on the interconnection of gender, labor, coloniality, and cultural legitimation. Produced by women, within a large feminist labor union with an overwhelming majority of women members, the dolls exemplified another model for the organization of solidarity in the workspace. As just one outcome of the Sindicato's strategy, the dolls were one product of years of consciousness raising and internal education efforts, mediation with internal and external actors, alliance building, and the seamstresses' own appreciation of their specialized knowledge. In a nutshell, these objects, now distinguished as worthy of aesthetic appreciation within major art institutions, came from a women-only group designed and constituted as a space of resistance against capitalist relations of production. The dolls were also a testament to other ways of organizing artistic work. They were a good example of how the production of objects of artistic merit can very well avoid patriarchal orderings of life and work, including the absence of men in the production process, in the governance of labor relations, and in internal decision-making processes. Beauty, in sum, could very well be a crucial outcome of feminist, anticapitalist, collaborative relations.

A Critical *Indigenismo*

The Bienal's mission to put forward a representation of cultural production by colonized peoples also included Indigenous nations from different parts of the world. In addition to the Mexican dolls and other forms of art and craft production by Indigenous artists exhibited in the 1986 and 1989 Bienals, the 1991 Bienal, celebrated in direct response to the five-hundred-year anniversary of Christopher Columbus's arrival in Cuba, featured a wide array of exhibitions directly devoted to valuing Indigenous cultural production. There was an exhibit titled *Cultura Popular Mestiza*, with objects from Peru, Chile, Mexico, and the Caribbean that "evoke[d] the inheritance of pre-Columbian cultures, manifest[ed] the European impositions, and express[ed] the Black presence" in the continent.[22] There was also an exhibition of contemporary art by nonwhite artists from the United States, Canada, and the United Kingdom; a show of feather art from Peru; and an exhibit of applied Native textile arts from Brazil. Very important in this effort to amplify the work of Indigenous artists was the show *Amerindios del*

Canadá (Indian Americans from Canada), curated by Edward Poitras, with artworks by Lance Belanger, Rebecca Belmore, Domingo Cisneros, Joseph Tehwaron, Richard Martel, Ronald J. Noganosh, and Edward Poitras. In an effort to include Indigenous cultural practices from outside the American continent, the 1991 Bienal included an exhibition of the traditional Bogolan textile-dyeing technique, practiced by the Mande people in contemporary Mali since before the days of colonial occupation.

This inclusion of Indigenous art played the crucial role of aligning the Bienal's mission with the Latin American program of *indigenismo.* Rooted in nineteenth-century postindependence nation-building efforts, indigenismo worked throughout the twentieth century mostly as a folklorist inclination toward rural life practiced by Latin American dominant classes. In its affiliation to the state, indigenismo allowed the symbolic incorporation of Indigeneity into the national project—a gesture most evident in the post-Revolutionary Mexican muralist program. Like folklorisms elsewhere, indigenismo functioned on the premise that greater visibility and validation of Indigenous culture would result in its accruing of political agency and ultimate emancipation from colonial subordination to the postcolonial national elites. In both its conservative and liberal forms, indigenismo represented an elite, most often urban, curiosity about Indigenous ways of life and culture. In art, it manifested in the representation of Indigenous subjects and cultural artifacts such as textile art, basketry, cuisine, and ceramics. Indigenista artworks often incorporated techniques and materials considered characteristically Indigenous. In other spheres of political action, indigenismo propelled a series of policies and social interventions that often interpellated the Indigenous subject as either an exoticized embodiment of precolonial ways of life or an oppressed subject in need of external liberation.

However, in its declared anticolonial stands, the Bienal de La Habana sought to ally itself with contemporaneous *critical* indigenismos developed in response to the increasing presence in Latin America of European and, chiefly, US-sponsored developmentalist projects. In the face of growing neocolonial relations, critical indigenismos amplified Indigenous struggles for recognition and political agency, aiming to correct their exclusion from national political life. One representative of this trend who influenced the thinking of Bienal especialistas was Paraguayan scholar and curator Ticio Escobar, who accused urban Latin American elites of siding with foreign-backed interests and rendering Indigenous life and culture as ahistorical and precapitalist. Escobar called instead for thinking of Indigenous ways of organizing social life and cultural production as alternatives to capitalist modes of production. Peruvian Mirko Lauer was another influential name on the Bienal curatorial team. He defended the indigenista program's potential as an emancipatory gateway toward socialist relations of production, where Indigenous subjects could become nation-building agents.[23] Lauer critiqued traditional indigenismos, in that they romanticized the crafts and the popular arts as avenues to idealized forms of cultural authenticity. Like Escobar, Lauer warned against the idealization of rural Indigenous life, its culture and, as part of it, its craft. Positing craft and popular art instead as categories subject to historical transformation, critical indigenismos recognized Indigenous authority to govern the development of cultural forms and, as a consequence, enact aesthetic judgments on their own terms. Hoping to avoid idealized romanticizations of Indigenous life and culture, Bienal especialistas chose to amplify objects' own situated meanings through a multifaceted approach: exhibitions exposed audiences to sensory-driven encounters with objects, theoretical events invited debate and public discussion, and workshops offered an opportunity to collaboratively engage with artistic production as a kind of aesthetic experience alternative to dominant visually driven approaches to aesthetic reception. Through this approach, Indigenous meanings, techniques, and notions of artistic merit became more easily accessible for Bienal audiences.

Although the Mexican fabric dolls successfully integrated artworks by Indigenous subjects in the Bienal, other objects in the exhibitions provide insights into the risks that come with embracing indigenista perspectives. Take, for example, Marta Palau's *Mis caminos son terrenales* (My paths are earthly; 1985), winner of the first prize in the category of installation at the second Bienal (1986). The installation featured 250 *estandartes*, baton-like objects wrapped in natural animal and vegetable fibers, ornate with feathers, shells, beads, and threads. The elongated cylinders echoed objects fabricated by nomadic Indigenous tribes of Baja California and featured bright saturated colors. Palau had found inspiration in Indigenous cultural work through her travels in Mexico. Her palette for this piece evoked that of Mexican crafts, especially the little devils of Ocumichu, Michoacán, and the Huichol embroidery from Jalisco and Nayarit.[24] Tightly hand-tied, they were positioned vertically together, shaping a cube-like structure that filled the central hall of the Museo Nacional de Bellas Artes. Compact and mono-

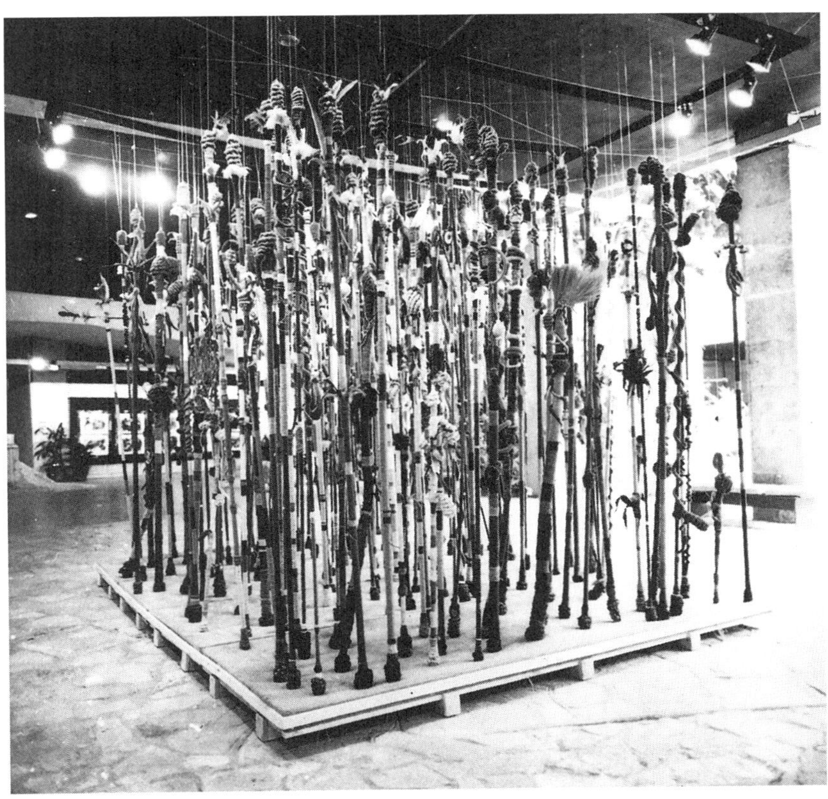

3.3   Marta Palau, *Mis caminos son terrenales* (My paths are earthly), 1985.
Courtesy of Llilian Llanes.

lithic, the 250 estandartes levitated over their pedestal, hanging from the museum's ceiling by thin, almost invisible threads. Reaching almost to the top, they forced the public to walk around the structure as they entered this central Bienal venue. Illuminated with ceiling spots, the estandartes were gracefully present. Their materials evoked a symbolism that reminisced the skill set of nonindustrial societies: wood, feathers, wool, cotton thread.

Unlike the dolls, which were produced by a collective of Indigenous seamstresses, Marta Palau's estandartes engaged with Indigeneity from the outside. Palau, a Spain-born artist established in Mexico, had learned the Indigenous techniques, symbols, and meanings in her work through travel and study. Albeit with much admiration and support for anticolonial

Indigenous struggles, she was not an Indigenous subject, yet her work featured predominantly conceptual and material aspects of Indigenous cultural production. In her *estandartes*, Palau walked a fine line between honoring Indigenous culture and appropriating it. Uruguayan artist Luis Camnitzer, a participant in the Bienal who was deeply knowledgeable about Palau's work, reflected these concerts in his review of the Bienal for *Arte en Colombia*. Camnitzer admitted that practices like Palau's helped bring institutional legitimation to art forms and materials formerly excluded from it, validating their "ethnic origins" and ultimately brokering the entrance of Indigenous artists and knowledges into the art museum. However, he claimed that these maneuvers risked "evading confrontation with contemporary problems, [which are] very different from those which initially created the conditions for craft"—that is, by dehistoricizing Indigenous cultural practices and reaffirming a link between Indigenous artists and the past, dispositions like Palau's risked erasing Indigenous agency in contemporary social life. Camnitzer's reservations were probably shared by others.[25]

A *Global* Aesthetics of Reception

The challenge of how to represent the wide diversity of approaches to cultural production throughout the planet in a single gallery space did not shape only the work of Cuban *especialistas*. Several exhibitions in the period pursued answers to this same problem, albeit with very different approaches than the Cuban one. If the Bienal de La Habana proposed a universalism that foregrounded an esthetics of production, curators elsewhere relied on programs that either presented face-value multiculturalisms or reenacted past metaphysical essentialisms around the art object. An important case study within this trend was *Magiciens de la Terre*, which opened in Paris, four months before the third Bienal de La Habana (1989). The one-hundred-artist show featured fifty contributions from "developed, capitalist countries" and the rest from "the peripheries."[26] Some crucial commonalities drew equivalencies between *Magiciens* and the Bienal: both pursued visualizing and validating the work of artists from outside elite, white-centric North Atlantic art worlds; they did so partially by surpassing museological categorizations such as art, craft, and popular art; and they based their artist selection process on a wide network of local informants cultivated throughout the world. The Paris exhibit amplified the period's multicultural vibes through new artworks commissioned to *magicians* (the word they used instead of artists) from different geographies. Even if two Bienal de La Habana iterations (1984 and 1986) preceded *Magiciens*, the exhibit was described by its curator, Jean-Hubert Martin, as "the first worldwide exhibition of contemporary art."[27] Although the show received accusations of reproducing North Atlantic–centric aesthetic criteria, it nonetheless managed to consolidate a lasting reputation in the contemporary curatorial canon as the exhibition that initiated "transnational" curating.[28]

Magiciens reactivated in post–Cold War Paris metaphysical concerns brewed in Western European art worlds between the 1960s and 1980s. Tacitly gesturing toward a nostalgia for postwar liberalism in Europe, it retrieved the legacy of neo–avant-garde French and German artists Robert Filliou and Joseph Beuys. Filliou's pursuit of a universal language through his work influenced Martin's idealization of the art exhibition space as a nonhierarchical realm. Beuys's incorporation in his performative practice of shamanist rituals as gateways to the metaphysical shaped the curator's conceptualization of the artist as a magician. In his attempt to avoid the canonical distinction between the arts and the crafts, Martin articulated a curatorial program centered around what he perceived to be a gnostic faculty essential to the role of the artist. In his view, artists had the innate ability to access the metaphysical, thus acting as interpreters of other-worldly mysteries, mediating between everyday life and inaccessible truths. Asked to filter local artists for the final selection, curators from the several regions had to "determine which artist had the most fantastic imagination to invent new formulas."[29] Huang Yong Ping, an artist from China, recalls that "the name of 'magicians' is, in my opinion, more important than that of 'artists' because it includes and surpasses the very definition of art, especially now, since the concepts of art and artist have died several times. *Magiciens* is a prophecy of what is to come, [where] the artist becomes a speaker of oracles."[30] Exhibiting "objects with aura" and stressing their "magical" attributes contrasted with the Bienal's emphasis on artists' capacity to engage in the production of beauty.[31] However, this emphasis was incompatible with the global vision that *Magiciens* pursued. Presenting artists as *magicians* reawakened the identification of the artist with the genius that is central to European aesthetics. This identification of the artist with the genius was already present in Immanuel Kant's program, where he characterized the latter as an innate faculty to give form to art. Traced back to the Greek form *enthousiasmos* ("to be taken in by the gods"), genius is for Kant a "particular spirit given to a person at birth, which protects and guides them, and from whom inspiration those ideas stem."[32] The myth of the artist as genius that backboned North Atlantic artistic modernity was reawakened by postwar Greenbergian modernism. This critical approach relied on the myth's pervasiveness in the modern imaginary to evoke a supposed natural talent in some artists to sidestep mimesis in representation and access metaphysical truth. This faculty was perceived in Clement Greenberg's program as a sort of teleological unfolding of artistic talent, the sublimation of narrative into negative, abstract, spontaneous form. Although Martin sought to open common spaces of signification with the artist-as-magician analogy to scaffold a *global* exhibition of art inclusive of art made all throughout the world, the anchoring analogy acted as nothing but a faux tabula rasa. In addition to the Eurocentric curatorial premise, Martin's model represented North Atlantic art worlds with institutionally legitimated artists, to the exclusion of popular art practices in the region. However, no distinction between so-called high and popular art applied to contributions from outside Europe and the United States. This characterization of artists as magicians with para-rational faculties inherited reductive colonial tropes of the non-European individual as a free, blissful, irrational *sauvage*.

Martin's model severed artworks from their contextual meaning, presenting them as itemized objects in the gallery. In a clear hint to early twentieth-century formalist attempts to curate together North Atlantic avant-garde art and cultural productions from outside Western Europe and the United States, such as Alfred Stieglitz's exhibition of African and European art at 291 Gallery in New York, *Magiciens* favored a formalist display of artworks that erased their emic value.[33] Comparing *Magiciens* and the exhibition *Primitivism in 20th Century Art* (MoMA, 1984), art historian Benjamin Buchloh argued that centering spirituality in the exhibition brought objects together "regardless of social and political context, regardless of technological development of the particular social formations," in clear denunciation of the exhibition's reductionism.[34] Other critics, like artist and theorist Rasheed Araeen, remarked on the importance of production over reception when drawing universalist constellations of contemporary art: "In order to understand the function of art, and the privileges of its producers (artists), in our modern culture, we need to confront the fact that the production of the commodity is fundamental (both materially and ideologically) to the very historical formation of this culture."[35] But Martin did not seem to worry about the "problem of context" caused by displacing objects from their original settings into the Parisian museum.[36] This displacement, and the erasure of meaning it entailed, was for him comparable to the one experienced by premodern European objects shown in contemporary museums. Narrative work in the exhibition catalog would fill in the gaps.

Magiciens offered an alternative to the Bienal's aesthetics of production, presenting aesthetic experience as an access to the metaphysical mediated by the artist-as-magician. Although this particularly unique approach did not recur in later attempts to curate global exhibitions of art, its structural vantage, as an exhibition organized by a major European museum, occluded the earlier Cuban attempts to provide an all-encompassing vision of the state of art production worldwide. Where *Magiciens* was indeed successful in helping perpetuate in contemporary curating the deep-held belief that access to the aesthetic experience is somehow not a capacity present in all human beings, but just of a select few—namely, socially distinguished actors such as those capable of accessing metaphysical truth: the geniuses and magicians. This elitist view clashed with Havana's democratic notion of the artist as producer, where aesthetic experience was widely accessible to all, through sensory-driven engagement with artistic techniques and materials. Although both exhibitions engaged in the aesthetic conversion of culturally distinguished objects into particular object categories—art-as-collateral-of-magic, Third World avant-garde—*Magiciens'* exclusivist position negated access to the making of art to wide audiences and further reproduced the superiority of aesthetic reception over its production dominant in modern aesthetics.

part two

Cosmopolitan Dreams at the US-Mexico Borderlands in inSITE94 and INSITE97

SAN DIEGO AND TIJUANA, 1994–1997

four

Sovereignty Claims over the Borderlands

Driving from San Diego, artist and singer Terry Allen arrives at the border fence in a white van emblazoned with the inSITE94 logo. He parks close to an obelisk-shaped border marker that sections a wire fence. His van is topped with a metal balcony; he hooks up a speaker to one of its metal poles and faces his standing mic southward. Two posters read "WELCOME TO ALL PEOPLE. You are cordially invited to climb up on this van and speak, sing, play music, etc.—FREELY—what is in your heart and your mind TO/AT/FOR the other side. CROSS THE RAZOR. This is offered with the hope that what happens here might encourage increased understanding and communication between the PEOPLE of the United States and Mexico."[1] Allen walks to the mic: "Test. One, two, three." On the other side of the fence, inSITE staff install a similar setup, with twin posters in Spanish. Surrounding the vans, under the same sunny sky, are kids and adults and the beach, which is split by the metal fence reaching west into the Pacific Ocean. On a rock near Allen's installation is Boundary Marker 258, a metal plaque commemorating the establishment of the first border markers between Mexico and the United States, installed on October 10, 1849. A man climbs on top of the van on the Mexican side and approaches the mic. Restless, he takes his time but finally speaks: "I want to get 'cross the border! Why can't I get through without having a job?" Signaling to the US side, he asks Allen: "How did you get there?" Allen replies: "I started here." Then the man calls out to the border park ranger on the north side: "Hey there! Can I cross... without being chased? My name is Fidel, and this is all I have to say." He leaves the mic, climbs down, and walks away (see plate 6).

At first glance, Allen's installation for inSITE94, *Cross the Razor / Cruza la navaja* portrayed the international border as a space pregnant with the possibilities of dialogue and conciliation. Providing platforms for the general public to communicate with the other side, Allen's piece amplified the voices of the diverse constituencies that coexisted in the region. It echoed the dialogical aspirations of many contemporaneous artists worldwide who, after decades of Cold War antagonisms, welcomed the optimism of a time perceived by many as the end of history, when the antinomies of the past would dissipate. Yet these longings for convivial cosmopolitanism contrasted with the rise in nationalistic sentiments alongside the United States–Mexico frontier. Citizen-led white-nativist brigades policed the border fueled by the anti-immigrant rhetoric of officials such as Pete Wilson (the former mayor of San Diego and US senator for California, who was governor of California in 1994) and backed by legislation like Proposition 187 among other efforts.[2] The North American Free Trade Agreement (NAFTA) established in January 1994 a new framework for the movement of capital, goods, and people between Mexico and the United States. The new regulations facilitated financial and commercial flows but further restricted demographic movement, accentuating already existing inequities that shaped life in the region. In spite of this violent climate, hopes for convergence and collaboration informed the mission of inSITE, a festival of site-specific and installation art celebrated in San Diego and Tijuana between 1994 and 2005 that sought to showcase via contemporary art the richness of a region long perceived as a land of conflict.

However, like other early-boom art biennials and despite its site-specific aspirations, inSITE's goal to reimagine territory glossed over the complexities of everyday life for most regional residents. The biennial boosted a partial and optimistic picture of everyday life in the United States–Mexico borderlands that mostly excluded the systemic inequities and negotiations with power that shape everyday life for most border residents. In its efforts to represent everyday life at the border through contemporary art forms in circulation within dominant art centers outside San Diego and Tijuana, inSITE's portrayal of the region seemed closer to the lived experience of regional elites and nonregional art publics than that of most borderlands residents. As art critic Kurt Hollander remarked, inSITE was "basically a two-part exhibition, revealing how a highly site-specific, geographically focused exhibition can be split between its local public and an international art world that is largely unaware of regional realities."[3] Since its beginnings, these tensions resurfaced in inSITE's organizational form, its alliances with extra-artistic regional actors, and its selection of artworks.

Despite the biennial's general oversight, some of its artworks did reflect the symbolic violence that shapes the US-Mexico borderlands.[4] Allen's installation, however idealistic it might have seemed at first hand, was clear about the structural and cultural limitations of the biennial's conciliatory goals. His piece was quick to render the contextual inequities that inform life in the region, where some have the privilege to travel, work, speak in public, and be presumed as innocent by authority whereas, for others, to engage in these actions means to risk their lives and livelihood. A Texan who had lived in Southern California and New Mexico, Allen was very familiar with the contradictions of life on the international border. His career-long multimedia work about the frontier preceded his intervention in its westernmost location. In 1992, for example, he explored the polarized mythologies surrounding the international border in *a simple story (Juarez)*, an installation he produced for the Ohio State University's Wexner Center.[5] *Cross the Razor / Cruza la navaja* juxtaposed the border fence's essential violence with the ideal of free speech, using platforms reminiscent of the soapboxes once used in public political addresses. Soapboxes bore a special place in San Diego's history. In 1912 the city approved legislation to prohibit free speech in so-called soap-box row in downtown San Diego as a way to suppress solidarity-organizing efforts by working class and poor San Diegans, led by groups such as the International Workers of the World, the Single Taxers, and the Socialist Party.[6] Allen's installation actualized this episode, stressing the belief that conversation can help overcome politically motivated physical barriers. The installation's title remarked on the unequal access to these exchanges, pointing to the metal fence cutting through Friendship Park that, during Allen's first visit to the area, was just being installed, laying land's divisiveness bare. In addition to Allen's, other artworks included in inSITE foregrounded the uneven conditions shaping life in the region. These included *Century 21* and *Toy-an Horse* (inSITE94, inSITE97) by Marcos Ramírez (known as ERRE), Louis Hock's *International Waters / Aguas internacionales* (INSITE97), BAW/TAF's installation *ESL: Tonguetied / Lenguatrabada* (inSITE94), and Rubén Ortiz Torres's *Alien Toy UCO (Unidentified Cruising Object) / La ranfla cósmica ORNI (Objeto rodante no identificado)* (INSITE97).

    Terry Allen's installation on the border fence exposed the shortcomings of then-popular conceptions of the public sphere as a realm of equal access to all. This belief permeated through biennial curatorial practice in the early biennial boom years, despite repeated challenges to it by efforts of biennial organizers worldwide to thematize particular enclaves. This widespread presumption of de facto universal access finds its basis in Jürgen Habermas's influential idealist model of the public sphere, where rational actors join in virtual community to construct a public opinion that reflects the convergence of their social needs.[7] Habermas's model enables beliefs in the art exhibition as a de facto inclusive medium in which different aesthetic legacies are able to coexist on equal terms. Fueling the worldwide expansion of biennials, this then-dominant presumption clashed with the forms of exclusion from art institutions experienced by nonelite constituencies around the emerging global art biennials.[8] As Allen made obvious, publics' capacity to access the art institution is always pre-inscribed in their preexisting unequal social positionalities. As he wrote in his recommendations for van drivers and installation translators,

> You will need to be sensitive to situations which may, in any way, jeopardize the safety of you, participants, or the public. If you sense a situation is at all tense or has the potential to get out of hand, for any reason, please turn the vans off. . . . The piece is not about hostility and aggression, but rather, it is about human interaction and communication across an international border. As you know, this site is on a combination of State, Federal, and City property, and there are numerous agencies who have jurisdiction, so it is very important to remember that we need to manage the project and work cooperatively with all others (state park rangers, border patrol, police officers, etc.).[9]

Before installing the piece, Allen found himself immersed in intensive negotiations with the US National Park Service and the US Border Patrol. In order to complete *Cross the Razor / Cruza la navaja*, the artist and an assistant paid several visits to the two agencies, during which they had to convince officers of the art status of his intervention and enacted a series of modifications to his installation plans in order to appease the two bodies' demands. Although Allen initially wanted a solid, unmovable structure, he and the National Park Service ultimately compromised on movable platforms on vans. For the National Park Service, this solution posed fewer obstacles to border patrolling than stable ones: they could be easily moved in case of altercations between agents and civilians. The bureaucratic nitty-gritty involved in producing Allen's installation highlights the maneuvers that even artworks backed by the San Diego cultural and political establishment needed to go through in order to navigate the complex degrees of governance over the international border—not to mention the anticipation, as part of the artistic process, of physical conflict around the installation.

However, not all artworks did, like Allen's, render visible the processes involved in the unequal valuation of human life permeating policy and everyday life at the US-Mexico borderlands. As this chapter and the following two show, the majority of art projects at inSITE, in the form of site-specific interventions and gallery installations, relied on artistic languages developed under interpretive regimes that favor art's formalism over its practiced engagement with social life. Some of these behaved like stand-alone objects and were almost exclusively produced by artists foreign to the region. In inSITE's two first iterations, artworks like Eugenia Vargas's *Bird's Eye View* (inSITE94), Nancy Rubins's *Airplane Parts and Building, a Large Growth for San Diego* (inSITE94), Mathieu Gregoire's *Blue Granite Shift / Transición del granito azul* (inSITE94), Anna Maria Maoilino's *There Could Be Many More Than These / Podría haber muchos más que éstos* (inSITE97), Spring Hurlbut's *Columna serpiente, autosacrificio* (INSITE97), and Quisqueya Henríquez's *Untitled* (INSITE97) converted selective aspects of the region into the codes of a nascent global contemporary art but did little to satisfy the truth-telling expectations placed on site-specific artworks, especially as these expectations related to the complex experience of life at the borderlands.

A Question of Sovereignty

The biennial conversions that took place in inSITE were tightly bound to the period's increasing anxieties about the border between the United States and Mexico. As with other material and symbolic forms of state interventionism, the ritualized acts of policing surrounding the international boundary soon after the signature of NAFTA evidenced the rising political attention to the cultural identities, economic regimes, and human bodies that meet at this liminal conjuncture.[10] Interventions in the borderlands were, and continue to be, a question of sovereignty. Allen's piece reminds spectators that at stake in every instance of state policing is the determination of who gets to live a respectable human life and who does not. Decolonial scholar Achille Mbembe explains that the logic of modern Western thought has unfolded to deliver an all-encompassing necropolitics fueled by the fundamental distinction between humans and savages.[11] In this hierarchical valuation of human life, borders and colonies are uneasy spaces of exception where negotiations about what is to be saved and what is to be sacrificed are surrounded by conflicts between civilizations and regimes that determine not only the value of human lives but also the value of cultural and sociopolitical legacies. Inscribed in its organic alliance with political power, institutionalized artistic expertise has long been invested in policing distinctions in art made by diverse constituencies, shaping an art canon that scaffolds extra-artistic constructions of taste and mirrors societal valuations of human life.[12]

If Mbembe is concerned with the crucial question of how necropolitics determines who becomes a subject, then questions about how this distinction translates to the realm of culture are paramount because they reveal how ongoing processes of coloniality are weighed in the valuation of place, identity, and history. The processes of coloniality shaping the valuation of human life and artistic work were redefined in the post-NAFTA context at the US-Mexico borderlands, a zone of transition not just for people and commodities but also for modernity projects and their aesthetic counterparts. These had grown in parallel throughout the twentieth century and now met through neoliberalism's porous borders.[13] Driving efforts to police the area (including its peoples and their culture) were perceptions of the region as a shaky field that required stabilization for efficient management. Peter Andreas explains that these repeated attempts to control and win over the region make "'successful' border management depend on successful image management."[14] An art biennial involved in the symbolic reframing of the region was a good example of this approach.

Crucial to these framings were questions about homeland and belonging. As the artworks discussed in this chapter show, claims to belonging to the borderlands had long shaped a tense regional art world. Art historian Jo-Anne Berelowitz has documented the changing orientation of claims on the border since the 1960s by tracing how imagining belonging to the border region materialized in art around the symbol of the home. Berelowitz establishes three periods: a first phase of Chicano art activism (1960s–1970s) fueled by the colonial displacement from the mythical Aztlán homeland and the subsequent fight to rebuild it; a second postmodern (1980s) phase of redefinition of such homeland as mobile, fluid, and portable; and a third and last stage (1990s–2000s) shaped by difference in a newly configured global space that she clearly identifies with inSITE.[15] As she states, "inSITE is part of and a contributor to the 'postborder' condition: it operates in a world in which 'the border,' having become a metaphor for a condition of deracinated subjectivity, has been disembedded from a literal connection to a site-specific border, and has in fact become a theme in art world discourse; at the same time, inSITE operates at the border—a significant place with a real purchase on social life."[16] Agreeing on an image of the borderlands for nonregional art-world publics would prove, as Berelowitz anticipates, a daunting task.

Binational efforts to imagine the border divide were not new. Historically, a number of actors have laid claim to the border and thematized such claims via art—including Mexican and US state commissions, regional activist artists, and foreign parachute artists. As Edward J. McCaughan writes, understanding the complex history of art production around the US-Mexico border allows for an understanding of its regional cultural and social history, with special focus on the reorderings of power that have shaped life in it and representations about it since the Mexican-American War (1848) and throughout the twentieth century. Representations of the US-Mexico border began in 1848, when after the signing of the Treaty of Guadalupe Hidalgo, a joint US-Mexican commission of surveyors, engineers, and cartographers surveyed the southwestern frontier lands to establish the boundary line.[17] Artists and botanists joined the US team, "gather[ing] extensive information about the people, animals, plants, and lands with which they came into contact and produc[ing] copious records, ranging from reports to oil paintings." The commission installed stone and metal markers, old precursors to inSITE's site-specific artworks, at regular intervals of five miles spanning between San Diego and Tijuana in the west and Brownsville and Matamoros in the east.[18] These landmarks, the product of binational expert collaboration around the definition of national boundaries, prefigured inSITE's symbolic address to the area: a marker of art-driven convergence that repurposed the borderline as signifier of the selective porosity of borders during globalization.

State efforts to map and legislate the border continued to change throughout the twentieth century, reflecting the economic and political needs of the neighboring countries. The post-1848 markers were followed by a string of policy interventions that reinforced the border as a rigid yet selectively permeable boundary between two nation-states. A series of bilateral labor and trade treaties anticipated late twentieth-century obsessive control of the borderlands: the Bracero program (1942–1964) imported low-paid manual labor from Mexican Indigenous communities to California's agricultural fields; this was followed in the 1960s by PRONAF (Programa Nacional Fronterizo), which was designed to change the mainstream image of Mexico's *frontera norte* (northern frontier) from a land of moral diversion and backwardness to a land of modernized industrial productivity and progress, prompting the first *maquiladoras* to open.[19] Reconfiguring relations of production around the borderlands, these programs inscribed the region's permeability to the logic of capital.

These measures continue to shape present inequities informing life in the region. Since the 1980s, collateral free-trade and tax-exemption policies have accentuated regional inequities, making the borderlands home to some of the wealthiest districts in the United States and home to thousands of migrant workers who rent out their labor for the lowest prices in the national labor market. The extreme economic disparity between North and South reinforced through the neoliberal policy framework has fueled already existing structural racism and anti-immigrant sentiment from the US federal government and factions of its civil society—an attitude that Ronald Mize terms "neoliberal nativism," wherein "the political economy of free trade ideology [meets] state-sanctioned violence against migrants and *maquiladora* workers."[20] Since the early 1990s, the escalating militarization of the area has led to the subsequent deployment of military technology and personnel to the southern edge of San Diego and Imperial counties. This context of militarization and anti-immigrant fervor was the grounds for inSITE, a festival of site-specific and installation art. In contrast with the denunciatory nature of earlier civil-rights–derived art production in the area, inSITE was "designed to facilitate exchange, discovery, and dialogue among multiple audiences in this dynamic region."[21] The biennial's emphasis on conciliation contrasted with the on-the-ground manifestations of systemic violence shaping the everyday life experience of many border residents.

Throughout the region's history, civil society has repeatedly morphed to adapt and resist attempts from both sides to police and regulate everyday life, making control of the borderlands more of an idealist project than a successfully materialized enterprise.[22] In spite of their selective exclusion from the processes informing the region's cultural, economic, and political life, border communities make strategic use of the benefits of living on the international border—to the extent that individuals are allowed, in different capacities, to go to work, participate in public festivities, shop for everyday supplies, and make use of educational and medical services across the border, in both directions.[23] Border scholar Lawrence Herzog calls San Diego and Tijuana a "global metropolis" made of, on the one hand, "spaces formed by global economic actors," such as factories or *maquilas*, shopping malls, tourist areas (or an art biennial, in this case), and, on the other, "spaces that represent regional and local responses to globalizing forces" like neighborhoods and community spaces. He remarks on the importance of what he calls "invented connections," fictionalized narratives that accentuate the region's interconnectedness over other aspects of border life at play in the fragmentation of space at the borderlands.[24] Herzog's emphasis on the produced character of these narratives bears a clear resonance with Eric Hobsbawm's concept of "invented tradition," albeit directed, in the case of inSITE, to the naturalization of a new order of things around the border in the present tense.[25] Like Hobsbawm's invented traditions, which designate symbolically loaded practices meant to imbue specific values and support claims to historical precedent in efforts to naturalize concrete moments in our experience of social life, the invented connections that followed the signature of NAFTA around the US-Mexico borderlands document the balance of forces at struggle in the region. These ritualized, invented claims to an order of things perceived as natural conceal the interests of specific actors at times of drastic social transformations. They produce commonsensical narratives about life in the region bolstering, in this case, the fiction of the US-Mexico border as an essentially cohesive and interconnected region for all. In its organic affiliation with regional elites, inSITE emerged as one of many symbolic productions involved in the reimagining of the borderlands through contemporary art, facilitating a number of biennial conversions that impacted the representations, values, and status of territory, people, and culture.

Before inSITE

Before inSITE, the label "Border art" had been used to depict a kind of art very different from the one exhibited in the biennial. Its direct precursor was art by Chicano and Chicana artists who, since the civil rights period, worked to describe the conditions of their own oppression and propose joint action forward.[26] Born out of the emancipatory drives of the period, Chicano art was originally community based, democratic, and activist in nature. According to art historian Jennifer A. González, Chicano art constituted a parallel aesthetic genealogy that was inherently anticolonial—denouncing the oppressive colonial subjugation of their people by both the United States and Spain. For González, during this period, "Chicanos and Chicanas allied themselves with a specifically activist project that included a celebration of Mexican Indigenous cultural traditions, a nationalist return to territorial claims, a general critique of racism, and a rejection of unfair labor conditions for the working poor."[27] Extending across the southwestern United States, yet galvanized with more intensity in California, the movement put art in the service of expressing the realities of Mexican and Mexican American communities. Chicano art's representations of its communities' lived experience worked to strengthen group consciousness against everyday forms of racialized and classed repression. Yet through the following decades, Chicano art morphed and widened to incorporate the manifold ideological and artistic orientations of self-defined Chicano and Chicana artists—a widening that was partially motivated by the desires of some younger members of the community for validation from the Anglo-dominant cultural establishment.[28] In San Diego the liberatory intentions of the movement galvanized first in Barrio Logan, a majority Chicano and Chicana neighborhood south of downtown, to amplify and strengthen community cohesion around residents' protests in response to their displacement and land expropriation by the state of California to build the Coronado Bridge and Interstate 5. Activists and artists joined to reclaim the land under the bridge as a neighborhood commons. The struggle eventually resulted in the creation of Chicano Park (1970). Members of the Chicano art movement, including the Congreso de Artistas Chicanos de Aztlán (CACA), painted murals on the bridge's supports that displayed Mexican, Latin American, Indigenous, and Chicano emancipatory symbolism over the utilitarian cement of urban-segregation public works (see plates 7 and 8).[29]

Through these and related practices, Chicano art slowly took root as an approach to art making that was specific to the border region. After holding informal meetings in the Ford building in Balboa Park (today's San Diego Aerospace Museum) for six months, in 1970 a group of regional Chicano and Chicana artists received city authorization to use an abandoned water tank in the park as a permanent venue for the Centro Cultural de la Raza, "a sacred space instrumental in Chicano, Latino, and Indigenous art and culture" in San Diego.[30] This new institutional home prompted the community to increasingly turn its focus toward the changing socioeconomic conditions of the border region, and artists used the term *Border art* to designate their work. Latinos, Chicanos, Indigenous artists, and allies from other identities gathered in the Centro to turn the international border into an object of artistic inquiry, a marker of state violence and international capitalism. Art historian Amy Sarah Carroll notes that Border art responded to the increasing (and often conflicting) cries for dominance in the region that came from US, Mexican, and Chicano nationalisms at the time.[31] Although an overarching sense of solidarity informed their practice, practitioners of Chicano art and Border art were far from homogenous groups. The different approaches to art making found in these collectives were as diverse as their individuals, and they offered representations of Chicano identity, first, and the border, next, grounded on subjective and structural accounts of these realities, individual and collective approaches to art production, and overtly and tacitly political intentions and reflections.

Yet the growing political attention directed to the borderlands also attracted interest from the mainstream art world. As Claire F. Fox explains, Border art soon became a highly contested category, approached by curators and artists from a variety of positionalities with varying interests, used by some "to celebrate the U.S.-Mexico border's capacity to juxtapose and absorb disparate cultural elements, while others criticize[d] the former perception as an appropriate fascination with the daily life and experience of border dwellers."[32] Especially active in this rising attention toward the border were binational artist collectives like Border Art Workshop / Taller de Arte Fronterizo (BAW/TAF) in the 1980s to the mid-1990s, and the collective formed by Elisabeth Sisco, Louis Hock, and David Avalos in the early 1990s. Working from their situated knowledge of the region, these collectives often articulated critiques of the racialized and classed biases shaping new relations of coloniality at the borderlands.

Relationships between critical Border artists and San Diego's predominantly white cultural establishment were not smooth. A conflict involving BAW/TAF member and prominent performance artist Guillermo Gómez-Peña and the Museum of Contemporary Art San Diego (MCASD) director Hugh Davies exemplifies the tensions between these communities.[33] In 1989 the MCASD received a quarter of a million dollars from the National Endowment of the Arts to organize the curatorial project Two Cities / Dos ciudades. Although this series of exhibitions explored the border region through art projects, almost none of the commissions went to local artists who had long been producing work about the border region. Instead, MCASD invited nonregional artists often based on the East Coast or abroad, such as Jeff Wall and Alfredo Jaar. The conflict about who got to practice Border art became a "struggle for ownership."[34] Members of the regional Chicano art community accused MCASD curators of neutralizing the liberatory intentions behind their work by appropriating the label and its referentiality to the border region, only to ground the exhibition's discursive apparatus into a sense of authentic Chicanoness that clashed with the foreignness of artists included in the exhibition. This struggle for ownership would perpetuate through the following years, permeating inSITE's several iterations.

These contested claims of cultural authenticity foregrounded the question about who could claim to create Border art. At the time, most answers to this question were based on actors' biographical kinship with the region or their racial and ethnic identity, a reading that understandably favored local claims to ownership and discredited Border art made by artists who were not from San Diego and Tijuana. However, other actors, such as Mexico City–born Gómez-Peña and the inSITE organizers, understood the border as a more abstract, portable notion and were thus in principle open to nonregional actors producing Border art. But Gómez-Peña and the inSITE organizers supported their positions with very different arguments: Gómez-Peña's openness owed to his postmodern understanding of the border as a postcolonial wound embodied by the subaltern subject. His border was not a physically situated one but an inherited colonial severance carried in him throughout multiple settings. In contrast, the inSITE organizers were beneficiaries of the mobility that neoliberalism was affording to an incipient global elite. In their travels throughout the world, they might have *seen* borders, but they had probably not experienced the same wounds as those whose experiences of colonialism were embodied and rooted in concrete struggles in the border region. As Carroll documents, inSITE director Michael Krichman portrayed inSITE as "a natural evolution" from his art-collecting trips to Eastern Europe immediately after the fall of the Iron Curtain—another recently opened border highly appealing to biennial organizers, which I address in chapter 8.

One good example of how the original critical spirit of Border art survived through inSITE was *For Our Environment* (1997), by the Chicano Park Artists Task Force. This was an intervention in Chicano Park comprising an altar as information center, an arrow planted in the garden symbolizing Indigenous claims to land, the planting of trees, and the restoration of murals to protest against Caltrans's plans to retrofit the bridge over the park. In addition to these players were many artists who were not Chicanos or Chicanas, who had not been born in the borderlands, but who had spent significant amounts of time living in the region and learning its culture, cultivating strong ties with nonelite border residents. Despite not having been born in the borderlands or being Chicanos themselves, inSITE artists like Louis Hock, Rubén Ortiz Torres, and Terry Allen were able to engage with the borderlands condition in their practice by developing artistic methodologies that came closer to rendering the region as experienced by many border inhabitants. Given the harsh inequalities shaping life at the borderlands, questions about who could claim to make Border art also occluded unuttered fears concerning the social position of claimants. If Border art had emerged as an anti-oppressive program rooted in resistance organizing, shouldn't its emancipatory intentions be protected against the wrong class alliance?

Transborder Collaboration, Institutionalized

This important conflict between regional constituencies about who could claim to create Border art precluded and framed the conversions taking place within inSITE, a well-furnished festival that, in its own way, reawakened dormant antinomies in the area. First was IN/SITE92, an exhibition of installation art organized by the nonprofit Installation Gallery in downtown San Diego (1992). Run in itinerancy by a group of artists, curators, and academics from the region, Installation Gallery sought to promote art from the San Diego area. Although the artistic community around Installation Gallery changed over time, it represented a wide array of San Diego's smaller art scenes, including members of the Galería de la Raza, University of San Diego (USD), San Diego State University (SDSU), University of California at San Diego (UCSD), Mesa College, and local galleries and museums. In the spring of 1992, board members—gallery owner Mark Quint and UCSD visual arts professor Ernst Silva—invited regional artists to exhibit their work during September and October that year. The resulting IN/SITE92 was "cooperatively curated" and had as its main venue the Mission Brewery building in downtown San Diego, with smaller peripheral exhibition spaces elsewhere in San Diego and Tijuana.[35] Given its success, soon after IN/SITE92 ended, planning for inSITE94 began. With an anticipated budget of $600,000 and almost 24 months for preparations, this second iteration was significantly more ambitious. Scaling up required financial support from a diversity of agents, including private donations from board members, grants from US philanthropic foundations (the Rockefeller Foundation, Andy Warhol Foundation, James Irvine Foundation, Nathan Cummings Foundation, and Lucille and Ron Neeley Foundation), and support from public organizations (the city of San Diego's Commission for Art and Culture, Tijuana's city government, Instituto Nacional de Bellas Artes [INBA], and Consejo Nacional para la Cultura y las Artes [CONACULTA]). Ten fund-raising events and one fund-raising gala provided supplemental financial support for inSITE94. In-kind support came from regional organizations such as the Tijuana Chamber of Commerce, San Diego's Pan Pacific Hotel, Granger Associates, Ninteman Construction Company, and the Catellus Development Corporation. Finally, exhibition space and an additional preparation budget were provided by institutions such as the Tijuana Cultural Center (CECUT), the MCASD, UCSD, Southwestern College, the California Parks Commission, and the Casino Aguascalientes. At the time of inSITE94's preparation, Installation Gallery had a thirty-one-member board of directors and a sixty-three-member arts advisory board that reflected all participating institutions in the festival. InSITE went from handling an operating budget of $20,000 in 1992 (as Installation Gallery) to an estimated budget of $1.5 million in 1997.

For Silva, IN/SITE92's foundational ethos of "synergy [and] collaboration" was the "driving force behind inSITE94."[36] However, the larger scale and ambitions of inSITE94 provoked a transition from IN/SITE92's original collaborative work model to a hierarchical organizational structure, with specialized roles differentiated within the six-person staff and distinct funding and publicity branches within the organization. The initial emphasis of IN/SITE92 on local art expertise changed to incorporate a growing amount of recognizable international art-world names. For inSITE94, curators

Olivier Debroise, Walther Boelsterly, and Carmen Cuenca from Mexico City and Tijuana were incorporated into the team and played an important role in the selection of artworks. Catalog essays were written by local USD professor Sally Yard, Debroise, rising Mexican curator Cuauhtémoc Medina, and US art critic Dave Hickey. This trend toward the import of nonregional expertise in the conceptual apparatus continued in INSITE97. This time, Installation Gallery invited four curators: Canadian Jessica Bradley, Mexico-based Israeli Debroise, Brazilian Ivo Mesquita, and Yard. Catalog essays for this iteration were authored by reputed names in the international roster, such as philosopher Susan Buck-Morss, sociologists Néstor García Canclini and José Manuel Valenzuela Arce, and musician and composer George E. Lewis.

Following the conflicts between Chicano artists and the regional predominantly white cultural establishment some years before, the intentions of inSITE organizers to convey a conciliatory representation of life at the borderlands also shaped the biennial's ethos and its structure. In tune with the post–Cold War optimism, the festival incorporated into its organization contextual myths of efficiency and growth that had become a creed for the borderlands' political and economic elites since the signing of NAFTA. For example, inSITE94's catalog framed the festival's origins in "San Diego/Tijuana's intertwined history, in a space defined by both cartographic juncture and rift, amidst a political momentum marked by the conflicting signals of NAFTA and Proposition 187.... [Collaboration between artists] echoed the disparities and cohesion of this borderland terrain."[37] This conciliatory position was reflected in the organization's own language, goals, and criteria of valuation. An internal document stated the following programming guidelines for inSITE94: "to plan and coordinate exhibitions related to inSITE94 in at least fifty places of the San Diego–Tijuana region; to plan and coordinate work residencies for artists from the region and elsewhere in sites of San Diego–Tijuana; to coordinate the installation of temporary work sites around the Tijuana–San Diego region . . . ; to plan and coordinate bilingual tours to sites participating in inSITE94 for Tijuana and San Diego residents, as well as for tourists who visit the region during the time of the exhibition; to plan and coordinate at least five key public openings in 'key places' in the city of Tijuana and the city of San Diego."[38] The document's emphasis on the two cities permeates inSITE94's internal and public-facing literature. The interest in the two locales is evidenced by the even distribution of artworks in Tijuana and San

Diego; the bilingualism of organizational literature; the careful selection of government, nonprofit, and private-sector participants from both cities; and the equal attention given to press outlets in California and Baja California. Public funding for inSITE came from both the US and the Mexican federal governments, the states of California and Baja California, and the municipalities of San Diego and Tijuana. Private contributors were cultural institutions such as the MCASD, universities, and individual donors. Affiliations with civil-society organizations included temporary concessions of exhibition venues at cultural centers, such as San Diego's Centro Cultural de la Raza and Tijuana's CECUT, collaborations with public universities to invite artists and lecturers into the exhibitions, and the organization of workshops with a Tijuana mental health institution for one of the projects commissioned years later by inSite_05.

Yet it was mostly with its artwork selection that inSITE reproduced preexisting conflicts on how to represent the region. As Ila Nicole Sheren argues, through its curatorial choices inSITE "reinforc[ed] the notion that anyone can be a border thinker, border dweller, or border subject."[39] To sustain its vision that Border art could be accessed and practiced by anyone, regardless of their biographical relation to the area, as long as they took the borderlands as object, inSITE developed sophisticated organizational tactics that foregrounded the smooth border-spanning experience of organizations benefiting from the new policy framework. As with many other contemporaneous early-boom art biennials, inSITE's claims to site-specificity were scaffolded in tacit ways. George Yúdice and Carroll have described how inSITE's curation of community-engaged art and participatory projects worked to deflect potential critiques that the organization was disconnected from local publics. In the words of Yúdice, "To show that its programs are relevant to nontraditional publics, inSITE accommodated an already existing bureaucratic rhetoric whereby 'community' functions as a code word for poor and racialized people."[40] A border-spanning venture, inSITE joined other efforts by regional political and cultural elites to recode the borderlands, emphasizing the region's connectedness over the systemic forms of violence and exclusion that shape everyday life at the borderlands. The contrast between inSITE's organizational ethos and the lived experience of the borderlands for its majority of inhabitants merits pause. Would inSITE94's image of smooth transborder life be, after all, an "invented connection," to borrow Herzog's term?

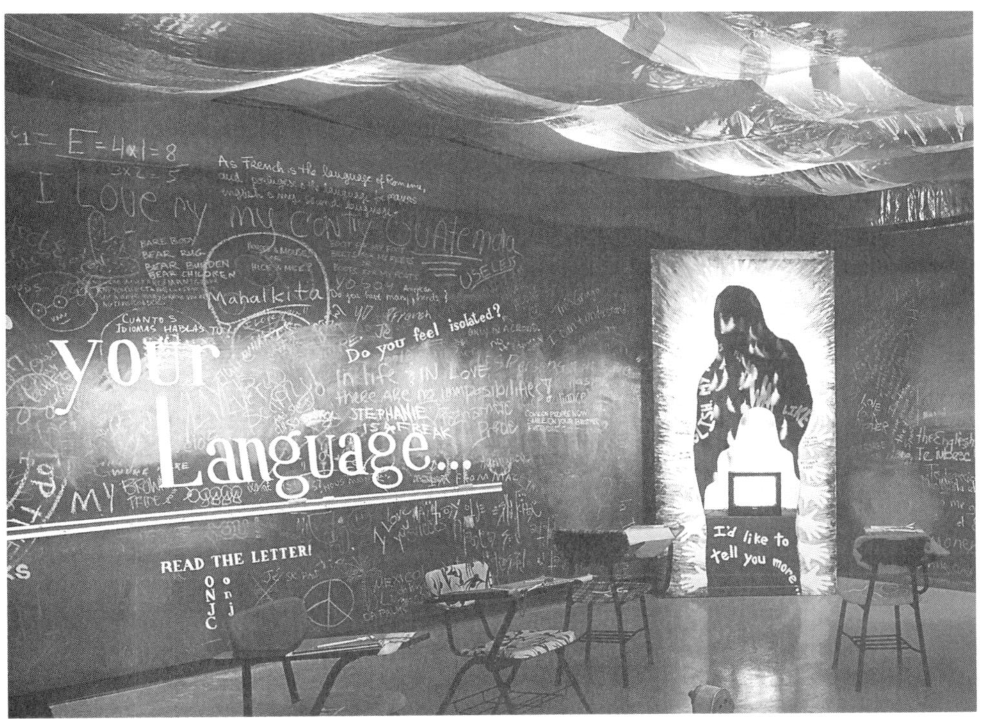

4.1 Border Art Workshop / Taller de arte fronterizo, ESL: *Tonguetied / Lenguatrabada*, 1997. Source: inSITE Archives, Special Collections Library, University of California, San Diego.

Lived Border Life

For inSITE94, the regional collective BAW/TAF produced the installation *ESL: Tonguetied / Lenguatrabada*. The piece, set up at Palomar College's Boehm Gallery in San Diego County, recreated the space of a classroom, in which all of the walls had been turned into blackboards. On them, handwritten messages addressed the audience: "SPEAK ENGLISH!" "What language do you think in … ?" "Do you feel insulted?" A television monitor displayed the testimony "I learned my English on TV." With this installation, the collective directed attention toward the institutions and media involved in identity formation, including the school, and portrayed the region as a land of unequal valuation of its cultural legacies. BAW/TAF's installation pointed to the role played by schooling in the disciplining of subaltern identities, partly through the policing of language. As Mbembe recounts, in addition to managing land, in its expansion the Western necropolitical regime also requires the governing of the people. What he calls "the management of the multitudes" consists of the categorization and spatial fixation of populations otherwise unruly—or, one might say, un-reifiable.[41] The biopolitical anxiety that was rightly felt by subaltern communities at the borderlands was registered by some artists featured in inSITE, such as BAW/TAF, primarily in the festival's early iterations. Despite inSITE's optimism, some projects, such as *ESL: Tonguetied / Lenguatrabada*, Marcos Ramírez / ERRE's *Cartolandia* and *Toy-an Horse*, and the film and video series curated by Norma Iglesias and Rita González several years later for inSITE2000, portrayed everyday life as a space of resistance to globalizing forces. These projects practiced what Jeff Kelley has described as an "art of place," in which "a place, a condition, an occasion is seen and worked as the materials of human or social exchange."[42] Like *ESL: Tonguetied / Lenguatrabada*, several of these early inSITE commissions focused predominantly on exposing the institutionalized disciplining of life and related devaluation of cultural diversity, by which Anglo-American cultural norms function as normative standards. This systemic cultural policing makes the borderlands a site of ongoing colonization where competing narratives about the experience of place clash in a struggle to define commonsensical understandings of the US-Mexico border.

Art's capacity to represent ongoing social life necessarily implies the selective valuation, bracketing, and abstraction of the myriad minutiae that inform it. Yet this freezing of unfolding life must be considered carefully, especially when contextual inequities—including those relating to race, class, ability, and gender—determine relations between artists and the referents in their creations. In his methodological contributions to the study of everyday life, Henri Lefebvre provides clear guidance on how to study what he calls the "proletarian condition." Lefebvre situates the proletarian condition in a dialectical fold: on the one hand, the proletarian individual is permanently addressed by forms of institutional policing that "crush [the subject] under the weight of the toil, the institutions and the ideas which are indeed intended to crush him." On the other hand, he has the embodied knowledge of his world that comes from everyday contact with the conditions of his life and work. Seeking emancipation, the proletariat articulates this tacit knowledge objectively as class consciousness, which is in turn articulated through the production and enjoyment of culture, in a wide diversity of forms. In his analysis, Lefebvre warns against attempts by nonproletarian actors who, despite their removal from the conditions of life and work that shape the proletarian condition, articulate the latter in cultural and intellectual productions, such as novels, artworks, and philosophical treatises. These actors, cautions Lefebvre, conceal their structural distance from the proletariat in different ways: some retreat into subjective abstractions of the proletarian condition, "withdrawing into private consciousness," whereas others "are lucid enough to create a political machine designed to extend their control" over the proletarian condition and develop sophisticated strategies to bridge this divide.[43]

Influenced in my thinking by Lefebvre's method, the "borderlands condition" might be a term better suited to encompass the variety of class positionalities of borderlands residents. This condition is caught in the dialectical bind defined by, on the one hand, the institutionalized processes that discipline the bodies, culture, and time of border dwellers (like those made visible by BAW/TAF in their installation). On the other hand, it is shaped by subjects' everyday experience of work and life at the borderlands, which grants border dwellers the embodied, firsthand knowledge of their world. Different kinds of cultural production, the most relevant for this analysis being Chicano art and early manifestations of Border art, had historically worked to render this dialectical bond visible. They also helped forge a group consciousness that in its description of the oppressive forces at play and the proposal of a call to action was inherently emancipatory. In words of artist Guilbert Sánchez Luján, member of the collective Los Four, "The problems inherent in the development of Chicano art and the Chicano artist are largely that of overcoming (1) the destruction process that the U.S.A. institutions have placed on the Chicano identity, and (2) the inability to affirm a unique culture as is manifest in the great reluctance of most Chicanos to say 'Soy Chicano' with pride and with conviction."[44]

Although not a Chicano, Border artist Louis Hock's installation *International Waters / Aguas internacionales* (INSITE97) directly referenced how borderlands inhabitants negotiated with the state policing of their everyday lives. The installation featured two pitched metal pipes installed as drinking fountains on both sides of the international border fence. It was set up at the same location as Allen's three years before, and people from Tijuana and San Diego could peep through a small hole cut in the fence as they

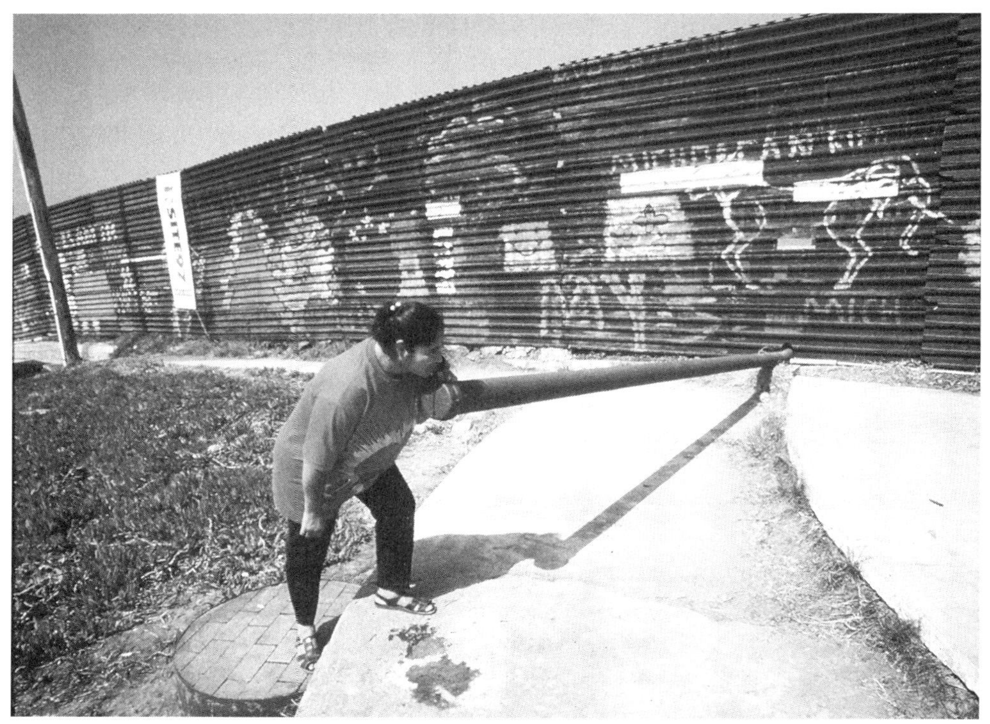

4.2   Louis Hock, *International Waters / Aguas internacionales*, 1997. Source: inSITE Archives, Special Collections Library, University of California, San Diego.

drank from the spouts, facing the physicality of the fence as an unavoidable presence. In its original formulation, Border art was thus an analytical tool for borderlands artists to engage with their embodied knowledge of life in the region, through which to expose its historical contradictions, articulate group consciousness, and propose joint emancipatory paths forward.

A small number of artists in inSITE's early iterations continued early Border art's driving spirit to signal globalization's impact on the everyday lives of borderlands residents. One of these was Tijuana artist Marcos Ramírez (ERRE), who participated in the 1994 and 1997 iterations. For *Century 21* (inSITE94), ERRE recreated a precarious housing unit—like those found in the informal residential areas of Tijuana—outside the Tijuana Cultural Center (CECUT). Before CECUT was built, in 1982, the area where it stood had been part of Cartolandia, a settlement of cardboard and

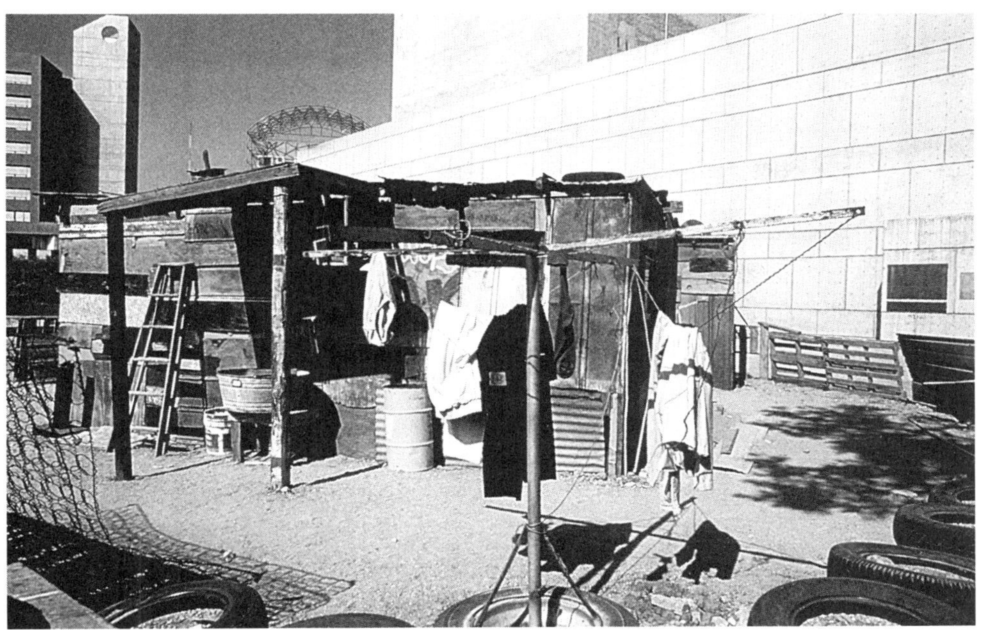

4.3 Marcos Ramírez (ERRE), *Century 21*, 1994. Source: inSITE Archives, Special Collections Library, University of California, San Diego.

wood houses along the Tijuana River that was mostly inhabited by Mixteca migrants from Central Mexico. In order to clear the area for high-end commercial redevelopment of the "Zona Río" in 1970–1976, local government authorities displaced Cartolandia's residents by intentionally flooding the area with water from a nearby dam, making way for the construction of shopping malls, hotels, and nightlife in commercial areas in this section, which is close to the San Ysidro international border crossing. ERRE's *Century 21* featured discarded wood panels, cardboard, and corrugated metal sheets. Old tires fenced its perimeter. Inside, mismatched kitchen cabinets next to a mattress and a round table with four chairs offered a view of the everyday scenarios of Tijuana's poorest residents. This recreation of everyday life in precarity is reminiscent of Mexican cultural critic Carlos Monsiváis's notion of "cultura de frontera," the practiced forms of life that reformulate the personal and national histories of those whose lives are severed by the geopolitical border. For Monsiváis, the cultura de la frontera is characterized by "its resistance to isolation (from the forgetfulness or dismissal of [Mexican] centralism), and the precarious settlement before the contiguous reality of the *American Way of Life*."[45] Such an acknowledgment of the simultaneous condition of isolation and forbidden aspiration makes Tijuana, yet another stop on the western frontier, a contested limit of state sovereignty, imagined and material, that has sustained through time expansionist ventures and justified exceptionalist economic policy frameworks such as NAFTA.[46]

Another piece that grew from an embedded appreciation of regional culture was Rubén Ortiz Torres's *Alien Toy UCO (Unidentified Cruising Object) / La ranfla cósmica ORNI (Objeto rodante no identificado)*. Shown in INSITE97, the piece was an inventive variation of a bed-dancer car fashioned after a Border Patrol vehicle. Ortiz Torres worked with Salvador, Chava, Muñoz, a car transformation expert and four times radical bed dancer world champion, who remodeled his own vehicle, inspired by the lowriders that they both had seen in car shows in San Diego and Los Angeles, to make its parts lift and spin in the air while retaining its ability to drive long distances. The piece hinted at the period's extraterrestrial fever, which had materialized in San Diego County around the Uranius Academy of Science, a spiritual community headquartered in the city of El Cajón that awaited the arrival of a spaceship fleet in 2001, and the unrelated 1997 Heaven's Gate mass suicide episode, where victims had been led to believe they would be rescued by alien spaceships and taken "to the next level."[47] Besides the obvious reference to extraterrestrial scatologies, the sculpture's title was a wink to the "alien status" used to designate non-US citizens. Relabeled as Space Patrol with the words "Alien Toy" on its shield, the motorized object lacked any explicit mention of the Border Patrol. However, the car mocked the agency—recognizable in its colors and design to those used to seeing its vehicles patrol their everyday lives. If you knew, you knew.[48]

The piece was a direct expression of the symbolic hybridity found in the region's culture and referenced, in addition to lowrider car shows, the harassment of nonwhite communities in California by immigration patrols and local police.[49] The car also emulated the fake handicrafts sold in Tijuana for United States visitors, a kind of pastiche authenticity designed to please north-of-the-border tourists' ill-informed expectations about Mexican culture. Its resemblance to TV cartoon transformers also rooted the vehicle in domestic media culture. Ortiz Torres, a classically trained painter, spoke of the cars as "Venetian paintings": sensuous, colorful, and thick with matter, rooting the project in an approach to image making

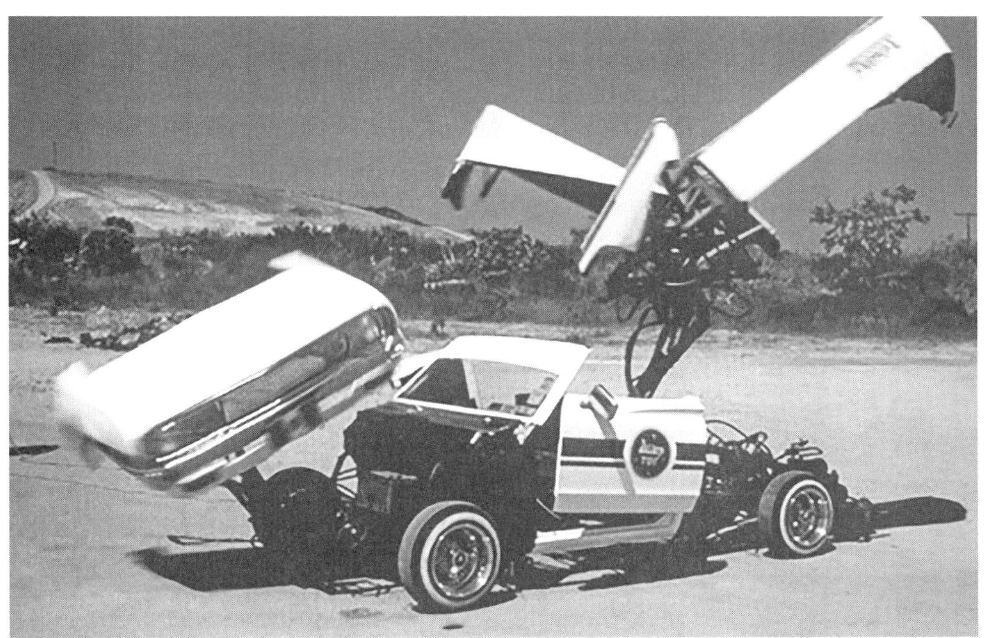

4.4   Rubén Ortiz Torres, *Alien Toy UCO (Unidentified Cruising Object) / La ran-fla cósmica ORNI (Objecto rodante no identificado)*, 1997. Source: inSITE Archives, Special Collections Library, University of California, San Diego.

that disregarded drawing's purportedly detached rationality and instead embraced painting's materiality as a sensuous, empirical engagement with the world. *Alien Toy UCO (Unidentified Cruising Object) / La ranfla cósmica ORNI (Objeto rodante no identificado)* was one of the Mexican artist's early transgressions of medium-specificity, following his move to California in the early 1990s to study at CalArts. For INSITE97, *Alien Toy UCO* was exhibited (and danced) in a garage in Barrio Logan, at the epicenter of San Diego's lowrider scene.

Through the years, fewer artworks featured in inSITE would echo the quotidian practices of reciprocity and recognition that inform life at the US-Mexico border. Most if not all of these were by artists living in the borderlands, including David Avalos, BAW/TAF, ERRE, Louis Hock, Patricia Patterson, Norma Iglesias and Rita González, and Elizabeth Sisco.

Although some inSITE artists in later iterations made explicit reference in their works to the economic unevenness and social contradictions of life in the region, the artistic forms that most of these later critiques adopted show how the organization increasingly favored aesthetic trends that were becoming prevalent in the nascent global contemporary art world. The border receded to a secondary plane. As inSITE's organizer Krichman told journalists, "[inSITE94] is not a Border art show" and will not lead to controversial expenditures on art. "There is some inSITE94 art that addresses the border, but surprisingly little," guaranteed Krichman. "In a number of subtle ways our artists have been interested in issues of the border, but not necessarily in the political sense." InSITE's guiding principles shared this partial optimism for the region's perceived binationalism.[50]

This progressive depoliticization of the border through biennial conversions favored global art trends to the detriment of cultural codes and practices bred in the rich local history of art production, such as Border art and forms of socially oriented conceptual art. Francis Alÿs's work for INSITE97, discussed in the next chapter, was a good example of how some foreign artists attempted to represent the borderlands condition through evasive poetic licenses—echoing Lefebvre. Yet many other actors involved in inSITE developed, in good faith, manifold strategies to remediate their nonbelonging to the region, such as long-term research stays and ongoing relationships with local informants. Often, however, what their good faith did not let them see were the enduring repercussions that their work would have in the regional cultural landscape and in the archives of art history: their biennial conversions at the border came to replace earlier emancipatory formulations of Border art in canonical contemporary art narratives.

five

Fears of Provincialism
and the Desire to Be Global

It's about time San Diego's cultural community does something to get us on the map. Let's face it—as the sixth largest city in the nation, San Diego should be one of the major "artopolises" right up there with San Francisco, Chicago, or at least Santa Fe or Seattle. What has kept us back? What keeps us back? Will we always hold ourselves back? How will we change this?

—Sonja H. Johnson, "Thank the Lord for inSITE94" (1994)

These words opened a story in the local publication *Arts Monthly*. The author, Sonja H. Johnson, blamed what she perceived as San Diego's cultural isolationism on the military and the tourism industries, but also on the "transient nature of our residents," which in her view impeded the formation of a solid cultural fabric. Johnson's longing for the cultural cachet of modern metropolises like New York, London, and Paris spoke to deep-seated insecurities among certain members of the local elite regarding San Diego's status. This view contrasted with another pervasive position among members of this group, who instead perceived the region's biculturalism as an untapped resource with big potential. Proponents of this latter position believed that greater investment in cultural tourism to the region would help leverage the borderlands culture to benefit the regional economy. In the words of a local gallery owner, "San Diego is perfectly poised to reap the benefits of recognition to our artists, museums, and galleries, to the border, to expanding other cultures via the art form medium. The financial wherewithal is here too. San Diego is a resort town. That attraction has pulled in lots of culture. People are coming in from New York, San Francisco, bringing growth to all businesses. This makes San Diego a prime site for a culturally awakened Mecca."[1] InSITE94's organizers seemed to agree that the region's cultural diversity had high potential for attracting cultural tourists seeking encounters with art comparable to those they could experience in other global art destinations. Under this view, the borderlands' "bicultural strength" was an unexploited resource that, if processed through the laws of the market, promised great potential benefit. Using George Yúdice's analogy, inSITE would work as a *maquiladora*, a site for the transformation of regional difference into a commodity whose surplus value derived from its placement in the exceptional space of the border region.[2]

Yet gains in reputation seemed to bear higher stakes for the cultural establishment than mere economic profit. Moved by their love for art and their personal collecting histories, regional elites saw the biennial as an opportunity to put their art connoisseurship into the service of what, in their eyes, was the greater good: showcasing the positive aspects of their home region and changing its image from a site of conflict into a pacified and beautified corner of exceptional bicultural difference, appeasing their own insecurities about San Diego's cultural cachet. Their partnership with experts such as art curators, academics, and artists would remediate uneasy feelings of provincialism that, in San Diego's case, dated back to the city's century-long competition for economic prominence with other Californian urban enclaves, such as Los Angeles and San Francisco. In Tijuana's case, these feelings reflected entrenched tensions with the Mexican state, which, despite its federalist structure, held a close grip on a region that had long pursued autonomy from Mexico City, as the next chapter details.

However, reliance on large-scale exhibitions to boost San Diego's reputation was an old trick. As Davis, Mayhew, and Miller explain, local elites in San Diego have repeatedly turned to grand exhibitions in an attempt to beautify the city and attract national and international investment.[3] Almost a century before inSITE, San Diego and San Francisco competed to host an international exposition to celebrate the opening of the Panama Canal, a large-scale engineering achievement that demonstrated the US's growing influence in Latin America. The canal was seen by many an example of techno-utopianism in the early twentieth century—proof of man's technical dominance over nature and of the US's geopolitical ascendancy. Although it was completed in 1914, local leaders in the industrial and real-estate sectors had been lobbying officials in Sacramento and Washington since the canal's early planning stages to host a large-scale event that would position their cities as international hubs for transpacific trade, commerce, and culture. Having lost to San Francisco, which was ten times larger in population and had been a mythical manifest destiny destination since the gold fever years, San Diego transportation and real estate magnate John D. Spreckels affiliated with Ulysses S. Grant Jr.—a son of the late US president who relocated to San Diego and became a prominent real estate developer and political player—to sponsor the celebration of the Panama-California 1915 Exposition in Balboa Park. The exposition relied, already then, on a series of aesthetic operations that romanticized San Diego and erased the contentious aspects of its violent colonial past, a framing that Jim Miller has called "an Anglo-Saxon interpretation of Spanish California."[4]

This earlier episode of local boosterism was revisited by inSITE94 artists Janet Koenig and Gregory Sholette in their installation *disLOCATIONS/desUBICACIONES*, with which the duo sought to amplify episodes of class struggle neglected in dominant historical accounts of the borderlands. Their project resuscitated the film archive of early twentieth-century cinematographer Lyman H. Howe, who filmed in San Diego in the early to mid-1910s but whose reels had been lost by the city. In their installation, Koenig and Sholette included four shadow-box dioramas and eight filmstrips, mounted on translucent plastic and hung from the Mandeville gallery's ceiling at UC San Diego, allowing audiences to walk through the set and "expose the fabricated nature of the constructions" by getting a glimpse of the different objects informing each scene.[5] The dioramas were handmade by Sholette, using polystyrene plastic sheets, aluminum brackets, fabric, styrene, clay, silicone, and model miniature figures. The newsreels, produced by Koenig, were color prints processed to resemble old black-and-white film stills, inserted in thin Plexiglas and airbrushed to mimic film pockets on their sides. The images in the newsreels came from postcards and two local newspapers, *San Diego Union* and *San Diego Tribune*, which Koenig retrieved from the archives of the San Diego

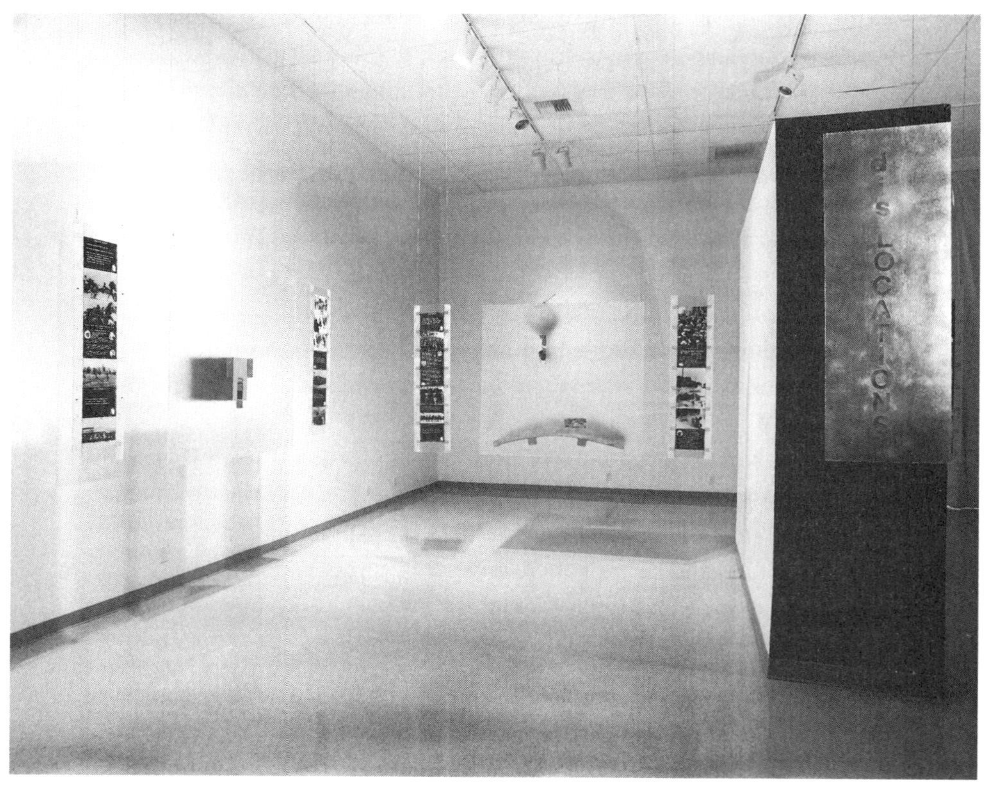

5.1   Janet Koenig and Gregory Sholette, installation view, *disLOCATIONS/ desUBICACIONES*, 1994. Courtesy of Janet Koenig and Gregory Sholette.

Historical Society.[6] The installation recreated episodes in local history such as the opening day of the Panama-California Exposition in Balboa Park. It also amplified the Pueblo Village exhibition of live human "specimens" at the California-Panama Exposition, for which Native Americans from the San Ildefonso Pueblo in New Mexico were forcibly removed by the Santa Fe Railroad Company from their lands and were brought to San Diego to build a makeshift Indigenous town in which they performed for exhibition visitors a fictionalized account of Indigenous everyday life. A note in the *San Diego Tribune* reported on how the "toiling redskins [were] glad to labor on structures in [the] 'Painted Desert'" exhibit—a clear sign of the dehumanizing toll of the exposition on its captive Indigenous performers.[7] Other episodes brought by Koenig and Sholette to the gallery included an exhibition of human anatomical types (also displayed in the Panama-California Exposition) by Smithsonian Institution anthropologist Dr. Ales Hrdlicka, a scene of Lowe's crew filming the Tijuana Revolution of 1911, and a display that documented the riots that followed the San Diego Free Speech fight in 1912, where local authorities banned political speech on the streets as a way to stop labor organizing and reduce working-class solidarity in the border region.

Koenig and Sholette had been investigating the classed dimension of historical narratives since before their arrival in San Diego in 1992. The artists were members of New York-based REPOhistory, a collective concerned with unveiling and honoring the histories of the US working class, working to "retrieve and relocate absent historical narratives at specific locations . . . through counter-monuments, actions and events."[8] A continuation of their work with REPOhistory in the border region, *disPLACEMENTS/ desUBICACIONES*, rendered visible the historical service that large-scale exhibitions had played for local boosterism. Alongside the shift of Border art away from its liberatory beginnings in Chicano civil rights activist organizing and into the powerhouse of a well-funded arts festival (see chapter 4), San Diego's political and economic elites soon identified an opportunity to leverage regional difference, reposition themselves within a growing global economy, and access often overlapping networks for the circulation of capital and culture—including art. Moved by different goals from those behind other early-boom biennials, including the Bienal de La Habana and Manifesta, the desire of borderlands elites to overcome long-held feelings of provincialism channeled their support of global contemporary art through an art biennial during this period of neoliberal expansion.

InSITE: A Boundary-Spanning Opportunity

The sense that the borderlands presented untapped opportunities to raise the region's cultural cachet on the global stage was widely felt. On May 14, 1993, the now defunct business publication *San Diego Daily Transcript* published "A Border-Spanning Extravaganza," an article that announced the celebration of inSITE94: "It's 'hands across the border' with an artistic emphasis. 'inSITE94,' . . . gives a new and deeper meaning to 'cultural exchange.'" After a brief description of the show and its binational collaborative model, the *Daily Transcript* cited the director of the Tijuana

Cultural Center (CECUT), Pedro Ochoa: "While people on both sides of the border are well aware of the importance of building business relationships between the United States and Mexico because of the NAFTA, I believe it is also a good time to take an approach through art and culture as well."[9] Ochoa and the *Daily Transcript* singled out inSITE94 as an extension of the business sector's enthusiasm about bilateral collaboration into the cultural field. References in the San Diego and Tijuana press to the opportunity that free trade afforded to cultural enterprises were frequent. In addition to inSITE94's organizers, other San Diego cultural institutions joined in this enthusiasm. For instance, the San Diego Opera's general director, Ian Campbell, said that "we consider Tijuana, and Baja California in general, are definitely part of our market. . . . We have that very real thing—the border—that often limits one's thinking. It forces you to think of it [Baja California] as a foreign country rather than a geographic extension of the same area, so we're trying to ignore the border and look at this as a general catchment area for all the performing arts." Similarly, the San Diego Symphony's executive director, Michael Tiknis, said that "Baja is a natural, close market with all sorts of people who love good music. . . . We're going to make every effort to build as much interest [among Mexicans] as possible."[10] These accounts demonstrate how ingrained that market-based thinking had become at this moment as a framework to explain the benefits of cultural cooperation.

This belief in the expediency of cross-border collaboration and exchange was shared among local business elites, who saw opportunities for economic profit in NAFTA's free-trade legislative framework. On the governmental level, a multitude of state-, county-, and city-level governments on both sides of the border celebrated efforts to accelerate the flow of goods and capital by the two federal governments. In this climate, ideas about economic and cultural exchange got easily conflated as the former gathered momentum. By way of this conflation, cultural exchange and collaboration were increasingly figured in the terms and assumptions of economic exchange. For example, San Diego mayor Susan Golding proclaimed March 19, 1994, to be "inSITE94 Day," acknowledging that "inSITE94 will be the first large-scale collaborative undertaking by nonprofit visual arts institutions in Mexico and the United States since the adoption of NAFTA; and . . . [that] the collaborative structure of inSITE94 represents a new national model of resource sharing in a period of declining sources of funding for the arts; and . . . [that] inSITE94 will be promoted internationally and is expected to draw significant numbers of culturally oriented visitors and museum groups from both countries."[11]

The market opportunities that NAFTA created invited the emergence of a multitude of boundary-spanning organizations, extragovernmental institutions that, according to border studies scholar Glen Sparrow, produced "cooperation or coordination between the various branches, levels and forms of government," and external entities, such as civil-society organizations and the private sector, which often met needs that were left unaddressed or had been abandoned by the state.[12] The period's boundary-spanning enthusiasm, part of a larger optimism for post–Cold War supranational convergence, translated into cultural organizations that, like inSITE94, self-instituted the mission of promoting contemporary art on both sides of the border. InSITE94's organizers described "unprecedented" levels of collaboration, "enlisting the active participation of every nonprofit visual arts institution in the binational region." Simultaneously, business elites perceived the biennial as an opportunity for economic benefit. For instance, a spokesperson for Tijuana's Chamber of Commerce justified its support of inSITE94, stating that the exhibition "will project the Tijuana–San Diego region to the world . . . , will notably improve the region's public image, will attract national and international tourism, [and] will generate economic flow with the arrival of national and international visitors."[13]

Scholars of globalization have long noticed the implication of inSITE in larger market schemes. Most remarkably, sociologist Néstor García Canclini described the operation as a metaphor for NAFTA, which "can, like [a] movie set, be conceived of as an artistic maquiladora whose executives (the directors of the art event) contract with managers (the curators) to map out the agenda for flexible workers-for-hire (artists) who in turn produce or extract (cultural) capital by processing a range of materials"—chiefly, the physical landscape, the endemic cultural practices of its inhabitants, and the many narratives about the borderlands circulating in local and foreign media.[14] García Canclini's account registers a general symptom of the period. Post–Cold War beliefs about market-driven supranational convergence were fueled to a significant degree by the success of operations like inSITE and other art biennials in institutionalizing particular cultural forms and, in so doing, multiply financial, social, and symbolic gains.[15]

Allan Sekula's work for INSITE97, *Dead Letter Office*, addressed globalization's impact in the border region, continuing the artist's commitment to unveil the conditions of labor and life in global capitalism's ocean economies (see plate 9).[16] The series of fifteen documentary photographs, some installed in diptychs and triptychs, record the unequal impacts of NAFTA in the borderlands: a Hyundai container factory outside of Tijuana, a shipyard welder cutting steel for a Hyundai truck chassis in Ensenada, the muscular suntanned son of a lobbyist at the Republican Convention in San Diego, metal workers employed by a Hyundai subcontractor voting to unionize in Tijuana, Marines and Navy photographers in an amphibious landing drill at the Camp Pendleton base, a man collecting recyclables in a shopping cart in downtown San Diego, an impounded migrant-smuggling ship flying a Chinese flag and an abandoned Russian fishing boat in Ensenada, a uniformed crew welcoming Republican Convention participants for a boat ride in San Diego Bay, young women working on the line at a tuna cannery in Ensenada, a coffin factory in Tijuana, and a backstage look at Twentieth-Century Fox's *Titanic* film set, next to mussel gatherers in precarious housing in the nearby coastal town of Popotla.

Fears of Provincialism

Deeper than the economic interests fueling transborder agency collaborations ran the desires of local elites to be taken as serious global players. But satisfying this longing would require recognition by those already established in the elite cultural circuits they sought to enter. Contemporary art would help mediate in that recognition. A hand-drawn portrait of a stylish woman on a fedora opens a gossip column in *619 Social Calendar*, a La Jolla society magazine. The column profiled glamorous Eloisa Haudenschild, a La Jolla arts patron, alongside her husband, CEO of a regional biotech computer systems company. It chronicled a March 19, 1994, fund-raising gala for inSITE94 hosted by the art collectors and chaired by world-renowned artists Christo and Jean-Claude, longtime regulars of MCASD. The column regretted San Diego's lack of "international events," reducing these to "the America's [Golf] Cup" and "Blue, White & Red parties," with "handsome, charming Italians; hand-kissing Frenchmen; and Crocodile Dundee look-alikes from the land down under." But things were about to change: "You are in for a wild international ride in 1994! . . . The San Diego–Tijuana region will be the binational location for inSITE94, a biennial exhibition of installation and site-specific art."[17] Urging La Jolla socialites to purchase $125 dinner tickets for the inSITE94 fund-raising gala, the column's author put her finger in a widely shared wound: local elites' anxiety about San Diego's supposed provincialism. The quotation—half-joking, half-serious—positions golf tournaments and episodic visits from European and Australian tourists as the most noteworthy moments of internationalization for La Jolla readers to date. By retreating to old clichés prevalent in tourism staging, the column thereby outed a biased understanding of cultural diversity. Remarkably, the piece ignores the high numbers of international residents living in the area, mostly of Mexican origin, but also Africans, Asians, and Central Americans. In the early 1990s, at least 510,781 residents (20.9 percent of the county's surveyed population, according to official records) were Mexican nationals.[18] In fact, San Diego County was a very diverse international region by the time of inSITE94.

This classed, racialized distinction between worthy and unworthy international alliances (and the implications that it bore for the valuation of human life and culture) quickly became obvious to many young artists participating in inSITE. In her performance *Inaugural Speech* (INSITE97), Los Angeles–based Andrea Fraser reflected elites' perceptions of the region's diversity. Humorously, Fraser took on the roles of different prominent socialites invited to deliver on-stage speeches at INSITE97's inauguration in downtown San Diego. In the guise of politicians, philanthropists, artists, and herself, Fraser mocked regional elites' disregard for the region's sociocultural diversity. Impersonating former San Diego mayor and then California governor Pete Wilson, she pronounced:

> Our region is a diverse region populated by many kinds of people. There are people who work in the fields and flower shops, in the hotels and factories, and there are people who vote. There are people who pay taxes and there are people who establish foundations. There are people who send their children to public schools and there are people who vote. And yet, despite this diversity, we are held together by our belief in diversity. We are devoted to that myth. It's our myth. It's all that many of us have.[19]

In her speech, Fraser also ridiculed arts patrons: "We want people to realize that there's a lot going on down here! We're the home to many, many internationally respected institutions, to Nobel Prize winners, authors, celebrities, custom ocean view homes, boutiques, luxury, charm, sophistication, jet-setters from around the globe." Later, when Fraser turned to

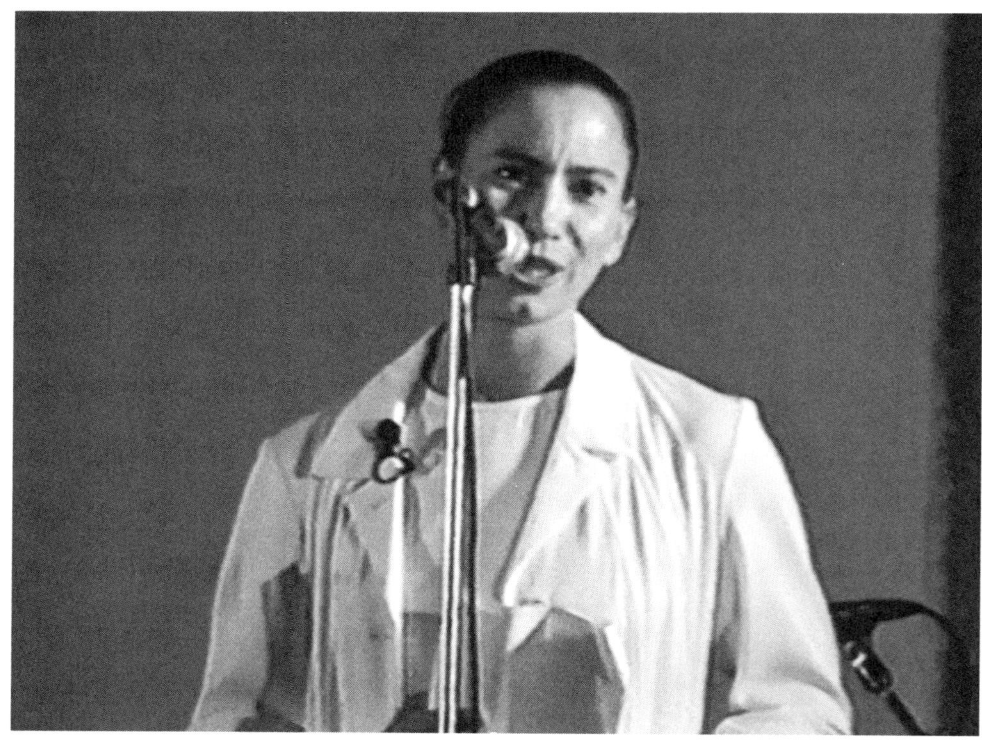

5.2   Andrea Fraser, *Inaugural Speech*, 1997. Source: inSITE Archives, Special Collections Library, University of California, San Diego.

performing as herself, an artist invited to produce an artwork for the arts festival, she exaggerated her indebtedness to the many arts patrons sponsoring inSITE and commemorated a fund-raising gala for INSITE97: "Who could forget that evening? A black-tie gala that equaled the raw creativity, exuberance, and international flavor of the exhibition itself. Music, dancing, super cuisine, all in a lavish and dramatic setting." Her concluding remarks listed the titles held by inSITE trustees, describing the classed alliance invested in the art biennial: "They have served as directors, executive vice presidents, state appointees, partners, brokers, planners, director generals, secretary generals, consul generals, vice presidents of development, cofounders, chairmen, owners, significant shareholders, chief financial officers, chief executive officers, and presidents throughout the Americas."[20]

The Haudenschilds' gala for inSITE94 and Fraser's parodic impersonations point to the rising political influence of private corporations in San Diego since the 1980s. During this time the biotech industry joined the military and tourism industries as influential players in the county's economy and politics. This growth of the biotech industry, which was perceived as experimental, risk taking, and science driven, changed the economic and political orientation of a new class of art patrons mostly based in north San Diego County. These transformations happened simultaneously with the active redevelopment of San Diego's downtown as a cultural center during the early 1990s, a phenomenon described as a "strong arts renewal" in downtown San Diego orchestrated by the newly formed Arts Downtown Council.[21] Among the cultural institutions contributing to this process of urban redevelopment were the downtown branch of MCASD, opened in 1993, the new Children's Museum, the New School of Arts and Architecture, and the B Street Pier gallery. However, the time's tentative plans for University of California San Diego Extension campus did not reach fruition for decades.[22] Susan Brown, then mayor of San Diego, attributed the higher visibility of art in public space to the rising "corporate response to art," which was "pull[ing] the artists out of their studios to participate."[23] Smaller art spaces that joined the momentum included Simayspace, Cafe Cinema, Taboo, Bravo Gallery, Sushi, Many Hands Gallery, and Installation Gallery, the artist-run gallery organizer of IN/SITE 92 and inSITE94.

Like Fraser, many other inSITE participants were aware of the contradictions that framed their work in the region. David Jurist's intervention for inSITE94, *Maíz/Maze*, directly acknowledged the important role played by real estate interests in the reimagining of San Diego in the period. With his two-part installation, Jurist drew condominium floor plans in empty twin lots in La Jolla and downtown San Diego, areas that were undergoing a process of real estate development at the time. In La Jolla, the artist traced the plan's contours by planting corn seeds that grew throughout the season to shape the walls of a house. In downtown San Diego, Jurist built a pyramid with cinder blocks. He planted corn in its holes, which grew to shape a live, green pyramid. Both installations were connected by a live video signal of the La Jolla piece, which was screened at the core of the downtown pyramid. In his piece, the fertile juxtaposition of cultures (mid-century California vernacular domestic and Mesoamerican monumental architecture) yielded development and growth.

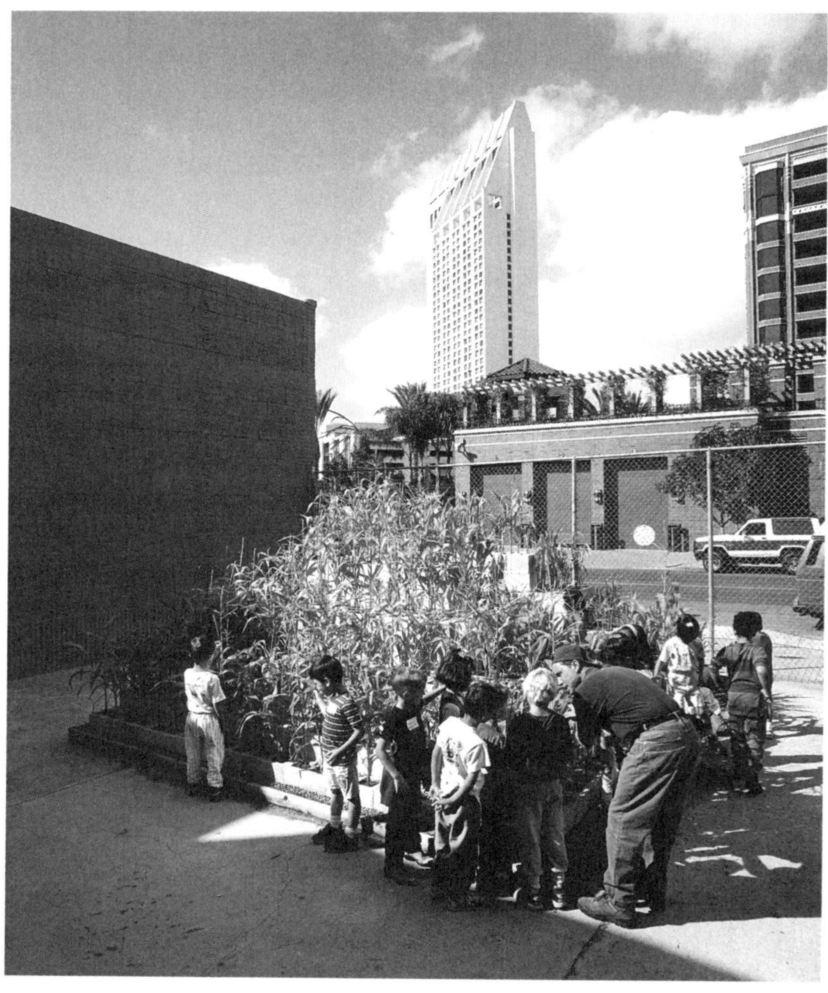

5.3   David Jurist, *Maíz/Maze*, 1994. Source: inSITE Archives, Special Collections Library, University of California, San Diego.

Creative Boosterism

These celebrations of cultural capital's potential to develop a city's economy signal the organic pairing of entrepreneurship and creativity under the neoliberal creed widely embraced by regional elite arts patrons. They also demonstrate how the importing of nonregional contemporary art forms was soon identified with the promise of bolstering local elites' own reputations as sophisticated cosmopolitans. This paradigm of profit-driven private-sector experimentation, widely held as a developmental model, found its apogee at the turn of the century in Richard Florida's theory of the "creative class." Florida celebrated the creative class not as a group that ought to be cultivated for its own sake but primarily because he believed that their activities raised the economic value of urban areas. Artists, cultural figures, and opinion makers, such as those involved in inSITE94 and other 1990s culture-led redevelopment ventures in downtown San Diego, differ from modern cultural elites in that they cherish individuality, meritocracy, diversity, and openness. Not unlike global contemporary artists, their work is transmutable between different sites because they themselves are movable and uprooted. Under this model, cities with a high density of "creatives" or "creative centers" are characterized by the presence of high-tech industries and diverse regional vitality. They "provide the integrated ecosystem, or habitat, where all forms of creativity—artistic and cultural, technological and economic—can take root and flourish," he explains.[24] Unsurprisingly, Florida repeatedly heralded San Diego as a creative hub, based on its active technology sector and high degree of tolerance for "diverse lifestyles." He even ranked San Diego as a top-ten creative city in the United States, owing in big part to the racial diversity of its creative class (in San Diego's case, residents of Asian and Hispanic heritage).[25]

Why would San Diego want to be a creative center? According to Florida's model and the dominant neoliberal creed, a growing creative class increased the overall quality of place: creatives brought diversity and a "better," more distinct lifestyle to cities, adjusting the quality of social interactions to the expectations of particular social groups—a framework that relegated cultural value to an economic demand. Though formulated at the turn of the twentieth century, Florida's model nonetheless matched the logic behind the alliance of cultural expertise and regional elites that made globally oriented art institutions such as inSITE take root in mid-1990s San Diego and Tijuana. Yet, as Sharon Zukin anticipated with her critique of what she called the "artistic mode of production," artists and professional creatives have been instrumental in processes of urban renewal and gentrification since the transformation of the urban fabric with the 1970s flight of industrial production to the peripheries, often unknowingly helping ease the importation of cultural and service activity for the rehabilitation of urban enclaves following periods of economic decline.[26] The tragedy, as Zukin shows, is that artists neither became the beneficiaries of the capital gains they helped produce nor were preserved on site and cultivated as a social group worthy of care. As transformers of a region's purported raw potential into culturally infused surplus value, often aware of their role, artists were brought in to contribute to the reattribution of meaning and value to sites. The collateral commodities derived from the process—artworks—entered the collection vaults (with accrued surplus value), while artists' bodies, their time, and their labor moved on to the next art commission elsewhere, as in the García Canclini metaphor at the beginning of this chapter. This tragedy repeated itself in the US-Mexico borderlands as inSITE failed to deliver the long-term transformation of the regional art scene it promised but managed to swell private collections in north San Diego County.

A New Class for Itself

By welcoming contemporary artists from Los Angeles, New York, Mexico City, and other international art-world capitals as translators of regional difference, borderlands economic elites articulated a desire to render the region legible and attractive to art patrons in global art capitals. In doing so, Border art—which had been understood until then as practices variously linked to Chicano political activism—was largely emptied of its original criticality and antiestablishment intentions. The local arts benefactors who came together in support of inSITE engaged in acts of distinction that articulated their perceived social class through the selective valuation of culture. Following Pierre Bourdieu's theory of cultural distinction, by selectively conferring the status of art to some objects over others, social actors express their belief that certain objects are distinguished from others by inherent qualities.[27] In doing so, they position themselves as capable of identifying and valuing those inherent qualities, implying an inclusive group kinship articulated around those presumed capacities, and excluding from it those who do not position themselves as able to partake in the same acts of identification and valuation. It is by performing belonging to a community with shared cultural tastes that subjects validate claims for their distance from the broader social mass, which they perceive as unable to interpret and value inherent differences between seemingly incompatible cultural repertoires. For Bourdieu, this latter point is of extreme importance because claims for the autonomy of expertise have repeatedly been made in order to support and reproduce contextual social hierarchies. In our case, this detachment of artistic expertise from the local social fabric was evidenced through the importing of curators, artists, and critics from the global circuits of artistic distinction, at the expense of existing cultural expertise. For example, Border artists from New York were often preferred to render the borderlands over Border artists from the region, at least when it came to strategically placing San Diego and Tijuana on the global art map. The former's organic affinity with artistic styles established in dominant art institutions implied, for better or worse, a distance from endemic cultural forms. This move ultimately disassociated the Border art label from the latter group and displaced it to new signifiers.

Relying on culture to change the region's image affected the urban fabric as well. The creative ventures that took place in downtown San Diego in the 1990s were indicative of a more widespread approach to urban renewal that was becoming hegemonic alongside the establishment of NAFTA and neoliberal optimism. San Diego in the 1990s participated in a particular form of urban boosterism that was becoming increasingly common in US cities during this period, one that was characterized by largely privately funded and culturally driven urban renewal. Geographer David Harvey describes this transition as a move from a management model of urban development to an entrepreneurial model in which "traditional local boosterism is integrated with the use of local governmental powers to try and attract external sources of funding." Under this paradigm, urban transformation is no longer motivated primarily by the social, political, and economic interests of the state. Instead, it is urban capitalist elites who pursue a return on their investments in the form of tourism, real estate valuation, or indirect symbolic benefits such as reputation, influence, and cultural capital. For Harvey, in this climate "urban administrators seek to build up symbolic capital through the development of so-called cultural, knowledge-based, or simply spectacle-driven industries. The marketing and selling of a city's reputation in itself becomes a big business."[28] A well-funded art biennial proved to be an attractive and effective means for enhancing and accumulating this form of symbolic capital.

These acts of distinction ultimately helped articulate a class consciousness that was crucial for emerging forms of group self-identification. By signaling a preference for nascent global art forms over local ones, art-supporting elites from across the world could recognize one another as sharing cultural dispositions and affinities despite their regional, national, and cultural differences. Designating and appreciating objects as global contemporary artworks helped an emerging globally oriented elite articulate a new sense of self. Simultaneously, the staging of exhibitions that featured and celebrated this incipient category of artworks in different locales provided members of this class with familiar and welcoming places to visit as they moved around the world. William Robinson portrays this new class as integrated by internationally oriented elites from regions that aspired to join the new circuits of capital accumulation, a class that understood economic and cultural development in terms of their accessibility to and agency within an increasingly global economy and its parallel governmental and cultural spheres.[29] This new bloc simultaneously included the global capitalist class that owned the means of production on a global scale, the professionals who managed the means of production, and the regional elites (political, economic, and/or cultural in nature) who aspired to be perceived in proximity to the propertied core.[30] In San Diego, Tijuana, and many other locales worldwide, artists, cultural officials, designers, architects, business owners, academics, and others engaged (knowingly or not) in practices that signaled their awareness of and appreciation for the cosmopolitan ideals of a new global capitalist class. Their support for and involvement with new art institutional operations such as inSITE was one promising way to signal that cultural distinction.

This aspirational cosmopolitanism among differently situated local elites was rooted in long-standing fears of being perceived as provincial. As Andrea Fraser and other inSITE artists understood very well, these anxieties prompted many elite art patrons in San Diego to enthusiastically support inSITE. Andrea Fraser was not alone in wielding humor as a way to draw attention to and make sense of the contradictions supporting her work as an artist. Thomas Glassford's video *City of Greens* (INSITE97) offered an ironic commentary on San Diego's self-image insecurities. Its eleven minutes feature Glassford, in the guise of a tourist/detective, on a mission to unveil the city's obsession with the color green. He finds golf greens, green buildings, green manicured lawns, green neon lights, green margaritas, green Bermuda pants, green beauty stores, green grocery-store signs, green palm trees, and green eyes, plus a failed sexual encounter with a woman covering her nipples with golf-green pasties topped by American flags. Glassford moves in a mysterious rush through a slow city centered around the golf course, rendered both as a sport field and as many other inventive iterations, such as a cell phone antenna and a urinal cover, a

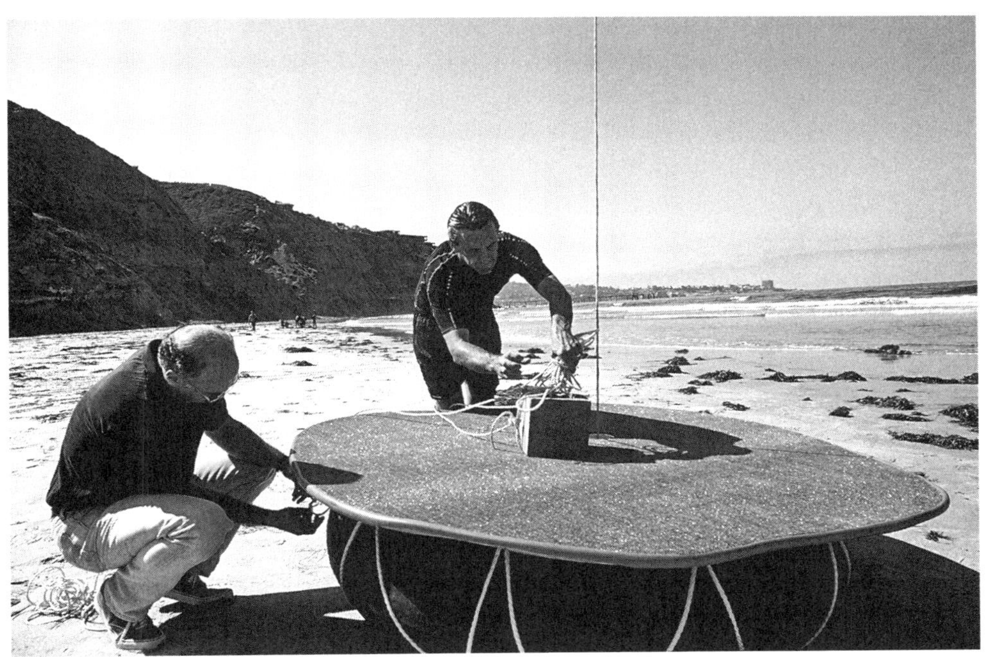

5.4   Thomas Glassford, *City of Greens*, 1997. Source: inSITE Archives, Special Collections Library, University of California, San Diego.

helicopter landing pad and a tiny ocean buoy. It was thus the region's reputation, and the commonsensical meanings widely associated with it, that were at stake. Predominant narratives about the borderlands as a site of division and oppression could be sidestepped, placated, and mended through a myriad of processes that included, among other operations, a festival of site-specific art.

The Artist as Tourist

The abnegation of local experience by art biennials to pursue globally legible renderings of site was not uncommon in this period, in part because of the expansion of international tourism. This industry of global reach became widely accessible to middle classes across the world and promised encounters with local authenticity in a growing variety of locales. Parallel to the globalization of the art industry, the globalization of tourism compelled cities and regions across the world to compete as tourist destinations. They did so in large part by rendering their essential difference in ways that presented these places as attractive for international visitors. The rapacious nature of this industry—determined by its quick capacity to enact substantial structural change, its ability to redraw social relations in the long term, and the consequent difficulties of expelling it once it has settled in—has been described by anthropologist Matilde Córdoba Azcárate as the "stickiness of tourism."[31] Participating in this stickiness, the nascent global art tourism industry became responsible to a high degree for the attribution of an aesthetic imperative to a place; this in turn justified the adoption of artistic tropes that would be legible to nonregional visitors as forms able to convey the truthfulness of a locale in its supposedly natural, cultural, and social idiosyncrasies. However, and as we have seen, these same tropes also obscured the processes involved in the social production of space. In this scheme, artists, curators, and collectors found themselves in permanent itinerancy, temporarily imported in locales throughout the world as touring interpreters of local difference.

Several inSITE projects engaged with the all-encompassing presence of tourism in the region. Melanie Smith's *The Tourists' Guide to San Diego and Tijuana / La guía turística de San Diego y Tijuana* (INSITE97) underscored the increasing importance that tourism optics played for the creative reimagining of the borderlands (see plate 10). Drawing on the legacy of documentary photography and travel guides, it directly addressed the region's reliance on self-advertising as a vacation destination with a tourist guide, a series of postcards, posters, leaflets, T-shirts, and other souvenirs. A storefront on Fifth Avenue in downtown San Diego served as the public-facing office for *The Tourists' Guide*; Smith was stationed in it most of the time, informing tourists and passersby about the several attractions to visit. In the guidebook, she satirically educated readers with bits of local knowledge, such as how to make a margarita cocktail, why Horton Plaza is "the Disneyland of shopping," and why Mission Beach is "the ideal place for the family."[32] *The Tourists' Guide* spoke to the marketing of the borderlands as a tourist destination, documenting unstaged scenes of beach life and other vacation-photography tropes. The project underscored tourism's prevalence in San Diego and Tijuana through the optics of the middle-class traveler. Smith, a prominent member of the Young British Artist group living in Mexico City, presented herself in the guise of the middle-class American family, a common visitor to the region, rendering in her prints cheap souvenir photographs of animals at the zoo, kids waiting in line at a Burger King in Tijuana's bus station, a forced view of the Horton Plaza mall, margarita glasses on paper napkins, fish at the Birch Aquarium, and beachgoers playing in the sand at Mission Beach.[33]

Amateur in their finish, Smith's documents of the borderlands as a vacation destination offered a seemingly spontaneous take on its potential, as filtered through familiar touristic devices. This tongue-in-cheek approach to documentary photography by an institutionally sanctioned artist poked at the long history of imagining San Diego and Tijuana as escapist horizons, diversion lands—a history that preceded Smith's work by almost a century. Her selective renderings of place foreclosed all commentary on the relations of production and policing of the border that upheld the touristic device. Excluding from the frame hints of the impact of the tourist's gaze in the region, Smith instead amplified tourism's aesthetic imperative to place, parodying a contradiction that might have seemed obvious to visitors like her. Smith's intentionally kitsch documents likely had no quantifiable impact on the regional tourism industry. Like other site-oriented biennial artworks of the time, *The Tourists' Guide to San Diego and Tijuana / La guía turística de San Diego y Tijuana* was another piece in the broader operation of making the San Diego–Tijuana region an alluring stop in the global biennial tourism scene.

Contrasting with Smith's role-play as a middle-class tourist, Francis Alÿs produced a hyperbolic image of the biennial artist's globe-trotting itinerance. Alÿs's *The Loop / La vuelta* mirrored the social rituals and sensibilities developed under the global-tourism paradigm. Though originally conceived as a tour through the many art biennials celebrated in 1997, *The Loop / La vuelta* became a long tour around the Pacific Ocean in which Alÿs departed from Tijuana and arrived in San Diego twenty days later, never crossing the border fence.[34] From his stops in Mexico City, Peru, Australia, Hong Kong, China, Japan, Canada, and the United States, Alÿs sent postcards to inSITE97 curator Olivier Debroise in Mexico City, which were then displayed on a pedestal for biennial audiences to peruse. In his identification with the spatial borderlessness of a detached jet-setter traveler, Alÿs personified the inherent class conflict that shaped the figure of the global itinerant artist in the mid- to late 1990s. But the parallel between the itinerant spatiality of contemporary artists and tourists was an old theme for Alÿs. A Belgian settled in Mexico City, his early works were performative gestures that mimicked, with a twist, social practices already taking place in the city. For instance, in *Turista* (Tourist [1994]) he had joined a group of day laborers in Mexico City's central Zócalo Square, advertising his profession, "Tourist," on a handwritten sign next to theirs: "Electrician," "Plumber," "Painter." A color photograph documenting the action shows the artist, wearing a white cotton shirt, loose khaki pants, and a light-brown jacket, casually smoking and leaning against the fence surrounding Mexico's Cathedral, chatting with a man offering his services as a painter. Regarding this work, Alÿs has stated: "I was denouncing but also testing my own status as a foreigner, a *gringo*. How far can I belong to this place? How much can I judge it? Am I a participant or just an observer? By offering my services as a tourist in the middle of a line of carpenters and plumbers I was oscillating between leisure and work, between contemplation and interference."[35] The questions behind *Turista* are not infrequent to those who move and relocate to a different culture. Making sense of one's belonging to a place requires a long inquiry that, in some cases, occludes the privilege of migration by choice. Yet by turning carefree notes on his foreignness into a central theme of his mobile tool kit, Alÿs resuscitated—in *Turista* and later in *The Loop / La vuelta*—the careless modern wandering of a *flaneur*, rekindling, maybe on purpose, a tacit nostalgia for the class habitus of leisurely bohemians who, a hundred years before him, had claimed the lead of suspicious objectivity in their cultivation of detachment from urban working-class life.

A permanent name in mid- to late 1990s global art biennials, Alÿs increasingly came to embody what has come to be known as the "parachute artist," a figure characterized by their temporary migration to work in unfamiliar contexts, often producing documents of their actions, to be exchanged, at a gain, in the global art market. This enactment of the global elite's facility to travel, briefly settle, and move on speaks to Alÿs's beliefs about the societal function of the artist. The artist is, for him, socially expected to practice "poetic license," a hiatus, a "suspension of meaning," during which they are expected to "issue a statement without a demonstration." These poetic licenses are for Alÿs "more about creating a sensation of meaninglessness, one that shows the absurdity of the situation."[36] Alÿs's cynical portrayal of the US-Mexico borderlands for INSITE97 offered a hyperbolic gesture toward his boundless mobility as a global contemporary artist. This five-week-long extended performance aligned with his "walking pieces," walking tours of Mexico City that framed specific aspects of life in the city and were later exhibited as documents of his actions. For *The Loop / La vuelta*, receipts, boarding passes, journal entries, photographs, and collected ephemera

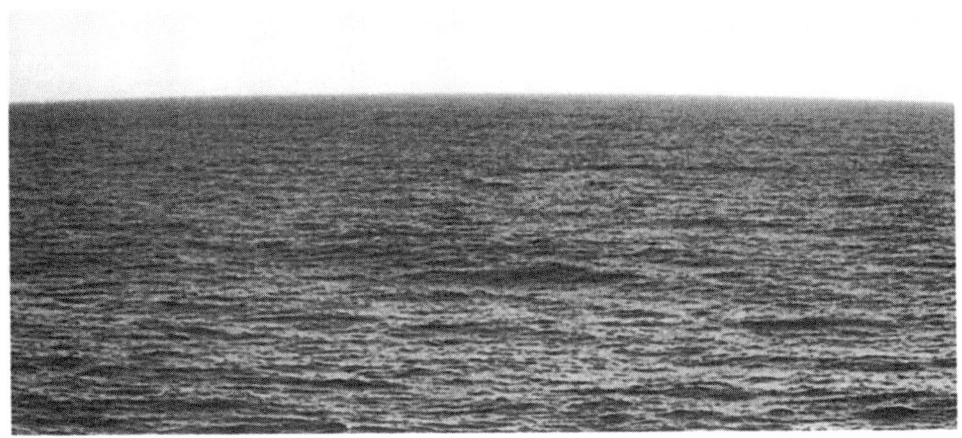

5.5   Francis Alÿs, *The Loop / La vuelta*, 1997. Source: inSITE Archives, Special
Collections Library, University of California, San Diego.

testifying to his flights and hotel stays were all displayed inside a file box
at CECUT in Tijuana, open to the curiosity of the public as a bureaucratic
trail of his detachment from the messiness of border life. Aware of his
privileged status as an artist, Alÿs wielded the display conventions of 1970s
institutional critique, albeit exempt from their critical and denunciatory
goals regarding the contradictions of the art institution, providing instead
snippets of impressions gathered in his travels.

Through the years, more poetic licenses would be featured at inSITE to
help mitigate local elites' fears of provincialism. During inSITE's history,
the border hosted the ceremonial release of a thousand white balloons
(Alfredo Jaar, *La nube / The Cloud*, inSITE2000), a proposal for a tropical
island on the fence (Acconci Studio, INSITE97), a large radio telescope
searching for alien life (Íñigo Manglano-Ovalle, *Search*, inSITE2000), a town
fair with a human cannonball launch (Javier Téllez, *One Flew over the Void*

[Bala perdida], inSite_05), and many more site-specific projects. Like other art biennials, inSITE partnered with foreign experts, including artists, academics, curators, and critics, who traveled to the region to translate local phenomena into global codes. As I describe in chapter 4, their enthusiasm affected the local cultural fabric by facilitating a renewal of the artistic forms labeled as "Border art" to favor mostly nonregional contemporary artists who, inexperienced in the complexities of the borderlands condition, thematized the border via artistic conventions developed elsewhere. This move not only displaced the imagined reference behind this disputed signifier, the border, but would also eventually divest structural support for local practitioners of Border art who did not abide by artistic repertoires then trending in the global contemporary art industry. Relying on the site-specific art biennial for this purpose inadvertently subjected the region to an aesthetic imperative that stressed the perception of the frontier as a pacified theme and occluded the complex processes involved in rendering such an illusion. In this operation, an emphasis on reception occluded the importance of community engagement and alliance building in the early production of pre-inSITE Border artists. As a result of this process, pre-NAFTA renderings of the borderlands as a site of conciliation crafted from the vantage point of activist artists' lived experience were eventually displaced and replaced by a global boosterist vision of the region as a land of economic potential that amplified the desires of outwardly oriented elites on both sides of the border.

Yet like other contemporaneous biennials, inSITE also developed many mechanisms to ground its offerings on site while securing regional visibility in a nascent global contemporary art circuit. Artworks were commissioned for specific enclaves of the local landscape, educational and outreach programs were set in place to connect with local publics, and alliances between different social actors set the stage for a festival that still relied upon regional reciprocity to exist. InSITE's transformation from a low-cost and artist-run exhibition in 1992 to an organizationally complex, transnational, and multiyear venture grew from the desire of regional art patrons to compete with other art biennials on a global stage. In the words of inSITE president Michael Krichman, "We are certain that the scale, quality, and uniqueness of inSITE94 will put us on par with other international art events."[37] As a result, since 1994, inSITE has been internationally recognized as "the border biennial." After its last iteration in 2005, inSITE went dormant for a time, resurfacing years later as a neighborhood center in Santa María de la Ribera, in downtown Mexico City.

InSITE's organizational transformations captured the progressive conventionalization of art biennials' internal division of labor, funding mechanisms, forms of expertise, and outreach modes at the turn of the century. The diverse forms that inSITE adopted between 1992 and 2005 also testify to a changing economic landscape characterized by new possibilities of international cooperation in the post-NAFTA era for a specific social class.

six

Globalizing Mexican Art

For inSITE94, Mexican artist Silvia Gruner installed 111 copies of a sculpture of the Aztec goddess Tlazolteotl on the southern side of the border fence in the Tijuana working-class neighborhood of Colonia Libertad. Photographs of the piece, *The Middle of the Road / La mitad del camino*, show the long series running along the fence, the miniatures squatting on tiny benches birthing new life. Gruner located the replicas near an incomplete section of the metal fence that had become a frequent crossing zone for northbound migrants. On a sign that accompanied the figures, Gruner explained that the goddess Tlazolteotl "protected women in labor, and those involved in lost causes; she recycled the world's filth, and pardoned the bad loves of men. The work placed in this site, a crossroads, is dedicated to those who live here and those who cross through."[1] Colonia Libertad was home to migrants from all over Mexico and Central America who arrived in Tijuana. While most stayed permanently to work in the area (often in the regional maquiladora sector), many others would eventually cross north (see plates 11 and 12).

If the vertical metal plates marked the international boundary between Mexico and the United States, the 111 Tlazolteotl figures accompanied the migrants in their transition as citizens in their nations of origin into another form of being human: that of the subordinated unauthorized migrant in California. As talismans, they signaled the fence as a transitional threshold between ontological states. Gruner installed these objects weeks before California voters approved Proposition 187 on November 8, 1994, a ballot measure that denied foreigners living in California without legal permission access to public services such as education and health care. Although Proposition 187 was ultimately declared unconstitutional by the US Supreme Court, then, as today, migrant lives in Southern California were framed by a climate of neoliberal nativist violence, in its state-sponsored and individually enforced manifestations.[2] In the words of border scholar Robert DeChaine, "The transgressive act of unauthorized border crossing produces a double exclusion: it renders migrant persons both legally and morally abject."[3] For many in this part of the world, life takes place in a liminal regime of questioned ontological and moral legitimacy. But the liminal line that is the border fence marks a threshold for transmutations of an aesthetic order as well. Artistic programs, including the forms and processes involved in the imagining of land, transpire through the porous fence. In the words of writer and filmmaker Jesse Lerner, *The Middle of the Road / La mitad del camino* "completes a circuitous migration that corresponds to imperial claims on Latin America, first from the Old World, then from the Yankees."[4] The location: inSITE, a festival of site-specific art seeking to display the specificities of land and life at the US-Mexico borderlands for foreign art audiences.

At stake in site-specific art are assumptions about art's capacity to convey the authentic features of place. Gruner's project cast a direct doubt over this assumption. As Lerner establishes, the 111 figures that she brought to the fence were replicas of a sculpture of the goddess Tlazolteotl, presently housed at the Dumbarton Oaks Pre-Columbian art collection. The statue is of dubious authenticity: archaeological research carried out since the 1980s shows the use of modern stone carving techniques all over the statue, shedding doubt over its origin. The object bears strong technical and formal differences from other pre-Columbian artifacts from present Mexico, including the figure's unique facial expression, the absence of dressing and ornaments on it, and its straight hair lines, which are dissimilar from other Aztec carving examples.[5] Current scientific consensus indicates that the artifact is probably a fake, fabricated in the mid-nineteenth century and introduced by a Parisian dealer into the buoyant European market for pre-Columbian artifacts. The aura of originality that for decades had distinguished this supposedly authentic representation of the Aztec goddess of motherhood and transitions represented in the 1990s a different sort of traffic. As Tlazolteotl specialist Jane MacLaren Walsh states, institutionalized cultural artifacts such as museum objects and commissioned artworks record not only material aspects from their contexts but also important immaterial elements such as the expectations and aesthetic aspirations that publics and experts set forth as conditions for their acceptance into the art institution. In this case, the item that served as model for Gruner's 111 copies was itself a modern idealization of a "pre-contact" Mexican past in Western Europe and the United States, an idealization shaped to fit the stylistic demands of turn-of-the-century transatlantic art collectors.[6] Contemporary art objects are not exempt from these interpellations. If inSITE94, a festival of site-specific art, sought to unveil the borderlands' nature truthfully to international audiences, then Gruner's inclusion of this nineteenth-century Tlazolteotl fake was a reminder of the heavy impact that aesthetic claims to truth can have on how we make sense of the world.

By placing the series along the US-Mexico border fence, Gruner's piece brought to Colonia Libertad two important genealogies in modern Mexican art. The miniatures enacted a feminist critique on recurrent *indigenista* gestures throughout twentieth-century Mexican art, by which cultural forms of the Indigenous inhabitants, past and present, of what is contemporary Mexico were incorporated into elite, non-Indigenous cultural circuits, often with the support of the state and dominant classes. Gruner critiqued this legacy by exposing the instrumentalization of archaeology in post-Revolutionary state-formation efforts. In the words of Amy Sarah Carroll, during the 1990s, "Gruner targets indigenismo as a racialized, sexualized, classed, and gendered ideological state apparatus, interrupting its operation with a de- and reallegorization of the Woman."[7] As well, Gruner's intervention linked back to the rich history of Mexican feminist performance and action art since the 1960s, claiming the legacy of artists like Magali Lara, Maris Bustamante, and Pola Weiss, and collectives such as La Revuelta. Emphasizing the labor by which a body tears and breaks apart to deliver new life, *The Middle of the Road / La mitad del camino* actualized a feminist art tradition characterized, in words of Karen Cordero Reiman, by "the development of iconographic, material, and conceptual vehicles to express women's corporeal experience and subjectivity; experimentation with artistic strategies to counter patriarchal constructions of the female body . . . ; critique of patriarchal relationships with nature and the nation . . . ; the frequent recourse to series as a way of advancing distinct narrations and modes of experiencing time and the body; [and] the creation and reactivation of archives with reference to the representation of women."[8] Gruner's explicit wrestling with Indigenous precolonial symbolism, in this fake collectible version, belonged to a broader program in her 1990s body of work, visible in projects such as *Fetiches Domésticos* (Domestic fetishes, [1992]), *Don't Fuck with the Past, You Might Get Pregnant* (1995), and the video performance *In Situ* (1996).

Gruner's installation at the US-Mexico border fence joined the work of other contemporaneous Mexican artists who instead adopted a more nihilist disposition toward the forces at play in state formation. These competing approaches to site-specific art turned the fence into a liminal line for negotiations between parallel modern art genealogies, mirroring the generational renewal that was ongoing in the Mexico City art scene at the time. This chapter dissects the diverse approaches to site-specific art from Mexico City that gathered at inSITE's early iterations. In so doing, it illustrates how shifting aesthetic trends within the art institutional complex directly influence the work of young artists at times of structural change. A platform that helped promote young Mexican artists into the new global art circuits, inSITE staged the biennial conversions that facilitated these artists' alignment with global contemporary art codes.

Internationalization

The redrawing of relations among nations in modern history has often prompted moments of artistic internationalization. In these instances, art initially relegated to local and national scenes moves beyond its original context to access international circuits previously off-limits. As art historian Andrea Giunta explains with regard to the internationalization of Argentine art in the 1960s, these processes follow structural conditions wherein the asymmetrical power balance between actors results in the success of particular interests (economic, political, and artistic) over others.[9] In these scenarios, organizations mediating convergences of local culture with nonlocal codes facilitate the introduction of extra-artistic ideologies into the spaces of artistic production as new normative and valuative frameworks. This book establishes how the processes of internationalization that triggered late twentieth-century globalization of art were similarly subject to the extra-artistic interests shaping new social relations on the supranational level. Early-boom art biennials, as well-funded organizations in organic affinity with political elites, played a crucial role in these processes. Through paradigms of artistic value and display conventions that were, in most cases, organically present in the period's curatorial toolkit, these exhibitions asserted important influence in these moments of artistic internationalization. The biennial conversions facilitated by these exhibitions often set the formal inheritances of North Atlantic modernisms as conversion standards for a wide diversity of artistic repertoires, inciting transformations in artworks to adapt them to the systems of meaning and value dominant within their newly accessed circuits.

In the post–Cold War years, these biennial conversions were common at the frontiers of liberalism, where they helped ease the entrance of artistic legacies initially excluded from the northern Atlantic capitals into the nascent global art circuits while simultaneously helping expand Western European and United States influence to new regions. These dynamics were clear in inSITE, where, in addition to the displacement of regional Border artists in favor of nonlocal artists invited to represent the border, a new generation of artists from Mexico City was prompted to enter nascent global art circuits. The biennial conversions taking place within inSITE helped reorient the Mexican avant-garde genealogy toward the expectations and interests prevalent in the art institutional complex of its northern neighbor. This legacy had unfolded throughout the twentieth century with a dominant southern orientation, in organic affinity with other internationalist and anti-imperialist avant-garde and neo–avant-garde programs across Latin America. Although it had always existed in deep awareness of New York and California modernisms and their aftermaths, the political commitments underpinning the Mexican avant-garde genealogy had kept it relatively autonomous from the northern gravitational force throughout the century. This changed in the 1990s when, partly through ventures like inSITE, the Mexican contemporary art world progressively abandoned its historical emancipatory agenda and veered northward to synch with approaches to art-making in US art worlds. Mexico City's art scene in the 1990s was eclectic and diverse. In the mainstream were the "neo-Mexicanistas," a group mostly composed of painters who gained wide visibility and collector acclaim in the 1980s. Also established, but of marked political commitment and international acclaim, were artists from the neo–avant-gardes of the 1960s and 1970s, such as Helen Escobedo and

Felipe Ehrenberg. Responding to their legacy, a much younger generation toyed with the formal and thematic repertoires trending within a nascent global contemporary art world in—initially—marginal artist-run spaces like Temístocles 44 and La Panadería. Amid this climate, inSITE helped propel abroad the work of a younger generation of Mexico City artists who, if alien to the borderlands, would soon become staple names in the global biennial roster and would enter a global contemporary art canon-in-formation. Facilitating this globalization of Mexican art was, for inSITE organizers, a desired outcome.[10]

Tijuana, *La Frontera Norte*

This reorientation on the level of artistic praxis responded to systemic changes in Mexico's society and its political economy that framed the individual practice of cultural actors—including artists, curators, critics, and administrators. Parallel to this younger generation of Mexican artists *becoming global*, the nation experienced a deep questioning of its state structure and ideology that prompted key transformations in the cultural institutional sphere and redrew the relations of production sustaining the making of contemporary art. The end of the so-called Mexican miracle (a period of autocracy and sustained economic growth between the 1940s and the 1960s) had seen the weakening of the single-party system and the plummeting credibility of government institutions. State disapproval had been growing since the crises of the Tlatelolco Massacre (1968) and the Mexico City earthquake (1985).[11] In response to the 1980s financial crisis, during the 1990s Mexico experienced a series of important market-oriented policy reforms as an orthodox neoliberal agenda gained traction among members of the Partido Revolucionario Institucional (PRI), aligning national economic policy with US goals in the region while reinforcing the power of central state agencies.[12] In 1988 Baja California elected a new state governor: Ernesto Ruffo Appel, from the pro-business Catholic liberal party Partido de Acción Nacional (PAN), marking the first time since the Mexican Revolution that a state governor was not affiliated with the PRI. This election prefigured the end of the PRI's single-party rule in Mexico and turned the central government's focus toward Baja California as a region that needed to be won back.

But the *frontera norte* had long been a region to win back—and it wouldn't be the first time that this effort was leveraged partly through state-sponsored cultural production. In February 1985, Mexican president Miguel de la Madrid created the Programa Cultural de las Fronteras (Cultural Program for the Borders [PCF]), which sought to "preserve and promote the different manifestations of our culture in the borderlands, with the goal of strengthening consciousness about our national identity and sovereignty." Actions within the program would be "inspired by the concepts of sovereignty, solidarity, and nationalism," with a special emphasis on "our artistic expressions, clothing, and language." The PCF sponsored the creation of new cultural institutions in the northern and southern borderlands, such as the Centro Cultural Tijuana (CECUT)—an institution that would become inSITE94's central organizational partner and exhibition venue in Tijuana. During this period, Mexico's Instituto Nacional de Bellas Artes (INBA) increased its efforts to promote Mexican contemporary art abroad. INBA worked closely with Mexico's diplomatic delegations, sponsoring a growing number of exhibitions of Mexican art internationally, such as the blockbuster *Mexico: Splendors of Thirty Centuries* at the Metropolitan Museum of Art in New York (1990–1991). The show was described in the *Los Angeles Times* as "a campaign for a more positive national image, a push for prosperity, the latest evidence of an ongoing quest for national identity and an effort to inspire respect by educating North Americans about Mexico's cultural heritage."[13] In the mid-1990s, mirroring the economic opportunities opened by NAFTA, the United States and Canada became countries of special interest for INBA's cultural diplomacy. Alongside this mission, inSITE94 and its later iterations acted as important avenues for the internationalization of art made by a younger generation of Mexico City artists. This was especially the case during Gerardo Estrada's tenure as president of INBA. An August 1994 fax sent from the Center for US-Mexican Studies at the University of California, San Diego, explains that for INBA, "One important and vital initiative that will strengthen the cultural ties between Mexico and the United States will take place on the Tijuana–San Diego border. This initiative is inSITE94, which will bring together from both sides of the border artists and galleries dedicated to all facets of the visual arts. InSITE94 will serve as a model to be emulated at other points of the border, and even in other areas of culture and art, through the support and participation of the private sectors of both countries."[14]

As a consequence, thanks to the centrally governed CECUT in Tijuana and INBA-sponsored efforts to turn the borderlands into a gateway to the global for Mexican art, Mexico City's cultural establishment reaffirmed its grasp of Tijuana. Despite the conflating goals driving the central government's centralism and Baja California's pursuit of autonomy, fruitful instances of collaboration took place between the two levels of government. The regional press celebrated collaboration among representatives from the PRI and PAN parties as an unprecedented instance of compromise between unlikely stakeholders, often signaling inSITE94 as the cause driving their convergence. Whereas cultural delegates in Mexico City perceived inSITE as an ideal platform to promote a vision of contemporary Mexican art as young, playful, and attuned to the aesthetic codes of an emerging global art community, Tijuana elites had much to gain from welcoming an international festival of contemporary art to their region: cultural cachet, a renewed image of the borderlands, and capital influx into the regional tourism sector. To both interest groups inSITE offered an opportunity to publicly signal Mexico's realignment with its northern neighbor and trade partner. Together, the federal and state governments leveraged the new free-trade framework to their advantage, fostering a smoother integration of the capital's and the frontera norte's art scenes.

The embrace of the neoliberal creed by state officials throughout Mexico during the late 1980s and early 1990s translated into widespread market-oriented reforms inscribed in the General Agreement on Tariffs and Trade (GATT) and NAFTA, opening the national industries to foreign capital. This neoliberal turn was backed by the economic elites of the nation's economic centers (Mexico City, Monterrey, Guadalajara, Tijuana) and had a direct impact on the sphere of culture through the creation of new public and private ventures. These new funding avenues deeply transformed the Mexican contemporary art scene, significantly increasing funding for art institutions and production grants, and helping cultivate a new collector class.[15] As art historian Daniel Montero has explained, the Mexican private sector saw a double potential for investing in culture: private investors gained symbolic capital and simultaneously benefited from new tax-exemption stimuli.[16] Key new organizations of the time were CONACULTA (National Council for Culture and Arts, established 1988), which governed national public art institutions, including museums, libraries, and publishers; and FONCA (National Fund for Culture and Arts, established 1989), a private-public partnership to support, promote, and disseminate Mexican art production and the nation's heritage.[17]

This new cultural policy framework, wherein subsidies from the private sector financed FONCA art production grants, created a fertile ground for independent artist-run spaces that often functioned with autonomy from institutional cultural initiatives spearheaded by INBA. This precarious yet dynamic para-institutional field freed younger artists from local art-collecting preferences, nourishing spaces of autonomy from which they increasingly tuned their practices to the art trends of a new global contemporary art world. Further, these partnerships between private and public arts sponsorship opened new avenues to represent Mexico's refurbished state project abroad through a lens that had incorporated the principles of globally oriented market efficiency that were driving NAFTA and similar neoliberal policies. This new framework for foreign relations shaped young artists' access to educational and professional opportunities abroad, chiefly in the United States. InSITE strongly benefited from these joint public and private promotion efforts, especially for the 1994 and 1997 iterations, when Estrada was president of INBA.[18] In words of Debroise,

> Mexican official cultural institutions have been designing and financing mega shows to export—including, for example, the reinstallation of the British Museum's Pre-Hispanic collection, set to open in the fall of 1994—while failing miserably to keep their own house in order, devaluing when not completely ignoring intellectual work and professional education. In contrast, private foundations seem to stand in the avant-garde, pressing for diverse alternatives, and often supporting those most critical of the current regime. Thus emerges an ironic situation whereby the institutional critique in Mexico is financed mainly by American foundations, thus discreetly contributing to the dismantling of Mexico's outdated cultural system in the new atmosphere we still call the post–Cold War era, but we should eventually rename the NAFTA era.[19]

The Mexican Avant-Garde Legacy at the Border

Back at the border, Gruner's site-specific installation against the fence, with its simultaneous quotations of the indigenista and the feminist art legacies, invited a critical revision of the Mexican avant-garde genealogy. This legacy can be traced back by almost a century to the independent and state-affiliated avant-garde factions active in the post-Revolutionary period. This diverse scene included the anti-academicism, techno-utopianism, and cosmopolitanism of groups such as the *estridentistas* and *¡30–30!*; the state-sponsored *muralista* program that, with its public and pedagogic orientations and related multimedia multiples, sought to aid state efforts toward social and educational reform; the rich production of surrealist painters and documentary photographers; and the incorporation of non-urban cultural production into urban artistic circles, including the cultural production of Indigenous Mexicans through indigenista programs.[20] As art historians David Craven and Harper Montgomery have described, these practices set the grounds for a modernist tradition that would be essentially anticolonial, democratic, and transnational. This genealogy blended urban and Indigenous motives in support of state ideology through the incorporation of subaltern actors—such as industrial and agricultural workers and Indigenous subjects—into its thematic repertoire.[21] Epic murals fixed Indigenous cultures into the official built environment, and archaeological artifacts from precolonial times were gathered in the new stages of national representation, tying the new state to a mystified Aztec imperial past and supporting a process that Mary Coffey describes as the nationalization of the avant-garde.[22] As I explain in chapter 3, the aesthetic conversions that helped draw Indigenous culture, past and present, into elite cultural spheres often involved the problematic concessions of the values, meanings, and worldviews coded in objects into forms that were legible to members of the receiving avant-garde art circles. As Gruner sig-naled with the Tlazolteotl replicas, this post-Revolutionary effervescence of Indigenismo was supported with the production of multiples that included, among others, archaeological artifacts, political publications, and widely circulated educational printed materials.

After several decades of depoliticization of this original avant-garde program, the rise of alternative art scenes in 1960s Mexico City reawak-ened a slow process of bottom-up politicized art practice throughout the capital's cultural scene. This opening was made possible, in large part, by the emergence of private art galleries and new forms of public art sponsor-ship, chiefly via the Universidad Autónoma Nacional de México, and was fueled by the growing student-movement discontent with the cultural institutional establishment.[23] This neo–avant-garde art scene galvanized around exhibition spaces such as Salón de Arte Independiente (1969, 1970, 1971), Museo Universitario de Ciencias y Arte (MUCA [1970s]), and a growing number of artist-run para-institutional spaces. Its protagonists were the emerging *grupos*, autonomous artist collectives that worked in articula-tion with the specificities of urban life, actualized the emancipatory tone

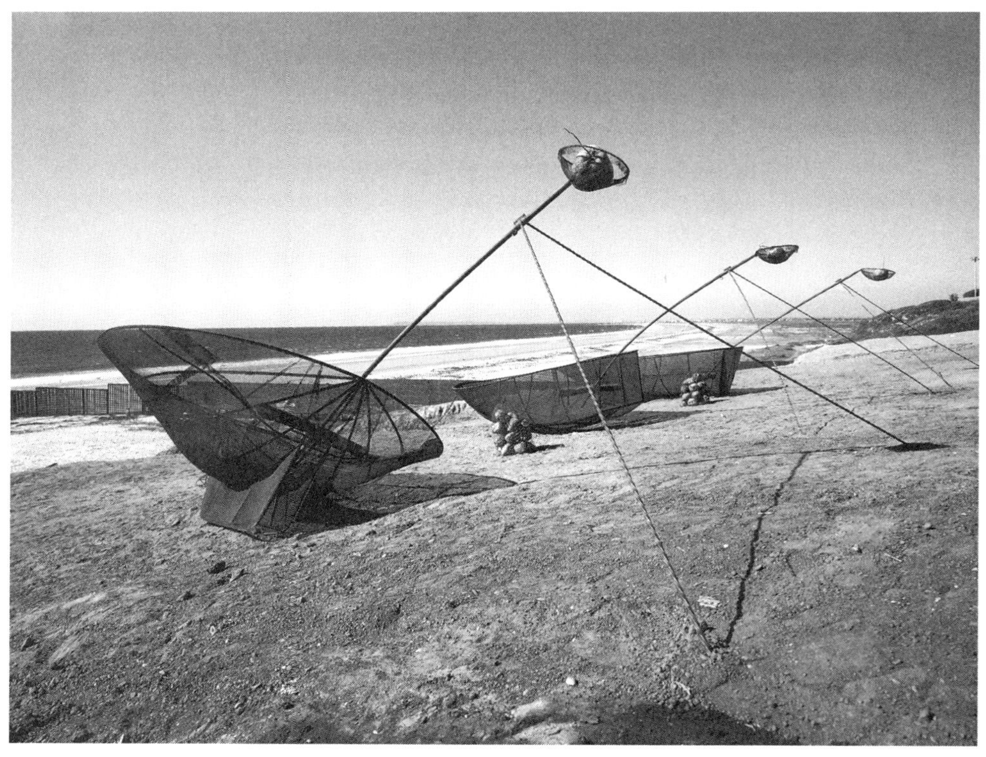

6.1   Helen Escobedo, *By the Night Tide / Junto a la marea nocturna*, 1994. Source: inSITE Archives, Special Collections Library, University of California, San Diego.

of the post-Revolutionary avant-gardes, and sought detachment from the elitist habitus of mid-century official culture. The grupos' dematerialized praxis offered renewed avenues to reconcile artistic work with the diverse urban subaltern subjectivities forged during Mexico's Cold War industrialist modernization program. As Karen Benezra argues, the grupos' deskilled collectivism "attempt[ed] to transform and potentiate the postrevolutionary project of art's socialization," offering a variety of models for the conciliation of art with everyday life.[24] These neo–avant-garde collectives, influenced by Marxist and feminist approaches to art-making, contributed to Mexico City's prominent role within the broader Latin American art scene. For some decades, the Mexican capital hosted international exhibitions, such as the Bienal Interamericana (1958), an itinerant exhibition of drawings and prints that began in Mexico City, and the Ruta de la Amistad (1968), a public sculpture festival coincident with the 1968 Olympics.

Present at both inSITE94 and INSITE97, Helen Escobedo had been an important curator, sculptor, and key name in the Mexico City art scene since the 1960s. A participant in earlier efforts to internationalize Mexican art, she brought an important delegation of the grupos to the X Biennial of Young Artists in Paris (1977) and participated in the Bienal de La Habana (1986). Escobedo's practice aligned within a tradition of site-oriented art parallel to but distinct from the one unfolding in the US art capitals in the period. Deeply influenced by Bauhaus notions of integrative design, her monumental sculptural arrangements often worked as total works of art. Escobedo had been exposed to this approach through her periods of life and study abroad, as well as through her repeated collaborations in Mexico with Bauhaus-influenced German artist and architect Mathias Goeritz. Her pursuit of "total ambients" through "plastic integration" hinted at *muralismo*'s totalist synthesis with the built environment and its address to a wide array of audiences. It also echoed Walter Gropius's ideal of "total architecture," a principle of balanced organicity between man and technology, where art, in its capacity to speak to the diversity found within human experience, would lead to a democratically integrated social fabric.[25] Yet through her environmental sculptural work, present in highly visible Mexico City sites such as the Ruta de la Amistad (1968) and Espacio Escultórico at Ciudad Universitaria (1979), Escobedo sought to transform urban life through the integration and subjugation of structures into their natural environment. Three decades later, these goals still shaped her installation for inSITE94. *By the Night Tide / Junto a la marea nocturna* (1994) consisted of three large boat-shaped wire structures with coconut-loaded catapults, aiming northward, just south of the fence at the shore of Playas de Tijuana. The ships were named *El Topo* (the Mole), *El Sapo* (the Toad), and *El Pollo* (the Chicken), in direct reference to border crossing jargon. Curator Sally Yard described the structures as symbolic attacks on the "barricade" that was the international border fence. Echoing this sentiment, Cuauhtémoc Medina remembered in his catalog essay how, in one of his visits, "someone had replaced the coconuts with stones," underscoring the commitments behind Escobedo's program, her "desperately Latin American war game."[26] In a somewhat nostalgic move, Escobedo activated in inSITE94 the anti-imperialism of the post-Revolutionary avant-gardes and the 1960s grupos, in the dawn of the NAFTA era.

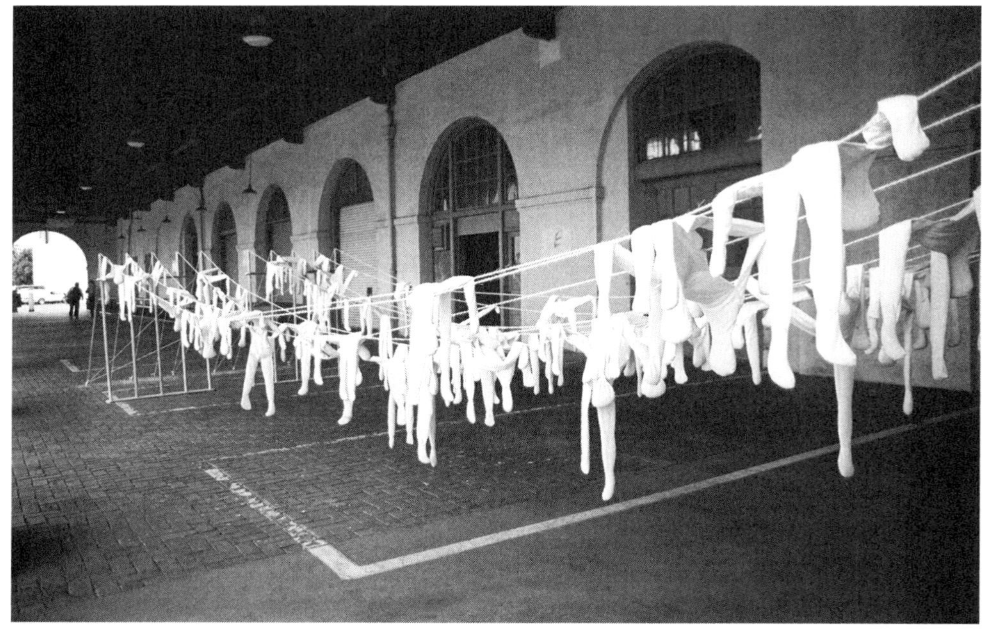

6.2   Felipe Ehrenberg, *Curtain Call / Tercera Llamada*, 1994. Source: inSITE Archives, Special Collections Library, University of California, San Diego.

Felipe Ehrenberg was another key figure from the grupos period who participated in inSITE94. A close colleague of Escobedo, Ehrenberg's internationalism had shared her commitment to emancipatory solidarity efforts. Affiliated with Fluxus while in London in the 1960s, Ehrenberg had helped forge ties between European and Mexican left-wing conceptualist art programs as an active member of the grupo Proceso Pentágono during the 1960s and early 1970s.[27] Ehrenberg held lifelong commitments to wielding art in the practice of communal emancipation, beliefs that would shape his two projects for inSITE94 and INSITE97. For inSITE94, Ehrenberg produced *Curtain Call / Tercera llamada*, a double installation at the Santa Fe Depot (San Diego) and CECUT (Tijuana) that featured ten clothes rack–like ropes from which hung a series of humanoid figures of white cotton and pillow filling. The large structure measured forty feet long by thirteen feet wide and six and a half feet tall. The forms caught in the ropes resembled humans who had tripped and deflated while jumping over a wire fence:

many lives lost to tense, deployed structures. Ehrenberg's assemblages worked metaphorically to fill the public space with narratives of systemic violence and continued early iterations of this theme in his work, such as *Light Up Our Border I* (1990) and *Light Up Our Border II* (1990), two interventions in the Texas section of the US-Mexico international border that addressed the power imbalance shaping the relationship between both countries.

These two artists' sustained interest in art's capacity to unveil systemic contradictions became more evident in their works for INSITE97 three years later. This time, Ehrenberg helped facilitate a community-engagement project that relied on the medium of installation to map the city of Tijuana. The artist and a group of participants met to discuss the capacities of artistic processes to intercept place-formation processes. Collaborating in the design and production of twenty-six installations located around the city of Tijuana, their interventions featured a long line of toy cars tracing CECUT's outside patio, a cubic structure made of two-by-four lumber painted red, with embedded display cases and a wooden picture frame, painted green, and strategically located to frame a fraction of a park. Meanwhile, for her 1997 participation in inSITE, Escobedo and three collaborators reimagined an abandoned building in downtown San Diego as a simultaneous critique of the dairy and art industries. Their site-specific installation, titled *Milk at the L'Ubre Mooseum* (see plate 12) was a satirical commentary that equated these two industries. Its title, pun intended, evoked the canonical Paris-based museum. The piece pointed to the presence in both industries of standardized serialized production standards, a shared whitewashed aesthetics, and their ultimate delivery of purified, reliably digestible products. Escobedo's intervention addressed the systemic extractivism prevalent throughout the borderlands and beyond, commenting on the new conditions of production for art under global neoliberalism.

The presence of Escobedo and Ehrenberg in both iterations of the biennial marked inSITE's acknowledgment of a critical Mexican neo–avant-garde legacy that by the end of the century occupied solid canonical status in the Mexican cultural establishment. The two artists, active during the Cold War in Mexico City's Left-leaning cultural circles, had been long-inscribed in broader operations to systematize a Marxist aesthetic program that, as I explained in chapter 3, was spearheaded by, among others, Adolfo Sánchez Vázquez and extended to include other Latin American artistic scenes, such as those in Cuba, Argentina, and Venezuela. The last lingerings of these emancipatory neo–avant-gardes made their presence in inSITE, through Escobedo's and Ehrenberg's work. But this Marxist legacy soon passed the torch to other understandings of site-oriented art practice. A central scenario for this takeover was inSITE.

A Formalist Production of Site

A very different genealogy of site-oriented art also came to plant itself in the borderlands via inSITE, echoing several large-scale exhibitions in Europe and the United States that relied on site-specific art to intervene in narratives surrounding particular urban enclaves. In 1977 curators Kaspar König and Klaus Bussman organized the first Skulptur Projekte Münster, inviting fifty artists to respond to the built environment of the German city in their work. In 1992 US curator Mary Jane Jacob curated *Places with a Past* for the Spoleto Festival in Charleston, South Carolina. This festival of site-specific art worked to make visible hidden collective histories of Charleston, including the city's history as a slave-trade hub and its foundational plantation economy. Like others at the time, inSITE's organizers found direct inspiration in these events, informing the biennial and its peripheral programming. In these exhibitions and many other ones to come, site-specific art worked toward the attribution of meaning to a place, intervening in its formal qualities, its historical narratives and perceived identity, and the experience of local and foreign actors in it.

This was a big responsibility to delegate on contemporary art, especially during the drastic geopolitical changes of the early to mid-1990s. If successful, site-specific exhibitions could help heal the social fabric from deep historical wounds. For many in Western Europe and the United States, site-specific art symbolized an opportunity to finally escape the constrictions of the gallery space and actualize the long-held promise of blending art with everyday life. Yet in order to intervene in public memory, these large site-specific exhibits often required the mobilization of important resources not readily available in everyday forms of cultural production. As Barbara Kirshenblatt-Gimblett explains, site-specific exhibitions occupy the conflicted middle ground between "real environments of memory," where historical memory is shared and sustained through everyday life, and "official sites of memory," such as museums and monuments, which uphold a fixed historical narrative. As chapters 4 and 5 show, inSITE was not exempt from these tensions. During its five iterations between 1992 and

2005, the biennial fostered a diversity of strategies, such as artist residencies, curatorial research trips to the area, and meetings with local actors, designed to attune foreign participants to the everyday lived experience of the borderlands. However, many of its site-specific artworks failed to meet such intentions, unknowingly becoming monuments to the period's borderlands elite in San Diego and Tijuana.

Since the 1980s, practitioners and commissioners of site-specific art in the North Atlantic art capitals have celebrated it as an art form capable of unveiling the true essence of a locale. Motivated by the belief in the potential of this form to convey isomorphic representations of a place's essential traits, this type of art takes its location as its object of analysis and intervenes in it, addressing its physical, institutional, or discursive characteristics. Underlying these defenses is a belief in its truth-telling potential and capacity to render a site's authentic features visible. Art historian Miwon Kwon has traced site-specific art's genealogy since its origins in the 1960s US neo–avant-gardes. Kwon describes site-oriented art's ability to "extract the social and historical dimensions out of places to variously serve the thematic drive of an artist, satisfy institutional demographic profiles, or fulfill the fiscal needs of a city." Similarly, Nick Kaye asserts that "site-specific work might even work to assert a 'proper' relationship with its location, claiming an 'original and fixed position' associated with what it is."[28] Underlying these claims is the belief that site-specific art, as a revelation of the true features of place, enhances the latter for public perception. This view resonates with Martin Heidegger's concept of authenticity as "ownedness," wherein the authentic self is a relation between what one is at a specific moment and what one can be in different manifestations through time.[29] In this framework, authenticity is an unfolding succession of episodes that add up to narrate the self's trajectory through concrete manifestations through time. The stakes of this unfolding are high: it is through this succession of images that one's self—or a place, I might venture, in this case—enacts its being in one way or another. Further, for Heidegger, authenticity occurs in the practice of truth-driven virtues, such as clearsightedness, perseverance, and integrity. Similar truth-oriented attributes would later be equally presumed by end-of-the-century art audiences of the site-specific artwork as this outwardly oriented art form engaged in the unveiling of a site's meaning.

The strong hermeneutic power conferred on site-specific art has high stakes because site-specific artworks, erected on putative truth-telling gestures, are seen by many to act as episodes in a locale's unfolding of itself. Like organizers of other large-scale site-specific exhibitions, those behind inSITE were aware of site-specific art's power to intervene in the production of place. As they wrote in a draft for the INSITE97 catalog, "The works included in INSITE97 investigate the ways in which the meanings of public space are constructed and construed. Artists have proceeded with passionate engagement, utopian idealism, self-conscious detachment, irony, humor—adopting strategies ranging from subtle subversion to willful spectacle. In choosing a site each artist has implicitly identified a specifically configured 'public' who will happen upon the work in the course of their daily routine."[30] Curator Olivier Debroise lamented that although a core concept for the festival was the notion of site specificity, "nearly all the artists invited to participate in inSITE94 ultimately mounted their installations in museum spaces, or spaces adapted for such use, in both San Diego and Tijuana; this largely neutralized the potential of the project itself to offer alternative mechanisms for perceiving works, a meeting point between an incursion on the landscape and public art."[31] This dominant gallery-centric approach tamed the organizers' aspirations to integrate contemporary art in the region's complex environment.

Site-specific art, as formalized in the North Atlantic–centric global exhibitionary complex in formation during the 1990s, was a direct unfolding of the formalist revisionism dominant in 1960s New York neo–avant-gardes. Following Miwon Kwon's account, site-specific art grew from minimalism's exhaustion of the objectivity demands of Greenbergian modernism and its subsequently presumed overcoming of art's formalist autonomy. An inherently "theatrical" form, to borrow Michael Fried's condemnatory depiction of minimalism, site-specific art further aggrandized the phenomenological engagement with the world that minimalist objects first hinted at, extending this contextual grasping beyond the gallery to include nonmaterial symbolic aspects of site as well. For Kwon, in their abandonment of the Cartesian dualism that hovered over the formalist avant-gardes and neo–avant-gardes, first minimalism, and then site-specific art, sought to break free from media-specific imperatives to find meaning in the relations between object and public that unfold, through time, in space.[32] Site-specific artists embraced this outward impulse, understanding space first in its physical dimensions but pushing it further by later including its cultural, ideological, and social facets as well. This disavowal of the visual implied, for Kwon, the de-aesthetization of the modernist legacy, transforming the artistic skill set in a simultaneous process of extreme deskilling and incorporation of extra-artistic techniques into the contemporary artist's repertoire.

Among the many examples of site-specific artworks featured in inSITE94 were Anya Gallaccio's two interventions, untitled and *Preserve: Maya / Preservación: Maya*, in which the young British artist embellished with gold leaf the fountain of an abandoned Tijuana resort for classic Hollywood stars; *Abandonado II*, a collaboration between San Diego artist Michael Schnorr and Swedish artist Ulf Rollof at Playas de Tijuana, consisting of a series of brick and concrete structures with an internal fireplace that served as heated urban furniture; Nina Karavasiles's installation *Saline / La salina*, a diagonal metal L-shaped structure containing ocean salt and water, installed at the Stephen Birch Aquarium-Museum in La Jolla; and *A Corner of the World... Land / Una esquina de un mundo... tierra*, a mural displaying a shipwreck by Tijuana artist Óscar Ortega on an abandoned building in Playas de Tijuana. For INSITE97, Dough Ischar's *Drill/Talador/ Adiestramiento* was an interactive project inside the Dolores Magdaleno Memorial Recreation Center in Logan Heights where three mediated installations guided viewers through the space, and Nari Ward's *Untitled Depot / Estación sin título* at Playas de Tijuana repurposed bedsprings, doors, and other found materials to build an interactive set of structures for children and visitors to play with. Their location in spaces not traditionally associated with the exhibition of art cast on these artworks a perceived aura of freedom from display conventions. However, the discursive agency of the art biennial compensated for the loss of gallery walls. In their compliance with the exhibition expectations of the art biennial, most site-specific artworks in inSITE reawakened the formalist inheritance of 1960s US neo–avant-gardes. These artworks set up shop in land unfamiliar to their authors, many of whom came from outside the region and were not familiar with immaterial valences of site. In the absence of situated knowledge, the formal and material qualities of place became the few elements in which many of these nonlocal artists could intervene. The biennial conversions entailed in these operations were not strategic choices by artists motivated to take advantage of or "trick" the system. Instead, they occurred through the organic incorporation in their practice of artistic norms upheld and valued in the institutional circuits they longed to access in their path toward professionalization.

A Generational Renewal

Marking these crucial transitions, Silvia Gruner's 111 copies of Tlazolteotl served as intermediaries between competing approaches to site-specific art. Her goddess of birth, trauma, and new beginnings stood between an older generation, represented in inSITE94 by Escobedo and Ehrenberg, and younger Mexico City artists, who gathered at independent art space Temístocles 44.[33] In the fall of 1993, Gruner had invited Michael Krichman and Kathleen Stoughton (inSITE director and Mesa College Gallery director, respectively) to *Calma*, a group exhibition at Temístocles 44 in Mexico City, where they coincided with artists Sofía Táboas, Abraham Cruzvillegas, and Pablo Vargas Lugo—all later featured in inSITE. This artist-run space emerged to fill a vacuum of exhibition spaces for young artists in the Mexican art institutional establishment. Its founding team included the artists above, along with Daniela Rossell and Eduardo Abaroa. An independent institution born out of everyday material and intellectual reciprocity between its members, the space helped this group continue its earlier experimentations with artistic developments trending locally and outside of Mexico.[34]

Situated in a house in the wealthy district of Polanco, Temístocles 44 was one among several alternative artist-run spaces, which also included La Panadería, Curare, and La Quiñonera, that emerged in the Mexico City art world during the 1990s. In these spaces, artists born in the late 1960s and 1970s exhibited work produced with meager subsidies from FONCA, supplemented with odd jobs, as they slowly gained name recognition and ultimately protagonized what Magalí Arriola describes as a move from alternative scenes to the institution.[35] With a tight-knit network of young artists, critics, and curators as their audience, their artworks featured a high degree of formal experimentation and playfulness. Their increasing access to international spaces of circulation because of INBA's growing efforts later in the decade allowed these younger practitioners to be in increasing synchrony with international art trends. Their conversion into *global* artists would be so successful that during the first decade of the new millennium this generation would become staple names of the global contemporary art industry.

InSITE was, for many of these artists, the first opportunity to show their work outside of Mexico City. The biennial's first two iterations in 1994 and 1997 included names such as Abraham Cruzvillegas, Táboas, Pablo Vargas Lugo, Diego Gutiérrez Coppe, José Miguel González Casanova,

Eloy Tarcisio, and Gabriela López Portillo (inSITE94); Rubén Ortiz Torres, Yolanda Gutiérrez, Eduardo Abaroa, and Miguel Calderón (INSITE97); and two Mexico City–based foreign artists active in these artist-run initiatives, Belgian Francis Alÿs and Briton Melanie Smith. For the most part this younger group evaded the explicit political commitment of early Mexican neo–avant-garde artists like Escobedo, Ehrenberg—and, later, Gruner—to adopt a position of overall political indifference in their work. This nihilism materialized in frequent quotations of the work by California and New York-based artists from the 1970s, 1980s, and 1990s. A clear interest in the physical and narrative dimensions of space coexisted, in some cases, with a will to develop neo-pop languages rooted in generational disillusionment. For instance, clear hints to Vito Acconci's work coexisted with nihilist neo-punk revisions of Jeff Koons's cynical pop objects in the works of Eduardo Abaroa and Daniel Guzmán. Their works also touched on the performative explorations of the abject in videos by artists such as Mike Kelley and Paul McCarthy. For others, like Cruzvillegas, apolitical indifference allowed for a reevaluation of the processes and materials of sculpture, an inquiry that led him to explore, at the time, dimensions of unskilled sculptural practice by artists such as Marcel Duchamp and Chris Burden.

A good example of this generation's formalist turn was Sofía Táboas's piece *Double Take / Doble turno*, an installation in the hallway of Tijuana's Casa de la Cultura's top floor (see plate 13). Exploring notions of spatial density, Táboas installed six modules built with curtains of nylon thread with blue plastic beads every four inches. The thick cube-like compartments blocked the hallway, forcing the public to circumnavigate them. Placed under ceiling-light boxes in an already well-lit space, the units shone in bright blue iridescence, changing with the natural daylight in the morning, afternoon, and night. Via the central enlarged cubes Táboas quoted the work of 1970s light artists, such as Dan Flavin and James Turrell, but also the minimalist canon, especially Donald Judd's boxes. Emphasizing elements of the built environment, such as light and the negative space of the hallway, she denoted the site in its physical attributes. Her installation echoed Kwon's first category of site-specific art: it directly addressed the architectural features of place, "insisting on the material fact of the gallery walls as 'framing' devices by notating the walls' dimensions directly on them; removing portions of a wall to reveal the base reality behind the 'neutral' white cube; exceeding the physical boundaries of the gallery by having the art work literally go out the window, ostensibly to 'frame' the institutional frame."[36] The intervention worked thus as an underscoring fixture, amplifying existing structures, in a restatement of the building's framing potential.

Táboas had visited the location six months prior to inSITE94 and sought to reference with her project the daunting repetitive labor that takes place inside *maquiladoras*. The many beads symbolized the mostly female labor force of these factories; the seriality of the grid alluded to the repetitious tasks at the production line. Táboas also incorporated a disposition not uncommon for US neo–avant-garde artists of the 1960 to comment on the dominant form of production in their contexts. The hints of white-collar, blue-collar, and domestic labor that art historians Caroline A. Jones and Julia Bryan-Wilson have identified in the practice of canonical neo-avant-garde artists Frank Stella and Carl André haunted the presence and grace of Táboas's light and translucent cubes.[37] With ready-made plastic playfulness, the cubes and beads pointed to the dominant mode of production in Tijuana's economy, the maquiladora.[38] Her descriptive formalism prompted a phenomenological relation among spectators, artworks, and the gallery's architecture.

Outdoors, in the same venue, Cruzvillegas installed *The Grass Is Greener / El pasto es más verde*. He filled each half of the building's front yard with thin steel rods fixed in the lawn. On one side, dried hummingbirds topped the rods; on the other were asthma inhalers. Cruzvillegas found the birds in a magic-supply booth at Mexico City's Sonora market. Traditionally used in love rituals, they worked as counterparts to the inhalers, which Cruzvillegas had kept following his own use of them. Although both evoked coexisting therapeutic traditions, their bond was mostly one driven by formal analogy, as, for the artist, their shapes, sizes, and materials complemented each other. The dried birds, deprived of life, and the inhalers, sustaining life, evoked for Cruzvillegas Marcel Duchamp's concept of the infra-thin (*inframince*). A condition of energy flow and liminality understood by art historians as the avant-garde artist's attempt to hint toward a fourth dimension in his two-dimensional and three-dimensional artworks, was perhaps a reference to the international border as a liminal line in Cruzvillegas's installation.

Eduardo Abaroa's participation in INSITE97 came as a result of his collaboration with Melanie Smith in the production of a site-specific installation for the show *Plantón en el Zócalo* (Protest in Zócalo [1995]), an exhibition in Mexico City's central public square. Olivier Debroise, an important

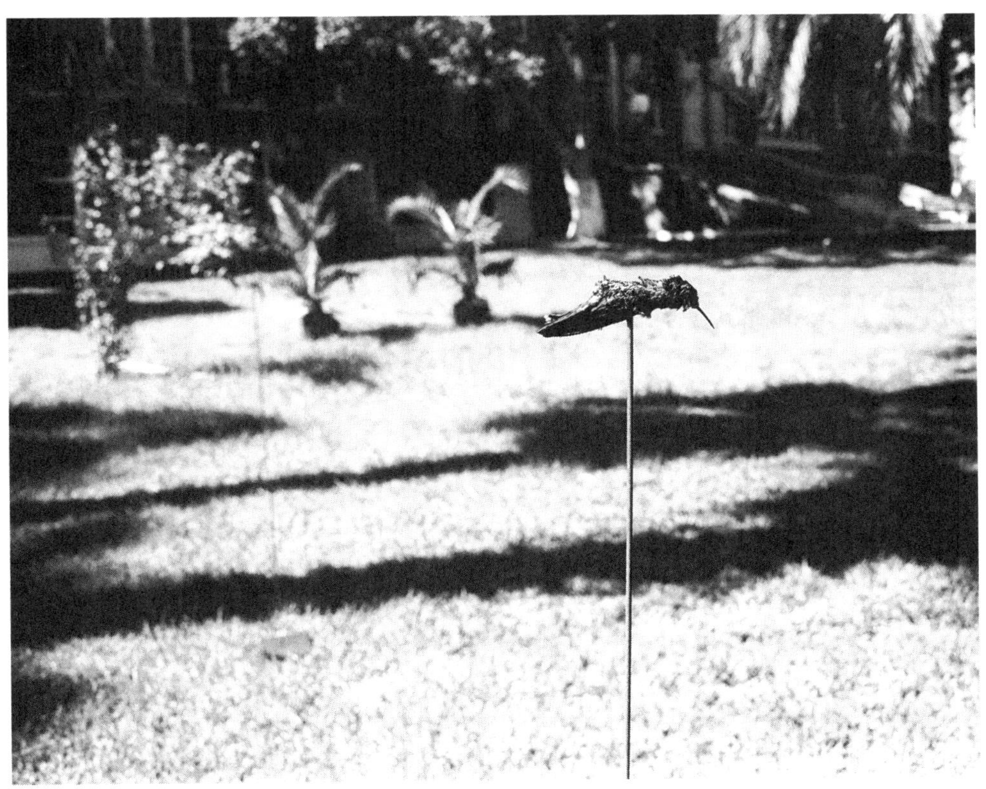

6.3   Abraham Cruzvillegas, *The Grass Is Greener / El pasto es más verde*, 1994. Source: inSITE Archives, Special Collections Library, University of California, San Diego.

player in Mexico City's art scene and curator at inSITE, invited the duo, who ultimately produced separate projects for INSITE97 (see chapter 5). Abaroa's piece, titled *Border Capsule Ritual Black Star*, consisted of five gumball vending machines that the artist filled with tiny plastic figurines. The five devices were positioned in strategic points within downtown San Diego, marking the vertices of a five-point star drawn throughout the city's map. Posters with instructions accompanied the "satanic capsules," which were activated with tokens provided by employees at their several locations: a barbershop, a second-hand bookstore, a 99-cent store, a café, and Smith's tourist booth installation. After completion of the five stages, audiences would retrieve their prize, a miniature plastic champagne

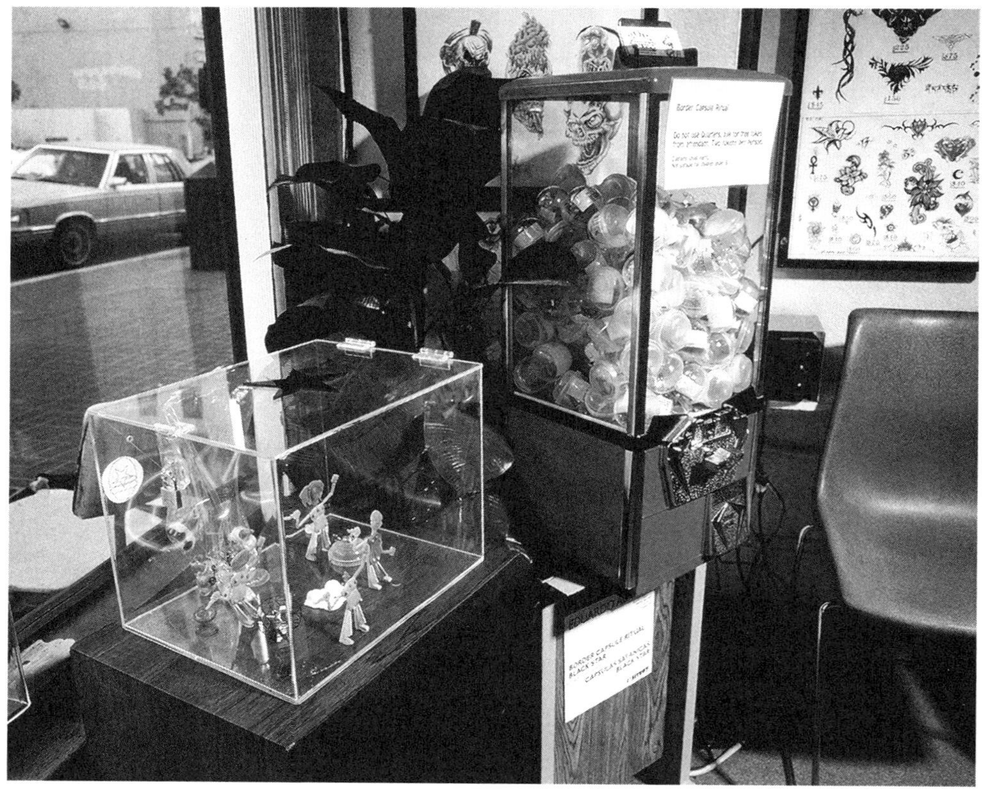

6.4   Eduardo Abaroa, *Border Capsule Ritual Black Star*, 1997. Source: inSITE
Archives, Special Collections Library, University of California, San Diego.

glass. Abaroa's proposal to explore the city of San Diego by tracing a set of
mysterious directions echoed myths of satanic violence in Mexico's northern frontier, a region that experienced escalating violence as a direct result
of the so-called US war on drugs. It also connected with the presence in
San Diego of several UFO-revering intentional communities (an element of
the local culture also referenced by Rubén Ortiz Torres). His site-specific
intervention in the cultural narratives of the region was a playful take on
the power of popular culture to shape the meanings attributed to place.
The map invited ironic reckonings of San Diego, infecting this manicured
city with the nihilist angst of gen-X urban myths. Whereas Táboas's and
Cruzvillegas's commissions remained in the level of the formal, Abaroa

engrained his work in popular narratives at the time in circulation in the region, valuing the rich popular culture of the borderlands and bringing some humor to his presence in the festival.

Neither Abaroa or Cruzvillegas recall having a special interest at the time in narratively addressing the border in their installations. In hindsight, however, they both admit that their site-specific interventions into the borderlands unintentionally mirrored, mocked, and underscored processes of splitting, circulation, and flow that at the time already informed the economies of life and death at the US-Mexico borderlands. The framework that they signaled, an instance of modernity's necropolitics, borrowing Achille Mbembe's term, is a framework concerned with the practice and performance of sovereignty, understood as the power to "dictate who may live and [who] must die."[39] As this and the previous two chapters have shown, the convergence of the two states, Mexico and the United States, around this international boundary invite magnified expressions of sovereignty whose affirmation require, in turn, the aid of institutions involved in the severing, reordering, and hierarchizing of life.

These expressions of sovereignty have deep implications for cultural production. Intentionally or not, by securing an artistic outpost in the northern frontier for the Mexican state, the art biennial became an institution involved in the reorientation of Mexican arts toward the expectations of a North Atlantic–centric nascent global art industry. The biennial conversions happening within and around inSITE helped shift the referent behind the Border art label to replace a decades-long legacy of emancipatory praxis with formalist approaches to site-specificity. At the end of history, one becomes a subject, Mbembe would say, through one's confrontation of death and one's ultimate conversion into the normative subjecthood set by neoliberal reason. One migrates, translates oneself, labors, maybe becomes a citizen, maybe *assimilates*—whatever that might mean. During the early biennial boom one became an institutionally sanctioned artist as one relinquished subaltern cultural legacies that were dismembered and broken, serialized and set up on a grid in the nascent global exhibitionary complex.

part three

Art for a
Unified Europe

MANIFESTA 1, ROTTERDAM, 1996

seven

Manifesta: Placenta Europa

If we had to do it all again, I would start with culture.

—Jean Monnet, quoted in Richards, *Cultural Tourism in Europe*

On Thursday, January 27, 1994, thirty-one representatives from European national cultural agencies gathered in the headquarters of the Rijksdienst Beeldende Kunst (the Netherlands Office for Fine Arts) in The Hague to discuss the European Art Manifestation, a project for a new exhibition of young European artists planned to move among European cities every two years. At the end of the gathering, the conveners signed a petition expressing their "firm conviction that the Ministers of Culture belonging to the European Union (EU) should seriously consider lending structural support to the European Art Manifestation."[1] Among those in attendance were the directors of art institutions, representatives of national and city governments, and directors of a series of Soros Centers for Contemporary Arts in Eastern European capitals.[2] Hoping to provide international visibility to emerging European artists, the organizers described the platform as a pioneer in the tracing of new channels of cultural cooperation between Western Europe and Eastern Europe in the aftermath of the fall of the Berlin Wall. The founders of the European Art Manifestation (EAM) echoed the celebratory promise of political proximity and European unification. They believed that renewed cooperation in contemporary art across the continent would not just strengthen supranational integration but would also help engrain regional cultural scenes with trending developments in the "international dialogue regarding contemporary art." This two-day gathering in The Hague would establish EAM as a new legitimizing platform for a younger generation of artists in order to celebrate "European talent," "quality," and "innovation," promising to "revitalize the artistic establishment" of the continent.[3] The final petition, signed by representatives of twenty-one nations at the meeting, was an extremely successful endorsement for financial-support requests to public and private funding agencies.[4] Ultimately, despite this emphasis on supranational collaboration, the aspirations of Manifesta and other coeval biennials to bring together different national publics predominantly relied on negotiations at the regional and local level.

The stakes were high. The period's goals for European convergence came together in Manifesta, an ambitious exhibition that brought together artworks from a diversity of Western, Central, and Eastern European art scenes to different cities every two years. The art biennial acted as a device within the cultural institutional field in the service of identity formation and supranational integration. Responding to a new cultural policy framework, it recruited contemporary art to support the daunting task of joining the culturally, ethnically, and politically diverse peoples living in the territory called Europe under a new felt sense of belonging to the territory and peoples informing what would be the EU. Yet this new Europe, imagined as a peaceful polity by its architects, had never been such. European history, old and recent, is shaped by ongoing tacit and explicit violence in the form of internal wars, class struggle, ethnic cleansing, patriarchal domination, and, chiefly, extensive colonialism beyond its nominal limits. As chapter 8 details, new conflicts in the post–Cold War years clashed with the spirit of pan-European unity that the art biennial helped envision.

The exhibition was conceived as an index of the artistic diversity to be found in this newly imagined Europe. The central exhibition venues of Manifesta's first iteration in Rotterdam (1996) were a good reflection of this effort. At Witte de With, artworks by Róza El-Hassan (Hungary-Syria), Carl Michael von Haussenwolff (Sweden), Eva Marisoldi (Italy), Jenny

Marketou (Greece), Hale Tenger (Turkey), Susann Walder (Switzerland), Henrik Plenge Jakobsen (Denmark), and Uri Tzaig (Israel) addressed the theme of migration as a process central to European history and essential to the late-twentieth-century global condition. At the Rotterdamse Kunststichting RKS (Rotterdam Arts Council), Joseph Grigely (US), Yuri Leiderman (Ukraine), Tracy Mackenna (UK), and Luca Quartana (Italy) reflected on translation as a necessary foundation for conviviality. At the Museum Boijmans van Beuningen, Vadim Fishkin (Russia), Dmitri Gutov (Russia), Christine Hill (US-Berlin), Soo-ja Kim (Korea-NYC), Maurice O'Connell (Ireland), Tadej Pogačar (Slovenia), Olafur Eliasson (Iceland), Arsen Savadov / Georgy Senchenko (Ukraine), IRWIN (Slovenia), and Didier Trenet (France) shared space with the museum's comprehensive collection dating back to the Middle Ages, anchoring the contemporary art biennial in the Western European artistic canon. Manifesta's catalog described these shows as celebrations of Europe's cultural diversity, crafting an image of the region as a linguistic laboratory nourished by peoples in permanent flux. These artwork arrays worked as indexes of their regional art scenes: artistic delegations gathered from all over the continent in Rotterdam to prefigure the potential of a strong and diverse union. Other, smaller peripheral exhibitions also reflected this conception of the art biennial as a synecdoche for Europe.[5]

In its invitations to participating artists, the organization defined itself as follows: "Manifesta is an exploration of the topographical and mental space of Europe. The curators of Manifesta feel that the definition of Europe will not be found on a map and the place of art today will not be found in objects or genres. The European boundaries are porous and therefore the process of discovery will take into account multiple introjections in one land mass and another, one people or another."[6]

Manifesta's first iteration took place between June 19 and August 9, 1996, in Rotterdam. By the end of the century, it would have traveled to Luxembourg (1998) and Ljubljana (2000). Even today, the biennial itinerates biannually around different European enclaves that bid to host the exhibition.[7] The project has successfully contributed to the formation of a European contemporary art circuit since the mid-1990s and is now perceived by many young contemporary artists across the continent as a natural step toward professionalization. The biennial has also been a useful regional rebranding tool, helping regions redefine themselves in terms of their service and cultural tourism economy after the geographical redistribution of production sectors within the EU since the 1980s. However, the biennial's cooperation with municipal governments and private capital has provoked repeated responses from local art communities, which often criticize the organization for its complicity with processes of gentrification and for failing to denounce political injustice. For instance, Manifesta 10 in St. Petersburg (Russia, 2014) provoked widespread protests in the local and international art community for its failure to denounce Vladimir Putin's 2012 annexation of Crimea, as well as for its silence with regard to Putin's and Vitaly Milonov's anti-LGBTQI legislation. In response to widespread outcry within the international art world, Manifesta's founder and director, Hedwig Fijen, stated that "Manifesta has historically 'chosen to operate within contested areas' and 'the organization often finds itself in a place of political non-alignment.'"[8] As the following chapters show, this programmatic choice to intervene in conflicted sites has been with Manifesta since its early days, when it saw itself as an art-mediated operation to help bring European art worlds together after a long twentieth century of war and division. This choice also points to an underlying trust in the medium of the art exhibition as a device intrinsically suited for conflict resolution. An analysis of its beginnings in Rotterdam in 1996 helps elucidate how this early-boom art biennial fashioned itself as a mediator within long-standing historical tensions, in this case supporting a new common European identity through aesthetic conversions.[9]

A European Cultural Policy

Cultivating a shared sense of belonging to a new European Union through contemporary art would require synchronized action by a wide array of stakeholders. Two months before the meeting described above, a more intimate gathering took place in the Netherlands Office for Fine Arts in The Hague. Dutch socialite, art historian, and EAM Foundation project manager Hedwig Fijen convened a group of cultural experts who would become the organization's advisory board: René Block, director of the Institut für Auslandsbeziehungen (Stuttgart); Henry Meyric Hughes, director of the South Bank Centre (London); Svenrobert Lundquist, director of NUNSKU, the National Committee for the Exhibition of Contemporary Swedish Art Abroad (Stockholm); Michelle Paris, cultural attaché of the French Embassy in The Hague; and Robert R. de Haas and Els Barents, director and consultant of the Netherlands Office of Fine Arts. At this meeting, the group agreed that the project required the active cooperation of cultural institutions from participating countries, as well as of the European Commission. Participation in the initial iterations would be limited to a smaller group of countries, but the group hoped that the selection's scope could broaden with time. The conveners of this meeting agreed that the first exhibition would be held in Rotterdam and would later move among different cities, potentially coinciding with the European Cultural Capital program in order to maximize its access to resources. Finally, the board had two tasks to complete over the winter holidays: first, it would nominate a new advisory board member from Eastern Europe, mirroring future European expansion plans; second, it would leverage the members' personal networks to "activate lobbyists in Brussels" and secure a hearing at the next semiannual meeting of the Cultural Committee of the European Commission to increase the likelihood of funding.[10]

From the beginning EAM was a top-down intervention in new niches opened by policy, launched by established cultural- and political-elite actors. In this sense, it did not differ much from other art biennials. EAM was conceived in a climate of renewed belief in the role that culture (including the arts) played in the transition from an economically driven European Economic Community (CEE) toward a politically unified EU, after recommendations for increased cultural action written in the Treaty on European Union (commonly known as the Treaty of Maastricht). Signed on February 7, 1992, the document advanced the process of European integration and created the EU. It set "firm bases for the construction of the future Europe" and sought to "deepen the solidarity between [European] peoples while respecting their history, their culture and their traditions."[11] Remarkably, Article 128 of the treaty was the first existing legislation to explicitly acknowledge the instrumentality of culture for European unification.[12] Its goal was to consolidate the EU as a political union, "celebrating diversity and promoting dialogue between national cultures" and transcending the economic determinism framing cultural action during the CEE period (1957–1993), to sponsor programs strictly on the basis of their "cultural value."[13] Although it is impossible to know what the authorities understood to be "cultural value," the text uses this term to evoke an intrinsic quality of cultural objects that is perceived as seemingly autonomous from their economic value.[14] Yet conflicting notions of cultural value clashed within and around Manifesta's exhibitions. Of particular relevance to the beginnings of EAM were two of the interest areas explicitly recommended for support in Article 128: "non-commercial cultural exchanges" and "artistic and literary creation."[15] As Monica Sassatelli explains, Article 128 opened a space of "delicate equilibrium between the drive for unity and the concern for diversity" in European cultural action, for both the sovereignty of member states and a shared European identity in formation needed to be acknowledged.[16] The tensions resulting from this double focus transpired in EAM, especially in its initial stages, when curators and advisory board members worked to include artworks from all European regions in the exhibition.

The complex, multilayered structure of this new EU demanded that for the EAM to be feasible, cooperation between cultural and political entities needed to occur at the local, national, and supranational levels. Simon Hix describes the European Union's multilayered governmental model as a two-dimensional model: on the one hand, European politics are driven by the goal of supranational economic, cultural, and political integration; on the other, national governments operate following the traditional Left-Right split in domestic intervention. As a consequence, EU governance often relies on interactions between private and public actors who, moved by informal norms and formal institutions and policies, join to collaborate and find solutions to specific challenges.[17] This dual approach to governance transpired within the biennial structure and its internal division of labor as administrators, curators, and artists navigated the competing interests and implicit norms that oriented the effort simultaneously in seemingly opposing directions: outwardly projecting an image of Europeanness and locally pursuing grounding and, to certain extent, validation in Rotterdam's cultural fabric.

Culture became an important source of soft power for European convergence. Internally, common cultural policy worked to integrate regional cultural differences in a shared set of supranational programs, appeasing historical conflicts between European nations.[18] But governments' reliance on culture to intervene in social life was, of course, far from new. Other parts of this book show how this reliance was a constant across the political spectrum in the period, helping trigger the so-called art biennial boom. More broadly, sociologist Tony Bennett has described this as an essential function of art institutions in the modern period, during which organic alliances among governments and cultural administration facilitate the coproduction of consent. In Bennett's words, cultural administration has "relied on means of acting in the social that respect the freedom and autonomy of individuals (or communities), seeking to govern them at a distance, and indirectly, by involving them as active agents in the processes of their own transformation and self-regulation."[19] Furthermore, under the right social conditions, specific articulations of high culture have historically helped to hold nations together by a dexterous incorporation of elements from folklore or popular culture into a unified program. These top-down mediations between low and high culture act as de facto repositories of legitimacy to nations—and, in this case, the nascent European Union—by providing a shared symbolic repertoire where diverse constituencies can articulate their "faith" in the new polity.[20]

In this vein, Manifesta was not alone in its dexterous handling of different artistic legacies. Echoing other early-boom biennials in their efforts to create consent around systemic political transformations, its mission to build a "structural platform for young European artists to redefine the value of European cultural heritage and to launch a search for the mental space of a redefining Europe" illustrates how elites participate in the formulation of new cultural categories that might at first glance seem inclusive to all.[21] As I explain in chapter 9, although initial efforts to incorporate fragments of Rotterdam's popular culture in Manifesta 1 were slim, the biennial organizers ultimately agreed to include in their plans initiatives designed by local artists. If in Manifesta's first iteration this incorporation was a last-minute concession made to appease the discontent of the local arts community, other editions since have featured elements from regional popular culture, mediated through the codes of contemporary art, as a key branch of the biennial's strategy to ground its discursive work in regional cultural repertoires.

Participating artists were well aware of Manifesta's mission. Some hinted at its political agency by reflecting in their practice on official culture's historical bond with power. One good example of this address was *Datacorridor (How to Change Your Wallpaper Daily)*, an installation that was part of the Art History Archives, a longer project by Romanians Călin Dan, Iosif Király, and Dan Mihălțianu, two artists and one art historian whose art practice addressed, often with irony, blistering myths about Romanian society. In *Datacorridor* the collective, known as subREAL, covered the walls and ceiling of a gallery in the Kunsthal Rotterdam with photographic

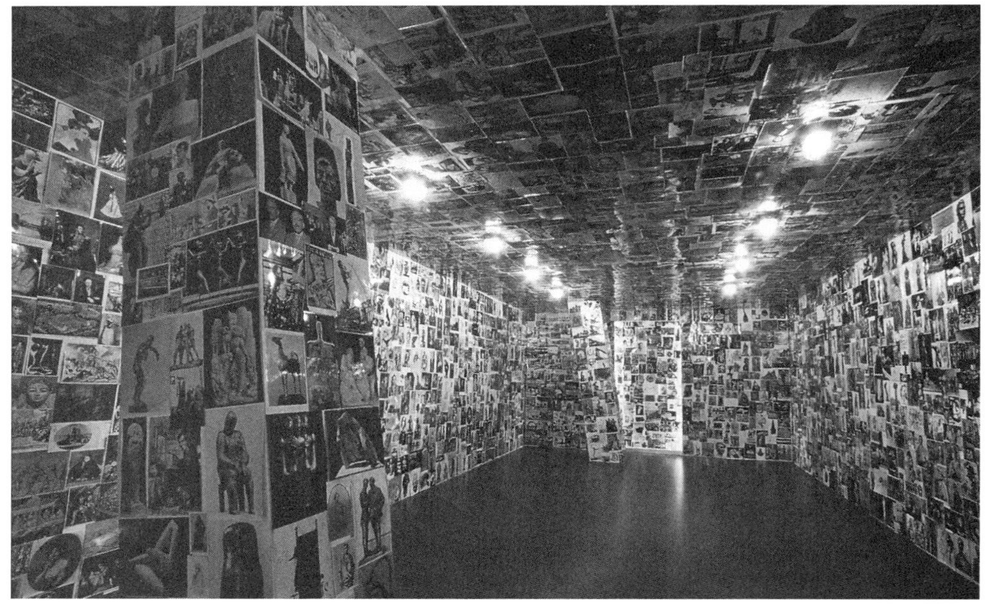

reproductions of artworks retrieved from eighteen crates discarded after the dissolution of Romanian state-controlled arts journal *Arta*, an official publication directed by the Romanian Union of Fine Artists between 1953 and 1990. Coating the Kunsthal's white walls with hundreds of reproductions of official Romanian art, subREAL underscored the ideological agency of the exhibition medium, stressing the pervasive ways in which national identity discourses haunt curatorial work.

In its monumental site-specificity, *Datacorridor* traced the physical coordinates of the exhibition space with a state-sanctioned classicist aesthetics deaccessioned in the aftermath of Nicolae Ceaușescu's overthrow in December 1989. *Datacorridor* had been previously shown in other venues outside of Romania, such as the Künstlerhaus Bethanien in Berlin (1995), where the three members of subREAL were artists in residence for the year 1995–1996, and then traveled to several other art venues in Europe. The installation was part of what Sven Spieker calls subREAL's "ironic monuments," constructions that "undermine their own readability as commemorative acts through the inclusion of elements—allusions or other subtexts—that contest the act's legitimacy or feasibility."[22] This compulsive totalist engagement with official Romanian culture's ruins highlighted the medium of the exhibition's own involvement in historical narratives. The black-and-white reproductions of sculptures, reliefs, painted and photographed portraits, medals, pieces of furniture, frescoes, and other art and archaeology artifacts formerly included in the state-sanctioned Romanian art canon stressed the crucial role that the production and maintenance of heritage plays in the legitimization of political power. SubREAL had been concerned with this very idea since its beginnings as a collective. Its first action, in August 1990, consisted of the installation of 120 commemorative metal plates along Bucharest's central East–West Avenue (formerly called Victory of Socialism Avenue). The plates, engraved with the words "rest in peace," honored workers who had died during Ceaușescu's drastic urban reform of Bucharest. Soon after this first intervention, the collective began to engage through its practice with the prejudices that it found in Western European art circles about Central and Eastern European contemporary art. In the words of curator Zoran Erić, following the end of the Cold War, the West's eagerness to engage in dialogue with Central and Eastern Europe created an assumption that Eastern European artists would adapt their work to the languages dominant in Western institutions at the time. I explore the pervasiveness of this assumption throughout Manifesta's integrative mission in the next chapter.

Euro-elitism and Europeanness

The new biennial's program reawakened regional political and economic elites' desires for economic, political, and cultural unification. After World War II, northern European industrialists had fostered the unification of the national markets of Belgium, the Netherlands, and Luxembourg. The resulting Benelux union relied on economic integration to pacify the long history of conflict in the three countries via a stable tax-free trade zone that would purportedly drive economic growth. Its successor, the financially driven CEE, widened the economic treaty's reach, leading the way to the formation of the EU decades later. In this context, and largely facilitated by a new cultural policy framework negotiated in Brussels, Europeanness, or the quality of being European, would materialize through projects such as Manifesta, shaping the cultural heritage of a new, unified Europe. This sentiment of supranational belonging echoes Benedict Anderson's concept of nation-ness as national identity, one of the myths of belonging through which political formations order relations among places, individuals, and power—informing the "imagined community" of the nation. As Anderson points out, in museums and other cultural institutions, objects and narratives facilitate the grounding of the abstract national and supranational identities, their imagined traditions and presents, into specific ordered displays.[23] This function scaled up from the national to the supranational after the Cold War. With time, elites across the continent organically embraced the myth of Europeanness as a complement to their national identities as a way of identifying themselves with increasingly neoliberal modernization programs, signaling their belief in the EU's advantage in the new geopolitical order.

Overcoming obstacles to internal cohesion by the production of shared sentiments is a prerequisite for the formation of polities.[24] Yet rendering valid this newly imagined union required elites *and* common citizens alike to coalesce under this new identity as the unification project moved forward through formal interventions and the overall permissive consensus of citizens. On the one hand, official interventions involved representative bodies, such as European government agencies, a new European legal framework, and European elections. On the other, consensus toward elitist formulations of Europeanness rested in the perception, widely amplified through media and culture, that European unification served the public interest on economic and social matters, settling for good a long history of intra-European wars and repression articulated via nationalist agendas.[25] In this regard, the Treaty of Maastricht's cultural-policy framework formalized a long-felt sentiment among regional elites, setting the legal and institutional conditions for its materialization.

Manifesta, whose initial working title was "Placenta Europa: Manifesta, the Rebirthing of Europe," was an instance of that effort. From the beginning described as a network "to redefine the value of European cultural heritage and to launch a search for the mental space of a redefining Europe," the art biennial became a platform for the cultivation of a specific kind of Europeanness among established regional intellectuals and new generations of art workers.[26] But rendering elite worldviews universal has crucial implications. As Étienne Balibar cautions, the universalization of elite interests satisfies a deep-seated need to forge "an ideological 'world' shared by exploiters and exploited alike," a consequence that requires the adaptation of the long-term interests and cultural repertoires of nonelite groups—a process reflected in the biennial conversions described in this book.[27] Balibar points to what, in hindsight, has proven to be the foundational mistake of the EU: an elite articulation of the cultural, political, and economic objectives driving unification that, in retrospect, has failed to satisfy the interests, including economic ones, of nonelite Europeans.

In the catalog for Manifesta 1, EAM director Hedwig Fijen and project office coordinator Jolie van Leeuwen remembered the biennial's beginnings: "In 1993 a piece of paper was lingering somewhere on an office desk in the Netherlands. It contained notes for a future art project, ignited by the belief in a Europe without borders. In November of the same year, five people from the field of the visual arts came together to discuss the possibilities for a 'different' platform for the presentation of young European art, a new type of biennial as an alternative to large-scale shows."[28] Yet young European artists had a different perception of Manifesta's mission. For example, despite the redeemable goal of supporting European unification, Manifesta's initial iteration was perceived as elitist and foreign by Rotterdam art actors, who were excluded from the art biennial, mostly conceived and executed by Amsterdam-based actors. Art critic Elly Stegeman noted these tensions from the biennial's early days. Despite organizers' intentions to address themes such as migration, cultural diversity, and communication, Stegeman felt that it was "a bit annoying to hear [about these themes] when the protagonists are narcissistic luxury children, post–avant garde tourists." Stegeman illustrated what she called a "culture of self-celebration" in the work of young British artist Catherine Yass, whose group portrait of the five curators was placed at the entrance of the auditorium at the Het Nieuwe Instituut in downtown Rotterdam. For Stegeman, the only project that "succeeded in penetrating"[29] Rotterdam into the official program was NEsTWORK, led by Rotterdam artist Jeanne van Heeswijk, which proposed a series of lectures, discussions, and tours around the city. I engage in detail with the whos, the whys, and the hows of NEsTWORK in chapter 9. Since this inaugural iteration, Manifesta has continued to support European integration by framing different approaches to contemporary art within the same exhibition space, reflecting the supranational polity's expansion, imagining a new Europe in the making.

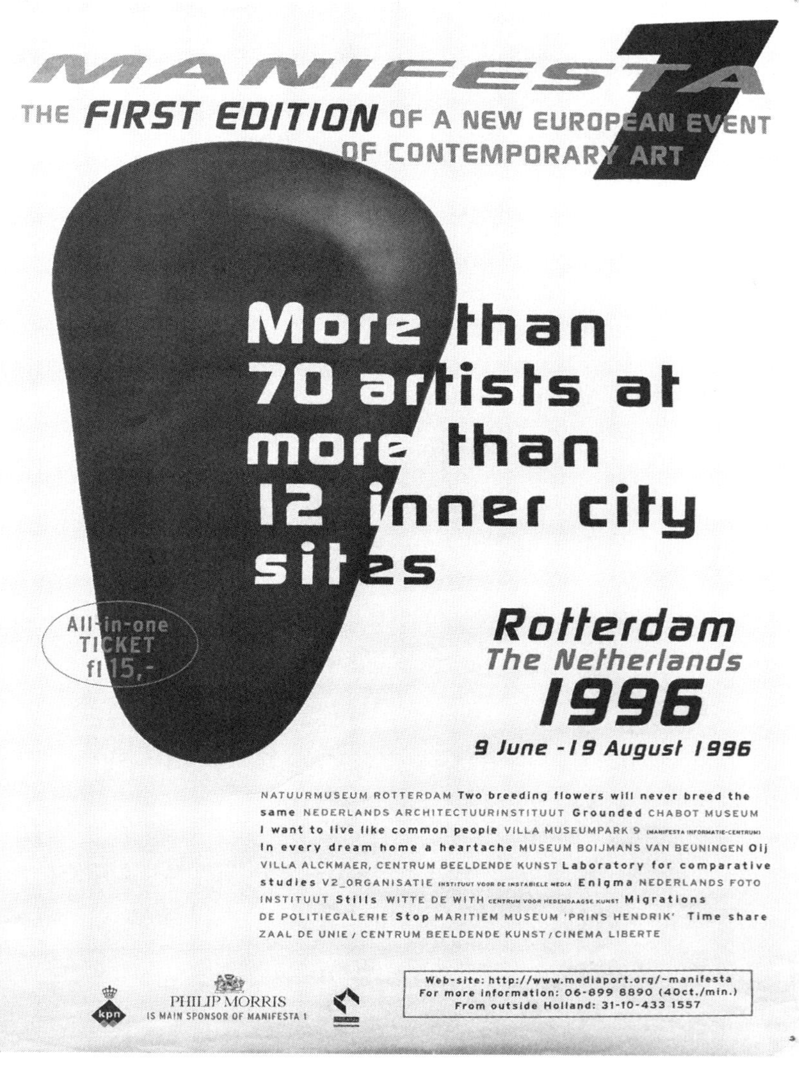

7.2   Event poster, Manifesta 1, 1996. Source: Witte de With Archives, Rotterdam Cultural Histories (renamed Kunstinstituut Melly).

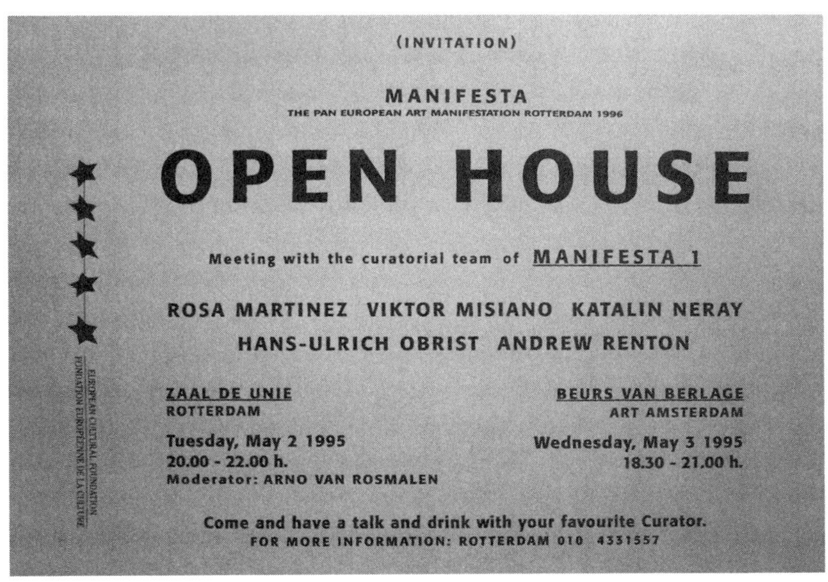

7.3   Open house flyer, Manifesta 1, 1995. Source: Witte de With Archives, Rotterdam Cultural Histories (renamed Kunstinstituut Melly).

It's Now or Never

Most artists and curators participating in Manifesta shared the organizers' appreciation of the historic opportunity that the biennial opened before them. Several of the artists conceived of their works as commentaries on their present. Henrik Plenge Jakobsen's diptych, *EVERYTHING IS WRONG*, included two murals facing each other inside a whitewashed gallery on the top floor of Witte de With Center for Contemporary Art (see plate 14). Two forty-three-square-foot "self-contained" circular targets, painted in bright primary colors, were crossed by the phrase "Everything is wrong." A "civilization critique" and a "protest" against worldwide environmental crisis, according to Plenge Jakobsen, the piece worked on a twofold reference to US color-field painter Kenneth Noland and New York electronic musician Moby. Noland's iconic paintings frequently feature concentric circular targets in primary colors, a pop response to abstract expressionism's uncensored gestuality. Moby's eponymous 1995 album was extremely popular in the mid-1990s rave scene. The diptych, celebratory of trippy night euphoria, was for the artist a sign of the Euro-optimism of the time, "a very positive period . . . after the fall of the Wall."[30] Biennial curators also felt the post-Maastricht feelings of historical urgency that followed the aftermath of the fall of the Berlin Wall. According to Manifesta 1 curator Katalin Néray,

> After many years of a "Sleeping Beauty Dream" we are at last present on the spiritual map of the world. The idea of Manifesta was created when the Iron Curtain of the Cold War was dismantled (indeed pieces of the barbed wire were offered by American department stores as collectible souvenirs) and its symbol, the Berlin Wall, had come down. It has taken some years until the idea became reality. Our endeavors as curators were to create a process which at a certain moment appears in the form of an exhibition. We will see our attitudes become form in Rotterdam.[31]

Like most art experts involved in the early biennial boom, the other Manifesta curators and organizers shared Néray's belief in the potential of art exhibitions to pacify historically divided regions. Curator Andrew Renton attributed the excitement around Manifesta to the exhibition's power to redefine the meaning of Europe.[32] Europe, for Renton, is "a place that's not defined by maps or political boundaries. Rather, it's something that could be held in the mind. It's a mental space. It needs to be defined by people and people in their spaces." Renton's characterization of Europe as a "mental space" reflects the idealism initially driving European unification within and beyond contemporary art worlds. To the challenge of how to successfully mediate among diverse worldviews, Renton explains: "The way you do this is that you center it on one place. You bring people together on a single site or a series of localities, Rotterdam. And in Rotterdam from elsewhere they'll come together and define themselves in relation to others."[33] Renton's characterization of the biennial as the joining of different voices for shared deliberation posited the exhibition as a polyvocality of disparate perspectives, invested, like their human counterparts, in the overcoming of differences for the sake of a greater good. Although art can indeed act as a space for resolution of long-standing conflicts, I show in chapter 8 how this Habermasian idealization of the exhibition space as materialized in Manifesta 1 would face important obstacles.

In addition to relying on the joint appreciation of art objects to support cultural unification, those involved in Manifesta's early days also saw this moment as an opportunity to rethink art exhibition conventions. In their pursuit of an exhibition design that could speak to their contemporaneous historical conditions, Manifesta organizers and the curatorial team hoped to avoid reproducing classic models, like the Venice Biennale, shaped over the centrality of the nation-state. Recent political events seemed to justify launching another biennial exhibition of art. As the advisory board of Manifesta wrote in the catalog for Manifesta 1, "The need for a new platform for artists was most keenly felt in 1989, after the fall of the Berlin wall. It wasn't hard to see then that there would be a new need for information, for open discussions, for new infrastructures and alternative exhibition spaces."[34] To this end, curator Viktor Misiano saw Manifesta as a timely innovation within the medium of the art exhibition: "I was convinced that our contribution to the contemporary art scene should be exactly the new mode of an art event, which is in a degree the loss of a clear paradigm, the age in between in-betweennesses."[35] Misiano's words and Manifesta's final form show an exhibition conceived of as a network. Though perceived by some in the public as unstable and disorganized, the biennial offered a decentralized alternative to Venice's national pavilion model, emulating the time's optimism for forms of networked communication brought about by recent technological developments such as the internet.

These years have been retroactively perceived as a time of renovation for curatorial practice: a "discursive turn," in the words of Paul O'Neill, during which curatorial work morphed from a culture of care and custodianship of objects toward an increasingly authorial and creatively discursive relationship with culture.[36] The timeliness of EAM reflected not just new directions in cultural policy or historical episodes; it also responded to recent changes within the Western European art world, such as the dissolution of the office within the Netherlands Office for Fine Arts in charge of distributing Dutch art abroad and the end of the Paris Biennial in 1985. The latter, envisioned as a space for young artistic innovation, had begun in 1959 as part of French minister of culture André Malraux's plans to reclaim Paris's centrality in the genealogy of modern art, hoping to recover the cultural protagonism that New York had purportedly stolen during the 1940s.[37] In his words, "France, which occupies a unique space in the domain of the arts, could not stay out of a movement of such a nature that brings wide information and extends intellectual exchanges."[38] As art historian Hannah Feldman has shown, Malraux's biennial anticipated Manifesta's pan-European ambitions by helping reimagine France's role within the emerging economic alliances preceding the European Economic Community—while simultaneously whitewashing French national identity at a time of colonial war in Northern Africa.[39]

The Master Plan

The guiding ideas behind Manifesta were formalized in August 1995 in a thirty-one-page master plan that detailed the objectives, structural organization, communication strategy, and budget for the art biennial.[40] Produced by the project office of the Foundation European Art Manifestation in consultation with the Bureau Menno Heling Cultural Marketing in Amsterdam, the dossier situated Manifesta in broader efforts to participate in the construction of European nation-ness at the local, national, and supranational levels. Although the initial master plan has been reviewed and altered many times since, this early version helps elucidate the original organization of this curatorial venture in its beginnings. This internal document was distributed among interested parties after the two initial meetings described at the start of this chapter, seeking to engage "participating institutions, subsidies, sponsors and the participating European countries." It set two objectives for Manifesta: "setting up and maintaining a European Network of artists, art institutions and art critics" and "organizing the Manifesta 1 1996 exhibition in Rotterdam, which aim[ed] to be the first exhibition of a series of biennales with contemporary European art." The first goal reflected the ambitions of the organizers, who saw in the post-Maastricht cultural-policy framework an opportunity to intervene in the field of so-called high art by unifying the distinct national and regional art scenes present in Europe at the time. According to the master plan, the network would, among other outcomes, "creat[e] a broad, structural platform for young European artists to redefine the value of European cultural heritage and to launch a search for the mental space of redefining Europe"; "initiat[e] a different form of cooperation and discussion possibilities with various target groups in Europe via the new media, Open House meetings and workshops"; and "[set] up a basic financing program to start the network."[41]

The operation would require complex organizational and financial support, as well as many open house meetings, colloquiums, laboratories, and workshops held all over Europe. Throughout these many meetings, EAM representatives aspired to reach a wide array of target audiences, including young European artists, artist-run organizations, visual art students, art history students, broad and nonspecialized audiences, national and European-level government representatives, private and public sponsors, and influential actors within international contemporary art circuits.[42] Other sections of the master plan provided general information about the exhibition catalog (structure and budget), calendar, proposed venues in Rotterdam, and ideal representations of European nations (both from the CEE and Eastern Europe). The document also compiled short biographies of curators for the Rotterdam exhibition: Néray (Hungary), Rosa Martínez (Spain), Viktor Misiano (Russia), Andrew Renton (United Kingdom), and Hans-Ulrich Obrist (Switzerland). Other sections outlined the composition and duties of the advisory board, the national committee, and the *projectbureau*. Last, the dossier included an estimated general budget and a section on EAM's financing model.

Sponsors and Partners

EAM's early finances reflected its ambitious plans. A January 1994 budget estimated the total cost of Manifesta 1 to be 845,000 guilders (US$435,052 in 1996). This figure, which comprised personnel (420,000 guilders), exhibition (220,000 guilders), and catalog expenses (205,000 guilders), would be satisfied via a combination of private and public sponsorship sources, in consistency with the multiple stakeholders involved in the enterprise.[43] Public sponsorship came from local, national, and European institutions. Recently established supranational funding agencies, such as the Council of Europe and the European Cultural Foundation, provided important support. On the local level, public sponsorship came from the Office of the Mayor of the City of Rotterdam, the Office of the Aldermen of the City of Rotterdam, the Office of the Director of Cultural Affairs of the City of Rotterdam, Rotterdam's Arts Council, and the Rotterdam City Development Corporation. Sponsorship from Dutch national public entities came from the Ministry of Foreign Affairs and the Ministry of Education, Culture, and Science. In addition to these sources, national agencies from supporting countries paid a participation fee of 10,000 guilders. In several cases, this fee was paid even if no artist from the country participated in the exhibition.[44]

The case of former socialist nations such as Albania, Bosnia and Herzegovina, and Belarus merits particular attention. These countries' participation fees were paid by the Open Society Foundation, a philanthropic organization directed by Hungarian-American billionaire George Soros that promotes liberal democratic values across the world. Founded in 1993, the Open Society Foundation sought to facilitate a transition to liberal democracy for republics formerly under the USSR's political and economic influence.[45] Aligned with this mission, in the 1980s and 1990s the foundation opened contemporary art centers in the capitals of former socialist nations. These centers were uneasy new actors in the regional art scenes: on the one hand they allowed for the emergence of rich experimental art scenes throughout the region but, on the other hand, they relied heavily on directives coming from the New York–based Open Society Foundation, often working under short-term operating budgets that curtailed the sustainability of these new art scenes. Art historian Izabel Galliera describes the work carried out by Soros Centers for Contemporary Art (sccas) in Central and Eastern Europe as involved in a broader process of normalization of liberal values such as individualism and entrepreneurship.[46] These organizations played a key role in mediating access for EAM curators in the region, facilitating the participation of artists from regional art scenes formerly under the USSR's influence.[47]

The sccas imported artistic programs into rapidly changing art scenes, often facilitating access to material and social resources off-limits to artists before the end of the USSR, and fueling effervescent local art scenes at times of regime change. These transfers of foreign means of production and systems of valuation to these sites required the recruitment of local art actors to mediate and translate foreign frameworks to local constituencies. For instance, Călin Dan, a member of the collective subREAL, had served as the first director of the Soros Center for Contemporary Art in Bucharest and had himself been charged with mediating in the transfer of expectations set in New York City for the conversion of contemporary art registers in Hungary to North Atlantic art-world expectations. Of special value to Bucharest artists was the importing of new media previously unavailable in the region via the local scca. Knowledgeable of these workings, subREAL addressed with its work the tensions provoked by these uneven cultural and aesthetic translations, embracing humor and relying on archival documents as source material for its installations. Yet even in the guise of jokes and documents, these aesthetic conversions became obligatory passage points into the time's supranational art networks.

Another uneasy partnership was the one developed between EAM and tobacco manufacturer and long-term sponsor of the arts Philip Morris. An undated document addressed to the Kunsthal Rotterdam lays the foundations of their private financial sponsorship model, stating that a quarter of Manifesta 1's budget would come from the private sector and explaining that "a main sponsor and a number of partial sponsors will be sought. This is thought to include national entrepreneurship that focuses on the European market."[48] After months of negotiations, tobacco giant Philip Morris became the main private sponsor of Manifesta 1 in Rotterdam. A contract from September 29, 1995, sets the conditions for the relationship between the EAM and Philip Morris.[49] The sponsorship bond would be active between September 29, 1995, and August 19, 1996. Philip Morris Holland paid a total sum of 300,000 guilders ($188,869) to be deposited in three parts on September 29, 1995, January 1, 1996, and June 9, 1996. The contract stipulated that Philip Morris would be the sole private sponsor of Manifesta 1 and clarified the forms of publicity that Manifesta would provide to Philip Morris in exchange for the sponsorship: chiefly, the association of its name with the art exhibition. Their partnership would be made explicit in "all written or spoken announcements, brochures, program booklets, posters, advertisements, stationery and similar" and would "take place where appropriate in the required colors as the colored printed matter, or in black, white, gray, when the black-and-white printing is concerned . . . stating 'Philip Morris main sponsor of Manifesta 1,' clearly and in a prominent place, although not perceived as disturbing by the public." In addition, the sponsor would receive admission tickets and catalog copies and could organize private viewings and educational tours of the exhibition before and after the opening date. Finally, Manifesta 1's programming autonomy was safeguarded by a contract clause which stated that "the sponsor [could] in no way influence the content and the concept of the exhibition, which could affect the independence of the curators of the exhibition."[50] Philip Morris's sponsorship of contemporary art was not new; the tobacco group has been an active patron of the arts since the 1960s. Overall, this reflected broader tendencies within private-sector brands to clean their otherwise troubling associations (in this case with lung cancer and other smoking-related diseases) through new affiliations with art and culture, *artwashing* their identities with positive and celebratory cultural manifestations.[51]

Soon after the fall of the Berlin Wall, policy-driven efforts to upgrade economic alliances into complex, socially integrated polities positioned culture as a unique field for the forging of common supranational identities. In this context, Manifesta unfolded as a response in the niche field of contemporary art, able to attract private and public interests across the continent in support of a renewed, unified European culture. Bringing art from different European regions together in the galleries, the art biennial realized widespread beliefs in art's potential to resolve entrenched political differences. Yet devising ways to reach beyond organically similar elite art publics to interpellate diverse local constituencies proved challenging and would require much more than grouping artworks in a shared exhibition space. Manifesta's own organic affinity with elitist articulations of Europeanness clashed with the many other understandings of what being a European artist meant at the time, within and beyond Rotterdam, East and West, North and South.

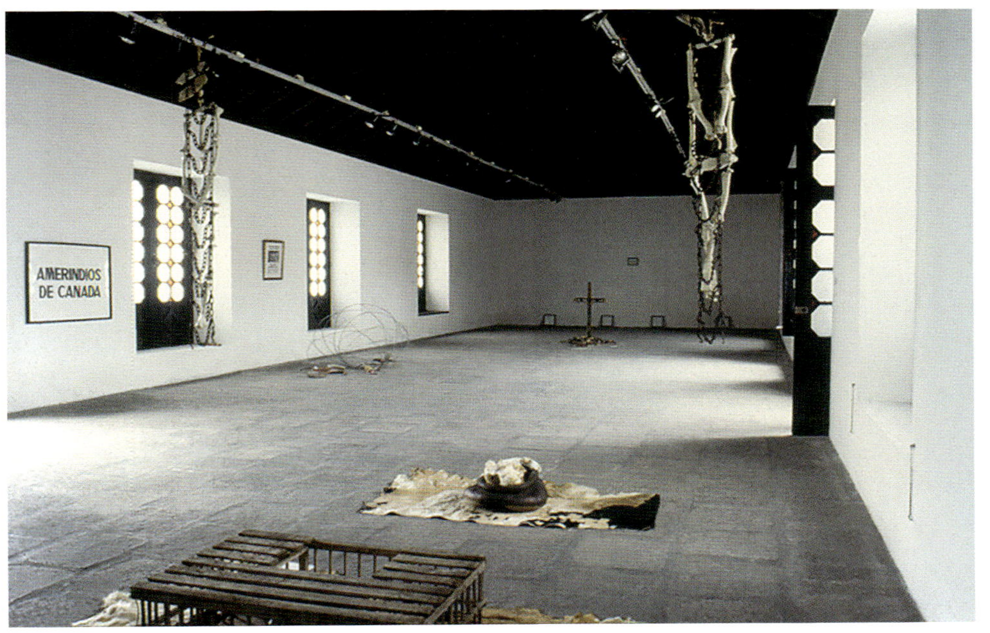

1 Installation view, *Amerindios del Canadá*, Bienal de La Habana, 1991. Courtesy of Llilian Llanes.

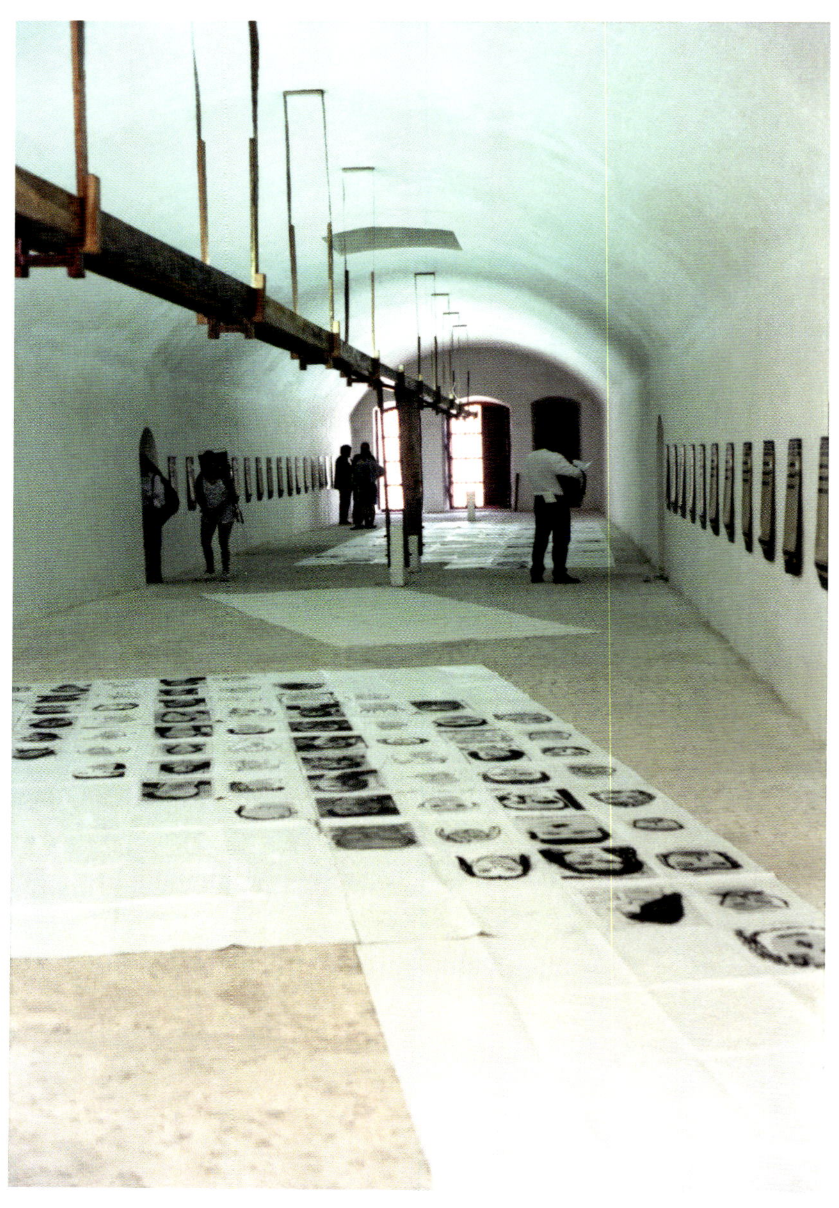

2   Eugenio Dittborn, *Aeropostal*, 1991. Courtesy of Nury González.

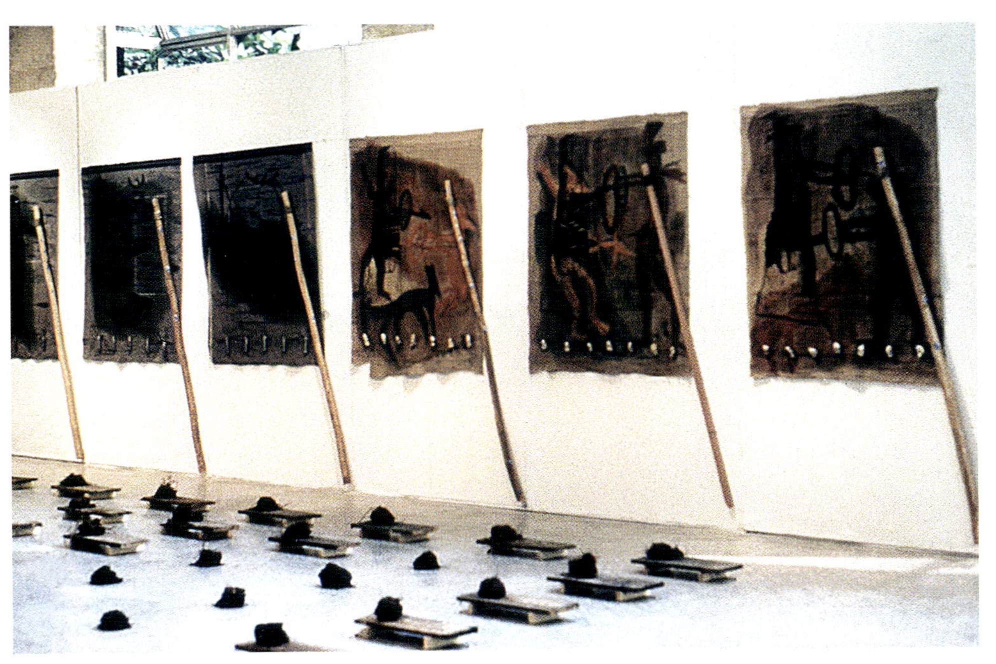

3   Nury González, *El sur total del mundo*, 1991. Courtesy of Nury González.

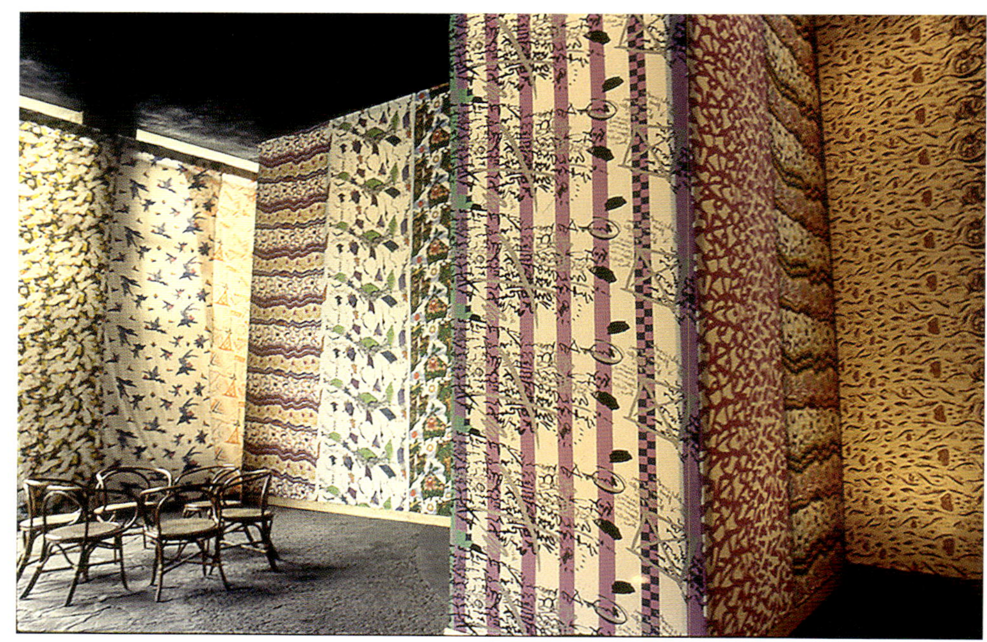

4   Textile designs from 2 Bienal de La Habana's *TELARTE* exhibit, 1986. Courtesy of Llilian Llanes.

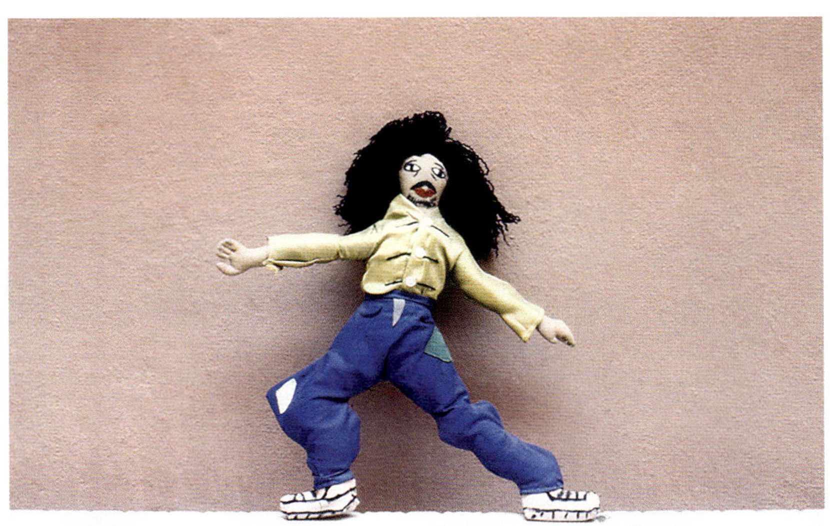

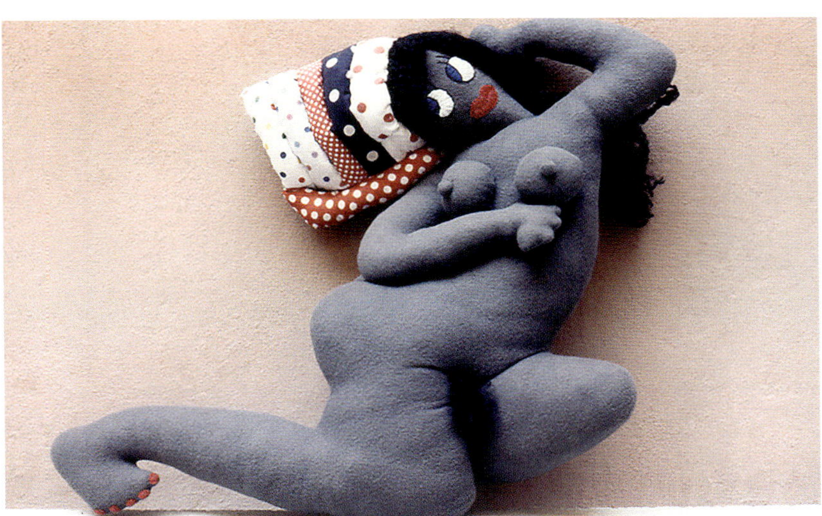

5   Sindicato de Costureras 19 de Septiembre, *Lucha y Victoria*, 1986. Courtesy of Llilian Llanes.

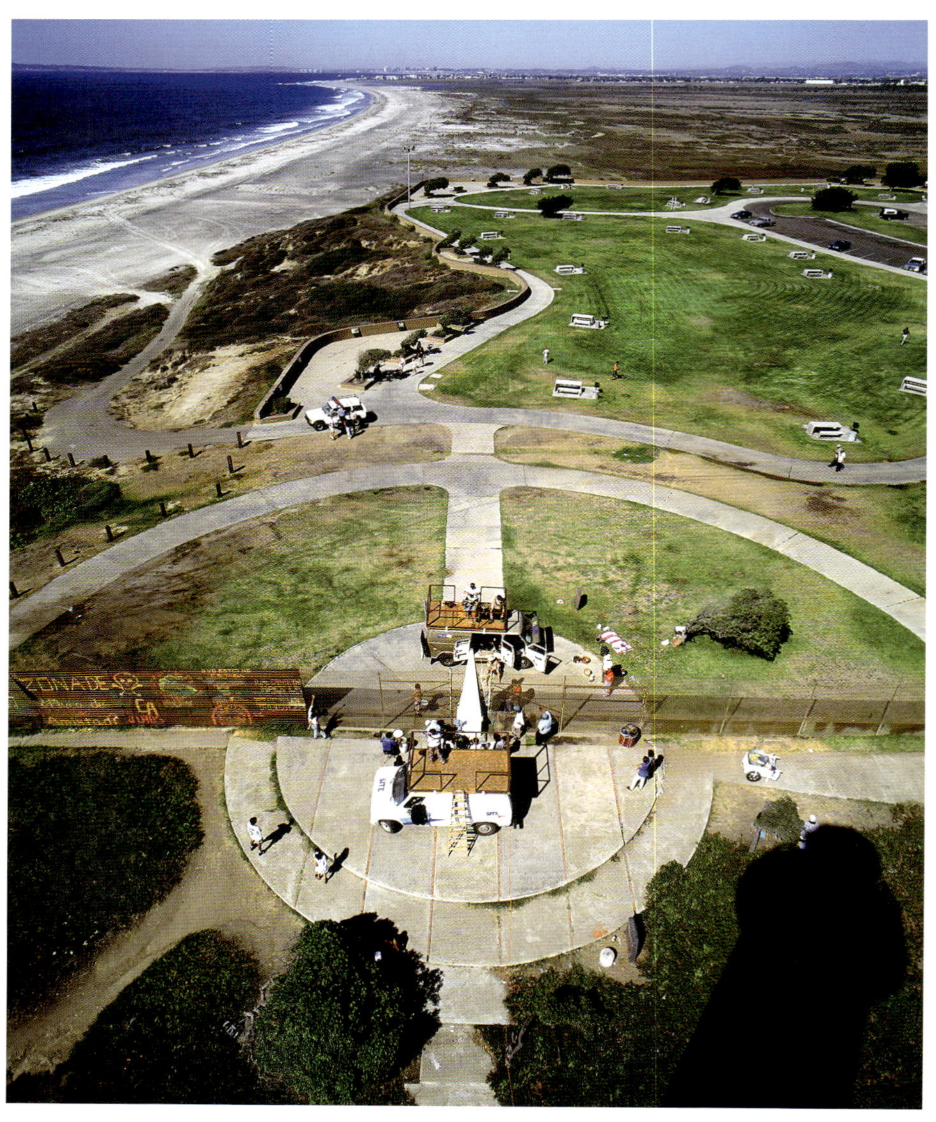

6   Terry Allen, *Cross the Razor / Cruza la navaja*, 1994. Source: inSITE Archives, University of California, San Diego.

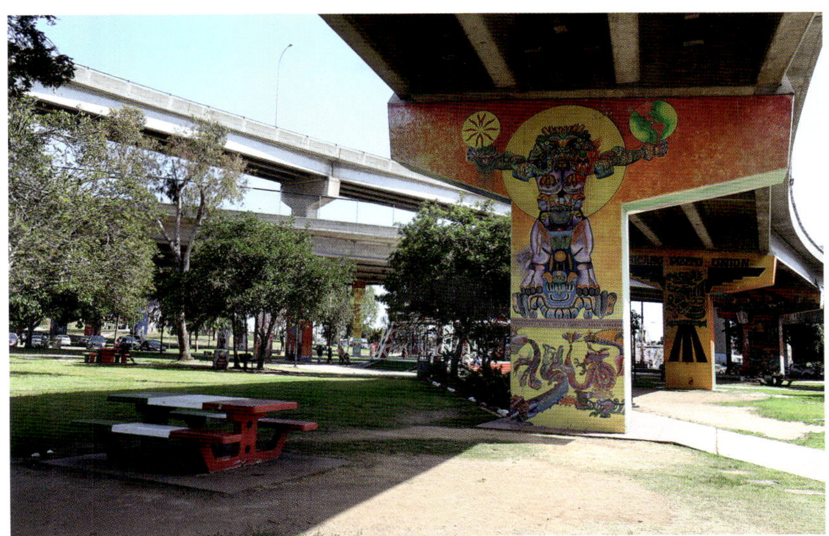

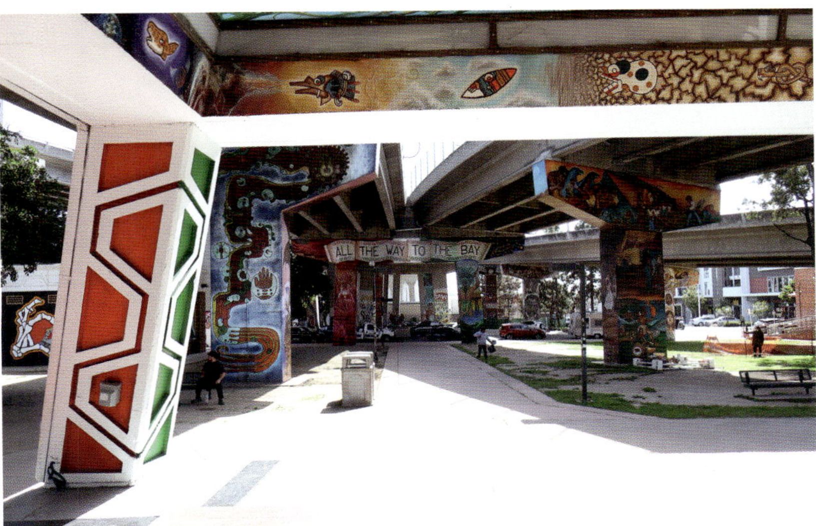

7 & 8   Chicano Park (two views), established 1970. Images by the author.

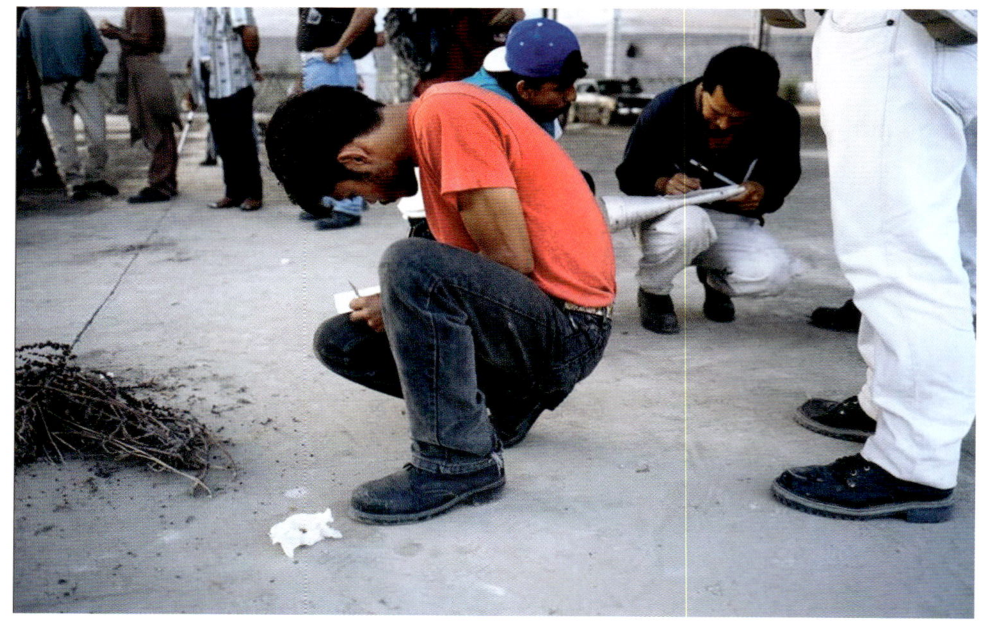

9   Allan Sekula, *Dead Letter Office*, 1997. Courtesy of Sally Stein, Sekula Studio.

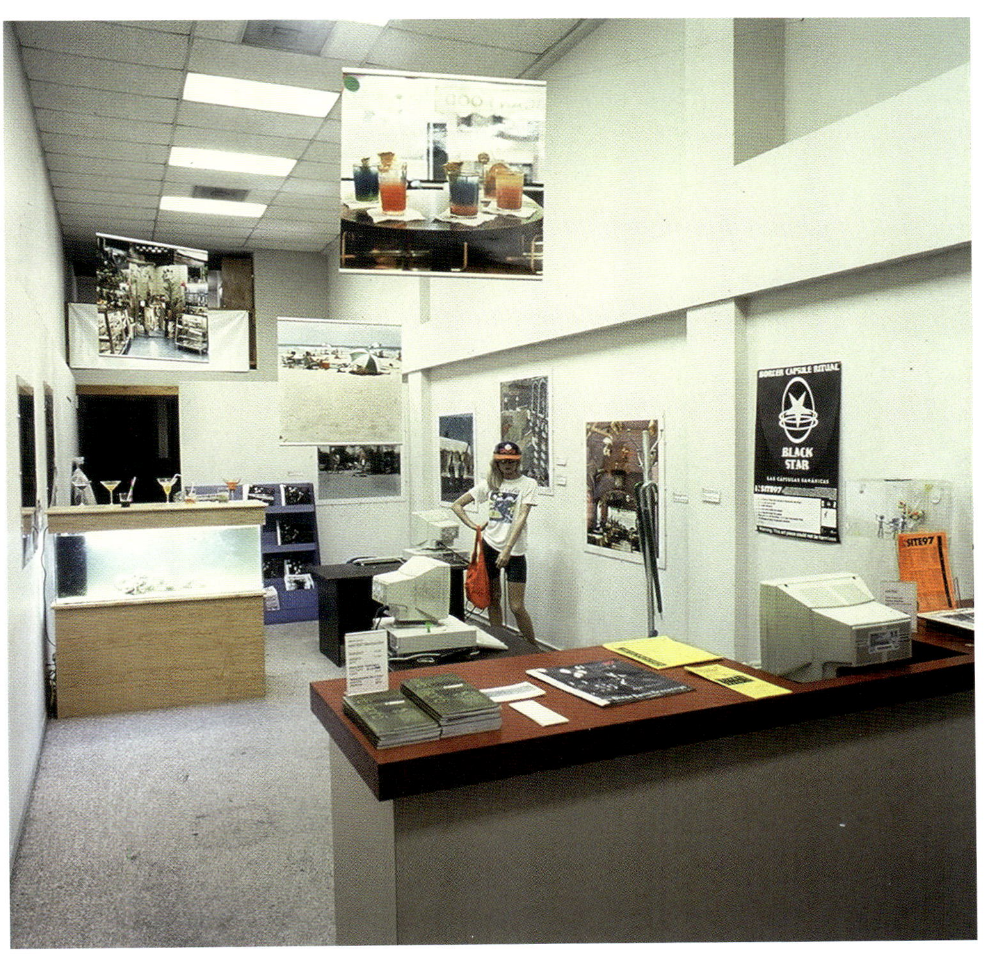

10   Melanie Smith, *The Tourists' Guide to San Diego and Tijuana / La guía turística de San Diego y Tijuana*, 1997. Source: inSITE Archives, University of California, San Diego.

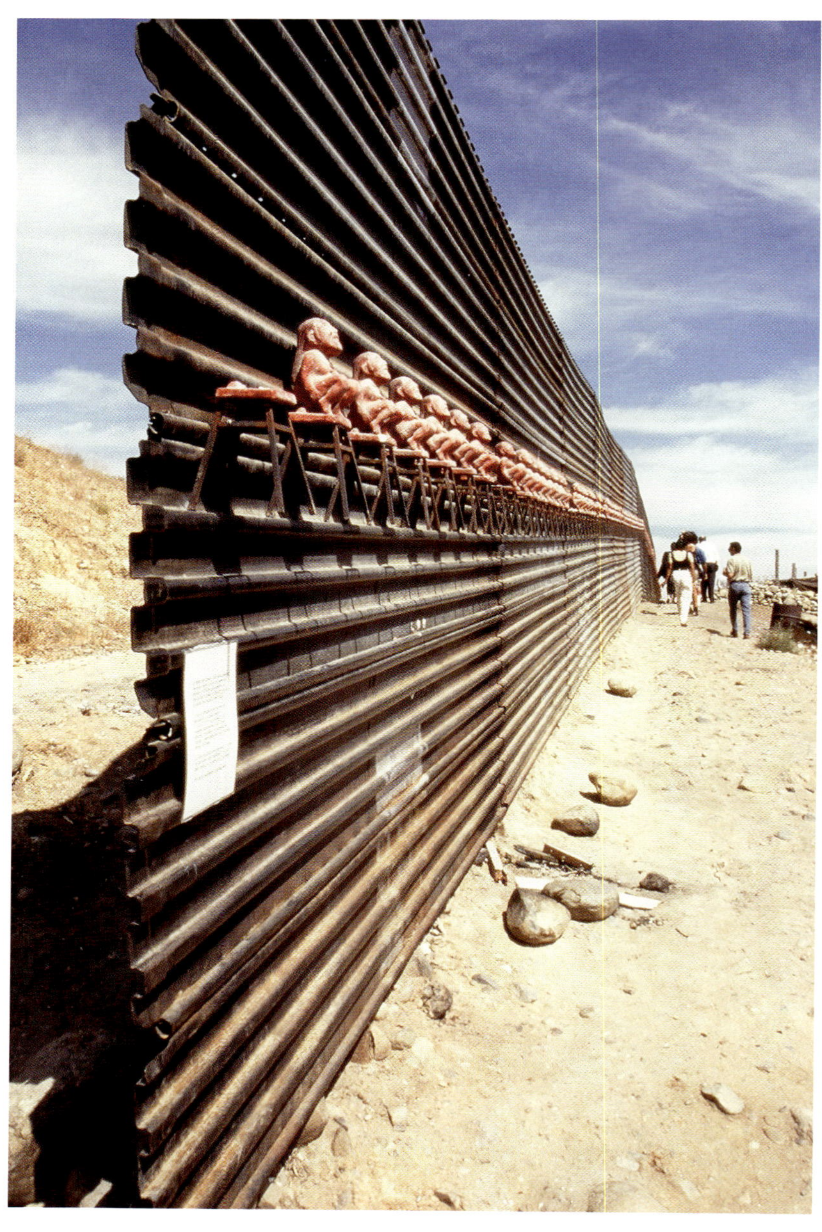

11   Silvia Gruner, *The Middle of the Road / La mitad de camino*, 1994.
Source: inSITE Archives, University of California, San Diego.

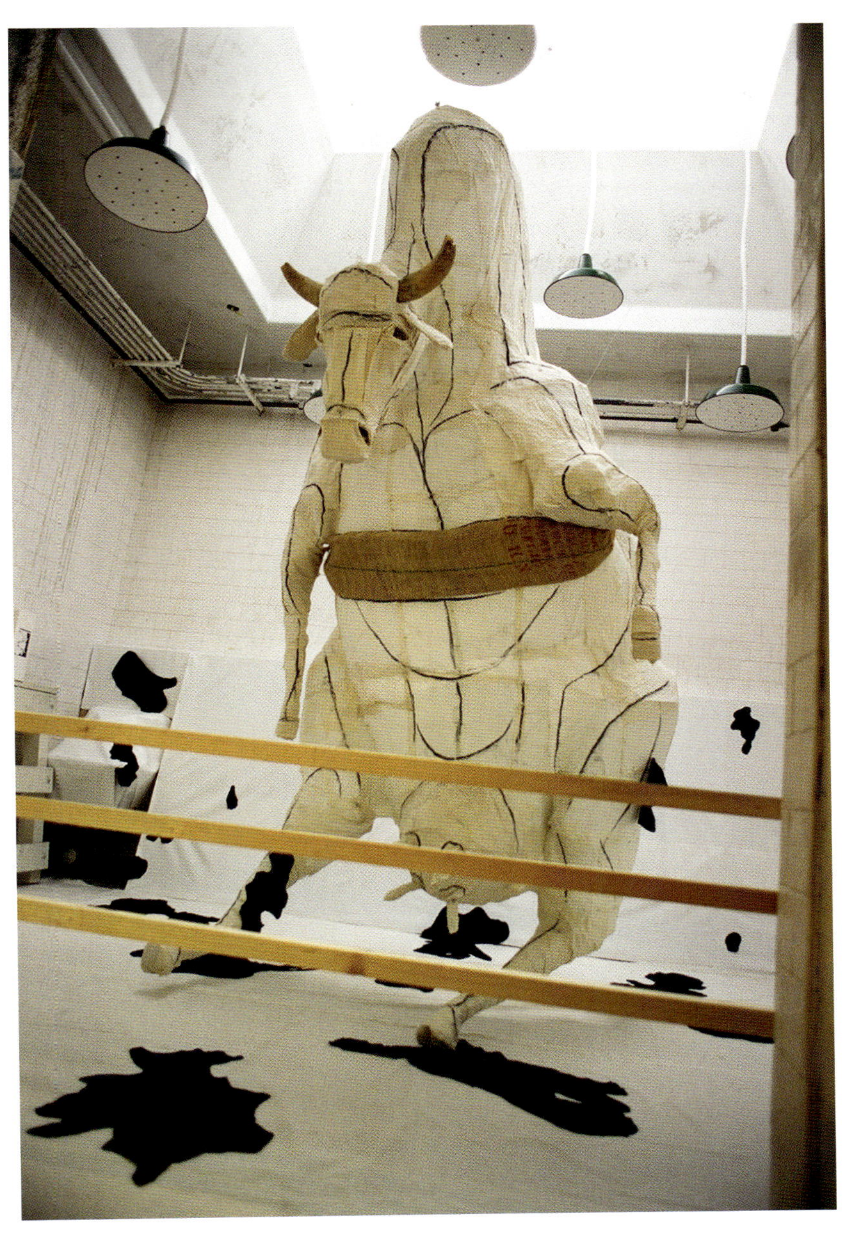

12 Helen Escobedo, *Milk at the L'Ubre Mooseum*, 1997. Source: inSITE Archives, University of California, San Diego.

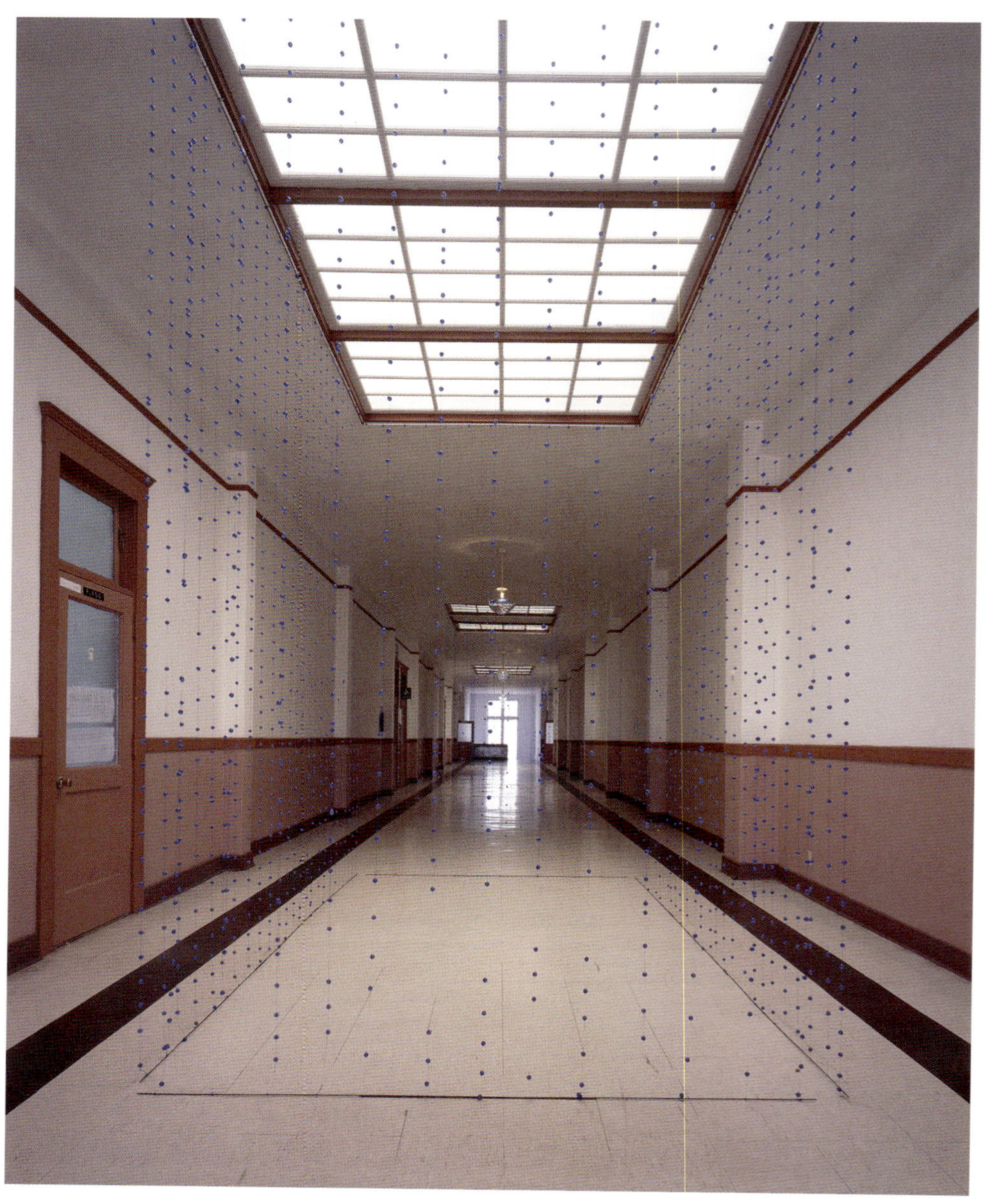

13   Sofía Táboas, *Double Take / Doble turno*, 1994. Source: inSITE Archives, University of California, San Diego.

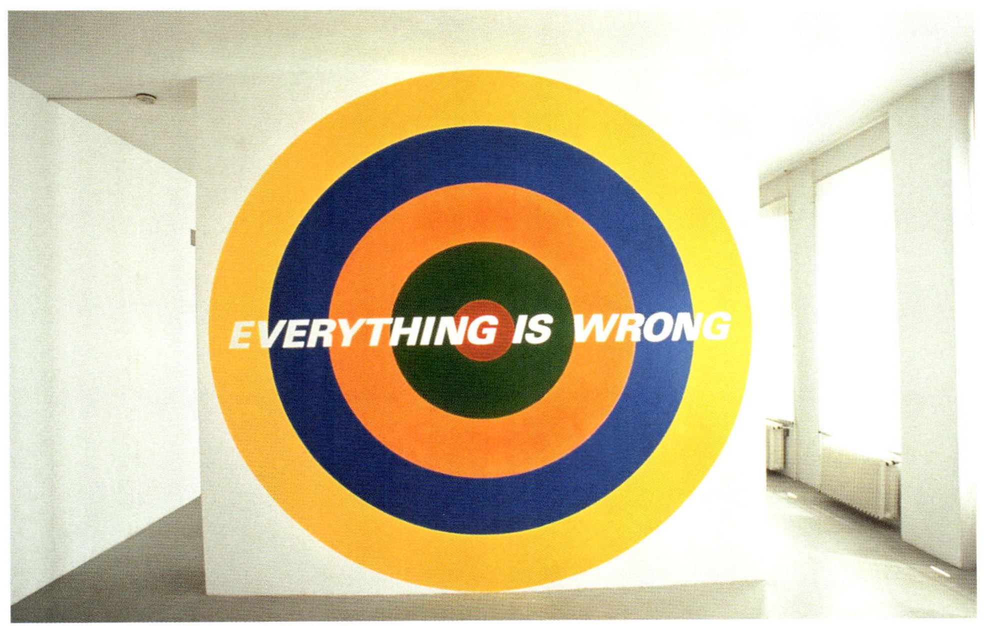

14   Henrik Plenge Jakobsen, *EVERYTHING IS WRONG*, 1996. Courtesy of the artist.

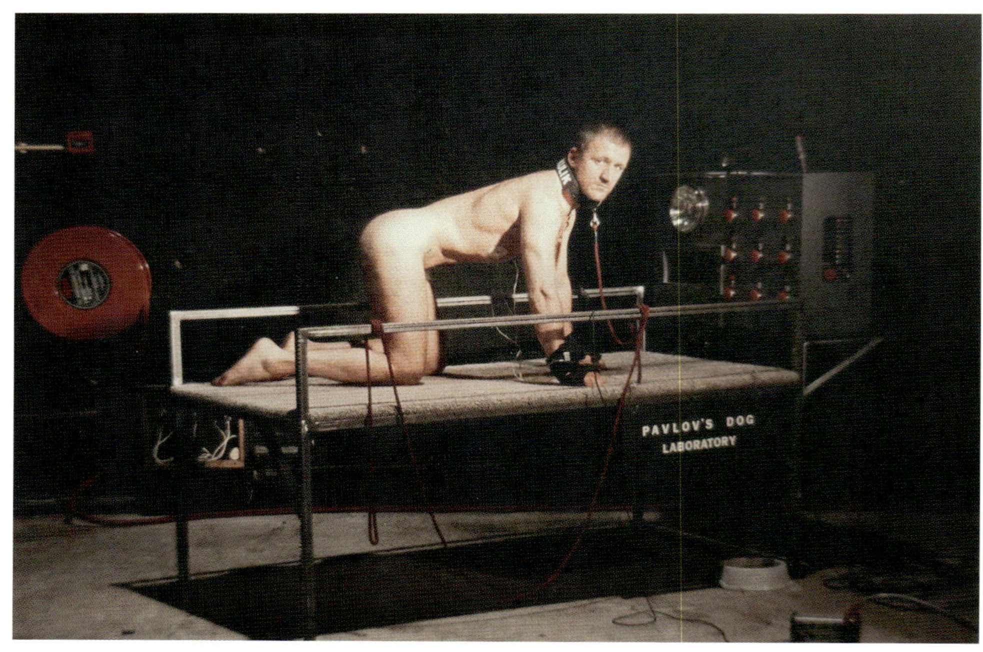

15   Oleg Kulik, *Pavlov's Dog Laboratory*, 1996. Source: Witte de With Archives,
      Rotterdam Cultural Histories (renamed Kunstinstituut Melly).

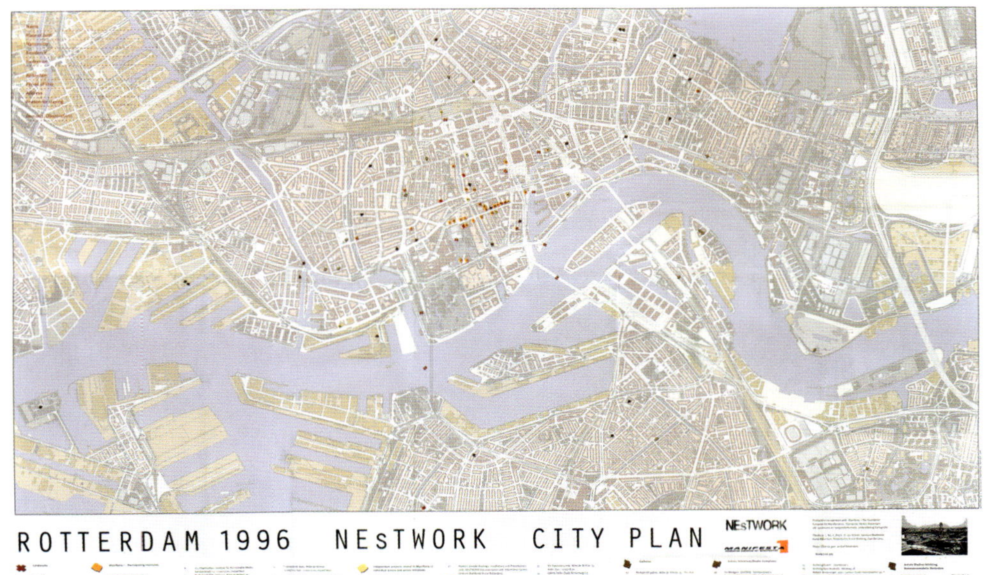

16   NEsTWORK, map of Rotterdam, 1996. Source: Witte de With Archives,
Rotterdam Cultural Histories (renamed Kunstinstituut Melly).

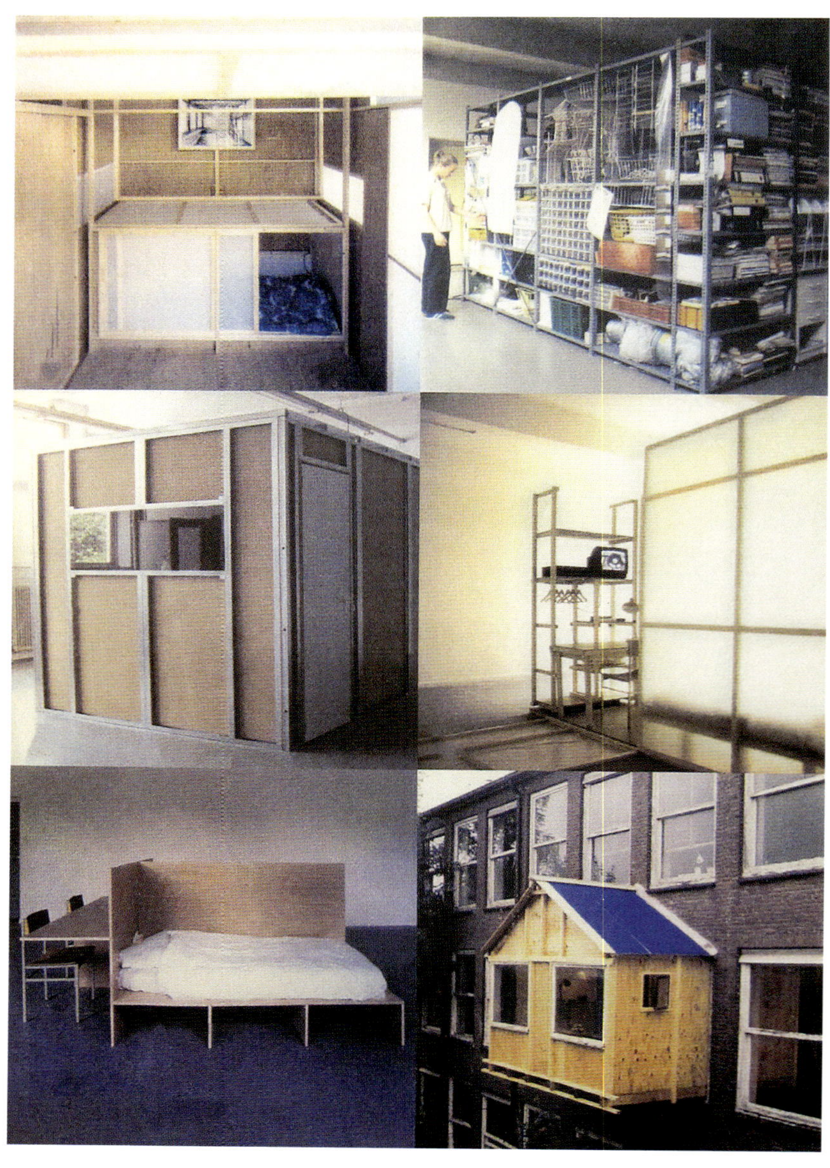

17   BAD Foundation, *My House: Your Home*. Page from booklet with dwelling designs, 1996. Source: Witte de With Archives, Rotterdam Cultural Histories (renamed Kunstinstituut Melly).

eight

Curating Conflict

Early-boom biennials across the world embraced the time's optimism for peace and political convergence. Their artist selection and artwork curation helped render the illusion of a pacified world, a widely desired outcome after the long Cold War. Through biennial conversions artistic genealogies from outside of hegemonic art worlds were adapted to the forms and values behind what would soon be called global contemporary art, a category then still in the making within the nascent global art industry. Manifesta's goal to deliver a new European art, as described in chapter 7, would entail the conversion of objects from diverse national and regional art legacies within Europe into the new umbrella category. But what, exactly, was understood as European art at that moment? Which of the many artistic legacies coexisting in Europe would act a conversion standard? The continent, marked by entrenched nationalist antagonisms, was just resurfacing from an eighty-year-long split between capitalist and socialist nations that had, in many cases, obstructed the flow of artistic programs, experts, and publics. Overcoming the impact of this Iron Curtain would ease the circulation of culture—including contemporary art—throughout Europe, signaling the end of conflict and proving the post-Maastricht integration framework as the logical consequence of a long and difficult path toward peace.

Beneath the veneer of a unified Europe existed layers of active conflict that were hard to ignore. Beginning in 1991 and extending throughout the decade, the perimetral regions of the former Soviet Union experienced frequent military confrontations, most harshly in the Balkans during the Croatian War of Independence (1991–1995), the Bosnian War (1992–1995), the Albanian War (1997), and the Kosovo War (1998–1999), but also in the Georgian Civil War (1991–1993) and the first Chechen War (1994–1996). German reunification began in 1990 as a process of incorporation of the territory formerly known as the German Democratic Republic into the Federal Republic of Germany, initiating a slow and difficult transition from socialism to capitalism that was as cultural and identitarian as much as economic. Central and Eastern European nations formerly under the USSR's influence embarked in difficult transformations from state socialism, in its many forms, to liberal democracy. The period's geopolitical reordering unveiled grave social and economic inequalities between East and West, and were responsible, to some extent, for the reawakening of nationalist struggles throughout Europe.

As this chapter explores, these tensions were well exemplified within and around Manifesta by the incorporation of art practices from Central and Eastern Europe into the art biennial. Yet conflict also shaped the very nature of curatorial work, which came to be idealized as an aspirational goal by a large faction of art workers at the time, partly thanks to the glamour associated in the 1990s with the new and exciting art biennial form. However, this idealization occluded the chief systemic tensions shaping the practice of curatorial labor, a predominantly precarious profession under neoliberalism. Evaluating the processes by which art from nations formerly under Soviet influence became integrated in the category of new European art helps illustrate how curators and artists made sense of the period's inclination to confer to culture the power to prefigure what for some was the logical unfolding of European history.

Curating Manifesta 1

Soon after its creation, the European Art Manifestation (EAM) appointed a group of five curators from diverse origins to Manifesta 1: Rosa Martínez (Spain), Katalin Néray (Hungary), Andrew Renton (UK), Viktor Misiano

(Russia), and Hans Ulrich Obrist (Switzerland). Coherent with EAM's main goal of celebrating European contemporary art, these five curators, by then rising stars of the continent's art scenes, would select and commission artworks from the region's diverse approaches to art-making into Manifesta 1's ten venues in Rotterdam. The curators signed their contracts with EAM in August 1995. From then until the opening date on June 9, 1996, they would work as a team to "deliver a concept and structure for the European Art Manifestation" and "realize the exhibitions."[1] Traveling throughout Europe's many art scenes, Manifesta 1 curators scoped out the multiplicity of contemporary art tendencies active in these regions, primarily seeking to connect with young artists. In order to render the ideals driving European unification relatable to art audiences, the curators embraced an exhibition paradigm that posited the gallery as a neutral middle ground for the encounter of diverse artistic genealogies.

Publicity materials produced for Manifesta's inauguration help clarify how the curators perceived their role. In a promotional video, they described Manifesta as an "attempt [at] a definition of what could be Europe today," a "laboratory where artists can meet, can interchange information, can get in connection with each other," and a platform from which they could "widen [their] research, [their] understanding... about European artists working in the Eastern countries."[2] Overcoming this East versus West split was a key goal for EAM organizers that mirrored the EU's ambitions to expand eastward and increase its influence in the former socialist republics. Curators' contracts listed as their main responsibilities "the selection of artists, the practical implementation of exhibitions in the specific spaces, the mental and artistic assistance to selected artists, and the assistance to the process of the implementation of the exhibition in Rotterdam institutions." Further, each of them was commissioned to write one catalog essay and participate in research trips around Europe during the fall of 1995.[3] During these travels they visited studios and met with local artists, curators, and critics. Néray, originally from Hungary, was assigned to visit Sweden, Croatia, Slovenia, the Czech Republic, Poland, England, Russia, Austria, and Turkey. Renton, from the United Kingdom, was assigned to Sweden, the Czech Republic, Estonia, Latvia, Russia, Slovenia, Belgium, the Netherlands, Portugal, Austria, and Turkey. Misiano, located in Russia, would go to Belgium, Italy, the Netherlands, Portugal, and Turkey. Based in Spain, Martínez had an itinerary that would include Sweden, Slovenia, Greece, Portugal, Turkey, Germany, Belgium, the Netherlands, France, and the United Kingdom. Obrist, who lived in France at the time, would visit Germany, Austria, Iceland, and Turkey. In exchange for these services, each curator received a fixed honorarium of 25,000 guilders (the equivalent of US $16,120 in 1995), plus a travel honorarium of 7,500 guilders ($4,836).

Research trips were a crucial component of the biennial conversions behind the production of "European art" in place for Manifesta 1. A fax from September 1995 provides insight into how these trips were arranged. It details EAM's plans to organize a tour in Eastern Europe for curator Hans Ulrich Obrist during the second week of October. During this trip, which would include visits to Moldova, Romania, Bulgaria, and Macedonia, Obrist would "be 'protected' and 'guided' by a special curator affiliated with the local Soros Center for Contemporary Arts [SCCA]."[4] This is just one example of how EAM organizers worked to enlist local art worlds in former socialist nations by working with local branches of transnational organizations, such as the Soros Foundation, an institutional partnership that I discuss in chapter 7. In these instances, local interpreters tuned to New York City–influenced approaches to contemporary art through the SCCA network would accompany Obrist in his research trip. This mediator would perform a crucial role: they would facilitate the linguistic and aesthetic translations that Obrist's foreignness might require while simultaneously grounding Manifesta's continental ambitions in the situated knowledge of local actors. These on-the-ground negotiations between worldviews were the foundations of Manifesta's operation. Although archival materials insinuate that this trip ultimately might not have taken place, the plan shines light on the scope of EAM's mapping aims and the favored approaches.

In addition to these research trips the curators also held a series of four open-house meetings to publicize Manifesta. Host venues included MUHKA Antwerp (Belgium), Kunstraum Vienna (Austria), the Gulbenkian in Lisbon (Portugal), and the South Bank Centre in London (United Kingdom). Their process might at first glance resemble other curatorial models described in this book—such as the research trips of the Bienal de La Habana specialists—where curators traced the extent of a regional interest network to survey the state of artistic production and forge relationships with regional art scenes. These research strategies helped the Manifesta curators present themselves (and the biennial) as a malleable body capable of mediating a multiplicity of artists, critics, and curators from all across and around the EU, mutually addressing one another as Europeans with commonalities that superseded local differences.

Curatorial Autonomy

Despite Manifesta's idealized vision of a team-based collaborative curatorial body, broader transformations were taking place in the cultural industries at the time that conditioned the work of biennial curators. The mid- to late 1990s saw the consolidation of the figure of the independent curator—as opposed to a museum-bound curator—who now worked by commission on a project basis. Positioned as an entrepreneurial free agent, the independent curator would rotate among art institutions, geographic regions, and object collections. In addition, independent curators would often be expected to mediate between locally situated and globally oriented publics. But independent curatorial practice was not new. Since the 1960s, independent curators had been increasingly visible in North Atlantic art worlds. Within art biennials the figure was most singularly exemplified in the figure of Harald Szeeman, an "exhibition maker," in his own words, and curator, among others, of canonical shows such as *When Attitudes Become Form* (1969) and documenta 5 (1972). By the end of the century, however, the figure of the independent curator had become more pervasive than ever. It embodied the general cosmopolitan optimism of a world no longer split by the Iron Curtain, and it personified the ideals of global mobility, in-demand production, and individual competition that underlie neoliberal ideology. In keeping with efforts to liberalize the movement of finance and goods across geopolitical borders, curatorial expertise was increasingly perceived as untethered from geographically and often nationally fixed cultural institutions. These broader shifts in the occupational conditions of curatorial expertise affected the work of early-boom biennial curators, including those working in Manifesta. Their practices were increasingly shaped by the tensions between organizers' collaborative aspirations and the highly individualistic models of curatorial expertise that were gaining traction in the global contemporary art world.

As the figure of the biennial curator became increasingly entrepreneurial, it also came to be widely perceived as desirable and glamorous, a sort of end-of-the-century high-art jet-setter. The job of the independent curator was even posited as a model of emancipated, self-directed labor in the popular imagination of the time because of the widespread misperception of these workers as owners and administrators of their time and labor. According to this popular view, freelance curatorial work embodied an ideal form of labor that was freed from the standardized workday, that was not bound to particular places, and that upheld creativity (and, later, innovation) as paramount qualities. As such, these professionals came to signify for many the promise of an eventual liberation from the perceived restrictive labor paradigms at place in the highly bureaucratized cultural institutions of modern nation states. Yet the aspirational aura that surrounded (and still does) the independent biennial curator occluded the conditions in which artistic expert labor happens for most—a delusion that mirrored other forms of acute inequality in neoliberalism. As the Italian *autonomista* tradition has explained, immaterial creative labor happens within pervasive conditions of precarity and subsumption to capital—that is, the tendency to incorporate everything into capital, including social relations, one's identity, subjectivity, and affects, as well as other aspects of life that had previously remained partially shielded from capital accumulation.[5] Immaterial postindustrial work produced not just the informational, thematic content of a commodity, it also contributed to creating an aura of cultural distinction around it.[6] Independent curators at the end of the twentieth century were expected to act as authors, arranging objects in unique and creative ways and providing skillful interpretations for these new combinations; their names and reputations also became subject to commodification, circulating in markets for immaterial labor.[7]

Despite its glamorous gloss, freelance curatorial labor was in fact at the time more precarious than stable curatorial positions at art institutions. This structural instability pushed workers to act more competitively in the labor market, permanently "hustling" for new jobs by renewing the services they could offer, staying up to date with new contemporary art trends, and distinguishing their profiles by identifying themselves with innovative artists. Compelled to leverage their social, cultural, and symbolic capital and increase their visibility to secure project-based work in competitive global markets, biennial curators had little choice but to engage in individualistic and frequently divisive processes that often clashed with the collaborative approaches favored by cultural institutions—as was the case with Manifesta. The conflation of a curator's name, personality, and skills as part of their personal "brand" facilitated a public perception (and often self-perception) of biennial curators as quasi-celebrities and stars, not unlike the artists they curated. These changing conditions for curatorial work under neoliberalism anticipated the acute precarity and geographical mobility that has been normative in cultural labor since the turn of the century and that has greatly expanded from the niche space of curatorial practice into other professional profiles in the networks of art production and circulation, such as those of the artist, the art administrator, the art critic, and the art historian.

The growing influence of freelance curatorial labor in this period often hindered Manifesta's goals for a dynamic and open research model based on curatorial collaboration and group cohesion. Although Manifesta 1 curators sometimes traveled together to host open houses and explore different local art scenes, the five individuals had differing interests and work ethics. They followed their own authorial agendas and cultivated their own growing reputations within the global art world. These individualized perspectives and ambitions were often at odds with those of Manifesta's organizers. On January 28, 1996, less than six months before the projected opening date, a member of the EAM organizing team sent a fax to the five curators, reminding them that "I truly dislike a position as your nanny and running a class-room. You are all independent curators being paid (a very serious amount of) money to make this exhibition and therefore you should act and work accordingly as professionals."[8] This administrator's frustration in this and other communications reflects a significant discrepancy between the organization's original plans for curatorial collaboration and a practiced reality that lacked synchronicity and cohesion. The participating artists were no strangers to these tensions and were sometimes caught between the organization's promises and what curators could individually deliver.[9]

This time of transition out of the Cold War was also a time for the systemic reconfiguration of relations of production worldwide, including those surrounding the production of art. In addition to producing idealized representations of regional stability, early-boom art biennials tended to gloss over the conflicts and inequities shaping immaterial labor under neoliberalism, romanticizing the increasingly precarious labor practices that sustained a growing global art industry. In Manifesta, conflicting authorial voices within the curatorial body did not come together in coordinated polyphony, as originally intended. Unlike the Bienal de La Habana's cooperative model, contextual relations of production that favored individualism and competitiveness jeopardized the formation of a cohesive curatorial choral consciousness. Manifesta 1 delivered instead a discordant artwork selection throughout the ten Rotterdam venues. But superseding Cold War antagonisms would not remain purely a labor question. This desire for convergence also translated into the symbolic realm in the form of earthshaking clashes between discordant artistic legacies within the biennial—tensions reconciled by gathering parallel artistic genealogies under the category "new European art," a regional stepping-stone into the umbrella category of "global contemporary art" just a few years later.

Curating the East

Manifesta's vision of a new unified Europe prompted biennial conversions between art genealogies, with particular emphasis on the incorporation of art from Eastern and Central Europe into the biennial as examples, too, of the "new European art."[10] Reaching beyond the former Iron Curtain divide was, in principle, an honorable goal, coherent with the Treaty of Maastricht's spirit of unification and conciliation—an invitation to join in greater union, in spite of past enmities, and for the sake of the common good. Yet the displacements required for this inclusion were greatly biased: they came at the cost of converting the original intentions, meanings, and values of Eastern and Central European artworks to artistic conventions set by Western European art-world institutions. Underlying these tacit expectations of conversion was the belief that liberal democracy, as practiced within the European Union, was the ideal culmination for the many political changes experienced in the region. This presumed universalism of Western European aesthetic frameworks and political norms, dominant in the North Atlantic–centric global art institution of the time, yielded a tacit imperative to "catch up" to its standards, in the words of Bojana Pejić, reproducing past instances of aesthetic conversion during political transitions in Europe.[11]

Manifesta joined a growing number of exhibitions of art from East and Central Europe that took place in Western Europe and the United States after the fall of the Berlin Wall in 1989. Art historian Claire Bishop has characterized this trend as one initially marked by the sense of discovery, nostalgia, and exoticism that propelled Western curators, in a sort of curatorial "safari," into regions of former Soviet influence in the early 1990s.[12] This interest gained urgency later in the decade because of the concerns about wars in the region and the resulting beliefs in the art exhibition as a symbolic pacifier. As art historian Mária Hlavajová has documented, efforts to "normalize" historical tensions between East and West were frequent in European art institutions between 1989 and 1999.[13] By the time that Manifesta 1 opened in Rotterdam in 1996, this sense of discovery and exoticism had materialized in exhibitions such as *Expressiv: Mitteleuropäische Kunst seit 1960* (Expressive: Central European art since 1960, artists from Central and Eastern Europe [Museum Moderner Kunst, Vienna, 1987]), *Der Riss im Raum* (The fissure in the room [Martin Gropious Bau, Berlin, 1994]), *Europa, Europa. Das Jahrhundert der Avantgarde in Mittel-und Osteuropa* (Europe, Europe: A century of the avant-garde in Central and Eastern Europe [Kunst- und Ausstellungshalle der Bundesrepublik Deutschland, Bonn, 1994]), *Artists of Central and Eastern Europe* (Mattress Factory [Pittsburgh, 1995]), and *Beyond Belief: Contemporary Art from East Central Europe* (Museum of Contemporary Art [Chicago, 1995]). These shows in North Atlantic art capitals were followed by many others, including a large number set in former socialist nations.[14] For art historian Piotr Piotrowski, this fever generated in artists from Central and Eastern Europe a feeling of being subject to public supervision in spaces regulated by Western European aesthetic and ethical norms, a tacit submission that reinforced hegemonic beliefs in the alleged universalism and impartiality of aesthetic judgments made in Western Europe.[15]

The nature of the projects by Eastern and Central European artists in Manifesta 1 varied greatly. Russian Dmitri Gutov proposed an artist-guided tour of the permanent exhibition of the local Museum Boijmans Van Beuningen in Rotterdam. In the same location, Russian Vadim Fishkin performed *Lighthouse*, during which a sensor on his chest synced the rhythm of his heartbeat with the light on the museum's tower. The Romanian collective subREAL brought to Manifesta *Datacorridor (How to Change Your Wallpaper Daily)*, a version of its project from the *Art History Archive* series discussed in chapter 7. Slovenian Tadej Pogačar participated in Manifesta 1 with an iteration of his *P.A.R.A.S.I.T.E. Museum of Contemporary Art*, an institutional critique project inspired by Marcel Broodthaers's portable museums in response to the art institutional vacuum of the post-communist Balkans. The *Museum*, established in 1990, often intervened in local art scenes to unveil institutionally naturalized processes of meaning making. For Manifesta, Pogačar curated an exhibition that combined his own images with artifacts from the city's natural and art history museums, interceding in their display with the editing and authoring of wall texts and captions. In a sort of forensic twist, he added to the array hair samples from the members of the biennial's curatorial team, which he had subjected to DNA tracing.[16] Ukrainians Yuri Leiderman, Arsen Savadov, and Georgy Sencheko were also included in the biennial.

Anxieties surrounding the aesthetic conversions between Eastern European and North Atlantic frameworks permeated through the different layers of the biennial, involving its curators as much as its artists. Exemplary in this regard was *Transnacionala: A Journey from the East to the West* (1996), a project orchestrated by Ljubljana-based artist collective IRWIN, in collaboration with Alexander Brener, Vadim Fishkin, Yuri Leiderman, Goran Đorđević, Michael Benson, and Eda Čufer. Departing from an exhibition of IRWIN's work in the Atlanta Arts Festival, the group toured the United States over the summer of 1996 in two RVs to engage in conversations with art and non-art actors about several topics, including lofty themes in theory, politics, and ontology, and more apparently pedestrian ones such as Americans' perceptions of Eastern Europeans.[17] Throughout the different tour stages they participated in events with local art communities organized by hosts Mary Jane Jacob, Catherine Gates, Randy Alexander, Charles Kraft, Robin Held, and Larry Reed. In Manifesta, *Transnacionala* was shown via a metal cart on wheels with four chairs and a monitor screening updates from the group's transcontinental tour.

Manifesta curator Viktor Misiano characterized *Transnacionala* as one of many projects that helped nourish relations of camaraderie, recognition, and reciprocity among artists in the early post-Soviet period. The mobile project was a good example of what Misiano had qualified as a model for the institutionalization of friendship: meetings of friends that allowed groups of artists with foundational disagreements to forge horizontal relations of mutual recognition.[18] Interpersonal trust fueled these ad hoc para-institutions that originated in artists living and working together in Moscow apartments. As Izabel Galliera argues, this model was highly influential at the time in Moscow and other art scenes in former Soviet republics, providing artists with important self-instituting models.[19]

But not all were smooth van rides. If *Transnacionala* was a sort of poster child, liked by audiences, of what Misiano had described as the institutionalization of friendship, other artists from this circle faced important public backlash. Misiano's participation in Manifesta was preceded by a notable art-world scandal. On February 2, 1996, the exhibition *Interpol—A*

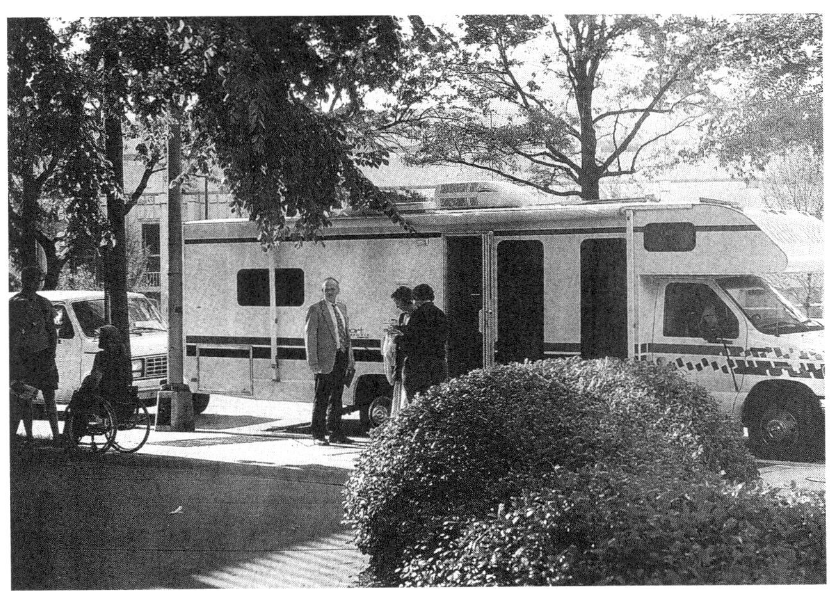

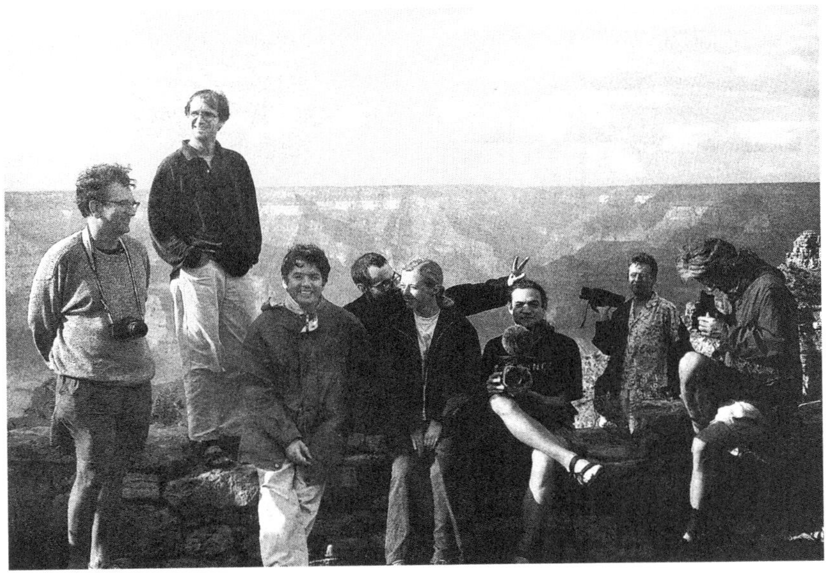

8.1 Participants in IRWIN's *Transnacionala: A Journey from the East to the West*, 1996 at its start in Atlanta, Georgia (*top*), and in Arizona at the Grand Canyon (*bottom, from left to right*): Dušan Mandič, Andrej Savski, Miran Mohar, Yuri Leiderman, Eda Čufer, Michael Benson, Roman Uranjek, Borut Vogelnik (not present are Aleksander Brener and Vadim Fishkin). Both images courtesy of the artists.

Global Network from Stockholm and Moscow, which Misiano co-curated with Swedish curator Jan Aman, opened in Stockholm's Färgfabriken Center for Contemporary Art. Conceived in November 1993, this exhibition rounded out two years of dialogues between the curators and artists from Western, Central, and Eastern Europe. The exhibition included diverse approaches to art making that would need to develop specific tactics in order to coexist in the gallery. The projects had a "quality of totality," by which the curators meant that, ideally, artworks would aspire to address the whole gallery instead of limiting their intervention to a fraction of the space.

As Manifesta would do months later, in the words of Misiano, "the staging of *Interpol* had become a metaphor for the establishment of a New Europe."[20] One of the artworks was by Kiev-born, Moscow-based Oleg Kulik, already scheduled to be featured in Manifesta 1 in Rotterdam the following summer. For *Interpol*, Kulik performed his dog-man persona under the title *Dog House: Nude.* Chained to a kennel, Kulik crawled around sniffing and licking objects in the gallery. Kulik-the-dog reacted violently to a curious audience member who pet him despite the many signs warning against it. The artist-dog jumped at the man and bit his leg repeatedly; then he refused to let go. In reaction, Aman called the police, who arrived at Färgfabriken to handcuff and arrest the artist. On that same opening evening, Russian artist Alexander Brener destroyed an installation by Chinese-American artist Wenda Gu as part of a longer "rock-star" performance that began with one-and-a-half hours of drumming and spewing guttural sounds. Following the incident, French art critic Olivier Zahm wrote a letter that was subsequently signed by Aman and others present that night and circulated widely throughout art institutions, art publications, and art professionals across Europe and the US. The document denounced Kulik and Brener, as well as Misiano, seeking to publicly expose "the consequences of collaboration with these people," among which was a revelation that Misiano's curatorial practice had, "in fact, nothing to do with art theory, but with hooliganism and skinhead ideology." The letter implied that the actions of these three individuals signaled an inherent faulty Russian quality and accused Misiano, Kulik, and Brener of wanting to destroy the art world, arguing that they posed a threat to conviviality because "Misiano [was] using theory to legitimize a new form of totalitarian ideology." Articulating the limits of tolerance for these Western European and US art actors, Zahm addressed Manifesta 1 curators Obrist, Renton, Martínez, and Néray and warned them against working with Kulik and Misiano in the Rotterdam biennial the following summer. These individuals were "a direct attack against art, democracy and the freedom of expression," he said.[21]

Yet despite the outcry, Misiano remained a part of Manifesta's curatorial team, and Kulik stayed on as part of the artist selection. Brener, not featured in the biennial, was present at the opening remarks, during which he stood up and yelled at a member of Manifesta's board while inciting others to follow. Despite the Stockholm incident, Kulik again performed a version of his dog-man piece in Rotterdam, now titled *Pavlov's Dog's Laboratory* (see plate 15). This time, however, there would be no incidents with the audience. A film produced by the local art initiative NEsTWORK and conducted by British Curatorial Assistant Jason Coburn documents a nude Kulik wearing a black leather collar and being walked around Rotterdam on all fours by his collaborator, Mila Bredikhina. The video also shows Coburn addressing Kulik in his room-sized cage inside the V2_: Institute for the Unstable Media (one of Manifesta's venues): his head and body shaved, Kulik is on his legs and arms on a platform, connected to a bracelet with sensors. The artist is taking a laboratory test. Bredikhina explains to Coburn that "the aim of the test is to check how long Kulik is able to hold on to this device. The aim of this test [is] to compare his results with the results of real dogs in these experiments."[22] The experiment, recalls art critic Daniel Birnbaum, "comprised a mechanism capable of turning humans into animals through the systematic application of pain."[23] While Bredikhina talks to the camera, Kulik crawls down the platform and approaches the lens, jumping and barking to attract the attention of his collaborator, who soothingly caresses his head. Kulik then leaves and returns to the platform, from where he climbs up on to a big rolling cylinder. Like a hamster, he stays on top for some minutes, arms and legs moving in synchrony to stay on top. Sensors send data back to the computer. In addition to Coburn, the spectators include a middle-aged couple and a man in his thirties with two young girls. They pat Kulik's head, then smell their hands and frown with disgust. By caressing Kulik-the-dog through the iron bars, the girls forced an uncanny throwback to Winston Churchill's 1946 imagined "iron curtain [running] from Stettin in the Baltic to Trieste in the Adriatic," dividing East and West.

The artist was tamed. Most reviews of Manifesta highlighted Kulik's piece as one of the best in the show. Whereas it is reasonable to expect art critics' curiosity about Kulik's practice not long after the Stockholm incident, it is important to scrutinize *Pavlov's Dog's Laboratory* on its own terms. The performer's capacity to endure the physical and behavioral challenge of impersonating a dog for several days is clear in the reportage on the piece. In it, for example, we see Kulik tirelessly chasing a ball in the park, back and forth, again and again, and going on walks through Rotterdam on his knees and hands, leashed and nude. This piece was an instance of "Zoophrenia," Kulik and Bredikhina's long-term artistic program that explored the subject of "the animal as the alter-ego of man." To the artist, in a context marked by the "specter of a global ecological disaster," Zoophrenia sought to integrate human and animal in one entity, opposing "human predisposition to superfluous thinking" and favoring "the irrational" as the only realm that could act as "source of something extraordinary, a new source of hope, . . . uniting people and animals in coalition for a better noosphere." This framework invited audiences to question the hierarchical valuation of humans over animals—prompting analogies between East and West. Aiming to transcend anthropocentric paradigms, Kulik and Bredikhina went on to state that "democracy, as it exists in the human world, is no worse than life in a jungle. Some inhabitants have an advantage, some are stronger, faster. . . . The problem of successful communication remains unsolved within the species of man. It is not our belief in fruitful communication that gives hope for the future to come, it is the confidence that universal collaboration is possible."[24] Tongue out, drooling with anticipation of an eventual treat—a metaphor for the artist's subjection to the unspoken norms of the contemporary art institution and the episodic rewards it may concede. Reenacting the master-slave bond with a clear BDSM inflection, disciplining and punishing the artist's body, dominating and turning it into the norms of the North Atlantic–centric art exhibition complex, *Pavlov's Dog's Laboratory* modeled a reconciliatory paradigm that grew from the uneven coproduction of master and subject subjectivities or, if we may, of subject and object artistic genealogies.

Soviet Modernisms

Audiences for *Interpol* had missed the point, Misiano argued. They failed to understand Kulik's and Brener's work because they ignored the conditions surrounding contemporary art production in regions formerly under Soviet influence.[25] In *Interpol* and in Manifesta, Kulik's sadomasochistic play with the audience stood for larger referents: in this master-slave bond, Kulik was an icon for Eastern Europe, watched and punished by the North

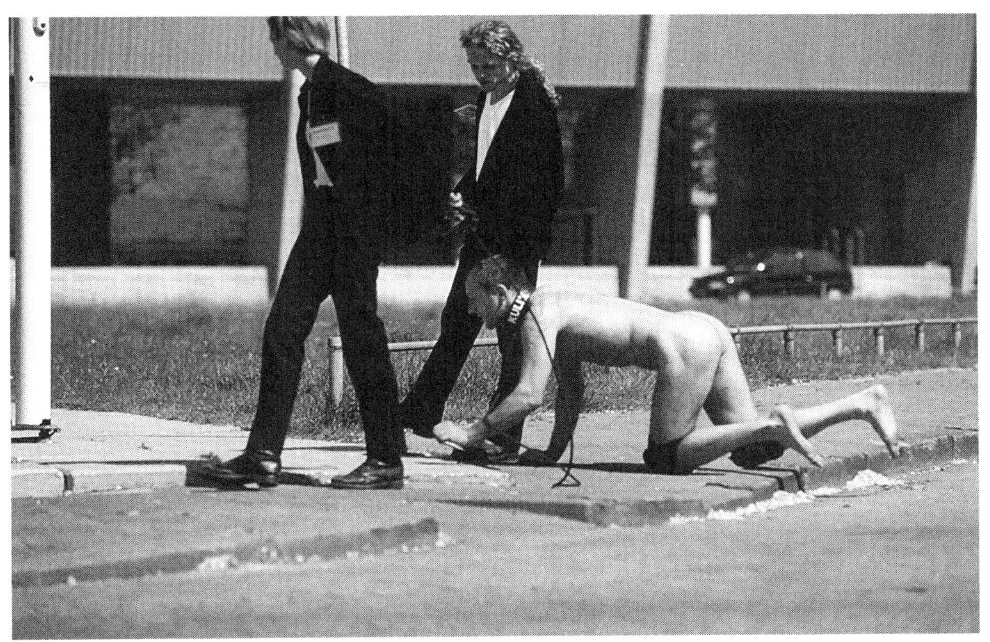

8.2   Oleg Kulik, *Pavlov's Dog Laboratory*, 1996. Source: Witte de With Archives, Rotterdam Cultural Histories (renamed Kunstinstituut Melly).

Atlantic contemporary art world. An opportunity for historical reconciliation in European elites' imaginary, the EU's eastward expansion would happen under the political and aesthetic conditions set by Western member nations. In the letter, Zahm's words reproduced entrenched Orientalist stereotypes of Eastern European backwardness and passion-driven behavior.[26] The Western European art and literary canon is populated with representations of physical ownership of the Eastern European body, including sexual domination and punishment, that echo Kulik's self-portrayal as a leathered animal-human to be tamed, controlled, and policed by Western European art audiences.

Understanding the clashes that surrounded Kulik's and Brener's work requires an evaluation of the coeval artistic paradigms that clashed within Manifesta. The legacies of modern art genealogies that ran in parallel for decades within very different ideological worlds were now enticed into entering a shared, representational space—as if they could do so on equal terms. As Igor Zabel explains,

> The sharp political division between the East and the West during the cold war period also implied a confrontation of two artistic models: the modernist art in the West and Socialist Realism in the East. Western art has presented itself as the "natural" development of genuine art as opposed to the politically suppressed art of Socialist Realism and its derived forms, which was not supposed to be genuine art but simply political propaganda. In light of this understanding, Eastern artists have been understood as a kind of underdeveloped and suppressed Western artists, and it was thought that they would immediately join the general developments in the West if they would be free to do so.[27]

Art in Central and Eastern Europe developed during the twentieth century under the spell of state socialism in its different historical articulations. In Russia, during the utopian bliss that followed the 1917 Revolution, artistic production was marked first by the coexistence of a multitude of formal and thematic approaches, as well as of a diversity of embodied dispositions to artistic practice. Groups as different as the representational painters that gathered under the Association of Artists of Revolutionary Russia, and avant-garde groups rejecting mimetic imperatives in the utopian pursuit of joining art and life in mutual reform, coexisted in Moscow and other cities. Modern in their themes and finishes, the 1920s Russian Constructivist and Productivist avant-gardes engaged the Leninist mission of society-wide reform, developing formal and material solutions, as well as new notions of artistic labor, that gravitated around the paradigm of industrial work as a motor of historical change, questioning individual authorship to mirror the collaborative deliberative ideal of the *soviet* as the foundational political unit. Simultaneously, other approaches to abstract and representational art continued pre-Revolutionary avant-garde artistic investigations. The fertility of this diverse art scene was, in part, a result of Anatoly V. Lunacharsky's cultural organizational model of the Proletkult, a multidisciplinary federation of cultural workers, autonomous from the state and party, that encouraged the embeddedness of culture in political change, regardless of its stylistic, formal, and technical aspects, under the belief that art's internal dialectics would contribute to the development of artistic forms.[28]

The effervescence of this influential initial period ended with Stalin's coming to power. Autonomous artistic associations were abolished in 1932, and artistic production was reorganized around discipline-oriented unions under direct state supervision (Union of Visual Artists, Union of Writers, etc.). The early postrevolutionary margin of artistic autonomy from the state collapsed under the strict control over form and content imposed by the Stalinist bureaucracy through the policy of socialist realism. This state art doctrine promoted an idealization of life in socialism via a simultaneous recourse to canonical Western European art styles such as realism, impressionism, and neoclassicism, and folklore and popular culture motifs from throughout the USSR. This official art had as its ideal audience the state and party elite, whom it sought to interpellate alongside the masses as actors in a time idealized as the culmination of historical logic. The state's heavy hand in this operation has led art critic Boris Groys to characterize the Stalinist state as an artist employing the everyday lives of citizens as medium.[29]

Although the subordination of artistic production to political power was exported, to different degrees, to other Soviet republics after World War II, socialist realism's stylistic codification was not the norm throughout the regions of Soviet influence. Art from Western Europe and the United States permeated and, to different degrees, influenced art legacies independent from Russia's in republics such as Yugoslavia, Czechoslovakia, and Poland. For example, Yugoslavia, which had detached from Stalinist doctrine as early as 1948, provided an important counterpart to Russia's approach to state control of the arts, sponsoring a Third World internationalist orientation that, to some extent, anticipated the nonorthodox socialist aesthetics unfolding in 1980s Cuba (see chapters 1–3). This diverse framework also allowed for the flowering of rich artistic scenes, as was the case of Ljubljana, in Slovenia, from where important names in the post-Soviet Eastern European art originated, such as the art collectives IRWIN and Neue Slowenische Kunst (NKS). However, the Stalinist collapsing of everyday life within the party's symbolic order did not last forever. As Aleš Erjavec explains, opposition to socialist realism within art circles and political spheres grew progressively after the 1960s, culminating with its abolition in the Soviet republics at different points in the following decades.[30] Often atomized and relegated to anonymity, participants in these circles had been trained under a socialist realist paradigm yet were to varying degrees cognizant of artistic developments in other world regions, chiefly Western Europe and the United States. A last stage of post-socialism followed after the late 1970s, when reformers began to believe in the possibility of transforming socialism from within, a relative relaxation from its authoritarian rigors that broadened the margins of tolerance for diverse formal and thematic repertoires in art production. In the 1980s and 1990s, artists in different socialist republics embraced, to varying degrees, pre-Soviet national art legacies, which were at times combined with elements from the North Atlantic neo–avant-gardes, including conceptualism, performance, installation, and new approaches to art making, such as conversation-based and site-specific art.

This moment of post-Soviet aperture happened simultaneously with the revision of national identities and the overall transformation of the sociopolitical realm in the former socialist states. As Misiano argued, what it meant to be Central or Eastern European became, now more than ever, defined in opposition to the idea of Western Europe, which simultaneously stood as a countermodel and an invitation for transformation for artists from these regions.[31] Through their work, Kulik and Brener engaged with Russia's historical exclusion from the category of Europe, an exclusion that, in their opinion, enticed Russian artists to enact a compulsive, fictionalized quality of Russianness, yielding totalist identity performances tainted by the haunting Western art institutions. Art historian Ekaterina Degot explains this conflict as highly determinant for practices that, like Kulik's and Brener's, explored what it meant to be Russian in relationship with Western Europe, often through aggressive gestures. The violence coded in systemic expectations of aesthetic conversion positioned Central and Eastern European artists in a state of permanent state of conflict between, on one hand, their identity (which as artists was already a contested one within Soviet history) and, on the other, institutional expectations to satisfy their demi-Orientalist othering and comply with the period's dominant North Atlantic–centric expectations:

> In Russia, where twentieth-century art with its ideology of individualism and unrestrained freedom is still a foreign phenomenon of invested dreams, being a "contemporary artist" means to represent Western culture (with all its connotations), as shown by mass media

shows in order to appear "up to date," more Western-like. In the West, on the other hand, a Russian artist must inevitably represent Russia. Western curators are almost never interested in him or her personally, but in having "an artist from Russia," best of all a typical one, i.e., a representative one, particularly one representing the political reality, chaos, and disruption.[32]

Conflict? What Conflict?

Despite Manifesta's goals to present a vision of a unified European art scene, on the ground things looked a tiny bit more complex. Degot's remarks on the ways in which chaos and disruption shaped access to a nascent global art institution for many Central and Eastern artists merits a close evaluation of the different approaches toward the inclusion of human relations within artworks that clashed within the biennial. Performative practices such as Kulik's and Brener's, which relied on the pursuit and execution of conflict, coexisted in Manifesta with very different yet seemingly related approaches to art making, such as Rirkrit Tiravanija's and Maurizio Cattelan's performances, which proposed a much more amicable version of human relations.

One such framework appeared in the catalog for the exhibition *Traffic* at CAPC Musée d'Art Contemporain de Bordeaux (March 1996), where French curator Nicolas Bourriaud articulated what he termed "relational aesthetics." In a sweeping attempt to make sense of a multitude of artistic practices that, during the 1990s, escaped the object-centered paradigm predominant within twentieth-century North Atlantic modernisms, Bourriaud attempted to broaden the category of art to include "art taking as its theoretical horizon the realm of human interactions and its social context." His was an effort to question the presumption of artistic autonomy from the social, where instead "being together" moved to center stage.[33] His proposal came from a belief that in making the aesthetic an issue of human relations rather than of objects, art would get closer to being an "interstice"—a term that Bourriaud borrowed from Marx to point to practices that reject capitalism by removing themselves from trade value. Reenacting past attempts to free art from capitalist relations, his move would afford a restoration of the avant-garde's original emancipatory purposes, lost, for him, in its eventual becoming a luxury commodity under capitalism. Artists like Vanessa Beecroft, Cattelan, Pierre Huyghe, and Tiravanija became exemplary illustrations of Bourriaud's theory and permanent fixtures in the mid- to late 1990s biennial circuit. Placing them in a longer avant-garde genealogy (even as he rejected teleological models of history), Bourriaud drew on earlier instances of emancipatory playfulness, such as dada, the International Situationists, and Fluxus. For him, relational art ought to be taken as a theory of forms, not as a theory of art. Like these groups' actions, situations, and happenings, relational artworks incited open-ended relations between humans and their contexts, wherein experimental freedom replaced the prescriptions for social change of other avant-garde genealogies. In their invitations to dine, drink, dance, and date, these gallery-bound relational artworks thus prefigured smoother human relations.

This framework was used frequently in the late 1990s and early 2000s to describe artworks that, since the previous decade, set up interactions between humans within the art institution. The vagueness of Bourriaud's theory (originally formulated as an exhibition catalog essay) prompted attacks from art-world actors who saw it as an aestheticization of the art party (or *arty parties*, as these approaches to art making came to be colloquially referred to) instead of a new art paradigm. Bourriaud's loudest critic was British art historian Claire Bishop, who disagreed with what she perceived as relational aesthetics' mistaken extension of extra-artistic ethical judgments into the aesthetic realm, a move that, in her view, assaulted artistic autonomy and limited art's potential to exist in criticality with social experience. As a countermodel to relational aesthetics, Bishop's own model of aesthetic antagonism espoused discord and strife within the exhibition space. Exploitation, if rendered through forms distinguished as artistic by the institution, was worthwhile because it played the important (and, yes, uncomfortable) role of rendering visible omnipresent social antagonisms. Positing conflict as an aspect of social life that ought to be cultivated within artworks, Bishop built from political theorists Ernesto Laclau and Chantal Mouffe's thinking, particularly their understanding of context as necessarily limited and exclusionary, and their defense of the role of politics as that of affirming "the contingency and ambiguity of every 'essence' and on the constitutive character of social division and conflict."[34] Against Bourriaud's arty-party relational artworks, Bishop's antagonisms reenacted the classic avant-garde shock as disruption and confronted audiences with the violence of social life, in a sort of magnified negation. Artists like Santiago Sierra or Thomas Hirschhorn were good examples of her approach. Antagonism in relational aesthetics "create[s] a kind of ethnographic realism, in which the outcome or unfolding of [their] action[s] forms an indexical trace of the economic and social reality of the place in which [they] work."[35] Like relational artists, Hirschhorn and Sierra propose relations between artist, audience, and participants within the gallery. Unlike them, they closed the art institution to extra-artistic challenges to art's autonomy, preserving its capacity to amuse, scandalize, and move in response to change.

Kulik's and Brener's disruptive actions in *Interpol* seem at first glance closer to Bishop's model. Yet against Bourriaud's naive idealism and Bishop's magnified negativity, Russian curator Viktor Misiano's own model of the institutionalization of friendship offered a more appropriate and contemporaneous framework.[36] Although the spell of Bourriaud's relational aesthetics undoubtedly hovered over *Interpol* and Manifesta's promotion of convivial human relationships as metaphors for a unified region, it would be a mistake to include the work of Kulik and Brener, seemingly contrary to the relational models idealized in these two exhibitions, under Bishop's model of aesthetic antagonism. Doing so would mean imposing an evaluative framework heir to a North Atlantic-centric theoretical genealogies upon practices, like Kulik's and Brener's, formulated in a post-Soviet scenario—contexts shaped by very different experiences of Marxism and avant-garde theory.

Responding to the period's art-world discussions, Misiano developed his own account of artistic relationality to explain practices that emphasized human relations in the historical specificity of post-Soviet Moscow. Misiano credits his development of a model of "relational curating" to his ongoing working relationship, since 1990, with Bourriaud, as well as to an important paradigm shift in Moscow from object-centered art to the comeback of socially oriented practices. The radical art institutional vacuum of early 1990s Moscow prompted a spirit of human interaction that permeated throughout the city's art scene, as mentioned above, driving artists to explore tactics of self-institutionalization to support their lives and work: "Whereas Western artists sought to construct an internal autonomy outside of official institutions, in Russia the construction of autonomy was meant to compensate for the 'flight of institutions.'" In the absence of institutions, Moscow artists gathered in *tusovkas*, informal circles of like-minded people with shared artistic interests and language. Unlike the atomized *dolce utopias* (to borrow Cattelan's term) of relational aesthetics' arty parties that joined periodically, pacing the global art calendar, tusovkas existed as ongoing social praxis in an institutional vacuum. In the words of Misiano, "Any relational project realized in the context of the tusovka was not only a form of constructing community; it was also an analysis of its social and economic dimensions."[37] Self-determination affected life as much as work: in addition to providing long-standing scaffolding for artistic production, members of these collectives lived following self-imposed principles that eroded distinctions between art and life.

These were the origins of Kulik's and Brener's clashes with Western European art worlds. Misiano attributed to Kulik's zoo centric actions a ceremonial quality capable of bringing the confidential community of the tusovka together. He conferred Kulik a protagonist role in Moscow's contemporary art circles of the period, during which the artist performed pieces such as *Pig's Snout Makes Presents*, a 1992 action in which the artist steamed a hog and offered portions of the animal as food to those present during its slaughter. If relational artworks, such as Tiravanija's communal food-centered projects, celebrate and strengthen already existing art-world cliques, Kulik's projects were "rituals of initiation into a community of the elect—a mafia, as it were—since otherwise there would be no community."[38] Others, like Gutov and Brener, shared Kulik's use of human relations as direct interventions, simultaneously symbolic and material, in the fractured social fabric left behind by the communist regime.

Thus, the conflict surrounding Kulik's and Brener's participation in exhibitions that, like *Interpol* and Manifesta, sought to render a conciliatory image of a unified Europe is twofold. On the one hand, their work was shaped by a foundational lack of institutional framing, an absence that the artists contended with through their self-determination as exceptional communities. The second dimension of conflict in their work responded to the aesthetic conversions expected, at the time, of Central and Eastern European artists who pursued access the nascent global art institutions conceived and run after Western European norms. As Misiano explained in response to the denunciation letter following the Stockholm incident,

> It soon became apparent that the West would only recognize Russia as a great power on one condition: that she would not behave as such. So Kulik was chained up at the Färgfabriken on [the] condition that he did not bite. When he did bite, he was accused of "imperialism and directly attacking democracy." Western political

correctness presupposes that the Other may receive an equal status and count on dialogue only when it shows itself to be humble, weak, ill-starred. If it departs from the victim's role, it is immediately seen as a fundamentalist and imperialist.[39]

Accessing Conciliation

If Manifesta was to be a space of dialogue between East and West, what would the terms of access to the conversation be? Whose model of reason and dialogue would prevail? Manifesta: Placenta Europa hosted the collision of the 1990s iterations of two separate modern art genealogies: one bred under socialist formalizations of the state and its relationship to culture, and another developed under the North Atlantic liberal democratic paradigm. Like other contemporaneous exhibition frameworks, its conception of the art gallery as a forum for the overcoming of historical differences is reminiscent of Habermas's model of the liberal public sphere. For Habermas, the public sphere is a historical formation in which private individuals gather to discuss issues pertaining to their common life, to monitor the state and hold it accountable in its regulation of social life. Actors in the Habermasian public sphere "behave as a public body when they confer in an unrestricted fashion—that is, with the guarantee of freedom of assembly and association and the freedom to express and publish their opinions—about matters of general interest," an ideal similar to Manifesta's conception of the exhibition space as a field for the overcoming of historical antinomies.[40] Nancy Fraser and other critics have denounced Habermas's model on the grounds that it idealizes accessibility to the public sphere by overlooking the preexisting biases and other exclusionary mechanisms keeping all from entering the forum on equal terms. Although the deliberative conference idealized by the Habermasian model is a laudable goal, Fraser condemns it as empirically faulty on the grounds that it ignores the all-pervasive hierarchical organization of social life. Fraser believes that Habermas's liberal model brackets actually existing "status distinctions" so that participating individuals can deliberate as if they were peers. But this suspension of social hierarchies turns the Habermasian public sphere into a "space of zero-degree culture, so utterly bereft of any specific ethos as to accommodate with perfect neutrality and equal ease interventions expressive of any and every cultural ethos." In a critique that might very well have been intended for Manifesta instead, Fraser sees this illusion of equality as the basis of a new mode of political domination. For her, the public sphere is "the prime institutional site for the construction of the consent that defines the new, hegemonic mode of domination."[41] Misiano was similarly concerned about this power imbalance. In his words, "Though we keep underscoring this idea of a multiplication of centers, we should not forget that the art scene still exists within the structure of power."[42] Misiano's perspective was shared by other voices who agreed Manifesta's incorporation of post-Soviet art within the exhibition space illustrates the forced biennial conversions occluded by mid-1990s umbrella art categories, such as "new European art" and, later in the decade, "global contemporary art." It would be through biennial conversions like these that names like Kulik, Brener, and subREAL would enter the European art institution.

The early-boom biennial, in abiding by the model of the Habermasian public sphere, often acted as a bracketed top-down enclosure wherein aspects of social life were constrained and suspended in artificial relationality. Like Bourriaud's relational art, the early-boom biennial relied on staged and mystified affinities dependent on the belief that the constant flow of actors, objects, and meaning that permeate art institutions' porous walls could be temporarily closed off. In its modeled Europeanness, Manifesta blurred the extant conflict of the post–Cold War years, delivering an illusion of equal access via the exhibition medium, and helping to render a mystified new Europe. Despite the organizational challenges, the biennial came to fruition and opened on schedule. Yet instead of functioning as the collaboratively cohesive group that EAM had dreamed of, the curatorial team behaved like an aggregate of independent curators who researched, selected, and brought to Rotterdam their own artists as contributions to the new Europe. As they produced a new European art, curators also engaged in the conversion of manifold modern art legacies of the region into a shared aesthetic program. But as chapter 9 details, other convivial notions of art and the home surged around Manifesta's porous walls and would become crucial for the development of the art biennial as we know it today.

nine

The Art of Belonging

I wondered how this was all going to take place and what role would be reserved for the artists' community of Rotterdam. Rotterdam has its own history of art events. . . . Was Manifesta 1 to become another traveling art circus, another quickie? . . . Artists have created their own basis in this city by means of exhibitions, exchanges, discussions and collaborative efforts in creating and maintaining spaces to work and think. How should this existing infrastructure relate to Manifesta 1? Would it be possible to give meaning to the idea of being the first host-city for Manifesta beyond merely satisfying the basic need for space and, of course, money? . . . What is the position of the local host when receiving an international platform? How can the international group of artists participating in Manifesta 1 be connected with their Rotterdam colleagues?

—Jeanne van Heeswijk, NEsTWORK artist collective (1996)

Despite Manifesta's ambitions to help forge a supranational sphere for the circulation of European art, since its early days the biennial has had to devise strategies to engage with local cultural scenes. The biennial now often involves regional art experts in its mediation strategies and tends to include in its program events that showcase local contemporary art to international visitors. However, as the passage above shows, in its first iteration in Rotterdam, Manifesta failed to consider local cultural actors—including contemporary artists. Initially, the biennial partnered exclusively with established museums and did not aim to feature active Rotterdam artists or noncanonical institutions in its original selection. This preference for established organizations excluded Rotterdam's contemporary art and culture from the exhibition, an omission that prompted strong reactions by local artists who fought against the biennial's criteria and proposed innovative strategies for their inclusion in the program. Manifesta's ultimate decision to acknowledge and remediate its initial misstep set a precedent for its later trajectory, and impacted other art biennials' strategies for local engagement.

Local Institutional Partnerships

Despite originating as a response to new policy imperatives on the European level, the biennial would require strong partnerships with Rotterdam's local cultural infrastructure. In the planning stages, EAM sought to partner with canonical art institutions in Rotterdam to secure exhibition space. Among these were the Kunsthal Rotterdam, Witte de With Center for Contemporary Art, Museum Boijmans Van Beuningen, the Natural History Museum of Rotterdam, and the Netherlands Architecture Institute as main exhibition venues. Yet despite its large-scale ambitions, the finish of Manifesta 1 differed from the polished standards of other big art events in the North Atlantic art capitals, leaving many in the public underwhelmed. Art historian Elena Filipovic recalls that Manifesta's first edition in Rotterdam was marked by a "remarkable fragility, informality, and tentativeness," mostly caused by its distribution around "subtle and small-scale" venues and its "unspectacular artworks and performances [that] hardly seemed to cater to the ambitions of a city looking to place itself on the cultural (tourist) map." These feelings were shared across the board. *Frieze* magazine stated that "Manifesta lacked clarity; had a confusing catalogue; included too many interventions, and abused the museum setting." Writing for *Artforum*, Daniel Birnbaum agreed, arguing that "as for Manifesta as a whole, one is left feeling that more energy went into the project than came out.... In the end, its emphasis on collaboration sounded better than it looked. Rather than providing a perspective on a Europe redefining itself,

Manifesta amounted to little more than another group show."[1] Although the central venues hosting Manifesta's exhibitions were anything but subtle and small scale, critics' dislike of the biennial was probably a result of its distribution through a wide array of additional settings, including several smaller exhibition spaces that supplemented the central shows, such as the Chabot Museum, Villa Museumpark 9, Rotterdam Center for the Arts, V2_: Institute for the Unstable Media, Nederlands Foto Instituut, the Policegallery, Maritime Museum Pins Hendrik Rotterdam, Manifesta's website, and, eventually, the artist-run BAD Foundation. Manifesta's spread in Rotterdam contrasted with what was, at the time, still the norm for large-scale exhibitions like the Venice Biennale, the Whitney Biennial, and documenta, all of which were centrally located at important museums or monumental fairgrounds.

Manifesta's confidence that it would attract international attention to Rotterdam helped broker partnerships with local established institutions. The terms for their collaboration were set in a standard contract on September 12, 1995. The document established that the "participating institute is responsible for the construction of the exhibition" and for "the state of the exhibited works." Partners would take on the responsibilities of "organiz[ing] and financing of the transports of the works of art of the participating artists from Europe, preparing and financing the art projects of participating artists 'in situ,' technical, construction and logistics, [and] organiz[ing] and financing the travels of the artists, stay and per diem according to the agreed amounts and terms." In addition, the host organizations would insure artworks, supervise their technical necessities, provide press-quality photographs of exhibitions and events to EAM, and organize a joint press conference on June 7, 1996.[2] Additionally, they would sell entry tickets for all Manifesta venues and exhibition catalogs, and were required to visibly display Manifesta 1's visual materials, including flags and banners, as well as Manifesta's logo. These partnerships between EAM and Rotterdam's cultural institutional complex were mutually beneficial. They afforded legitimacy to the new biennial. In exchange, local cultural institutions hosted content that had been preprogrammed for their venues, reshaping their otherwise traditional profiles to attract foreign and younger publics. For local established institutions, participating in this partnership also helped them accrue visibility in national, European, and international art media, affiliating themselves with the new European art world partly sponsored by Manifesta.

A New Cultural Heritage

In addition to shaping artistic trends and amplifying specific art gene-alogies, early-boom art biennials often participated in broader efforts to reimagine place. Manifesta's settlement in Rotterdam was part of a larger operation to transform the city's identity from Europe's largest industrial port to a cultural destination. This change reflected a broader tendency across the new Europe to spur urban service economies, continuing the reallocation of production sectors that began in the European Economic Community during the 1980s and the subsequent externalization of in-dustrial activity to non-European countries and peripheral new EU nation members.[3] This economic transition had provoked significant crises in former industrial enclaves such as Barcelona, Manchester, and Rotterdam, which saw a spike in unemployment, budget decreases, and subsequent quality of life deterioration. In this context, the Treaty of Maastricht's cultural-integration imperative helped fuel the European tourism industry, turning it into a driving economic force in depleted postindustrial regions. As chapter 5 details, during the 1990s urban planners and allied interest groups often perceived cultural tourism as capable of reimagining the social contract in ways that integrated impoverished and excluded groups into a city's identity, at times providing new tools for these groups to regain political agency and visibility at the city level.[4] Cultural initiatives that saw themselves as spaces for the conciliation of difference, such as Manifesta, became ready solutions in these urban transformation processes.

Yet years before Manifesta, Rotterdam's city council had already strategized ways to remediate what it perceived to be the city center's de-cline. Starting in 1986 with the production of the New Rotterdam Plan, a blueprint for urban regeneration designed to "halt urban decline and regain Rotterdam's position as a global player in world trade," planners intended to turn the city into Europe's "gateway to the world."[5] The plan echoed the neoliberal creed then gaining traction in European politics, promoting fast economic growth in the private sector motivated by beliefs that capital gains would eventually trickle down to improve quality of life in the city. Its primary goals were to increase the industrial port's competitiveness, transform older port facilities into luxury residential waterfront areas, and improve infrastructures for the international business sector, objec-tives that it hoped to meet by reducing social expenditures and subjecting culture to the service of economic growth.[6] Further, the plan united several existing yet disconnected regeneration ventures, establishing the urban renewal agenda for the next decade and ultimately re-inscribing Rotterdam into a changing global map.[7] However, in its implementation the agenda was criticized for lacking a strategy to improve life conditions, failing to accomplish integrated and sustainable city growth, and driving the rise of inequality.[8] It accelerated the exodus of the middle and upper classes to the suburbs and impoverished the downtown districts. Although in theory this shift toward a strategic planning model involved the participation of local government, the private sector, knowledge industries, and residents, the latter would have to wait to be included.[9]

These reforms included efforts to center Rotterdam's cultural heritage as a key ingredient in the reshaping of the city's identity. The City Tourist Office 1992–1994 tourism marketing strategic plan first articulated these desires around the city's architectural heritage.[10] Heavily bombed during World War II, Rotterdam lacked the centralized urban plan and centuries-old architecture characteristic of many European cities. The city's fast-paced mid-century reconstruction favored functionalist approaches to architecture, to the detriment of architectural forms traditionally perceived as historical and monumental. Yet a fraction of the prewar architectural heritage was still standing (not without significant reconstruction efforts) in the so-called Museum Quarter, a downtown area spanning in and around Museumpark. This area, which eventually became a central tourist destination in the city, houses the Natuurhistorisch Museum (Natural History Museum) of Rotterdam, the Kunsthal Rotterdam, the Museum Boijmans Van Beuningen, the Museum Chabot, and the Het Nieuwe Instituut (Netherlands Architecture Institute), all of which were Manifesta exhibition venues in the summer of 1996. Downtown Rotterdam's stylistic hodgepodge was reframed by cultural tourism campaigns as an asset. Drawing analogies between the absence of a clear "city center" in Rotterdam and the image of a center-less Europe devised by Manifesta, curator Andrew Renton commented on the biennial's dispersed structure: "It is very interesting that Manifesta should take place in a city like Rotterdam, incidentally, because one of the disconcerting things about the city is that you can keep walking and never find its center. When it was rebuilt from scratch it could never grow organically around a center. It kept on shifting. I think this is how Manifesta has evolved, too."[11] Renton's reflection helps naturalize Manifesta's homology with Rotterdam. In a sense, the biennial was an organic coming-to-being of the city's potential.

These processes of urban renewal set a good framework for Manifesta's first iteration in 1996. One important focus of Rotterdam's urban-redevelopment plan had been the area around the central Witte de With "cultural quarter," a district that would contain half of the biennial's exhibition venues.[12] As one local art curator described, Witte de With Street was a street "where you wouldn't want to go at night"—referring to the presence of prostitution and drugs—just a decade earlier. However, by the time of Manifesta 1 in 1996, and partly due to the opening in 1990 of the world-renowned Witte de With Center for Contemporary Art (renamed Kunstinstituut Melly in 2020), the area had already undergone a significant makeover. The local curator's impressions contrast with the experience of place coproduced by the projects installed in Witte de With Street, such as Douglas Gordon and Rirkrit Tiravanija's *Cinema Liberté*, an ephemeral discussion café and cinema for the screening of censored films, and a case of relational aesthetics (see chapter 8). This arty party piece exemplified the kind of social relations between art-world insiders favored by late twentieth-century relational aesthetics artists, and, frequently, tourism-driven cultural initiatives—like art biennials. Portraying the piece as a cluster for art tourists, Daniel Birnbaum characterized it in *Artforum* as a place where "Gordon shows films that were censored when they were released in the Netherlands. One can view these films while seated on great bean bags. During or after the film one can have a drink in the bar, designed by Tiravanija." Although *Cinema Liberté* opened with a well-attended all-night party, Birnbaum described it as "pretty dull" and agreed with local art critic Ineke Schwartz that it "remained dead and deserted after the opening weekend," failing to take root in the city's diverse art community, a community that mostly hung out elsewhere.[13]

Manifesta's location in the revamped Witte de With cultural quarter in the museum quarter invites questions about early-boom biennials' role in the production of heritage. As Stuart Hall has acknowledged, heritage is a contested category within cultural production, one around which nationalism, invented traditions, and moral programs join to support authoritative claims about the present moment's links to selective pasts and futures.[14] Heritage is thus not only deeply ingrained in contemporaneous experiences of culture but also has deep implications for how such experiences are woven into historical narratives. Through the many discursive productions of reputable actors—such as artists, historians, curators and other cultural experts—contemporary art, as heritage,

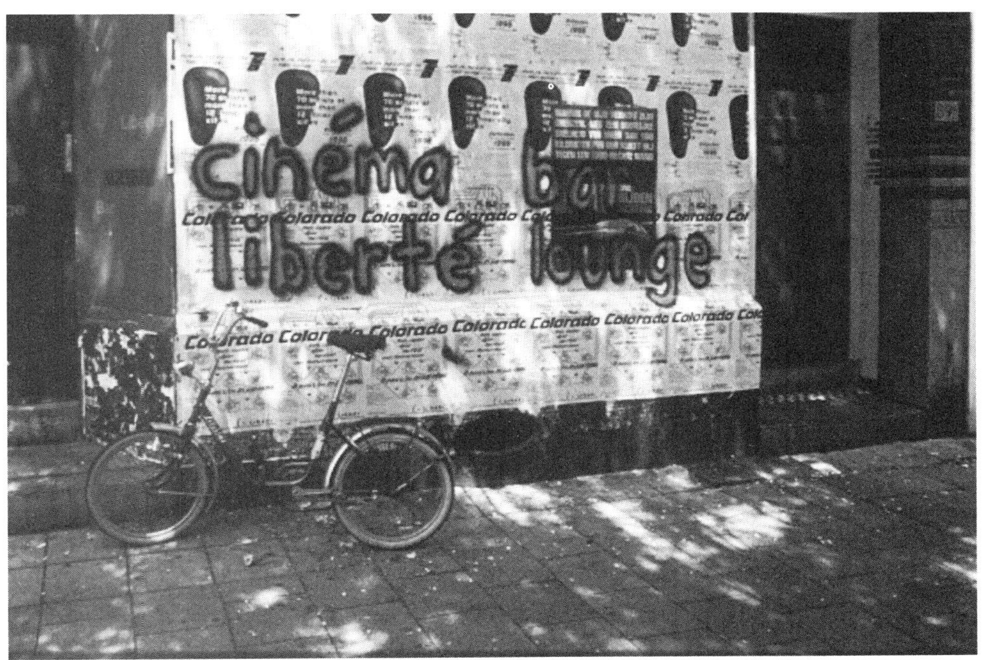

9.1   Douglas Gordon and Rirkrit Tiravanija, *Cinema Liberté*, 1996. Source: Witte de With Archives, Rotterdam Cultural Histories (renamed Kunstinstituut Melly).

selectively illuminates some worldviews while occluding others. This distinction encompasses immaterial and material aspects of culture, including the built environment, artistic production, traditions, and oral culture, all of which circulate within a heritage economy. Building from the classic Bourdieuan critique of the Kantian distinction between art and purposeful cultural forms, Luc Boltanski and Arnaud Esquerre describe this "heritage economy" as a function of contemporary capitalism, derived from a form of commodity enrichment that favors goods' claims to the past and their material uniqueness over other qualities as a way to distinguish them from standard objects. Boltanski and Esquerre argue that those who profit from the production of heritage "have an interest in maintaining the separation between ordinary things, whose trade is supposed to obey only economic laws, and exceptional things, which, although they are traded, are presented as if they somehow essentially elude the universe of commodities, conferring an extra value on them and supporting their price."[15] In their pragmatic approach to value they focus on instances in which objects change hands, exceptional moments in which their insertion in particular circuits is justified with discursive production—as when non-art objects undergo processes of aesthetic conversion by their inclusion in an art exhibition.

Early-boom art biennials such as Manifesta, inSITE, and the Bienal de La Habana were just one of the many institutional spaces involved in this sophisticated form of cultural distinction. In addition to explicitly participating in the production of heritage through the conferring of the artistic distinction to otherwise ordinary objects and practices, such as streets, buildings, and parks, early-boom art biennials helped synch these objects to selective historical narratives. As I have shown throughout this book, these selective claims to history bear important extra-artistic repercussions, especially regarding the uneven valuation of a population's lived experience of a particular enclave and its role in the enclave's history. The authoritative voice of early-boom art biennials was articulated in the form of discursive elements such as exhibitions, public and private statements, catalogs, display texts, and publicity materials—which in turn contributed to the partial canonization of aspects of regional culture in the popular imagination.

Where Are the Locals?

However, local artists had a different perspective on the biennial's arrival in Rotterdam. Excluded from the exhibition's original selection, members of the local arts community disapproved of Manifesta's selective partnering with canonical cultural institutions on the grounds that the alliance misrepresented Rotterdam's culture for nonlocal visitors. Members of the local arts community believed that by excluding local artists from the exhibition Manifesta would not be able to showcase the city's culture truthfully. This is how artist Jeanne van Heeswijk articulated Manifesta's selective rendering of Rotterdam: "Manifesta 1 did not choose Rotterdam by accident. An industrial city, living off one of the world's largest ports, Rotterdam is in cultural terms building itself. Spread out along the river, it is a vast city with multiple centres, constantly reshaping itself. Manifesta 1 will take place in the cultural centre, which is situated around the Museumpark, north of the river. This means that some of the aspects that give the city its character and shape its cultural climate will remain invisible."[16]

The biennial's partnership with Rotterdam's established cultural institutions contrasted with the absence of the city's rich contemporary-art community from its artist roster. Notably, no artists in Manifesta's initial selection were actually from Rotterdam. Although many efforts had been put into bolstering the biennial's pan-European credentials, members of the local art community were excluded from the organization's original outreach efforts. Through public hearings and communications to the organization members of Rotterdam's art community characterized Manifesta's failure to recognize them and their work as a sign of disregard. At first, EAM seemed uncertain about how to respond to these reactions. For instance, in a fax from January 3, 1996, a representative of EAM's Rotterdam project office shared a statement (now lost) written by Rotterdam artists with the curatorial team, explaining that "these seem to be the common local problems generated by such a project. Please, reply at your wish, because you don't have to answer all questions. You can also forward some questions back to the project office. You can give as much or as little information as you please."[17] Yet recognizing the opportunity before them, Manifesta's organizers ultimately heeded the demands of the local art community and sought to remedy its original exclusion with symbolic amends, such as by posting on the biennial's website a list of artist-run initiatives and gallery exhibitions happening simultaneously with Manifesta.[18]

Naturally, local artists were deeply offended by their exclusion from this first comprehensive exhibition of new European art to be celebrated in their city. Their offense grew from two unmet expectations. On the one hand, they sought professional legitimation through the insertion of their work into the art biennial; on the other hand, local artists hoped to be acknowledged as reputable experts in the local cultural scene. In their view, they could offer a perspective on Rotterdam that, informed by a situated knowledge of place, would be closer to the lived experience of the city than those produced by established cultural institutions affiliated with the Amsterdam-based biennial administrators. The epigraph opening this chapter, part of a report written by van Heeswijk after attending a meeting with Manifesta's organizers in May 1996, registers the concerns widely felt among members of the local art scene regarding EAM's oversight of the existing local art community. Van Heeswijk was concerned with the long-term sustainability of this exhibition and the kind of exchanges between foreign and local artists that it would facilitate. Her words also signal the interest of Rotterdam artists to develop proposals that would position them as translators of local culture to non-Rotterdam biennial artists and visitors.

The demands for recognition from artists also worked as instances of mutual solidarity that helped them organize as a bloc. Organized to counter Manifesta's mishap, the many resulting activities included open studios, conversations, and exhibitions, all of which had important repercussions in the local art scene and the final exhibition. A large number of Rotterdam artists came together against Manifesta's affront, forming something similar to what Daniel Loick calls a "counter-community."[19] Building from new and preexisting relations of friendship and camaraderie, they worked cooperatively to procure mutual artistic legitimation, propose alternative forms of connecting with Manifesta artists, and self-determine in para-institutions to counter the new biennial's position in the city's cultural scene. The artist-run initiative NEsTWORK united most of the responses against Manifesta's ellipsis, becoming the main vector for local art organizing in the wake of the biennial. Founded in November 1995 following plans for Manifesta announced for the following summer, NEsTWORK was a gesture of self-determination, a subjugated sociality that grew out of a desire to welcome Manifesta artists into Rotterdam and act as mediators of their interactions with the city, fostering connections between local and foreign art worlds, moved by their defense that "the place already exists before the guest arrives."[20] The collective was formed by artists van Heeswijk, Karin Arink, Wapke Feenstra, Edwin Jaansen, Menna Laura Meyer, and Kamiel Verschuren, as well as philosopher Ruud Welten. It self-defined as a "hospitable group which aims to foster connections and be a sounding board for the local and international art world."[21] Members often gathered in Zaal de Unie, a 1985 replica of the 1925 coffee shop designed by De Stijl architect J. J. P. Oud. During Manifesta's run, between June 8 and August 18, 1996, NEsTWORK organized forty-three events corresponding to five categories: Portable Art / Local Art, a series of conversations about art; NEsTWORK Ad Hoc, a video program about Manifesta; Going Places, a set of tours around Rotterdam; Neighbourhood Rotterdam / NEsTWORK City Plan, a map of Rotterdam's art community; and Stratego, a conversation series with artists. NEsTWORK ran the Information and Documentation Center at the Rotterdam Center for Visual Arts, providing Manifesta's audiences with information about artists' initiatives and special events in the

9.2   NEsTWORK, poster for a party, 1996. Source: Witte de With Archives, Rotterdam Cultural Histories (renamed Kunstinstituut Melly).

Rotterdam art community, and distributed *Lokaal Europa*, a publication produced by Rotterdam artists during the spring and summer of 1996 that provided information on local art events.

NEsTWORK's actions reached far. In addition to providing a cohesive response to, in their words, the "exclusiveness of the official Manifesta 1 programme," many of the collective's events hoped to correct what, in their view, were the biennial's distorted portrayal of the city of Rotterdam.[22] Part of NEsTWORK's efforts, the Portable Art / Local Art program featured a series of conversations on art theory with local art actors. Organized at the café Zaal de Unie, these gatherings set the theoretical framework for NEsTWORK's actions.[23] The discussions followed Welten's theory of portable art and local art, which circulated in a manifesto published in *Lokaal Europa*. According to Welten, artworks can move back and forth between the categories of portable and local art as they negotiate their engagement with place. His approach provides a framework in which culture is always heteronomous, a model that, in his words, "counterbalances 'autonomy,' and acts as a critique of the idea of the artist as independent or self-determining."[24] In its programming, NEsTWORK helped visibilize areas and populations negatively affected by the reforms brought about by the New Rotterdam Plan and sought to remediate Manifesta's homogenizing rendering of the city through events that amplified its diverse demographics. Rotterdam was, at the time, characterized by a large percentage of foreign-born individuals; it had a large Muslim community, a high presence of Dutch Antilleans, and a considerable Chinese population—groups also excluded from Manifesta's vision of a new Europe. NEsTWORK's programming accentuated Rotterdam's class and ethnic diversity, directing art audiences to the work of nonwhite cultural producers, including those originally from postcolonial states. For instance, during Manifesta's opening night, NEsTWORK's counterprogramming included a series of rap performances titled Representing the Rotterdam Docks at the Museum Boijmans Van Beuningen, during which biennial audiences and participating artists could engage with the local underground music scene through the work of musicians and performers from the predominantly working-class immigrant community south of the river.

For NEsTWORK Ad Hoc, artists, critics, and curators produced eight short documentaries about the works featured in Manifesta 1. The films were produced and narrated by a diversity of individuals, including artist and curator Jason Coburn, the Via-Via group, art patron Frits Smith, artist Ben Schot, art critic Ineke Schwartz, management consultant and writer Shirley Azimullah, musician and composer Arthur Sauer, and art critic Riki Simons. In them, the camera follows guest presenters as they tour a selection of Manifesta venues, engaging in conversations with the artists, production assistants, and members of the audience. One video shows musician Sauer as he walks down Witte de With Street, the center of downtown Rotterdam's urban remodeling, and enters Witte de With Contemporary Arts Center. The camera follows him up the stairs to the fourth floor, where he greets "Goedendag!" to a receptionist before entering the gallery to discuss two large-scale paintings by Danish artist Henrik Plenge Jakobsen. The artworks, featuring big circular targets in rainbow colors, have the text "Everything is wrong" superimposed on them. Another video, narrated by Ben Schot, shows a project by Tracy Mackenna and Joseph Grigely installed in the Villa Alckmaer: Post-its, pens, pencils, paper sheets, teacups, books, flower bases, desks, and chairs, all materials for their conversation-based artworks.

A number of additional programs sought to mediate the encounter between foreign artists and the city of Rotterdam. Every Tuesday evening between June 11 and August 13, 1996, Rob Beentjes guided the public to "a large number of locations, unknown places and non-existent worlds." For over two hours, "the idea of 'place' [would] be mapped out in varied and entertaining ways."[25] Each iteration took a different form and featured guest speakers. For example, on June 11 the "Museum of the Banal" was "an evening looking at the charm of 'ugly' and 'everyday' places." Three speakers came to this iteration: curator of the Chip Hut Museum Paul Ilegems gave a lecture on Belgian chip huts, designer Tom Matton presented on "strange situations that . . . set you thinking," and journalist Rob Sijmons used photographs by Wout Berger to show members of the audience some of the Netherlands' most toxic landscapes. "Invisible Cities" (June 18) addressed the relationships between existing cities and their mythical representations. Some cases discussed were heavenly Jerusalem and real Jerusalem, Paris, Rome, and New York. "A Flat Existence" (June 25) was devoted to regions unacknowledged by maps, such as deserts and ocean valleys. Guest speakers included a desert nomad and author, a speleologist, an aviation expert, and a deep-sea biologist. "Synthetic Cities" (July 2) promised to "enter the world of speed, realism, violence and interactive user-convenience" by exploring computer-designed spaces. The evening showcased the DOOM software and CD-ROMs, "which the public [would] later be able to explore

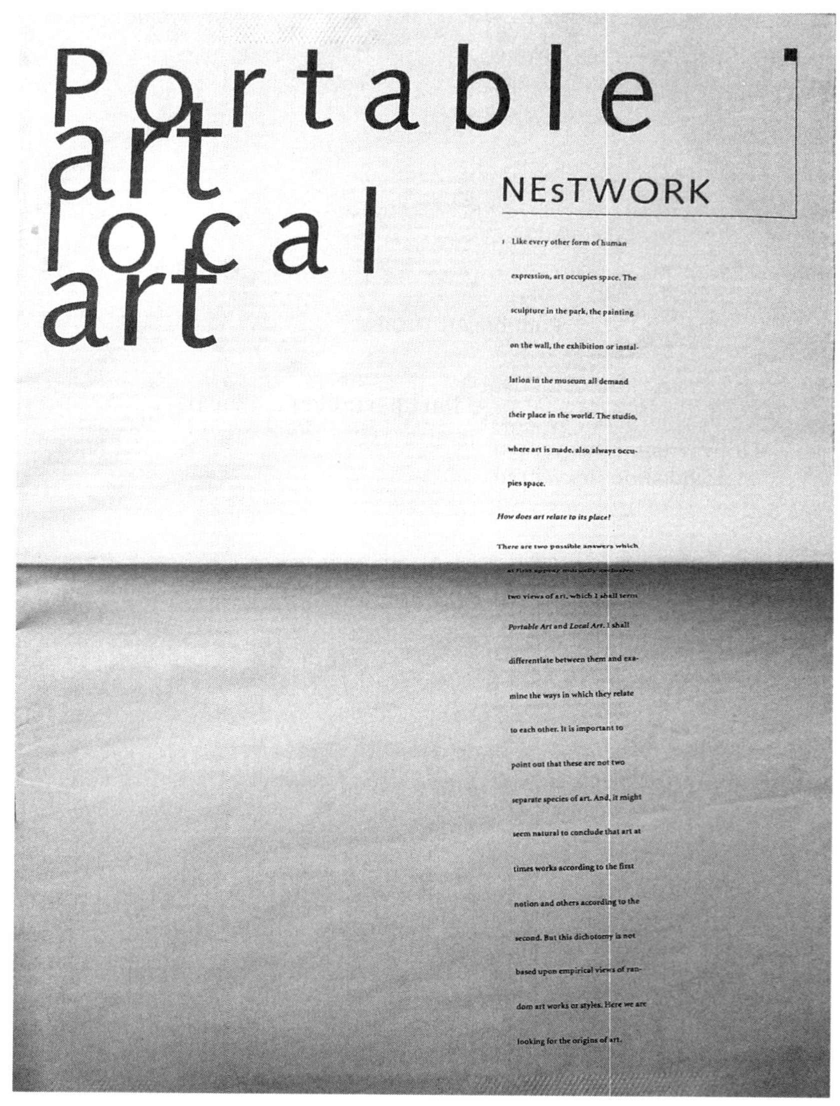

9.3 NEsTWORK catalog page for *Portable Art / Local Art*, 1996. Source: Witte de With Archives, Rotterdam Cultural Histories (renamed Kunstinstituut Melly).

themselves." Stories told in "From Micro to Macro Landscapes" (July 9) were accompanied by stereoscopic slides of fantasy photographer Wim van Engold and artist P. H. Connaughton. Archaeologist W. H. Metz and geographer Roel Sneider showed images of archaeological sites and the inside of the Earth. "The Cell" (July 16) was an evening devoted to discussing "the charm of imprisonment." Presentations by artist Alicia Framis, criminologist Herman Franke, and psychologist Hans van de Sande prompted discussions about solitary confinement with the audience. The evening of July 23 was devoted to exploring Spokania, a remote archipelago nation not known to many. During the gathering, participants learned about the country's music, its beer industry, and language. A meeting titled "The Stretchable City" (July 30) was devoted to discussing suburbs. It included a conversation with designer Lucas Verweij and discussion of an interview with author Robert Vernooy. On August 6, "The Private Domain" explored the "confusing territory" of one's body space as defined by cultural and individual boundaries. Guest presenters included Arjen Mulder, who spoke about sensory-deprivation tanks, artist Karin Arink, and publicist Karin Spaink. The last meeting (August 13) was titled "Tour du Monde / The Grand Tour." It sought to "seduce and stimulate the audience with an excess of unknown stories and smells in order to take them to the furthest reaches of thought and taste." Presentations featured a talk by philosopher Elsbeth Brouwer on paradises and utopias, stories by Josien Laurier, an exposition on Dutch eighteenth-century fantastic travel stories by historian Marleen de Vries, and discussions on the mutability of the kitchen through history by food sociologist Anneke van Otterloo. The Going Places series closed that evening with a dinner of world foods prepared by Zaal de Unie's chef, Rien van der Waa. This rich and enjoyable series not only mediated between foreign and local artists but, most importantly, it helped consolidate the counter-community of local artists who came together as a result of their exclusion from the biennial, promoting a mutual relationality between them that was highly valuable—as art and as social relation.

In addition to these programs, NEsTWORK produced Neighbourhood Rotterdam / NEsTWORK City Plan (see plate 16): a map including the city's downtown and the southern district of Charlois. Distributed among the biennial's audience, it included nine landmarks with views of the city, Manifesta 1 venues, NEsTWORK projects, projects affiliated with Manifesta 1 (individual artists and artist initiatives), galleries with a program related to Manifesta 1, and other galleries, artist initiatives, and studio buildings.

Of the several thousand copies of this comprehensive map, five hundred had no street names on them. These were distributed among eighty artists living in Rotterdam or who had spent some time working in the city, with an invitation to intervene in the maps and send them back with comments about the city. Responses from foreign artists included, for instance, that of Sylvie Reno, who lived in Marseille but had been an artist in residence in Rotterdamse Kunststichting in 1995; Ari Gold, a nomad between Los Angeles, New Mexico, and San Francisco, who was in Rotterdam intermittently between 1991 and 1996 and wrote "please don't tear down the old cinema-houses"; and Karlos Lydon, from London, in Rotterdam during the summer of 1996, "recovering from broken heart, making art." By visualizing aspects of the city left out by Manifesta's organizers, NEsTWORK artists hoped to provide international participants in Manifesta and tourists with a representation of the local fabric produced by locals, thus correcting an image of Rotterdam produced by Manifesta that, in their opinion, "[invisibilized] some aspects that give the city its character and shape its cultural climate."[26]

My House: Your Home

In the face of institutional exclusion, local artists resorted to cultivating hospitality. Through the many dialogue-based events, artist members of NEsTWORK offered a model by which art can function as a means to resolve conflict. In addition to directly targeting Manifesta, the artists saw their counterprogramming as a way to remedy the neglect of local cultural expertise that they found to be pervasive among globally oriented contemporary art events at the time. As van Heeswijk remembers, "In a period when nomadism and traveling art circuses are being welcomed as an important quickie, NEsTWORK wants to focus attention on the place where work is done. Occupying space and offering space is a form of reciprocity between guest and host.... Space is not a blank page. Every space—and therefore also the space of the art work and the artistic activity—has its own history.... At Manifesta 1 NEsTWORK will be linking the stories of people from here with the stories of the guests."[27] Van Heeswijk's framing of the encounter between biennial visitors and local artists as a reciprocal meeting between guests and hosts signals to the general willingness among members of the collective to turn Manifesta's mishap into a generative opportunity. In the spring of 1996, some months before the opening of the biennial, Manifesta organizers agreed to deliver a letter to participating biennial artists from a third party until then unknown to them: fourteen artists from the BAD Foundation, a Rotterdam-based artist-run space, had written an invitation to Manifesta artists to live with them during their time in Rotterdam. The BAD Foundation was an art center at a squat in a former public school in Oud-Charlois, a majority working-class and immigrant district south of the Mosa River, within walking distance to Port of Rotterdam facilities.[28] Working autonomously, this group was involved in most of NEsTWORK's activities. Members of the BAD Foundation did not yet know which artists would be featured in Manifesta but, in their disagreement with the biennial's curatorial concept, wanted to help shape "Rotterdam's role as the host to the venue of Manifesta 1" by fostering "exchange and discussion on a visual level and in a direct way" among guests and hosts.[29]

In order to achieve this, the BAD Foundation launched the project *My House: Your Home* (see plate 17). Their letter invited visiting artists to coproduce what they called "dwellings," little habitacles for guest artists inside of their own studios at the building. To construct the dwellings, they suggested a process of collaboration articulated in three stages. First, each guest artist would send initial ideas for their dwelling space. In response, a host artist from BAD would interpret these guidelines and send back a drafted design. Ultimately, when guest artists arrived in Rotterdam, the two parties would collaboratively finalize the design, fabricate the habitacle, and get it ready to be inhabited. In addition to the dwellings, the main building would feature common areas and spaces for projects and discussion. In the evenings, collaboratively cooked meals and informal events open for everyone to participate would help the group "get to know each other," "hopefully leading to culinary exchanges and informal contacts."[30] Peripheral events would include an "Introduction Evening," a "Mystery Tour of Rotterdam" (co-organized with NEsTWORK in the BADmobile, a van rented for the occasion), and a closing party, where all dwellings would be open to the outside public. Most invited artists welcomed the invitation and agreed to stay at BAD during at least some of their time in Rotterdam. These included Călin Dan and Augustin Kiraly (members of collective sub-REAL), Jaan Toomik, Eulália Valldosera, João Tabarra, João Louro, Tamara Grcic, Jenny Marketou, Yuri Leiderman, Pavel Kopřiva, Tadej Pogačar, Oleg Kulik and Lioudmila Bredikhina, Joseph Grigely, Tracy Mackenna, and Jazon Coburn. Coburn, who worked in Manifesta's curatorial team, wrote in his diary that "today about 35 of us went on a mystery tour as part of

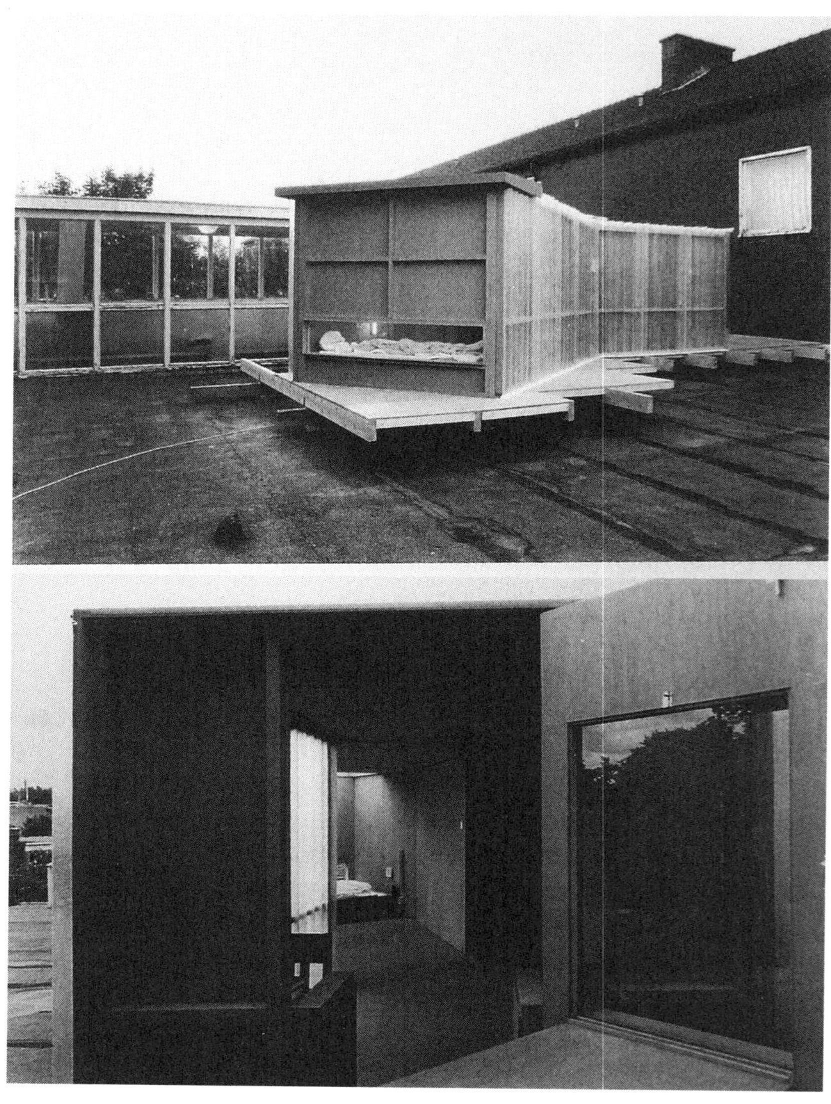

9.4   BAD Foundation, *My House: Your Home* (dwelling designs), 1996. Source: Witte de With Archives, Rotterdam Cultural Histories (renamed Kunstinstituut Melly).

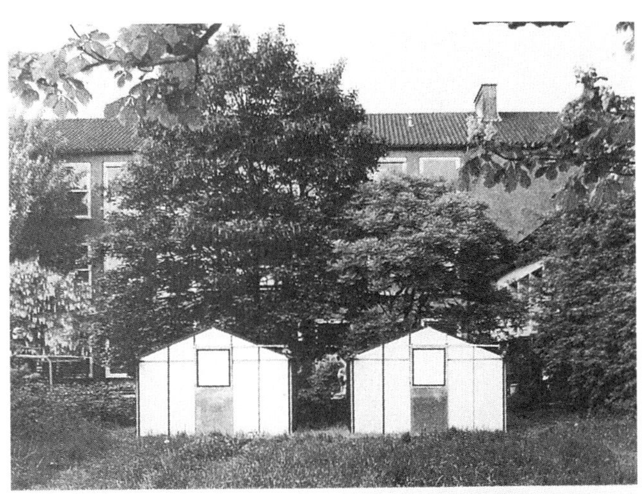

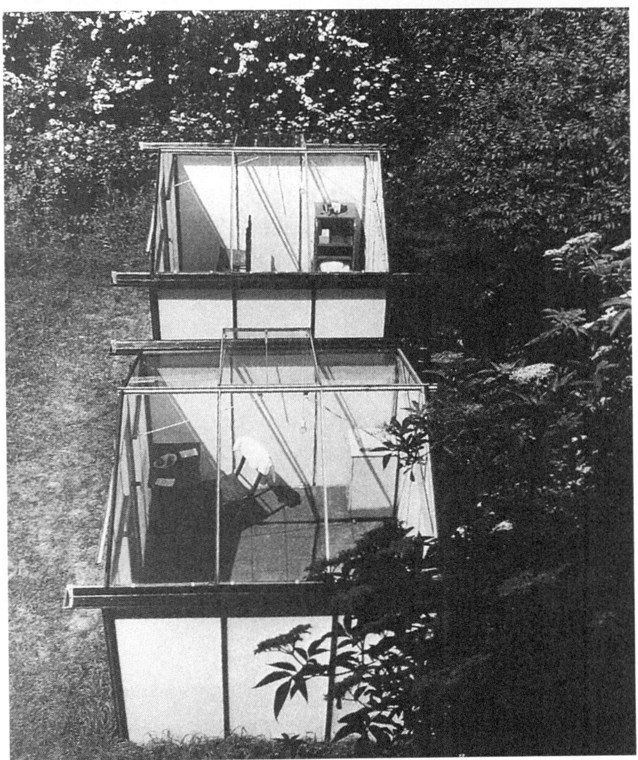

9.5 BAD Foundation, *My House: Your Home* (dwelling designs), 1996. Source: Witte de With Archives, Rotterdam Cultural Histories (renamed Kunstinstituut Melly).

the *My House: Your Home* project. Drove along scenic roads, ended up at the Slufter beach and after watching the sunset we all enjoyed a supper of salmon, gambas, eel, trout, salad, pasta, and champagne. Martin and Laurien cooked for Holland. Tomorrow should be fun as I am assisting Andrew Renton for the day."[31]

This model of hospitality provided a formal recognition framework to mediate in the encounter between foreign artists in Manifesta and the human, cultural, and physical specificity of Rotterdam. As the BAD Foundation artists explained, "Through this gesture of hospitality you will be able to learn more about the artists working in Rotterdam and about Rotterdam itself.... Construction and placing in our building should give visual expression to the maker's personal idea of hospitality and his/her views on living/dwelling/being."[32] Unlike other artworks in the biennial that fit under the relational aesthetics umbrella, *My House: Your Home* transcended the exhibition walls to foster sustained reciprocity between local and foreign artists. Within the dialogical exchange started by the BAD Foundation, locals and foreigners learned about others' work and worldviews, regardless of their formal status within the biennial. The temporary community forged around *My House: Your Home* enacted collective resistance to Manifesta's exclusion and its partial representations of Rotterdam. The social relations that resulted from this project extended beyond Manifesta's program and constituted, for many of the foreign participants, the most valuable part of their experience in Rotterdam. Friendships, flirtations, work partnerships, and spontaneous exchanges afforded the truthful representations of site that the well-afforded art biennial was not able to engineer. In the words of artist Joseph Grigely,

> As one of the artists participating in *Manifesta 1*, I spent a total of almost six weeks as a guest at B.a.d. It was, I should say, an extraordinary experience, and quite defied my expectations. For these six weeks I lived, slept, and ate with other visiting *Manifesta* artists and with the artists of B.a.d. I found everyone to be very generous with time and with resources, and the members of Stitching B.a.d. were helpful in every possible way: they loaned me furniture for my installation at CBK, made phone calls for me, helped find and deliver supplies, cooked, provided advice, and—most important—provided for me a home for six weeks.... I am hopeful that Stitching B.a.d. will continue to make itself available as a site of continued exchange, a

site where artists like myself can continue to visit and work. I would certainly like to return again, and I would like to think that the opportunity to have the sort of experience I had is one that will be available to other artists in the future. It is not just the building as a site that was important, or the greenhouse that for six weeks was my "home," but the people who helped make this possible—their spirit, their energy, and their ideas are very special, and deserve continued support by others.[33]

My House: Your Home's emphasis on communication and collaborative production offered a counterexample to other Manifesta artworks that relied on human relations, such as Douglas Gordon and Rirkrit Tiravanija's *Cinema Liberté* and Oleg Kulik's *Pavlov's Dog's Laboratory* (discussed in chapter 8). The proposals for joint design, coproduction, and conviviality that informed NEsTWORK's and the BAD Foundation's efforts to root the experience of foreign artists in the local cultural scene grew from already existing forms of practiced solidarity among local art-world members, who engaged in resource redistribution and mutual support as they worked and lived in Rotterdam.

NEsTWORK's general programming and, more concretely, the BAD Foundation's conviviality project echoed Grant Kester's model of dialogical aesthetics, a framework that values the processes of communication constitutive of artworks over their formal and material qualities.[34] Influenced by Mikhail Bakhtin's diagnosis of the dialogic work of literature, where characters engage in open-ended dialogue to listen and echo others' expressions of their experience, in Kester's model the dialogue involved in the coproduction of the artistic experience brings together unlike actors in their finding of reciprocal common ground as a basis for mutual learning and transformation. In this model, communication between participants in the artwork follows an honest desire for empathy with and recognition of the other. Although those involved in the communicative exchange often come from different social positions, it is through empathy-driven exchanges that common knowledge, situated in the specificity of their commonality, can be achieved, providing a solid foundation for eventual instances of material reciprocity. Informed by Mary Field Belenky's model of "connected knowledge," a paradigm of procedural knowledge based on the recognition of the existence of multiple sources of knowledge, Kester's dialogical aesthetics allow an appreciation of human relations beyond their inscription within the art institution, offering a conceptualization of relational aesthetics very different from the ones formulated by Nicolas Bourriaud, Claire Bishop, and Viktor Misiano discussed in chapter 8. Participants in the dialogical artwork are driven by the pursuit of empathy and recognition. The connected knowers involved in the exchange do not depart from oppositional dispositions. Instead, they are aware of the role of context in the shaping of one's worldview, and they pursue an understanding of others' positionalities and their rationales as relative to their conditions.[35] It is through these processes of shared reevaluation of the competing epistemic frameworks that meet in conversation that, Kester argues, participants in dialogical artworks can reach mutual empathetic identification.

The designs produced within this dialogical process were as diverse as the actors involved. One, placed at Judith Schoneveld's studio, was a house-shaped three-dimensional wooden platform protruding from the outside of the building's second-floor facade. It featured two square windows on its front and side. The structure remains there to this day. A second, more minimal design featured translucid walls made of clean canvas stretched on wood frames. Inside, it had a single bed, a TV set, and a desk. Placed inside an artist's studio, the walls of this structure could be propped open at a 90-degree angle during the day and closed at night for privacy. Proposing a less individualistic approach to cohabitation, a dwelling with four single beds invited guests to share their sleeping quarters. Pictures show a group of four men chatting from their beds at night, with bath towels hanging from the bed frames as curtains. Other dwellings featured wooden walls that emulated a small apartment: one bedroom, a living room, and a small entrance. Joseph Grigely (the only US artist in Manifesta 1) stayed in twin house-shaped greenhouses located in the back garden of the building. Grigely used one as a studio and the other as a living space. Photographs show the two structures surrounded by tall, lush green grass and trees, with white walls and translucent glass ceilings. Reflecting on his own experience as a guest, British assistant curator Jason Coburn wrote the following in his travelogue:

> I was invited by Aletta de Jong, whose studio was unoccupied, to take her place. The house is a cube that occupies the centre of her studio and it is constructed from grey metal shelving units which have been packed with stuff from Aletta's studio. A gap in one of the

cube walls allows access to a modest room which has a bed and a desk, these have also been constructed from shelving. Several empty shelves have been reserved for me to put my belongings. What I have is a room within a room—the inner being dense and concentrated, whilst the outer one is sparse and light. I have returned early so I can enjoy the unique atmosphere that comes with this wonderful space.[36]

Although the encounters with the local scene that Manifesta facilitated for guest artists were limited to events organized at the nine collaborating art institutions, BAD and NEsTWORK provided an all-encompassing programming that offered opportunities to forge meaningful interpersonal bonds. The instances of collaborative design, conviviality, and exchange that *My House: Your Home* fostered paved the way for several lifelong friendships between hosts and guests, and at least one enduring romantic liaison. The artist-run initiative grew from an appreciation of already existing forms of relationality in the local cultural scene as a legitimate starting point for organically welcoming guests. Additionally, it sought the recognition of a certain universality in the artist experience, an experience that diverged from that of the elite art-world actors behind the biennial—such as the donors, benefactors, and lobbyists. This shared experience was one of reciprocity and mutual recognition that valued the many forms in which artists rely on one another in their professional and personal lives.

The activities proposed by NEsTWORK and the BAD Foundation were a big success. They compensated for Manifesta's avoidance of the local art scene, providing welcoming spaces for the encounter between foreigners and locals. These two collective projects emphasized the importance of locally situated cultural expertise, drawing attention to the worthiness of Rotterdam artists as reliable interpreters of their city. Importantly, the programs orchestrated by NEsTWORK and the BAD Foundation were among the few events within and around Manifesta that actually practiced the goals of conference, unification, and conciliation driving the biennial and, more generally, the broader European unification agenda. As Grigely wrote in a fax from his studio in New Jersey upon his return from Rotterdam, "By converting their studios into houses for the visiting artists of Manifesta, the artists of BAD quietly but effectively articulated the principal theme of the exhibition and did so in a way that most art did not do. And Stichting Bad [the BAD Foundation] did this by emphasizing the importance of the process of transnational exchanges—exchanges that involved words, ideas, gestures, actions, and ultimately homes."[37]

In its involvement in the production of heritage, the early-boom art biennial helped bracket fragments of everyday life as worthy of memorialization and appreciation, distinguishing them as exemplary indexes of the present. By initially partnering with Rotterdam's cultural establishment, Manifesta conveyed to its contemporary art selection the legitimacy and reputation of institutionalized cultural expertise, offering audiences a new pan-European art exhibited alongside the Western European artistic canon. Yet as this chapter recounts, Manifesta offered only a partial account of Rotterdam's culture, one that excluded its rich and diverse art scenes. It would be through the eventual incorporation into the biennial program of the para-institutional actions of a counter-community of artists, that Manifesta managed to broaden its restrictive approach to better reflect the everyday experience of place. Manifesta curator Andrew Renton recognized that NEsTWORK and the actions at the BAD Foundation were "singled out by other organizers as one of the most positive and beneficial elements in this 'new' concept of international exhibition making. I really begin to see it as a model for other projects elsewhere." Specialized art-world media agreed. An article in *Frieze* magazine concluded that "on the level of sheer personal exchange, [Manifesta] may have succeeded well enough to make its rivals reconsider their own tactics."[38]

Epilogue

In this book I have traveled back to the early moments of late twentieth-century art globalization. Zooming into the processes that prompted the art biennial to become the dominant exhibition form at the end of the Cold War, I have foregrounded culture as a key playing field for the realignment of hegemonic forces. Through the study of artworks, forms of curatorial labor, and artistic genealogies, I have shed light on the aesthetic conversions occurring between different artistic programs within *early* boom biennials—that is, those at the beginning stages of the fast-paced multiplication of the form. I have referred to these transformations as "biennial conversions" as a way to differentiate them from other instances of aesthetic conversions in the history of art in modernity. These biennial conversions synched artistic practice to the global art industry's accelerated two-year calendar and made a variety of approaches to contemporary art production legible to a nascent global collector class. In my engagement with debates on cultural policy, class and identity formation, and international border management, I have demonstrated the implication of the art biennial boom in the period's abrupt geopolitical changes and the subsequent redrawing of colonial relations worldwide.

The previous chapters excavate the desires and longings that helped legitimate and animate this exhibition form as especially suited to stage the connectedness and conviviality that many thought would come with the end of the Cold War. They also show how these longings for peace through cultural exchange occluded historical and ongoing conflict across the world. Early-boom art biennials had several important consequences for artistic production and its histories, some of which I account for in this book. They helped strengthen new cultural identities that superseded former nationalisms in the pursuit of supranational unity between peoples. At a time of crisis for the modern Westphalian state, supranational formations such as the European Union, the North American Free Trade Agreement, and the Non-Aligned Bloc offered hopeful pathways for overcoming nationalist antagonisms. Emerging first at the boundaries between capitalist and socialist nation-building projects, early-boom art biennials recorded these longings and offered art as a field for the negotiation of new common senses. My analysis records how early-boom art biennials sprouted out of new alliances between art experts and regional elites who jointly desired to access emerging networks for the supranational circulation of culture. It details how cities in a number of world regions relied on art biennials to cultivate thriving art scenes and promote cultural tourism. These chapters also account for the many ways in which contemporary artists, working in a diversity of media, grappled with a changing industry as they widened the scope of what dominant art worlds recognize as art to include methods, symbols, and constituencies that were formerly off-limits. I have traced how these processes affected the meanings, forms, and values of contemporary art, often yielding new regional art categories that mediated conversions between local and supranational art genealogies—categories such as "Third World avant-garde," "Border art," and "European art." Artworks in these resulting categories were often diverse in their themes and values yet those who joined a global contemporary art-canon-in-formation often did so by embracing the formal inheritances of elite, white-centric, North Atlantic modernisms.

The aesthetic conversions that I describe and analyze coincided with the culmination of a century-long conflict between capitalism and socialism that shaped social, political, and economic life worldwide for decades. This ideological clash also materialized in the cultural field, crucially shaping commonsensical present agreements on how dominating groups distinguish this thing they call "art" from other forms of culture. The artist workshops, curatorial meetings, artwork installations, and instances of public engagement that I center in this book exemplify the extent to which the crisis of authority that followed the end of the Cold War altered cultural production worldwide—even the seemingly apolitical and ahistorical niche field of so-called high art. These changes in the level of the superstructure mirrored late-capitalist reorganizations of production worldwide under a new colonial order where the widespread inequality between players—at the national, intranational, and international level—was often washed out with the "global" qualifier.

Emerging first at the borders of liberalism, early-boom art biennials foreshadowed a new period of North Atlantic–centric world hegemony that transformed how art was produced, exhibited, and valued across the world. Some of these exhibitions, such as the Bienal de La Habana, were created in an explicit attempt to resist the expansion of liberalism; others, such as inSITE and Manifesta, anticipated and aided liberalism's ultimate spread worldwide. In their concern with art matters, early-boom art biennials engaged in political praxis by openly embracing ideological positions, by participating in the reimagining of site and everyday life, and by helping construct new cultural identities. Sites as dissimilar as Cuba, Mexico, the United States, and the European Union institutionalized these shifts via new cultural policy frameworks and regulatory mechanisms. Art biennials' cyclical temporality, the boundlessness of their collections and their site-specific orientation allowed this previously marginal and infrequent exhibition form to become an ideal malleable display solution for the wide array of world pictures being imagined in this crucial time in recent history. These porous exhibitions filtered into the artistic field the forms of production, symbols, and social relations shaping life in their surrounding locales. Predominantly public facing, they helped situate cities on a new world map, partly by orchestrating encounters between foreign and local art actors, but also by tapping into the thirst for cultural and material difference of a new class of global cosmopolitan tourists hopping around what they now experienced as a seamless world.

Furthermore, early-boom art biennials were critical sites for experimenting with and developing new techniques and social relations in the field of curatorial practice. The many approaches to curating envisioned and exercised in these exhibitions set the foundations for what "curating" looks like today in noncollecting, globally oriented art institutional spaces—a large and influential subset within the contemporary exhibitionary complex. In the early-boom biennials I trace the consolidation of today's predominant paradigms in contemporary curating: "collaborative" and "freelance" curation models—models that, in turn, inherited competing conceptions of expert labor in socialism and capitalism. Moreover, because curatorial practice in early-boom biennials was explicitly deployed to mediate between logics internal to the art field and others that were contextual to it, these early-boom experiments continue to be important references for art actors who wrestle for autonomy from and/or engagement with social life in their work.

Many of the forces that I record in this volume are structural in that they condition artistic work at many levels, including that carried out by artists, curators, critics, and historians. But their structural character doesn't annul actors' agency. Throughout this book I show how artists, curators, administrators, and community members selectively engaged in biennial conversions to the extent that they could, negotiating their own mediations with history, territory, and, ultimately, art, within a nascent exhibition complex that was predominantly oriented toward global elite audiences. More generally, aesthetic conversions selectively bracket cultural elements from outside the "art" category and incorporate them into historically dominant, but ultimately contingent, frameworks of artistic distinction. Aesthetic conversions are neither good nor bad per se; they are simply part of the work that art does, as a category in permanent transformation and often expansion, by forces both inherent *and* external to art worlds—including not only the logics underpinning curatorial practice, the art market, academia, and the actual making of artworks but also the broader social and economic forces that govern life in contemporary capitalism. Touchstones in the genealogies of modern and contemporary art, aesthetic conversions have been tactically wielded through history with a diversity of purposes. These conversions were constitutive of turn-of-the-century avant-gardes, for they resignified elements from everyday life as art. They were also integral to decades-long efforts to label as art the production of nonwhite artists who experience colonial exclusion from mainstream art institutions on the basis of their race and ethnicity. These conversions have also been key to the groundbreaking work of feminist and queer artists fighting to make room for a diversity of bodies and affects, community-making practices, and maintenance and care work within the patriarchal museum.

As I describe throughout this book, early-boom biennials repeatedly relied on aesthetic conversions that amplified widespread desires for social cohesion and world peace after a long and difficult twentieth century. Biennials were moved by an interest to showcase the cultural specificity of the hosting sites—including their constitutive material and immaterial elements. Consciously or not, these longings reflected the rise of a new end-of-the-century global cosmopolitanism, a feeling of belonging to a supranational culture in the making shared by members of elite groups who were benefiting from (or aspiring to benefit from) post–Cold War geopolitical arrangements. In some cases, these biennial conversions responded to deeply held desires to leverage a city's advantage in a new world order. By showing local and foreign art together in ways that were legible to global art audiences, as happened with inSITE in San Diego and Tijuana, biennial conversions could help local boosters in their efforts to insert their cities and regions in emergent and valorized circuits of economic and cultural exchange. In other cases, biennial conversions helped amplify policy makers' goals of cultural unification by representing diverse modern art genealogies as manifestations of a shared identity, as was the case with Manifesta in Rotterdam and its many other venues since.

At other points, biennial conversions were consciously wielded to carve spaces of artistic legitimacy for practices and peoples that had previously been denied artistic distinction by North Atlantic modern art institutions, as with the first iterations of the Bienal de La Habana. Curators helped craft new aesthetic labels, such as "Border art," "European art," and "Third World avant-garde," to facilitate the conversion of endemic art genealogies into the emergent category of *global* art. In the process, these early-boom biennial conversions set the stage for the accelerated boom of art biennials throughout the 1990s and early 2000s, not only by establishing these new labels for art that would consolidate in the category of "global contemporary art" but also by developing exhibition forms that proved, symbolically at least, to be effective at mediating tensions between the global and the local, at least for art tourists and patrons of dominant art worlds. These transformations ultimately eased the consolidation of the art biennial as the dominant exhibition form in the period.

The inclusionary ethos of early-boom biennials was often well intentioned, and it ultimately helped broaden what contemporary art worlds value as art, while fostering regional art scenes and increasing artist diversity worldwide. However, I argue that a large number of the biennial conversions that these exhibitions facilitated negatively affected the worlds surrounding the art institution. In many cases, these globally oriented exhibitions have sometimes been complicit in processes of urban gentrification and have often excluded local art constituencies and endemic cultural forms from their exhibitions and organizations. Despite their attempts to support heteronomous, site-specific, and socially oriented artistic practices, the alliances that developed between biennial curators, their organizers, and supporting political and economic elites often had the effect of neutralizing the liberatory orientation of the dialogical aesthetic frameworks that had propelled many to conceive of art biennials as conciliatory spaces. This book explains how, in spite of organizers' good intentions, early-boom art biennials often helped appropriate the aesthetic repertoires of subaltern groups in specific regions, placing them in the service of monumentalizing the historical victories of regional and global elites. Many of these biennial conversions rid the appropriated aesthetic repertoires of their original emancipatory intentions, reproducing earlier formalist co-optations of emancipatory avant-garde art practices by hegemonic institutions and actors.[1]

Importantly, the biennial conversions of the early-boom years paved the way for the ultimate emergence of what we now recognize as "global contemporary art." I have used this term throughout this book to refer to a diversity of art practices found within and around boom art biennials. But what is "global contemporary art"? Answers to this question have been multiple in the past two decades.[2] To start, as other art historians do, I recognize that one of the features of living in contemporary times, as opposed to *modern* times, is our incapacity to find reassurance in a totalizing and unifying discourse that explains the whole of present human experience—including the experiences of artists producing art and those of art historians studying their work. The postmodern erosion of modern historical metanarratives invites the open embrace of a time shaped by not only multiple, coeval cultural paradigms but, importantly, of *many* contemporary arts. Living with contemporaneity involves acknowledging the variety of arts and worldviews as well as the limitations of different situated attempts to understand them. Contemporary arts actively engage these multiple ways of being alive, diagnosing these many presents, which are fragmented, multiple, and in permanent change. Within them coexist, in unstable equilibrium, parallel and interconnected historical processes and their aftermaths. Like other cultural productions, contemporary art objects are embedded in the arrangements of forces that frame life in the present. They adopt myriad attitudes toward it: some seek to render transparently how things truly are; others glimpse to what these forces could yield if arranged otherwise. Here and there, artworks pop through the clefts reclaiming ways of life that are forbidden, dehumanized, chastised, muted, labeled untrue. Although they all speak of our presents, they hold countless possible futures within.

If the category of contemporary art designates the many approaches toward art making that exist in contemporaneity, I use the term *global contemporary art* to designate a subset within that larger category. As I see it, global contemporary art is a direct product of the abrupt realignments of power that occurred at the end of the twentieth century. Global contemporary art is that subset of contemporary art practices produced within the relations of production drawn in the global exhibitionary complex. The "global" qualifier is not descriptive of its material geographical reach but, rather, of aspirations to be legible to audiences self-identified with the global. The years described in this book inaugurated two decades of significant historical transformations, during which economic globalization and the spread of neoliberal ideology shaped new relations of production in the post–Cold War world order, consolidating dominating aspirations of the European Union and the United States for global reach. This time was also marked by the consequences of recent postcolonial processes in Africa and Asia, which placed so-called global South states as actors in the new supranational circuits—not as equal players, but beholden to refurbished colonial relations with the northern powers. These tectonic shifts had important implications for cultural production, favoring new strategies for the institutionalization of art that centered the global as idealized and experienced by a new elite class in the making. As I show in this book, more often than not, the *global* qualifier conceals forms of coloniality in a neoliberal world order.

Spreading throughout the planet during the 1990s, art biennials became the dominant exhibition form worldwide, shaping the production, circulation, valuation, and experience of art in the contemporary moment. In words of art historian Chika Okeke-Agulu, "Contemporary art as we now know it is characterized by two contrapunctual forces: the globalization of sameness (what some have cynically referred to as the biennial aesthetic) and the contestation of this sameness through these very biennials, many of which have the mandate to promote and to assert the imagined uniqueness of national, regional, or continental contemporary art and visual practices."[3] Contemporary art, broadly understood, is produced by the many frictions between these two complementary forces, in enduring tension with each other, caught in what I have called the centrifugal and centripetal litanies that shape hegemony.[4] With this in mind, throughout this book I consciously use the term *global contemporary art* to designate a new contemporary art canon produced within globally oriented art institutions that became dominant in many parts of the planet during the late twentieth and early twenty-first centuries. Global contemporary art, in its distinction within the global exhibitionary complex, registered the idealized promise of global seamlessness, a particular aspiration of unity through differences. Although the category is a direct result of the neocolonial relations that cemented during the period—ones that upheld a revamped dominating elite, white-centric, North Atlantic culture—not all global contemporary artworks celebrate such superiority. Indeed, many artworks that were showcased in the early-boom biennials critiqued the hegemony of North Atlantic art worlds and proposed much-needed alternatives.

Yet the category of global contemporary art became hegemonic at the turn of the millennium not despite but rather in part through these artistic critiques. Although global contemporary art incorporated material, processual, and symbolic elements from subaltern artistic genealogies, it was still predominantly white and North Atlantic–centric at the turn of the century because its formal, representational, and display repertoires were still rooted in the legacies of twentieth-century art in Western Europe and the United States. In particular, and regardless of its forms and themes, global contemporary art was subject to the aesthetic expectations, interpretative frameworks, and evaluative practices of curators, critics, art historians, and, importantly, collectors who were, for the most part, attuned to North Atlantic–centric parameters of aesthetic value. Several chapters in this book detail the conversions that artistic practices originating from nondominant worldviews had to undertake in order to be deemed worthy of inclusion in the globally oriented exhibition spaces of early-boom art biennials. These conversions included art by Indigenous artists reframed as magicians in *Magiciens de la Terre* (Paris [1989]), the production of young Mexican artists becoming global through their inclusion in inSITE (San Diego / Tijuana [1994, 1997]), and the adaptations that the work of Russian performance artists had to undergo in order to exhibit in Manifesta

(Rotterdam [1996]). The chapters on the early iterations of the Bienal de La Habana show the complex efforts that went into proposing an alternative to modern European aesthetics, a proposal for an anticolonial avant-garde that was as enthusiastic as it was short-lived.

The biennial conversions facilitated by these new globally oriented art exhibitions ultimately asserted an aesthetics of reception that was anchored in solutions to representational problems that had been developed within North Atlantic modern art throughout the nineteenth and twentieth centuries. During the realignment of hegemonic forces at the end of the Cold War, early-boom biennials helped rehabilitate the sanctity of the exhibition space as a visually centered standard for the contemplation and judgment of beauty, a standard that had been consolidated during previous centuries of colonial expansion by Western Europe and the United States. The result was the reinforcement of a spectacular, formalist ecumenism that was far from new: it had been inscribed in the foundations of European aesthetics and the discipline of art history all along. At the turn of the millennium, this formalism surfaced again as a solution to the challenges of trans-cultural communication, imposing itself over other proposals for how to jointly appreciate diverse cultural productions in a common framework. As Amelia Jones reminds us, despite motley efforts to counter and topple it, this legacy has achieved hegemonic status and is still widely celebrated today as the quasi-teleological summit of artistic progress.[5]

In the decades that followed the early biennial boom, art biennials mutated to conform to what was becoming an increasingly standardized form. In spite of the diverse local specificities that had initially prompted the boom, the globalization of the art industry facilitated the progressive homogenization of the forms of labor, conceptual frameworks, and relationships with locality that shape dominant standards in the art biennial form. The Bienal de La Habana, inSITE, and Manifesta outgrew their original configurations to adapt to a changing world. As Cuba wrestled with the deep economic and social crisis of the Special Period in Times of Peace and its aftermath, the Bienal struggled to survive. With declining economic support from the state, the organization relied on episodic private foreign sponsorship and the sustained devoted effort of its staff. Its curatorial focus changed to synchronize with global art trends while preserving its original focus on a southern perspective that progressively incorporated artists from Europe and the United States—changes that have largely evacuated the Bienal of its original anticolonial tone. InSITE continued to take place in Tijuana and San Diego until 2005. During its lifetime, the festival developed an increasingly sophisticated approach to the complexities of life in the region, organizing research residencies for artists prior to their interventions, involving a growing number of regional actors in decision-making processes, and reaching broader audiences with a robust community-outreach agenda. Although most of its commissions still went for nonregional artists, favoring spectacular interventions in the area, in the twenty-first century the organization supported a growing number of socially engaged art projects that intervened in the complex inequalities shaping life at the borderlands. Manifesta still takes place every two years in a different location within the European Union. It moves back and forth among sites in Central, Southern, Western, and Eastern Europe, faithful to its original goal of helping articulate a unified European field for contemporary art. With a rotating roster of guest curators who assume authorship and artist selection for each occasion, the exhibition has become one among many platforms for the showcase of contemporary art in Europe. Throughout its long life, Manifesta has maintained the original structure developed in Rotterdam, featuring a central foreign-curated core supplemented with locally situated peripheral projects.

The post–Cold War optimism for world peace that fueled the art biennial boom has since vanished. Early-1990s desires for world convergence and unity have been replaced by a more skeptical and critical orientation toward both globalization and art, given a more widespread awareness of the abstract and material casualties produced by neoliberalism in its planetary advance. Further, artists, historians, curators, and critics worldwide now wonder about the long-term feasibility of the biennial model as questions about the art world's aesthetic and social exclusivity, its environmental sustainability, and its affinity with ethically corrupt actors such as the fossil fuel, big pharma, and military industries surface in the public debate.[6] As a result, efforts to decolonize the art biennial and to embed it in local fabrics are widespread.[7] A good sign of how timely many of these critiques are is that even those in leadership positions within the global exhibitionary complex have begun to respond to calls for change and to anticipate them in their own defenses of the art industry.[8] This new and bubbling angst does not come as a shock: as I have shown, the biennial form became dominant in a globally aspirational world that no longer exists. The hegemony of the previous period has fractured, and whatever rearrangement of forces is to become dominant has yet to calcify. As such, the future of biennials, and art worlds more generally, remains uncertain. The transformations they will experience are yet to be seen. What is sure, however, is that whatever cultural institutional models become prevalent, artists, curators, art historians, and exhibition forms will play a big part in its construction as they continue to partake in aesthetic conversions in their engagement with history and territory, beauty and joy.

NOTES

Biennial Conversions at the Borders of Liberalism: An Introduction

1   During the 1950s, several regionally oriented art biennials emerged, most of which existed for only a handful of editions. These included Bienal de São Paulo (São Paulo, Brazil, 1951), documenta (every five years, Kassel, German Federal Republic, 1955), Biennale de la Méditerranée (Alexandria, Egypt, 1955), Biennale Grafike (Ljubljana, Slovenia, 1955), Muzički Biennale Zagreb (Croatia, 1961), and Biennale de Paris (France, 1959). After these came Bienal de Arte Coltejer (Medellín, Colombia, 1968), Triennale-India (New Delhi, India, 1968), Bienal del Grabado Latinoamericano (San Juan, Puerto Rico, 1970), Bienal Americana de Artes Gráficas (Cali, Colombia, 1971), Bienal Internacional de Arte de Valparaíso (Valparaíso, Chile, 1973), Biennale of Sydney (Sydney, Australia, 1973), and Arab Art Biennale (Baghdad, Iraq, 1974). The inauguration of the Bienal de La Habana in 1984 triggered a phenomenon of repetition and adaptation of the form worldwide, including Africa (Dakar Biennale, 1990; Biennale de Bamako, 1993; Johannesburg Biennale, 1995; etc.), Latin America (Mercosul Visual Arts Biennial, Porto Alegre, 1990; inSITE in Tijuana and San Diego, 1994; San Juan Biennial of Latin American and Caribbean Engraving, relaunched as San Juan Poly / Graphic Triennial: Latin America and the Caribbean, 2004; etc.), Asia (Gwangju Biennale, 1995; Fukuoka Triennale, 1999; Asia Pacific Triennial of Contemporary Art, Queensland, 1993; etc.); and Europe (Istanbul Biennial, 1987; Manifesta, 1996; Berlin Biennale, 1996; Liverpool Biennial, 1999), etc.

2   Rafal Niemojewski calls them "perennials." Niemojewski, *Biennials*, 26.

3   Jones, *Global Work of Art*. As I have explained elsewhere, biennials often work as mediators of a fictionalized experience of authenticity for art tourists. Checa-Gismero, "Global Contemporary Art Tourism," 313–28. See also Wang, "Rethinking Authenticity," 349–70.

4   For a foundational framing of the art exhibition as a discursive operation, see Greenberg, "Exhibition as Discursive Event," 118–25.

5   Smith, "Biennials."

6   Jones, "Longer History," 69.

7   Francis Fukuyama famously declared the 1990s the end of history—an announcement that has long been proved untimely. See Fukuyama, *End of History*. The Scorpions' song "Winds of Change," composed by the West German rock band following a visit to Moscow in 1990, became an instant hit in Europe and the United States.

8   Throughout this book I use the term *North Atlantic* to refer to the modernist art genealogies dominant in elite, white-centric art worlds in the United States and Western Europe throughout the twentieth century. My choice is motivated by a desire to concretize and provincialize the region otherwise referred to as *the West* or *Euro-America*. Though not perfect, this term underscores the centrality afforded to the cities of Paris and New York in the myths of origin of dominating art-historical master narratives. Similarly, it encapsulates the hegemonic role played by elite universities in the United States and Western Europe in the production and reproduction of these accounts. Last, *North Atlantic modernisms* underscores the imbrication of this art genealogy in nonartistic collaborations developed between Western European nations and the United States throughout the twentieth century, such as those exemplified by military and economic alliances like nato and the Marshall Plan. My avoidance of the term *Euro-America* was in great part influenced by reading Flores, "'Latinidad Is Canceled,'" 58–79. My choice of *North Atlantic* was influenced by Elkins, "Leading Terms."

9   This book joins ongoing debates within the discipline of art history on the nature and genealogy of "global contemporary art." Relevant book-length studies in this discussion include Lotte Philipsen, *Globalizing Contemporary Art* (Aarhus: Aarhus University Press, 2010); Harris, *Globalization and Contemporary Art*; Hans Belting, Jacob Birken, Andrea Buddensieg, and Peter Weibel, *Global Studies. Mapping Contemporary Art and Culture* (Karlsruhe: Hatze Cantz, 2011); Demos, *Return to the Postcolony*; Ring Petersen, *Migration into Art*; Smith, *Art to Come*; and Joselit, *Heritage and Debt*. Additional resources can be found in de Duve, "Glocal and the Singuniversalae, 681–88; Carroll, "Art and Globalization," 131–43; Dimitrakaki, "Art, Globalization," 305–19; and Miller, "Modern Global Art," 35–53.

10   By selecting 1989 as a benchmark date in my analysis, I do not seek to claim its universal validity but to point to how the events surrounding the end of the Cold War contributed to the shaping of supranational

political efforts, class identity, and cultural circuits in an influential, but niche, sphere of global aspirations dominated by the interests of Western Europe and United States. I look forward to periodizations that do not take 1989 as a point of reference and that, in so doing, supplement my intention to show how calls for universality of the visions encompassed under the "global" label are always only partial in their scope.

11   See, for example, Cachia, *Curating Access*; Sandell, Dodd, and Garland-Thomson, *Re-Presenting Disability*.

12   See, for example, the controversies surrounding the exhibition "*Primitivism" in 20th Century Art: Affinity of the Tribal and the Modern* (Museum of Modern Art, New York, 1984–1985). Important critiques include Foster, "'Primitive' Unconscious," 45–69; and Clifford, "Histories," 164–215.

13   Boltanski and Esquerre, "Economic Life of Things."

14   For the origins of formalism, its dominion over twentieth-century North Atlantic–centric master art narratives, and its early twenty-first-century prevalence, see Jones, "Form and Formless," 127–44.

15   Throughout this book I use the now outdated term *Third World* to refer to nations that, during the Cold War, remained unaffiliated with the United States and the Soviet Union. This political movement called for unity and solidarity among these nations, most of which came together in political alliances such as the Non-Aligned Movement (1961) or the Group of 77 (1964). I have chosen to use this term because it was the self-designation used at the time by organizers and participants of the Bienal de La Habana. For an emic explanation of this word choice, see Llanes Godoy, "Bienal de la Habana," 9. For a genealogy of the term and suggestions for alternative terminology, see Tomlinson, "What Was the Third World?," 307–21.

16   Kwon, "One Place after Another"; Kester, *Conversation Pieces*; Yúdice, *Expediency of Culture*. As Kester recognizes, for many artists and critics the collaborative component of dialogical aesthetics can trigger questions such as "Collaboration with whom and what?" as well as fears from dialogical art practitioners and defenders about institutional co-optation of their emancipatory goals and formal registers. Kester, *One and the Many*.

17   Jones, "Longer History," 69. See also Jones, *Global Work of Art*.

18   See Jones, "Longer History"; Alloway, *Venice Biennale*; Filipovic, van Hal, and Øvstebø, *Biennial Reader*; Ricci, *Starting from Venice*; and Coates, "From the Margins," 113–32.

19   Green and Gardner, *Biennials, Triennials, and Documenta*, 9, 19–24.

20   Green and Gardner, 51.

21   For an insightful analysis of the Bienal de São Paulo's early days and its role in connecting Brazilian art with other international art currents, see Nelson, *Forming Abstraction.*

22   See, for example, Gardner and Green, "Biennials of the South," 442–55.

23   Niemojewski, *Biennials*, 17.

24   Mignolo, *Local Histories / Global Designs.*

25   Wu, "Biennials without Borders."

26   Bennett, "Exhibitionary Complex."

27   Balibar, "World Borders," 71–78. See also Mezzandra and Neilson, *Border as Method.*

28   Smith, *Art to Come*, 60–61.

29   Harvey, *Spaces of Global Capitalism*; Harvey, *Cosmopolitanism.*

30   De Duve, "Glocal and the Singuniversalae."

31   My thinking about taste has been informed by the work of sociologist Pierre Bourdieu. Bourdieu, *Distinction.*

32   See, for example, Okwui Enwezor's work as curator of documenta 11 (2002) alongside Octavio Zaya.

33   Camnitzer, "Art and Literacy"; Camnitzer, "ALPHABETIZATION, Part I"; Araeen, "Art and Postcolonial Society"; Calhoun, "Class-Consciousness of Frequent Travelers," 869–97; Calhoun, "Cosmopolitanism and Nationalism," 427–48; Jones, "Ethnic Envy and Other Aggressions," 96–110.

34   Angela Dimitrakaki has explored the conditions for art production when capital operates fully as a social relation, with special emphasis on how these relations shape, and are shaped by, the exhibition form of the art biennial. Dimitrakaki, "Art, Globalization," 305–19.

35   Harvey, "From Managerialism to Entrepreneurialism"; Robinson, "Global Capitalism Theory."

36   Gramsci, *Selections from the Prison Notebooks.* For a classic anthropological account of common sense as a cultural process, see Geertz, "Common Sense," 5–26.

37   Marchart describes documenta as a "hegemony machine." See Marchart, *Hegemony Machines.*

38   Alberro, "Response in Questionnaire," 55–60; Jones, "Ethnic Envy and Other Aggressions."

39   González, "Cultural Fronts," 108.

40   My thinking is influenced by Mary Louise Pratt's concept of the "contact zone" in Pratt, *Imperial Eyes*; and James Clifford's formulation of the museum as a contact zone in Clifford, "Museums as Contact Zones," 188–218.

41   For a recent generalist account of this exhibition form that responds to some of the critiques that I and others articulate, see Niemojewski, *Biennials*.

42   Spivak, "Resistance That Cannot Be Recognized," 61.

43   In addition to the studies referenced throughout this introduction, relevant titles include Filipovic, van Hal, and Øvstebø, *The Biennial Reader*; Osborne, *Anywhere or Not at All*; Eilat et al., *Making Biennials*; Kompatsiaris, *Politics of Contemporary Art Biennials*; Harris, *Global Contemporary Art World*, especially chapter 3 ("Globalizing Indian Contemporary Art: The Biennial as Rhetorical Form"); Rojas-Sotelo, "Cultural Maps"; Christov-Bakargiev, "Biennale Syndrome"; and Ferguson, Greenberg, and Nairne, *Thinking about Exhibitions*.

44   My account of the Bienal de La Habana and inSITE include their first three and two iterations, respectively, but I decided to limit my analysis of Manifesta to its first iteration because questions about the organization's relation with its context changed as the biennial relocated to different cities.

Chapter One. Polyphonic Internationalism

1   Álvarez, *Noticiero ICAIC Latinoamericano*.

2   See note 15 of the introduction for an explanation of my choice to use the term *Third World* in this book

3   As this chapter and the next one describe, cultural institutions in Havana had worked to position the Cuban capital as the center of left-leaning Latin American intelligentsia since 1959. These efforts were driven by Casa de las Américas and ICAIC. In the visual arts, internationally oriented exhibitions before the Bienal included the Salón de Mayo (1967) and many others organized in Casa de las Américas.

4   Art collective Grupo Antillano included Esteban Guillermo Ayala Ferrer, Manuel Mendive, Rogelio Rodríguez Cobas, Claudina Clara Morera Cabrera, Manuel Couceiro Prado, Guillermina Ramos Cruz, Herminio Escalona González, and Rafel Queneditt. See de la Fuente, *Grupo Antillano*.

5   *Volumen I* opened on January 14, 1981, at Havana International Arts Centre (on San Rafael Street). It featured a selection of artists under twenty-five years old, including Flavio Garciandia, Tomas Sanchez, Jose Manuel Fors,

Jose Bedia, Gustavo Perez, Ricardo Rodriguez, Leandro Soto, Israel Leon, Juan Francisco Elso, Rubén Ortiz Torres, and Rogelio "Gory" Lopez Marin. The exhibition marked a moment of transition in Cuban contemporary art, exhibiting work by artists who grew up during the Revolution.

6   Ashton, "Havana, 1986," 38–39.

7   Romero Fernández, "La Rectificación," 178–95.

8   Hart, "Joseph Stalin."

9   For a detailed account of the Bienal de La Habana's early days, see Weiss, *Making Art Global (Part 1)*.

10   "Decree 113 of March 30, 1983, states the Bienal de La Habana's functions: (a.) to promote the study and promotion of Lam's work as a universal expression of contemporary art; (b.) to internationally promote the art work of artists from Asia, Africa, and Latin America, as well as of artists who struggle for cultural identity and who are related to those territories; (c.) to endorse international activities in the field of visual arts in order to develop and establish networks of cooperation; (d.) to facilitate the development of the visual arts in Cuba and to promote the contemporary manifestations of Cuban contemporary artists of most significance; (e.) to offer services of specialized information about contemporary art, artists, critics, and researchers; (f.) to enrich the cultural patrimony of the country through the creation of a permanent collection of visual arts and the systematic exchange of artistic and cultural documentation; (g.) to periodically present national and international events related to the visual arts and to give artistic recognition in the form of grants and prizes; and (h.) to promote a broader interest in the visual arts to society through didactic and artistic activities and the use of mass communication."

11   This initial mission would be modified in 1989, after the Centre d'Art Georges Pompidou in Paris opened the exhibition *Magiciens de la Terre*. See chapter 3.

12   The Special Period in Times of Peace (Periodo Especial en Tiempos de Paz) was an exceptional period in the Cuban economy that began in 1991 and lasted approximately one decade, until 2001. The Special Period forced a restructuring of the Cuban economy in response to the acute economic crisis that the nation faced after the dissolution of its primary trade partner, the USSR, and the increased US embargo.

13   For example, in 1981 he was a speaker at the Encuentro de Intelectuales por la soberanía de los pueblos de nuestra América (Encounter of Intellectuals for the Sovereignty of the Peoples of Our America), where

he gave a talk titled "Value: A Weapon for Cultural Penetration." See later sections for a discussion of his thinking.

14   I borrow the term *polyphony* from Mikhail Bakhtin, who uses the term to acknowledge the coexistence of multiple voices in Dostoevsky's novels. In polyphonic literary works, truth is produced through dialogical interaction between characters who articulate different visions of the world. See Bakhtin, *Problems of Dostoevsky's Poetics.*

15   The deployment of cultural relations in the fight for US influence began in 1940, when Nelson Rockefeller took office as coordinator of commercial and cultural relations with the American nations. See Fox, *Making Art Panamerican.*

16   *Boletín Divulgación*, "Visitantes extranjeros en la II Bienal de La Habana," November 27, 1986, Archivo Centro de Arte Wifredo Lam.

17   Llanes Godoy, *Salón de Mayo de París.*

18   Povey, "Segunda Bienal de La Habana," 82–84; Ashton, "Havana, 1986," 38–39.

19   Collier, *Repainting the Walls of Lunda.*

20   Garrido Gómez, "Tradición y contemporaneidad."

21   Weiss, *Making Art Global (Part 1)*, 30.

22   Cabrera Infante and Jiménez Leal, *P.M.* See "Conclusiones de un debate entre cineastas cubanos."

23   A compilation of documents from these debates can be found in Pogolotti, *Polémicas culturales de los 60.*

24   García Buchaca, "Consideraciones sobre un Manifiesto."

25   Zhdanovism: Soviet cultural policy (1946 and 1953), that classified the world into "Imperialistic" (aligned with the United States) and "Democratic" (aligned with the USSR). The policy set the ethical and legal framework to censor and prosecute artists accused of producing "bourgeois" art. Green and Karolides, *Encyclopedia of Censorship.*

26   Like Rio de Janeiro, Caracas, and Buenos Aires, Havana was an important hub for the development of Latin American modern abstraction in the 1940s and 1950s. For example, the journal *Noticias de arte* sought to "contribute modestly . . . without the prejudices that might tarnish the free expression of thought, to disseminate any cultural manifestations from this country or from abroad." See *Noticias de arte*, no. 1 (1957). In this line, issue 11 (1957) was entirely devoted to analyzing Cuban presence in the second São Paulo Biennial. It published essays by important Latin American critics of the time, such as Argentine Jorge Romero Brest. Important names in

Cuban abstraction at the time were Carmen Herrera (based in New York since 1934), Zilia Sánchez, Loló Soldevilla (who returned to Havana from Paris in 1957), and critics Juan Marinello, Pedro de Oraá, and José Lezama Lima. In 1957 Soldevilla curated the exhibition *Pintura de Hoy: Vanguardia en la Escuela de París at the Palace of Fine Arts*. She and critic de Oraá later opened Galería de Arte Luz Color, around which the group Diez Pintores Cubanos gravitated. See Weiss, "To Defend the Revolution."

27   Guevara, "El Socialismo," 266–67.

28   Bürger, *Theory of the Avant-Garde*, 36.

29   Other new cultural institutions that were the product of the postrevolutionary institutional reform were the Union of Writers and Artists of Cuba, the National Ballet of Cuba, the National Theater, the National Art School, and the Teatro de Arte Popular.

30   An established artist in the 1960s, Le Parc won the first prize for painting in the 1966 Venice Biennale. See Mazars, "La peinture se meurt."

31   Le Parc, qtd. in Christiane Duparc, "Julio Le Parc: Voulez-vous jouer avec lui?," *Le nouvel Adam*, December 1966, Le Parc Archive, Paris; cited in Plante, "Kinetic Multiples."

32   Greenberg, "Recentness of Sculpture"; Greenberg, "Where Is the Avant-Garde?"

33   Arnauld Pierre, historian of the Groupe de Recherche Audiovisuel, cites a 1960 letter from Le Parc: "It was necessary 'to learn about the physiological mechanisms of ocular movement and how it was interconnected with the mind, *in order to move on consciously, and step by step, to conquering the rest of the sensory and mental mechanisms* and to successfully configure visual elements in accordance with the knowledge attained about the *nature of the relationship between the human eye and the human being.*'" Le Parc, qtd. in Pierre, "Instability of Kinetic Environments," 94.

34   "Propuestas de Julio Le Parc," Archivos Centro de Arte Wifredo Lam, Havana. In Madrid the workshop was held at the Círculo de Bellas Artes, an independent cultural institution that throughout the twentieth century played an important role in connecting international artists with the Madrid cultural spheres.

35   Julio Le Parc, "Le Parc à La Havane," 1986, Julio Le Parc, www.julioleparc.org. Unless otherwise stated, all translations are by the author.

36   Julio Le Parc, "Guerrilla Cultural," March 1968, Le Parc Archive, Paris.

37   Julio Le Parc, "La valorización, un arma clave para la penetración cultural," 1981, Julio Le Parc, www.julioleparc.org.

38   Le Parc described the papier-mâché artist thus:

> If it shook its ears, it was to chase out false encouragements, un-founded criticisms, flattering; if it shook its eyes, it was to better perceive forms, colors, movements, changes; if it shook its tongue, it was to respond with arguments and to defend its ideas against conformism and, why not, to taste Cuban rum; if it shook its head, it was to see everything happening in its environment, to be informed of injustices, and to see the world in full convulsion and the peoples engaged in struggle; if it shook his brush, it was to underline that, in the arts like elsewhere, all advances come from hard work; if it shook its arm holding the palette, it was to invite everyone to participate in the act of creation, to not keep it egotistically for himself; if it made any noise it was to wake people up from their lethargy; if it had a big red heart it was to show that the creative act must be generous, towards the others, and not an individualistic search for sacralizing economic success. (Le Parc, "Le Parc à La Havane")

39   As a remedy to this damaging division of labor, Le Parc proposes changes in cultural policies, increasing the participation of artists, critics, and members of the general audience in the drafting of legislation. It is important to remember that Le Parc has lived in Paris since 1958. These notes do not reference cultural policies in Cuba but, more generally, cultural policy trends in the West. See Le Parc, "La valorización."

40   Mosquera, "Raíces en acción," 32–39, cited in Craven, *Art and Revolution.*

Chapter Two. Curating the Third World

1   Llilian Llanes, interview with the author, Havana, September 21, 2017.

2   Guevara, *Che Guevara Reader*, 120. From a speech at the meeting of the Central Organization of Cuban Trade Unions on August 21, 1962.

3   Guevara, *Guerra de Guerrillas.* Grant Kester has explored the similarities between the revolutionary organizational model of *foquismo* and the rhetoric and practices of disruption by Latin American artists during the Cold War. My analysis discusses, instead, the on-the-ground tactical openness of revolutionary curatorial practice to form transnational and trans-class alliances. See Kester, "Sound of Breaking Glass I" and "Sound of Breaking Glass II."

4   Olinde Rodrigues, "L'artiste, le savant et l'industriel," qtd. in Călinescu, *Five Faces of Modernity.* Originally published in *Opinions littéraires, philosophiques et industrielles*, Paris, Bossange père, 1825.

5   Becker, *Art Worlds.*

6   Kester, *Conversation Pieces.*

7   For an analysis of the figure of the freelance curator at the turn of the millennium, see chapter 8.

8   Marx, *Capital,* 451.

9   Hall, "Marx's Notes on Method," 113–49; Marx, *Capital,* 102.

10   See Decree no. 113, Executive Committee of the Council of Ministers, March 30, 1983. Decree signed by Armando Hart Dávalos (minister of culture), Fidel Castro Ruz (president of the Council of Ministers), and Osmany Cienfuegos Gorriarán (secretary of the Council of Ministers). In the 1960s, a time of institutional reform in Cuba's cultural industries, Paris-based Cuban painter Wifredo Lam reinstated his relationship with the island and declared his support of Castro's socialist program. Actively engaged in sponsoring artistic exchanges between Cuba and Europe, Lam quickly became a symbol of Castro's international avant-garde aspirations. The son of a Chinese immigrant and a Black Cuban peasant, Lam also embodied the nation's renewed will to overcome colonial race and class disparities. When Lam died, in 1982, Castro and Lam's widow, Swiss artist Lou Lam, envisioned the creation of the Centro de Arte Wifredo Lam, a national center of contemporary art, in his honor. The institution's first task was to organize an international exhibition of contemporary art in the Third World.

11   The Casa de las Américas was founded in 1959 by Haydée Santamaría, a revolutionary hero and party organizer originally from rural eastern Cuba. The Casa's mission was to overcome the restrictions on communications that the US embargo imposed on the island, using cultural cooperation to spearhead the formation of an emancipated pan-American consciousness. Close to Ernesto Guevara and his ideas, Santamaría was perceived as a liberal within the ccp, and Casa remained a sanctuary for free thought at times of intense political persecution in the 1970s, 1980s, and 1990s.

12   Lesbia Ves Dubois, interview with the author, Havana, October 2, 2017.

13   The list included Mexico, Cuba, Argentina, Colombia, Venezuela, Brazil, Chile, Nicaragua, Uruguay, Bolivia, Ecuador, Peru, Panama, Puerto Rico, the Dominican Republic, Costa Rica, El Salvador, Guadalupe, Guatemala, Jamaica, and Martinique.

14   In the initial years, "specialist" was the title given to those in charge of researching, selecting, and organizing the artworks in each iteration of the exhibition. Later on, this denomination was changed to "curator," mirroring trends in the international art industry.

15   The list of nations and territories is long: Algeria, Angola, Argentina, Belize, Bolivia, Brazil, Burkina Faso, Cambodia, Cameroon, Chile, Colombia, Congo, Costa Rica, Cuba, Dominican Republic, Ecuador, Egypt, El Salvador, Ethiopia, Ghana, Guadalupe, Guyana, Haiti, Honduras, India, Indonesia, Iran, Iraq, Jamaica, Kuwait, Laos, Lebanon, Malaysia, Mali, Martinique, Mexico, Morocco, Mozambique, Nicaragua, Nigeria, Pakistan, Panama, Peru, Philippines, Puerto Rico, Senegal, Seychelles, Sri Lanka, Sudan, Syria, Tanzania, Togo, Trinidad and Tobago, Tunisia, Uruguay, Venezuela, Vietnam, Zaire, Zambia, and Zimbabwe.

16   Jose Manuel Noceda, interview with the author, Havana, November 17, 2016.

17   Margarita González, interview with the author, Havana, June 17, 2015.

18   Gerardo Mosquera, interview with the author, Los Angeles, May 17, 2016.

19   Nelson Herrera Ysla, interview with the author, Havana, November 12, 2016.

20   Di Maggio, "La revolución en esencia no se cuestiona," 22 (translation by the author).

21   Noceda interview, November 17, 2016.

22   The Special Period in Times of Peace was a time of national exceptionalism defined by nationwide policy reforms that sought to remediate the grave economic impact of the end of USSR subsidies for the Cuban economy and the tightening of the US embargo on the island. During this period, Cuba introduced major changes to its foreign relations agenda, initiating an important reform of its economy to allow foreign tourism development on the island. The beginning of the Special Period, which eased the reorientation of cultural production to support a growing international tourism industry, coincided with the globalization of the contemporary art industry, triggering major transformations in the production, conceptualization, and exhibition of art throughout the world.

23   Llanes interview, September 21, 2017.

24   Llanes, interview, September 21, 2017.

25   *Fiesta de la imagen (I Bienal de La Habana).*

26   From a conversation with the artist, September 28, 2022.

27   Noceda interview, November 17, 2016.

28   Jorge Fernández, interview with the author, San Diego, October 31, 2016.

29   Magaly Espinosa, qtd. in Weiss, *Making Art Global (Part 1),* 17.

30   Noceda interview, November 17, 2016.

31   Although the Oficina del Historiador dates back to the 1930s, its present identity and mission was established in 1967, when Eusebio Leal became city historian. The office is directly financed by tourism revenue from its enterprise Habanaguex, the owner of restaurants, souvenir shops, hotels, and other tourist services. The office began a decades-long restoration project of the Old City following a master plan after UNESCO, which included the area in its World Heritage list. The master plan's main principles are "to safeguard national identity with the research, promotion, and development of culture. To protect heritage, rehabilitating territory with a legally binding Integral Development Special Plan. To avoid the displacement of the local population, protecting it from the tertiarization of economy. To grant the territory a basic technical infrastructure and services according to contemporary needs. To achieve the self-financed integral development of the restoration of heritage." See "Master Plan," 1981, Oficina del Historiador, Havana.

32   "II Bienal de La Habana, Egresos hasta 31 de diciembre de 1986," December 31, 1986, internal report, Centro de Arte Wifredo Lam archives, Havana.

33   Llanes interview, September 21, 2017.

34   Pagel, "ART."

35   Ves Dubois interview, October 2, 2017. The "boom" that she refers to is the "boom" that Latin American literature experienced in the 1960s–1970s and that propelled writers such as Gabriel García Márquez, Julio Cortázar, Carlos Fuentes, and Mario Vargas Llosa to international prominence. This phenomenon was an industry-led attempt to market a purported Latin American stylistic difference to North Atlantic audiences, galvanized around the formation and marketing of the genre "realismo mágico."

36   Kester, "Sound of Breaking Glass II."

37   Barreiro López, "Collectivization."

38   Gardner and Green, "Biennials of the South."

39   Gardner and Green, "Biennials of the South."

40   For a study on the impact of the Special Period in the development of artistic public spheres in Cuba, see Fernandes, *Cuba Represent!*

Chapter Three. An Aesthetics of Production

1   Weiss, *Making Art Global (Part 1).*

2   The complete roster included José Franco Codinach, Flora Fong García, Leandro Soto Ortiz, Sandra Ceballos Obaya, Raúl Santos Serpa, Pedro

Contreras, Manuel Mendive Hoyo, Flavio Garciandía de Oraá, Eduardo Rubén García Herrera, Mariano Rodríguez Álvarez, Moisés Finalet Aldecoa, Carlos Alberto García de la Nuez, Alberto Jorge Carol Yaniz, Fayat Jamis Bernal, Umberto Peña Garriga, Minerva López Díaz, Raúl Martínez González, Adelaida Herrera Valdés, Ever Fonseca Cerviño, Ernesto González Puig, Emilio Castro Mosquera, Nelson Domínguez Cedeño, Antonio E. Fernández (Tonel), Miriam Alejandra González, Tomás Sánchez Requeiro, Gilberto Frometa Fernández, María Eugenia Haya Jiménez, and Gustavo Acosta Pérez.

3   Herrera Ysla, "Textil Latinoamericano," 253 (translation by the author).

4   Herrera Ysla, 253.

5   See note 57 in "The Working Day" of *Capital*, where Marx cites a report by Dr. Richardson, "Work and Over-work," in *Social Science Review*, July 18, 1863. See also "Machinery and Modern Industry" in Marx, *Capital*.

6   Kant, *Critique of the Power of Judgment*, 114, 183.

7   My thinking has been influenced by Pierre Bourdieu's and Gayatri Chakravorty Spivak's critiques of Kant's *Critique of the Power of Judgment*. See Bourdieu, *Distinction*; and Spivak, *Critique of Postcolonial Reason*.

8   Checa-Gismero, "Collective Fabric," 275–92.

9   Although the manuscripts were compiled and published in German in 1932, they became difficult to access until after World War II, when they were translated into English (1956), French (1962), and Spanish (1963). Included in Marx, *Early Writings*.

10   Sánchez Vázquez drastically opposes, for example, the deterministic frameworks offered by Gueorgui Plejánov and György Lukács. See Sánchez Vázquez, *Invitación a la estética*, 66.

11   Sánchez Vázquez, *Las ideas estéticas de Marx*, 58, 59.

12   Mosquera, *El diseño se generó en octubre*, 33.

13   On March 1, 2020, as I wrote these lines, Ernesto Cardenal left this world.

14   Craven, "Art in Contemporary Nicaragua," 51–63.

15   Alewitz, "Havana Biennial," 25.

16   Ravelo Blancas, "Protagonismo y poder."

17   The full roster of collaborating artists included Marta Palau, Rogelio Naranjo, Vicente Rojo, Ofelia Murrieta, Silvia de Icaza, Lourdes Almeida, Helen Escobedo, Carla Rippey, Magali Lara, Teresa Morán, Ismael Guardado, Olga Dondé, and Beatriz Zamora. The exhibition toured Cuba, the United States, West Germany, Sweden, and other parts of Mexico.

18   As the director of Museo Carrillo Gil in Mexico City, Silvia Pandolfi played an important role in the early internationalization stage of Mexico's contemporary art scene in the early 1990s. Among the artists she showed in the museum were Lili Engel, Amelia Peláez, Felipe Ehrenberg, Joseph Beuys, Alejandro Prieto Posada, Jordi Boldo, Joan Duran, Perla Krauze, Masafumi Hasumi, Jorge Du Ban, Patricia Soriano, Joan Miró, Wolfgang Paalen, Ryuichi Yamabi, Gabriel Macotela, Silvia Gruner, Fernando García Correa, Miguel Chevalier, Patricia Londen, and Tomás Emde.

19   *Tercera Bienal de La Habana, 1989* (Havana: Centro de Arte Wifredo Lam, 1989).

20   Toni Piñera, "Muñecas con vida artística," *Granma*, November 15, 1991.

21   Marx, *Capital.*

22   "Cultura Popular Mestiza," 1991 Bienal.

23   Escobar, *El mito del arte*; Lauer, *Producción Artesanal.*

24   Marta Palau, interviewed by Ida Rodríguez Prampolini in Palau and Barrios, "Dear Marta," 213–33.

25   Camnitzer, "La segunda Bienal de La Habana," 84.

26   The event occupied galleries at two venues, the Center Georges Pompidou and the Grande Halle de la Villette. It took place between May 18 and August 14, 1989. See Steeds, "*Magiciens de la Terre*," 41.

27   Curatorial statement, 1989, box 95026/168, Center Georges Pompidou Archives, Paris.

28   See, for example, the issue of *Third Text* dedicated to the exhibition (vol. 6, Spring 1989). Steeds, "*Magiciens de la Terre*," 25.

29   Martin, "Preface."

30   Cited in Cohen-Solal, *Magiciens de la terre*, 126.

31   Martin, "Preface."

32   Kant, *Critique of the Power of Judgment*, 187.

33   See, for example, the exhibitions *Statuary in Wood by African Savages: The Root of Modern Art*, 1914, and *The Picasso-Braque Exhibition*, 1915, both curated by Alfred Stieglitz at Gallery 291, New York City.

34   Buchloh and Martin, "Interview," 21.

35   Araeen, "Our Bauhaus," 6.

36   Buchloh and Martin, "Interview," 21.

Chapter Four. Sovereignty Claims over the Borderlands

1   From "Cross the Razor: Project Documentation," date not available, MSS 707, inSITE Archive, Special Collections and Archives, University of California at San Diego, San Diego, CA (hereafter inSITE Archive).

2   Proposition 187, also known as Proposition Save Our State, was a ballot initiative approved in 1994 that granted power to local authorities to deny access to public services like health care and education to unauthorized immigrants residing in the United States. The initiative was found unconstitutional by a federal district court three days after it passed on November 11, 1994.

3   Hollander, "Crossover Dreams," 50.

4   Throughout this book I have chosen the term *borderlands* to designate the region that includes the cities of San Diego and Tijuana and their peripheries. This umbrella term designates a roughly defined geographic area around the borderline that allows for specific evaluations of the region's economy, its conflicts, or its specific culture. Yet, for reasons that will become obvious through this section, I share Glen Sparrow's reluctance to embrace the belief in the region's supposedly binational character and hope to provide instead a more nuanced examination of the complex relations between two cities whose populations, economies, and culture are unequally valued and only partially integrated. See Monsiváis, *La cultura de la frontera*; and Sparrow, "San Diego–Tijuana," 73–83.

5   Fox, *Fence and the River*.

6   See Davis, Mayhew, and Miller, *Under the Perfect Sun*, 169–97; and Shanks, "I.W.W. Free Speech Movement," 25–33.

7   Habermas, *Structural Transformation of the Public Sphere*.

8   See chapter 8 for a discussion of the aesthetic theories surrounding the symbolic conflict and antagonism within the art institution at the turn of the century.

9   Terry Allen, "Instructions for Drivers and Translators," date not available, MSS 707, box 16, inSITE Archive.

10   For Gloria Anzaldúa's account of the border as a liminality, see Anzaldúa, *Borderlands / La Frontera*.

11   Mbembe, "Necropolitics," 11–40.

12   Bourdieu, *Distinction*.

13   Sparrow, "San Diego–Tijuana."

14   Andreas, *Border Games*, 6.

15   I use the terms *Chicano* and *Chicana* instead of the most recent form *Chicanx* to reference the historical, self-denominated, Chicano movement of the civil rights period.

16   Berelowitz, "Spaces of Home," 341.

17   McCaughan, "'We Didn't Cross the Border,'" 6–31; John, *Line in the Sand*.

18   John, *Line in the Sand*, 25.

19   In 1965, at the beginning of the Plan de Industrialización de la Frontera, 12 factories employed 3,000 workers. In 1990, 1,920 factories employed around 460,000 workers. Since NAFTA was enacted in 1994 these figures have multiplied: 2,267 factories employed around 648,000 workers; in 2000, 3,251 factories employed an estimated 1,090,000 workers. Data from Instituto Nacional de Geografía y Estadística, Mexico City, 2004.

20   Mize, "Interrogating, Race, Class, Gender and Capitalism," 136.

21   "inSITE94 Organization Draft," date not available, MSS 707, box 209, folder 7, inSITE Archive.

22   John, *Line in the Sand*.

23   Vega Briones, "Población Commuter de La Frontera Norte," 207–38. At the turn of the century, 29,303 *tijuanenses* of working age commuted every day to work in San Diego. Data from "Muestra del 10% del Censo de Población y Vivienda 2010," INEGI, cited in Vega Briones.

24   Herzog, "Global Tijuana," 121.

25   Hobsbawm, "Introduction," 1–14.

26   Carroll, *REMEX*, 211.

27   González, "Introduction," 1.

28   See, for example, Salkowitz-Montoya and Montoya, "Critical Perspective on the State of Chicano Art," 3–7.

29   See, for example, Carroll, *REMEX*. El Congreso de Artistas Chicanos de Aztlán (CACA) was a Barrio Logan organization of artists active between the 1970s and the late 1980s. Among its members were Mario Torero, Pablo de la Rosa, Tomas Casteneda, and Felipe Barboza.

30   Among the original members were Salvador Torres, Viviana Zermeno, Delia Moreno, Leticia de Baca, Armida Valencia, Judith Baca, Guillermo Aranda, Tomas Castaneda, and Mario Acevedo.

31   Carroll, *REMEX*.

32   Fox, *Fence and the River*, 44.

33   For a fascinating account of the controversy, see Berelowitz, "Conflict over 'Border Art,'" 69–83.

34   Yúdice, *Expediency of Culture*, 289.

35   Ollman, "'IN/SITE 92' a Comeback."

36   "Installation Gallery," date not available, press clip from unknown source, MSS 707, inSITE Archive.

37   Yard, *inSITE94*, 6.

38   "Declaración de principios de inSITE94: Installation Gallery," date not available, MSS 707, inSITE Archive.

39   Sheren, *Portable Borders*, 91.

40   Yúdice, *Expediency of Culture*, 290.

41   Mbembe, "Necropolitics," 34.

42   Kelley, *Border Art Workshop*, 20.

43   Lefebvre, *Critique of Everyday Life*, 163.

44   Sánchez Luján, "Arte del Chicano," 11.

45   Monsiváis, *La cultura de la frontera*, 44.

46   See Nelson Limerick, *Legacy of the Conquest*.

47   Noriyuki, "Age of Unarius."

48   The piece, which became highly popular at the time, was even "danced" on *The Tonight Show with Jay Leno*. Ortiz Torres remembers that every time the car is danced outside of Southern California, its audiences miss the reference to the Border Patrol, yet they rejoice in the spectacularity and acrobatic dexterity of the vehicle.

49   Ortiz Torres credits the important role that car shows played for community cohesion in the aftermath of the 1992 Los Angeles uprising with his interest in cars as an art medium. Interview with the artist, January 20, 2022.

50   Turegano, "Binational Festival Celebrates"; "inSITE94: Mission Statement," undated, MSS 707, box 210, folder 1, inSITE Archive.

Chapter Five. Fears of Provincialism and the Desire to Be Global

1   Johnson, "Thank the Lord for inSITE94."

2   Yúdice, *Expediency of Culture*.

3   Davis, Mayhew, and Miller, *Under the Perfect Sun*.

4   Miller, "Just Another Day in Paradise?," 161.

5   Gregory Sholette, email to the author, December 27, 2021.

6   Janet Koenig, email to the author, January 13, 2022.

7   "Toiling Redskins Glad to Labor."

8   Greg Sholette, cited in Lippard, "Anti-amnesia," 4.

9   "A Border-Spanning Extravaganza," *San Diego Daily Transcript*, May 14, 1993, MSS 707, inSITE Archive, Special Collections and Archives, University of California, San Diego, San Diego, CA (hereafter inSITE Archive).

10   Preston Turegano, "border: Crossing the Cultural Frontier," *San Diego Union Tribune*, October 3, 1993, MSS 707, inSITE Archive.

11   "Proclamation," Office of the Mayor, City of San Diego, March 19, 1994, MSS 707, inSITE Archive.

12   Sparrow, "San Diego–Tijuana," 73–83.

13   InSITE94 internal document, n.d., MSS 707, inSITE Archive; "Cultura en Tijuana," *El Heraldo* (Tijuana, Mexico), July 10, 1994, MSS 707, inSITE Archive.

14   Néstor García Canclini, qtd. in Yúdice, *Expediency of Culture*, 287–88.

15   My thinking has been informed by Pierre Bourdieu's classification of the forms of capital. See Bourdieu, "Forms of Capital," 241–58.

16   Allan Sekula contextualized *Dead Letter Office* within his lifelong interest in the conditions of life and work at sea in his essay "Between the Net and the Deep Blue Sea," 3–34.

17   Olga Krasnoff, "Style," *619 Social Calendar*, March 1994, 6, MSS 707, inSITE Archive.

18   Ganster and Buj, "Percepciones de la migración Mexicana," 262.

19   Andrea Fraser, *Inaugural Speech* (1997), insiteart.org, https://insiteart.org/people/andrea-fraser.

20   Fraser, *Inaugural Speech*.

21   "Downtown Arts Rising."

22   A UCSD mixed-use building in downtown San Diego's East Village opened in 2021.

23   "Downtown Arts Rising."

24   Florida, *Rise of the Creative Class*, 218.

25   See Florida, "Rise of the Creative Class" and "Mapping the Diversity of the Creative Class."

26   Zukin, *Loft Living*.

27   Bourdieu, *Distinction*.

28   Harvey, "From Managerialism to Entrepreneurialism," 3–17; and Harvey, *Cosmopolitanism*, 67.

29   Harvey, "From Managerialism to Entrepreneurialism."

30   Robinson, "Global Capitalism Theory," 349.

31   Córdoba Azcárate, *Stuck with Tourism*.

32   Guidebook produced by Melanie Smith for INSITE97, inSITE Archive.

33   Melanie Smith, interview with the author, Mexico City, August 27, 2016.

34   *The Loop / La Vuelta* took place between June 1 and July 5, 1997.

35   A caption for this image reads: "On 10 March 1994 I went to the Zocalo and stood in the middle of a line of carpenters, plumbers and house painters, offering my services as a tourist." Medina, Ferguson, and Fisher, *Francis Alÿs*, 10, 11.

36   Medina, Ferguson, and Fisher, *Francis Alÿs*, 40, 39.

37   "Installation Gallery," date unavailable, press clip from unknown source, MSS 707, inSITE Archive.

Chapter Six. Globalizing Mexican Art

1   Fax from Silvia Gruner to Sara Maarchick, Installation Gallery, no date, MSS 707, inSITE Archive, Special Collections, University of California, San Diego, San Diego, CA (hereafter inSITE Archive). Unless otherwise stated, all translations are by the author.

2   Mize, "Interrogating Race, Class, Gender and Capitalism."

3   DeChaine, "Bordering the Civic Imaginary," 43.

4   Lerner, "Borderline Architecture," 1–8.

5   See, for example, Maclaren Walsh, "The Dumbarton Oaks Tlazolteotl," 7–43.

6   It was also through these nineteenth-century trade circuits that other objects that served as inspiration for canonical avant-garde movements such as cubism were appropriated by the white-centric North Atlantic art canon, mostly as formalist distortions severed from their original meanings. See, for instance, Blier, *Picasso's Demoiselles*.

7   Carroll, REMEX, 183.

8   Cordero Reiman, "Mexico," 271–72.

9   Giunta, *Avant-Garde, Internationalism, and Politics*.

10   Michael Krichman, interview with the author, San Diego, August 15, 2018.

11   Aguilar Camín and Meyer, *In the Shadow of the Mexican Revolution*.

12   Montero Fayad, *El cubo de Rubik*. Mexico entered the General Agreement
      on Tariffs and Trade (GATT) in 1986, under the presidency of Miguel de
      La Madrid. As the introduction to this chapter describes, in 1992 Mexico,
      Canada, and the United States signed the North American Free Trade
      Agreement (NAFTA). See Romero Sotelo, *Los orígenes del neoliberalismo
      en México*.

13   Muchnic, "Unmasking Mexico's Many Faces."

14   Krichman interview, August 15, 2018; untitled fax, Center for US-Mexican
      Studies, UCSD, August 25, 1994, inSITE Archive.

15   Yúdice, *Expediency of Culture*. See also, for example, Sánchez, "SEMEFO," 57.

16   Montero Fayad, *El cubo de Rubik*.

17   A CONACULTA report from 1994 describes FONCA as a "financial mecha-
      nism where the state, the private sector, and the art community volun-
      tarily come together [moved] by, on the one hand, their support to artistic
      freedom, and, on the other, the preservation and growth of [our] cultural
      heritage.... FONCA received a first sum of 5,000,000 new pesos from the
      Federal Government, an amount to which was added tax-deductible
      contributions from the private sector." *Memoria, 1988–1994*, 159.

18   Krichman interview, August 15, 2018.

19   Debroise, "Museums in Mexico."

20   Flores, *Mexico's Revolutionary Avant-Gardes*.

21   See Craven, *Art and Revolution in Latin America*; Montgomery, *Mobility of
      Modernism*; and Flores, *Mexico's Revolutionary Avant-Gardes*.

22   See Coffey, *How a Revolutionary Art Became Official Culture*.

23   See Debroise and Medina, *La era de la discrepancia*.

24   Benezra, *Dematerialization*, 104.

25   Eder, *Helen Escobedo*, 16; Gropius, *Scope of Total Architecture*; Gropius,
      "Architecture at Harvard University."

26   Yard, "Tagged Turf in the Public Sphere," 50; Medina, "Una línea es un
      centro," 62.

27   Acha, "Felipe Ehrenberg."

28   Kwon, *One Place after Another*, 87; Kaye, *Site-Specific Art*, 1.

29   Heidegger, *Being and Time*.

30   "Exhibition Framework," INSITE97, fax from Danielle Reo to Olivier De-
      broise, August 4, 1997, Fondo Olivier Dubroise, Arkheia MUAC, Mexico City.

31   Debroise, "By the Night Tide / inSITE94," 31.

32   Foster, *Return of the Real*; Fried, "Art and Objecthood"; Kwon, *One Place after Another*, 87.

33   Krichman interview, August 15, 2018.

34   As early as 1991, Daniel Guzmán, Pablo Vargas Lugo, Eduardo Abaroa, Damián Ortega, Diego Gutiérrez, and Abraham Cruzvillegas organized the group show *In Situ* at the Mexico City studio of US artist Michael Tracy, where they engaged with the language of site specificity.

35   Arriola, "¿A qué le tiras cuando curas mexicano?"

36   Kwon, *One Place after Another*, 14–15.

37   See Jones, *Machine in the Studio*; Bryan-Wilson, *Art Workers*.

38   To quote Hal Foster in his analysis of seriality in 1960s minimalism and pop, "To what order do these minimalist industrial objects and pop simulacra point? To work in a series, to serial production and consumption, to the socio-economic order of one-thing-after-the-other." Foster, *Return of the Real*, 62.

39   Mbembe, "Necropolitics," 11.

Chapter Seven. Manifesta: Placenta Europa

Epigraph: Reportedly said by Jean Monnet, pragmatic diplomat and one of the architects of the European Coal and Steel Community, predecessor of the European Economic Community, qtd. in Richards, *Cultural Tourism in Europe*, 95.

1   "Petition," January 27, 1994, Foundation European Art Manifestation, The Hague, Netherlands.

2   The directors of the art institutions were Katalin Keserü, director of Kunsthalle Budapest, Műcsarnok (Hungary); Anda Rottenberg, director of the National Gallery of Contemporary Art, Zacheta (Poland); Henry Meyric Hughes, director of exhibitions at the Hayward Gallery, South Bank Centre, London (United Kingdom); and Katalin Néray, director of the Ludwig Museum in Budapest (Hungary). Rosella Siligato, deputy director of the Palazzo dell'Exposizioni de Roma (Italy), had confirmed attendance but was not at the meeting.

      The government representatives at the meeting were Ebe Nomberg, counselor in the Department of Arts and Culture, Ministry of Culture and Education (Estonia); Markku Valkoonen, director of Frame, Finnish Fund for Art Exchange (Finland); A. Kontis, cultural attaché in the Greek embassy at The Hague (Greece); Thomas Meyerzu Schlochteren, counselor of visual arts at the Rotterdamse Kunststichting (Rotterdam, Netherlands); Robert Haas, director of the RBK, the Netherlands Office for Fine Arts (Netherlands); Boris Danailov, vice minister of culture (Bulgaria); Jan Verlinden, director of the Art and Museums Department, Ministry of Culture of Flanders (Belgium); Jane Balsgaard, painter and sculptor from the Danish Ministry of Culture (Denmark); René Block, director of exhibition exchange, Institut für Auslandsbezichungen (Germany); Martha Deneltova, arts officer, Ministry of Culture (Republic of Slovakia); Barbara Berce, senior adviser, Ministry of Culture (Slovenia); Olaf Fekkes, director of the Iceland Gallery, Ministry of Culture (Iceland); Svenrobert Lundquist, director of NUNSKU, Swedish National Commission for Art Exchange Abroad (Sweden); Mikael Adsenius, secretary of the board, NUNSKU, Swedish National Commission for Art Exchange Abroad (Sweden); Gheorghe Vida, director of the Visual Arts Department, Ministry of Culture (Romania); Sever Mesca, director of the Department of International Cultural Dialogue (Romania); Leonid Bajanov, director of the Fine Arts Department, Ministry of Culture (Russian Federation); Sarah Finlay, visual arts officer, Arts Council (Ireland); Barbara Tosi, cultural attaché, Italian embassy in The Hague (Italy); Ivan Saric, deputy minister of culture (Croatia); Gundega Cébere, art adviser to the Ministry of Culture (Latvia); Svein Christiansen, director of the Norwegian Commission for Visual Arts (Norway); Irina Kourolenko, chief specialist, Ministry of Culture (Ukraine); Victor Belein, art adviser, Secretaria de Estado da Cultura (Portugal). Those who had confirmed attendance but were not at the meeting were Hubert Wurth, ambassador of the Grand Duchy of Luxembourg in The Hague (Luxembourg); Joseph Secky, director of the Visual Arts Department, Bundesministerium für Unterricht und Kunst (Austria); M. J. Alonso, cultural counselor of the consulate, Spanish embassy in The Hague (Spain); Peter Schreiber, counselor to the Ministry of Welfare, Health, and Culture (Netherlands); Eleonora Stehower, cultural attaché to the Dutch Embassy in Rome (Netherlands); and Y. Martial, cultural attaché of the embassy of the French Republic in The Hague (France).

As part of the philanthropic interventions of the Soros Foundation, a series of Soros Foundation Fine Arts documentation and exhibition centers (Soros Centers for Contemporary Art, or SCCA) opened in the capitals of Soviet republics in the 1980s and 1990s. The first one opened in Budapest, the birthplace of investor George Soros, with the goal of "support[ing] modern Hungarian culture which was banned or at least forced into the background by official cultural policies; in essence, [of] support[ing] those Hungarian artists in 'counter-culture' circles." Soros Centers for Contemporary Art Network, accessed on January 10, 2018, www.c3.hu/scca. With the advising of prominent US and British curators such as J. Carter Brown (director of the National Gallery in Washington, DC), Thomas Messer (director of the Guggenheim Museum, New York), and Michael Compton (director of exhibitions, Tate Gallery, London), the center in Budapest sought to promote "avant-garde spirited art through scholarships, purchases, the organization of exhibitions and the publication of catalogs." Other centers followed: SCCA Zagreb (1993), SCCA Ljubljana (1993), SCCA Sarajevo (1996), and SCCA Skopje (1994). For a thorough study of the role of the SCCA in the art scenes of Eastern European nations, see, for example, Galliera, *Socially Engaged Art*.

3 "The European Art Manifestation," brochure, January 27, 1994, Foundation European Art Manifestation, The Hague, Netherlands.

4 National representatives, as mentioned in note 4, came from within the EU and aided in its eastbound growth.

5 For a description of the metaphors used to define Europe in the period, see Pejić, "Dialectics of Normality," 17–27.

6 See invitation to Rosa El Hassan, October 31, 1995, Manifesta Foundation Archives, Amsterdam (hereafter MFA).

7 Since 1996, Manifesta has taken place at Rotterdam (Netherlands), Luxembourg (Luxembourg), Ljubljana (Slovenia), Frankfurt/Main (Germany), Donostia / San Sebastián (Spain), Nicosia (Cyprus—canceled), Trentino / South Tyrol (Italy), Murcia (Spain), Limburg (Belgium), St. Petersburg (Russia), Zurich (Switzerland), Palermo (Italy), and Prishtina (Kosovo).

8 Hedwig Fijen, qtd. in Guskov, "Manifesta 10."

9 Originally, Manifesta was scheduled to take place at the end of 1994 and beginning of 1995 at the Kunsthal Rotterdam. Later, organizers moved it to April–June 1996. It finally happened in the summer of 1996 in several venues in the same city.

10 From "Minutes of the Meeting concerning the European Art Manifestation," November 8, 1993, Netherlands Office for Fine Arts, The Hague, Netherlands.

11 Treaty on European Union, February 7, 1992, Luxembourg Office for Official Publications of the European Communities, 3.

12 Before the signing of the Treaty of Maastricht in 1992, timid attempts toward cultural cooperation in the CEE had taken place at the initiative of the European Commission, although they were always subject to the economic framework set by the 1952 Treaty of Rome. As Nicoleta Lașan argues, in the absence of a shared cultural policy before 1992, the

recognition of the importance of the field of culture by European institutions responded to the "development of cultural industries, the wider consumption of cultural goods and services, the recognition that culture and commerce are not mutually exclusive and that in fact the Treaty of Rome affected also trade in cultural goods." Although subsequent communications of the commission acknowledged the importance of culture by defending the free circulation and improvement of living conditions for cultural workers (1977), the reduction of employment in the cultural sector, the growth of audiences, and the importance of conserving heritage (1982), these recommendations always obeyed the logic of improving the single market. See Laşan, "Article 128," 3.

13   See Laşan, "Article 128"; and Costa, "Culture as a Driving Force," 105–10.

14   See Laşan, "Article 128."

15   Article 128, Treaty on European Union, Maastricht, February 7, 1992, accessed January 12, 2018, https://europa.eu/european-union/sites/europaeu/files /docs/body/treaty_on_european_union_en.pdf.

16   Sassatelli, "Arts, the State, and the EU," 28–41.

17   See Hix, "Study of the European Community," 1–30; Hix, "Study of the European Union II," 38–65; and Hix, *Political System of the European Union*.

18   On the governing of diversity within unity through cultural policy, see, for example, Bonet and Négrier, "End(s) of National Cultures?," 18–34.

19   Bennett, "Acting on the Social," 1421.

20   Gellner, *Nations and Nationalism*.

21   "Foundation European Art Manifestation. Manifesta I. 1996 Rotterdam Nederland Masterplan (concept)," August 1995, MFA, Amsterdam.

22   Spieker, "SubREAL during the 1990s."

23   Coll, Dagnino, and Neveu, *Disputing Citizenship*; Anderson, *Imagined Communities*.

24   Checkel and Katzenstein, *European Identity*; Best, Lengyel, and Verzichelli, *Europe of Elites*, 5; Wallerstein, "Construction of Peoplehood," 81–82.

25   Best, Lengyel, and Verzichelli, *Europe of Elites*.

26   In English in the original. "Foundation European Art Manifestation," 7, 4.

27   Balibar, "Preface," 4.

28   Hedwig Fijen and Jolie van Leeuwen, qtd. in *Manifesta 1 Rotterdam*, 157.

29   Stegeman, "Manifesta 1."

30   Henrik Plenge Jakobsen, interview with the author, online, March 21, 2018.

31 Katalin Néray, qtd. in *Manifesta 1 Rotterdam*, 25.

32 In its first iteration, Manifesta had five curators: Katalin Néray (Hungary), Andrew Renton (United Kingdom), Rosa Martínez (Spain), Hans Ulrich Obrist (Switzerland), and Victor Misiano (Russia).

33 Introduction to "Manifesta 1: The Pan European Art Manifestation," 1996, promotional video, Witte de With Center for Contemporary Art Archives, Rotterdam, Netherlands.

34 *Manifesta 1 Rotterdam*, 12.

35 Introduction to "Manifesta 1."

36 O'Neill, "Curatorial Turn," 13–28.

37 See Guilbaut, *How New York Stole*.

38 *Biennale de Paris*.

39 Feldman, *From a Nation Torn*.

40 The document followed a closed-door meeting in Moscow with the curatorial team for Manifesta 1 in Rotterdam in 1996.

41 "Foundation European Art Manifestation. Manifesta I. 1996 Rotterdam Nederland Masterplan (concept)," August 1995, 3, 4. MFA, Amsterdam.

42 "Foundation European Art Manifestation," 4, 10–11.

43 "Budget Foundation European Manifestation Visual Artists 1994 for the Implementation of the European Manifestation Beeldende Kunstenaars Project from January 1994 to January 1995," MFA. The total sum increased with time to reflect unforeseen expenses.

44 Ministries of culture from the following countries paid the fee: Hungary, Finland, Portugal, Sweden, Belgium, Luxemburg, Slovakia, Russia, Macedonia, Ireland, Slovenia, Austria, Estonia, Denmark, Czech Republic, Romania, Germany, Italy, Spain, and the United Kingdom (the British Council).

45 From "Actual State of Participating Countries. September 1995," MFA, Amsterdam.

46 For a detailed account of the different Soros Centers for Contemporary Art and their actions in Central and Eastern Europe, see Galliera, *Socially Engaged Art*, 81.

47 As I write these words, the Central European University, funded by the Open Society, has been forced out of its headquarters in Budapest because of Hungary's prime minister Viktor Orban's attacks on Hungarian American philanthropist George Soros. See Novak and Santora, "University Backed by George Soros."

48   See "Sponsor Proposition Manifesta 1. Kunsthal Rotterdam 1995," no date, unsigned, MFA. Unless otherwise stated, all translations are by the author.

49   From "Sponsorship Agreement," September 29, 1995, MFA. Signed between the private company Philip Morris Holland BV, represented by G. L. de Bruin, and Stichting Europese Manifestatie Jonge Beeldend Kunstenaars, represented by its chairman, J. N. A. van Caldenborgh.

50   From "Sponsorship Agreement," September 29, 1995, 2, 3. MFA, Amsterdam.

51   In addition to receiving financial sponsorship from Philip Morris, EAM received funds from a series of private art foundations in the Netherlands and in-kind support from a number of private companies. Private foundations partnering with EAM included the Mondriaan Foundation and the Caldic Collection. In a letter from March 13, 1995, Melle Daamen, director of the Mondriaan Foundation, agreed to contribute 100,000 guilders ($63,428) to EAM. Similarly, in a letter to Joop van Caldenborgh, chairman of chemical and food distribution company Caldic and director of the Caldic Collection, EAM project manager Fijen requested a total sum of 150,000 guilders ($94,949). However, the Culture Fonds Foundation of the Bank Nederlandse Gemeenten denied EAM's sponsorship request on the grounds that the foundation's goals were to prioritize "the knowledge of municipal activities" already taking place in Dutch towns and cities. Other forms of collaboration were sought by EAM with transportation companies, such as NS Rail and Deutsche Lufthansa. See letter from Mondriaan Foundation, (no subject), Manifesta 1, March 27, 1995, BKVN 474/95.5, MFA; letter from Stichting Cultuurfonds of the Bank Nederlandse Gemeenten of November 23, 1995, MFA; letter from Hedwig Fijen to NS Rail Marketing Manager Marjan Kretz, November 16, 1995; and letter from Hedwig Fijen Deutsche Lufthansa Sponsorship Department of March 20, 1995, MFA, Amsterdam.

Chapter Eight. Curating Conflict

1   "Contract for the Members of the Curatorial Team," August 1995, Foundation European Art Manifestation, Manifesta Foundation Archives, Amsterdam (hereafter MFA).

2   Andrew Renton, Rosa Martínez, and Hans Ulrich Obrist speaking in Manifesta 1 promotional video, Rotterdam Cultural Histories, Witte de With Center for Contemporary Art, Rotterdam, Netherlands.

3   "Contract for the Members of the Curatorial Team."

4   Fax from Nicole Meijer (EAM) to Hans Ulrich Obrist, September 13, 1995, MFA.

5   See, for example, Brouillette, "Creative Labor."

6   Lazzarato, "Immaterial Labor," 133.

7   See Smith, *Thinking Contemporary Curating*, 131–32.

8   Fax to curatorial team, January 28, 1996, MFA.

9   See, for example, a fax from an artist initially considered for participation in the biennial about the difficulties of working with a member of the curatorial team. Fax to Nicole Meijer, February 27, 1996, MFA.

10   Artists coming from Eastern and Central Europe included in Manifesta 1 were Pavel Kopriva (Czech Republic), Mila Bredikhina (Russia), Vadim Fishkin (Russia), Dmitri Gutov (Russia), Róza El-Hassan (Hungary), IRWIN (Slovenia), Robert Jankuloski (Macedonia), Piotr Jaros (Poland), Ivana Keser (Croatia), Oleg Kulik (Russia), Yuri Leiderman (Russia), Roman Ondák (Slovakia), Valeri Podoroga (Russia), Tadej Pogacar (Slovenia), Arsen Savadov (Ukraine), Georgy Senchenko (Ukraine), subREAL (Romania), Nedko Solakov (Bulgaria), and János Sugár (Hungary).

11   Pejić anchors this "catching up" in a long history of staging, via internationally oriented art exhibitions, Eastern and Central Europe's adoption of Western European artistic languages as a sign of political normalization. Pejić, "Dialectics of Normality," 17.

12   Bishop, "Exhibiting the 'East' since 1989," 67.

13   Hlavajová, "Towards the Normal."

14   See, for example, Galliera, *Socially Engaged Art*.

15   Piotrowski, "Central Europe in the Face of Unification."

16   Burnham, "Tadej Pogačar's Persistent Perversion of Institutional Critique."

17   Transnacionala's tour started with an opening of an exhibition by IRWIN, curated by Mary Jane Jacob at the Castle, in Atlanta, on July 28, 1996. They continued to Richmond, for a night of conversations, screenings, and performances with Catherine Gates; Chicago, with events organized by Mary Jane Jacob and Randy Alexander at different locations; San Francisco, with a presentation and screening at SRL; and Seattle, for a conversation with local art actors hosted by Charles Craft, Larry Creed, Robin Reed, and others. See Čufer, *Transnacionala*.

18   Misiano, "Institutionalization of Friendship."

19   Izabel Galliera has traced the origins and afterlives of this model in post-Soviet republics. See Galliera, *Socially Engaged Art*.

20   See Misiano, "Interpol."

21   Zahm et al., "Open Letter to the Art World," 108, 109.

22   Mila Bredikhina, interviewed by Jason Coburn for an untitled video produced by artist collective NEsTWORK, 1996.

23   Birnbaum, "Manifesta 1."

24   Kulik and Bredikhina, "Pavlov's Dog," 107.

25   Misiano, "Response to an Open Letter."

26   Wolff, *Inventing Eastern Europe.*

27   Zabel, "Dialogue East–West."

28   See Mally, *Culture of the Future.*

29   Groys, *Total Art of Stalinism.*

30   Erjavec, "Introduction."

31   Misiano, "Institutionalization of Friendship."

32   Degot, "Revenge of the Background," 341, originally published in Eiblmayr, *Zones of Disturbance.*

33   Bourriaud, *Relational Aesthetics,* 14, 15.

34   Ernesto Laclau and Chantal Mouffe, cited in Bishop, "Antagonism and Relational Aesthetics," 74.

35   Bishop, "Antagonism and Relational Aesthetics," 70.

36   Misiano, "Institutionalization of Friendship."

37   Misiano, "Confidential Community," 459, 461.

38   Misiano, "Confidential Community," 461.

39   Misiano, "Interpol," 1–25.

40   Habermas, "Public Sphere," 49–55.

41   Fraser, "Rethinking the Public Sphere," 56–80.

42   Viktor Misiano in conversation with Araeen, "Manifesta 1," 149.

Chapter Nine. The Art of Belonging

Epigraph: Jeanne van Heeswijk, "A NEsTWORK Report from Manifesta 1," in *NEsTWORK Activities Blueprint during Manifesta 1, 1996,* edited by Jeanne van Heeswij (Rotterdam: Jeanne van Heeswij, 1998), originally published in *Lokaal Europa.*

1   Filipovic, "Global White Cube," 70; "Manifesta"; Birnbaum, "Manifesta 1."

2   See "Cooperation Contract Model," 2, 3, 4.

3   The forging of Rotterdam's identity as a modern port city began with the opening of the Nieuwe Waterweg in 1886, which increased maritime

traffic and accelerated the development of the port. These years also marked the first important wave of migration from rural Holland to Rotterdam. Unlike with other highly bombarded cities, post–World War II reconstruction plans in Rotterdam ignored the prewar urban landscape and sought to build a modern city center concerned with the development of port and traffic infrastructure. Residential development favored the suburbs, provoking an exodus of the middle and upper classes away from the city center. Although the city's economy has become increasingly service oriented, Rotterdam's port is still the biggest in Europe and one of the busiest in the world. Since the New Rotterdam Plan, the port has moved away from the city both geographically and organizationally: new facilities have been built west of Rotterdam and on the North Sea, and port infrastructures have been privatized. See Carmona, *Planning through Projects*.

4   Richards, *Cultural Tourism in Europe*, 68.

5   W. Albeda, *Het Nieuwe Rotterdam* (Gemeente Rotterdam, 1986), cited in Oude Engberink and Miedema, "Governing Urban Regeneration," 114–24.

6   Oude Engberink and Miedema, "Governing Urban Regeneration."

7   Carmona, *Planning through Projects*.

8   Oude Engberink and Miedema, "Governing Urban Regeneration."

9   Carmona, *Planning through Projects*.

10   See Brouwer, "Het Nieuwe Rotterdam," 31–43; and Richards and Wilson, "Impact of Cultural Events," 1931–51.

11   Andrew Renton, in conversation with Araeen, "Manifesta 1," 148.

12   Hitters and Richards, "Creation and Management of Cultural Clusters," 234–47.

13   Birnbaum, "Manifesta 1"; Schwartz, "Manifesta 1."

14   Hall, "Whose Heritage?"

15   Boltanski and Esquerre, "Economic Life of Things."

16   From a letter sent by Rotterdam artist initiative NEsTWORK to eighty Rotterdam artists inviting them to intervene in a map of the city, in *NEsTWORK Activities Blueprint*, 82.

17   Fax from EAM's Rotterdam project office to the curatorial team, January 3, 1996, MFA.

18   As of March 24, 2023, the long list was still available on Manifesta 1's website, http://m1.manifesta.org/projects.htm.

19   Loick, "Ethical Life of Counter-Communities."

20   NEsTWORK, press release, November 1995, Witte de With Center for Con-
      temporary Art Archives, Rotterdam.

21   Invitation letter sent by NEsTWORK to Rotterdam artists, July 4, 1996, in
      NEsTWORK Activities Blueprint, 82.

22   "A NEsTWORK Report from Manifesta 1," in *NEsTWORK Activities Blueprint*.

23   Participants in these conversations included Samuel Ijsseling, Renée
      van de Vall, Nathalie Houtermans, Henk Oosterling, Kees Vuijk, and
      Liesbeth Levy.

24   "Going Places," in *NEsTWORK Activities Blueprint*, 58.

25   "Going Places," in *NEsTWORK Activities Blueprint*, 58.

26   Invitation letter to Rotterdam artists, 82.

27   "NEsTWORK Announcement," in *NEsTWORK Activities Blueprint*, origi-
      nally published in *Lokaal Europa*, 1996.

28   Artist members of the BAD Foundation included Joris Fiselier, Job Backer,
      Aletta de Jong, Karin Arink, Martijn Brenninckmeijer, Bibo, Kamiel Ver-
      schuren, Robin Kolleman, Anneloes van der Leun, Judith Schoneveld,
      Arthur Brugman, Marco Douma, Janie Schrijver, and Laurien Dumbar.
      The BAD Foundation began in 1988, when its members were students in
      the Rotterdam Academy of Art. Its first headquarters were a bathhouse
      (hence the name: *Bad* means "bath" in Dutch), and the group later moved
      to an empty bank building and then a factory, ending up in their current
      location, the empty public school Rijnmond-Zuid, in 1991. The foundation
      is still active and in the same venue. The building features eighteen stu-
      dios, of which four are for guest artists; a gym; a kitchen; a project room;
      and a multipurpose central hall. It now also includes a gallery that was
      not available in 1996.

29   Quoted from invitation letter signed by Stichting Bad Ateliers and
      Projectruimten, no date, Witte de With Center for Contemporary Art
      Archives, Rotterdam.

30   Invitation letter signed by Stichting Bad Ateliers and Projectruimten.

31   Extract from Jason Coburn's Manifesta travelogue, "Extracting the
      Human," first published in *Lokaal Europa: Rotterdam in Dialoog met
      Manifesta* (number 3), in a booklet from Kamiel Verschuren's personal
      archive, Rotterdam.

32   Invitation letter signed by Stichting Bad Ateliers and Projectruimten.

33   Fax from Joseph Grigely, July 29, 1996, in a booklet from Kamiel Versch-
      uren's personal archive, Rotterdam.

34   Kester, *Conversation Pieces*, 113.

35   Field Belenky, *Women's Ways of Knowing*, 9–10.

36   Extract from Jason Coburn's Manifesta travelogue, "Extracting the Human."

37   See fax from Grigely to BAD Foundation.

38   Letter from Andrew Renton to BAD Foundation, August 2, 1996, in a booklet from Kamiel Verschuren's personal archive; "Manifesta: The Inaugural Manifesta in Rotterdam."

Epilogue

1   See Buchloh, *Neo-Avantgarde and Culture Industry*.

2   See, for example, the many responses to the "Questionnaire on 'The Contemporary.'"

3   Okeke-Agulu, "Response to 'Questionnaire,'" 45.

4   My thinking on hegemony has been informed by the work of Jorge A. González. See the introduction to this volume and González, "Cultural Fronts."

5   See Jones, "The Revolution Is Over," 376–79.

6   See the important actions and organizing by the collectives Guerilla Girls, Decolonize this Place, and Prescription Addiction Intervention Now (P.A.I.N.), among many others. For an artist's and art critic's perspective, see Gillick and Charlesworth, "Is This the End of Contemporary Art?"

7   Documenta, the impactful quinquennial in Kassel, Germany, made solidarity a core element of its controversial fifteenth iteration (2022). Its artistic directors, the Indonesian collective ruangrupa, applied the principles of lumbung, an agrarian-economy model anchored on collaboration and welcoming, and prompted those in their initial roster to invite additional participants. Similarly, the 2019/2020 Berlin Biennale enacted durational commitments with place, partnering with local organizations to support already existing social-justice processes in the district of Kreutzberg. Under the motto "Weaving Solidarity," they worked to address the unfolding crisis by visibilizing histories of racism in German schools, amplifying children's imagined visions of their neighborhood, educating residents on the alternative health-care movement of 1970s/80s Berlin, and illuminating histories of refugee resettlement in Kreutzberg.

8   A good example of this reformist attitude is the recent volume by Biennial Foundation director Rafal Niemojewski: *Biennials*.

BIBLIOGRAPHY

Acha, Juan. "Felipe Ehrenberg y la subversión conceptualista." *Diorama*, Suplemento cultural de Excélsior, México (February 1973).

Aguilar Camín, Héctor, and Lorenzo Meyer. *In the Shadow of the Mexican Revolution: Contemporary Mexican History, 1910–1989*. Austin: University of Texas Press, 1993.

Alberro, Alexander. "Response in Questionnaire on 'The Contemporary.'" *October* 130 (Fall 2009): 55–60.

Alewitz, Mike. "Havana Biennial: A Partisan Review." *New Art Examiner* 14 (June 1987): 24–25.

Alloway, Lawrence. *The Venice Biennale, 1895–1968: From Salon to Goldfish Bowl*. Greenwich, CT: New York Graphic Society, 1968.

Álvarez, Santiago. *Noticiero ICAIC Latinoamericano: Actualidades Nacionales e Internacionales*. Havana: Instituto Cubano del Arte e Industria Cinematográficos, 1986.

Anderson, Benedict. *Imagined Communities*. London: Verso, 1993.

Andreas, Peter. *Border Games: Policing the U.S./Mexico Divide*. Ithaca, NY: Cornell University Press, 2001.

Anzaldúa, Gloria E. *Borderlands / La Frontera: The New Mestiza*. San Francisco: Aunt Lute, 1987.

Araeen, Rasheed. "Art and Postcolonial Society." In *Globalization and Contemporary Art*, edited by Jonathan Harris, 365–74. London: Wiley-Blackwell, 2011.

Araeen, Rasheed. "Manifesta 1." In *Cahier 5*, October 1996. Dusseldorf, Germany: Richter, 1996.

Araeen, Rasheed. "Our Bauhaus, Others' Mudhouse." *Third Text* 3, no. 6 (Spring 1989): 3–14.

Arriola, Magalí. "¿A qué le tiras cuando curas mexicano?" In *Los museos de cara al futuro*, 117–20. Mexico City: Consejo Nacional para la Cultura y las Artes (CONACULTA), 2003.

Ashton, Dore. "Havana, 1986." *Arts*, February 1987, 38–39.

Bakhtin, Mikhail. *Problems of Dostoevsky's Poetics*. Translated by Carl Emerson. Minneapolis: University of Minnesota Press, 1984.

Balibar, Étienne. "Preface." In *Race, Nation, and Class: Ambiguous Identities*, edited by Étienne Balibar and Immanuel Wallerstein, 1–14. London: Verso, 1991.

Balibar, Étienne. "World Borders, Political Borders." In "Special Topic: Mobile Citizens, Media States," special issue, *Publications of the Modern Language Association of America* 117, no. 1 (January 2002): 71–78.

Barreiro Lopez, Paula. "Collectivization, Participation and Dissidence on the Transatlantic Axis during the Cold War: Cultural Guerrilla for Destabilizing the Balance of Power in the 1960s." *Culture and History Digital Journal* 4, no. 1 (2015): 1–15.

Becker, Howard. *Art Worlds*. Berkeley: University of California Press, 1982.

Benezra, Karen. *Dematerialization: Art and Design in Latin America*. Oakland: University of California Press, 2020.

Bennett, Tony. "Acting on the Social: Art, Culture, and Government." *American Behavioral Scientist* 43, no. 9 (2000): 1412–28.

Bennett, Tony. "The Exhibitionary Complex." *New Formations* 1988, no. 4 (Spring 1988): 73–102.

Berelowitz, Jo-Anne. "Conflict over 'Border Art': Whose Subject, Whose Border, Whose Show?" *Third Text* 11, no. 40 (Autumn 1997): 69–83.

Berelowitz, Jo-Anne. "The Spaces of Home in Chicano and Latino Representations of the San Diego–Tijuana Borderlands." *Environment and Planning D: Society and Space* 23, no. 3 (2005): 323–50.

Best, Heinrich, György Lengyel, and Luca Verzichelli. *The Europe of Elites: A Study into the Europeanness of Europe's Political and Economic Elites*. Oxford: Oxford University Press, 2010.

Biennale de Paris: Manifestation Biennale et Internationale des Jeunes Artistes… Musée d'Art Moderne de la Ville de Paris. Paris: Biennale de Paris, Museé d'Art Moderne de la Ville de Paris, 1959–1985.

Birnbaum, Daniel. "Manifesta 1: Rotterdam." *Artforum* 35, no. 1 (September 1996): 105–42

Bishop, Claire. "Antagonism and Relational Aesthetics." *October*, no. 10 (Fall 2004): 51–79.

Bishop, Claire. "Exhibiting the 'East' since 1989: Introduction." In *Art and Theory of Post-1989 Central and Eastern Europe: A Critical Anthology*, edited by Ana Janevski, Roxana Marcoci, and Ksenia Nouril, 67–71. New York: Museum of Modern Art, 2018.

Blier, Suzanne Preston. *Picasso's Demoiselles: The Untold Origins of a Modern Masterpiece*. Durham, NC: Duke University Press, 2019.

Boltanski, Luc, and Arnaud Esquerre. "The Economic Life of Things: Commodities, Collectibles, Assets." *New Left Review* 98 (March–April 2016): 31–54.

Bonet, Lluís, and Emmanuel Négrier. "The End(s) of National Cultures? Cultural Policy in the Face of Diversity." *International Journal of Cultural Policy* 17, no. 5 (2011): 18–34.

Bourdieu, Pierre. *Distinction: A Social Critique of the Judgment of Taste.* New York: Routledge, 1984.

Bourdieu, Pierre. "The Forms of Capital." In *Handbook of Theory and Research for the Sociology of Education*, edited by John Richardson, 241–58. New York: Greenwood, 1986.

Bourriaud, Nicolas. *Relational Aesthetics.* Dijon, France: Les Presses du réel, 2002.

Brouillette, Sarah. "Creative Labor." *Mediations* 24, no. 2 (2009): 140–49.

Brouwer, R. "Het Nieuwe Rotterdam: De Kunst, Het Beleid, de Zorg en de Markt, Vrijetijd en Samenleving." *Vrijetijd en Samenleving* 11 (1993): 31–43.

Bryan-Wilson, Julia. *Art Workers: Radical Practice in the Vietnam War Era.* Berkeley: University of California Press, 2011.

Buchloh, Benjamin H. D. *Neo-Avantgarde and Culture Industry.* Cambridge, MA: MIT Press, 2000.

Buchloh, Benjamin H. D., and Jean-Hubert Martin. "Interview." *Third Text* 3, no. 6 (Spring 1989): 19–27.

Bürger, Peter. *Theory of the Avant-Garde.* Minneapolis: University of Minnesota Press, 1984.

Burnham, Clint. "Tadej Pogačar's Persistent Perversion of Institutional Critique." *MOMUS*, December 15, 2014.

Cabrera Infante, Alberto, and Orlando Jiménez Leal, dirs. *P.M.* Havana: Instituto Cubano del Arte e Industrias Cinematográficos, 1961.

Cachia, Amanda. *Curating Access: Disability Art Activism and Creative Accommodation.* London: Routledge, 2023.

Calhoun, Craig. "The Class Consciousness of Frequent Travelers: Toward a Critique of Actually Existing Cosmopolitanism." *South Atlantic Quarterly* 101, no. 4 (Fall 2002): 869–97.

Calhoun, Craig. "Cosmopolitanism and Nationalism." *Nations and Nationalism* 14, no. 3 (July 2008): 427–48.

Călinescu, Matei. *The Five Faces of Modernity: Modernism, Avant-Garde, Decadence, Kitsch, Postmodernism.* Durham, NC: Duke University Press, 1987.

Camnitzer, Luis. "ALPHABETIZATION, Part I: Protocol and Proficiency." *e-flux*, no. 9 (October 2009). www.e-flux.com/journal/09/61367/alphabetization-part-i-protocol-and-proficiency.

Camnitzer, Luis. "Art and Literacy." *e-flux*, no. 3 (February 2009). www.e-flux.com/journal/03/68519/art-and-literacy.

Camnitzer, Luis. "La segunda Bienal de La Habana." *Arte en Colombia* 33 (May 1987): 79–85.

Carmona, Marisa. *Planning through Projects: Moving from Master Planning to Strategic Planning; 30 Cities.* Amsterdam: Techne, 2009.

Carroll, Amy Sara. *REMEX: Toward an Art History of the NAFTA Era.* Austin: University of Texas Press, 2018.

Carroll, Noël. "Art and Globalization: Then and Now." In "Global Theories of the Arts and Aesthetics," special issue, *Journal of Aesthetics and Art Criticism* 65, no. 1 (Winter 2007): 131–43.

Checa-Gismero, Paloma. "A Collective Fabric on a Cane Loom: A Weaving Workshop by Marta Palau in the 1986 Bienal de La Habana." *Journal of Modern Craft* 15, no. 3 (2022): 275–92.

Checa-Gismero, Paloma. "Global Contemporary Art Tourism: Engaging with Cuban Authenticity through the Bienal de La Habana." *Tourism and Development Journal* 15, no. 3 (2017): 313–28.

Checkel, Jeffrey T., and Peter J. Katzenstein. *European Identity.* Cambridge: Cambridge University Press, 2009.

Christov-Bakargiev, Carolyn. "The Biennale Syndrome." *Janus* 8, no. 22 (June–December 2007).

Clifford, James. "Histories of the Tribal and the Modern." *Art in America,* April 1986, 164–215.

Clifford, James. "Museums as Contact Zones." In *Routes: Travel and Translation in the Late Twentieth Century,* 188–218. Cambridge, MA: Harvard University Press, 1997.

Coates, Rebecca. "From the Margins to the Center: The São Paulo Biennial, the Biennale of Sydney, and the Istanbul Biennial." *Museum Worlds: Advances in Research* 2, no. 1 (2014): 113–32.

Coffey, Mary. *How a Revolutionary Art Became Official Culture: Murals, Museums, and the Mexican State.* Durham, NC: Duke University Press, 2012.

Cohen-Solal, Annie. *Magiciens de la terre: Retour sur une exposition légendaire.* Paris: Éditions Xavier Barral, Centre Pompidou, 2014.

Coll, Kathleen, Evelina Dagnino, and Catherine Neveu. *Disputing Citizenship.* Bristol, UK: Policy Press, University of Bristol, 2014.

Collier, Delinda. *Repainting the Walls of Lunda.* Minneapolis: University of Minnesota Press, 2016.

"Conclusiones de un debate entre cineastas cubanos." *La Gaceta de Cuba* 2, no. 23, August 3, 1963.

Cordero Reiman, Karen. "Mexico: Corporeal Apparitions / Beyond Appearances." In *Radical Women: Latin American Art, 1960–1985,* edited by Andrea Giunta and Cecilia Fajardo-Hill, 271–77. Los Angeles: Hammer Museum, 2017.

Córdoba Azcárate, Matilde. *Stuck with Tourism: Space, Power, and Labor in Contemporary Yucatan.* Oakland: University of California Press, 2020.

Costa, Carlos. "Culture as a Driving Force for Europe 2002." In *Culture: Building Stone for Europe 2002; Reflections and Perspectives*, edited by Leonce Bekemans, 105–10. Bruges, Belgium: European Interuniversity Press, 2001.

Craven, David. *Art and Revolution in Latin America, 1910–1990*. New Haven, CT: Yale University Press, 2006.

Craven, David. "Art in Contemporary Nicaragua." *Oxford Art Journal* 11, no. 1 (1988): 51–63.

Čufer, Eda. *Transnacionala: Highway Collisions between East and West at the Crossroads of Art*. Ljubljana, Slovenia: KODA, 1999.

"Cultura Popular Mestiza." In *Cuarta Bienal de La Habana, 1991: Desafío a la Colonización*, 186–88. Havana: Centro de Arte Contemporáneo Wifredo Lam, 1991.

Davis, Mike, Kelly Mayhew, and Jim Miller. *Under the Perfect Sun: The San Diego Tourists Never See*. New York: New Press, 2003.

Debroise, Olivier. "By the Night Tide / inSITE94: The Archipelago." In *inSITE94: A Binational Exhibition of Installation and Site-Specific Art*, 14–33. San Diego: Installation Gallery, 1994.

Debroise, Olivier. "Museums in Mexico: Between Autonomy and Dependence." Excerpt from presentation at Getty Foundation, Los Angeles, 1994.

Debroise, Olivier, and Cuauhtémoc Medina. *La era de la discrepancia: Arte y cultura visual en México, 1968–1997*. Mexico City: Museo Arte Contemporáneo (MUAC) and Universidad Nacional Autónoma de México (UNAM), 2007.

DeChaine, D. Robert. "Bordering the Civic Imaginary: Alienization, Fence Logic, and the Minuteman Civil Defense Corps." *Quarterly Journal of Speech* 95, no. 1 (February 2009): 43–65.

De Duve, Thierry. "The Glocal and the Singuniversalae: Reflections on Art and Culture in the Global World." *Third Text* 21, no. 6 (2007): 681–88.

Degot, Ekaterina. "The Revenge of the Background." In *Primary Documents: A Sourcebook for Eastern and Central European Art since the 1950s*, edited by Hoptman Pospiszyl, 340–44. Cambridge, MA: MIT Press, 2002.

de la Fuente, Alejandro. *Grupo Antillano: The Art of Afro-Cuba*. Pittsburgh: University of Pittsburgh Press, 2013.

Demos, T. J. *Return to the Postcolony: Specters of Colonialism in Contemporary Art*. Berlin: Sternberg, 2013.

Di Maggio, Nelson. Interview with Nelson Herrera Ysla. "La revolución en esencia no se cuestiona." *La república* (Montevideo, Uruguay), July 23, 1990, 22.

Dimitrakaki, Angela. "Art, Globalization, and the Exhibition Form." *Third Text* 26, no. 3 (2012): 305–19.

"Downtown Arts Rising." *San Diego Home/Garden*, October 1993.

Eder, Rita. *Helen Escobedo*. Mexico City: Universidad Nacional Autónoma de México (UNAM), 1982.

Eiblmayr, Silvia. *Zones of Disturbance*. Graz, Austria: Steirischer Herbst, 1997.

Eilat, Galit, Nuria Enguita Mayo, Charles Esche, Pablo Lafuente, Luiza Proença, Oren Sagiv, and Benjamin Seroussi. *Making Biennials in Contemporary Times: Essays from the World Biennial Forum 2, São Paulo, 2014*. Amsterdam: Biennial Foundation, 2015.

Elkins, James. "Leading Terms: Master Narrative, Western, Central, Peripheral, North Atlantic." In *The End of Diversity in Art Historical Writing: North Atlantic Art History and Its Alternatives*, 39–62. Boston: De Gruyter, 2021.

Erjavec, Aleš. "Introduction." In *Aesthetic Revolutions and the Twentieth-Century Avant-Garde Movements*, 1–18. Durham, NC: Duke University Press, 2015.

Escobar, Ticio. *El mito del arte y el mito del pueblo*. Asunción, Paraguay: RP Ediciones, Museo del Barro, 1986.

Feldman, Hannah. *From a Nation Torn: Decolonizing Art and Representation in France, 1946–1962*. Durham, NC: Duke University Press, 2014.

Ferguson, Bruce W., Reesa Greenberg, and Sandy Nairne. *Thinking about Exhibitions*. London: Routledge, 1996.

Fernandes, Sujatha. *Cuba Represent! Cuban Arts, State Power, and the Making of New Revolutionary Cultures*. Durham, NC: Duke University Press, 2008.

Field Belenky, Mary. *Women's Ways of Knowing: The Development of Self, Voice, and Mind*. New York: Basic, 1986.

Fiesta de la imagen (I Bienal de La Habana). Paris: Rogelio, 1984. Instituto Cubano del Arte e Industria Cinematográficos, documentary film.

Filipovic, Elena. "The Global White Cube." In *The Manifesta Decade: Debates on Contemporary Art Exhibitions and Biennials in Post-Wall Europe*, edited by Barbara Vanderlinden and Elena Filipovic, 63–84. Cambridge, MA: MIT Press, 2005.

Filipovic, Elena, Marieke van Hal, and Solveig Øvstebø. *The Biennial Reader: An Anthology on Large-Scale Perennial Exhibitions of Contemporary Art*. Bergen, Norway: Hatje Cantz Verlag, 2010.

Flores, Tatiana. "'Latinidad Is Canceled': Confronting an Anti-Black Construct." *Latin American and Latinx Visual Culture* 3, no. 3 (July 2021): 58–79.

Flores, Tatiana. *Mexico's Revolutionary Avant-Gardes: From Estridentismo to ¡30–30!* New Haven, CT: Yale University Press, 2013.

Florida, Richard. "Mapping the Diversity of the Creative Class." *Bloomberg City Lab*, May 11, 2017. www.bloomberg.com/news/articles/2017-05-11/mapping -creative-class-diversity.

Florida, Richard. "The Rise of the Creative Class." Keynote presentation at San Diego's Forum on the Future, August 25, 2003. Video of presentation, 59 min., www.uctv.tv/shows/Richard-Florida-The-Rise-of-the-Creative-Class -7714.

Florida, Richard. *The Rise of the Creative Class*. New York: Basic, 2002.

Foster, Hal. "The 'Primitive' Unconscious of Modern Art." *October*, no. 34 (Fall 1985): 45–69.

Foster, Hal. *The Return of the Real: The Avant-Garde at the End of the Century*. Cambridge, MA: MIT Press, 1996.

Fox, Claire F. *The Fence and the River: Culture and Politics at the US-Mexico Border*. Minneapolis: University of Minnesota Press, 1999.

Fox, Claire F. *Making Art Panamerican: Cultural Policy and the Cold War*. Minneapolis: University of Minnesota Press, 2013.

Fraser, Nancy. "Democracy's Crisis: On the Political Contradictions of Financialized Capitalism." Samuel L. and Elizabeth Jodidi Lecture, Weatherhead Center for International Affairs, Harvard University, November 5, 2018.

Fraser, Nancy. "Rethinking the Public Sphere: A Contribution to the Critique of Actually Existing Democracy." *Social Text*, nos. 25–26 (1990): 56–80.

Fried, Michael. "Art and Objecthood." *Artforum* 5, no. 10 (Summer 1967).

Fukuyama, Francis. *The End of History and the Last Man*. London: Free Press, 1992.

Galliera, Izabel. *Socially Engaged Art after Socialism: Art and Civil Society in Central and Eastern Europe*. New York: Taurus, 2017.

Ganster, Paul, and Lili Buj. "Percepciones de la migración Mexicana en el Condado de San Diego." *Revista Mexicana de Sociología* 53, no. 3 (1991): 259–89.

García Buchaca, Edith. "Consideraciones sobre un Manifiesto." *La Gaceta de Cuba*, October 18, 1963.

Gardner, Anthony, and Charles Green. "Biennials of the South on the Edges of the Global." *Third Text* 27, no. 4 (2013): 442–55.

Garrido Gómez, Martín. "Tradición y contemporaneidad en Roberto Feleo." *Juventud rebelde*, November 30, 1989.

Geertz, Clifford. "Common Sense as a Cultural System." *Antioch Review* 33, no. 1 (Spring 1975): 5–26.

Gellner, Ernest. *Nations and Nationalism*. Oxford: Blackwell, 1983.

Gillick, Liam, and J. J. Charlesworth. "Is This the End of Contemporary Art as We Know It?" *Art Review*, September 29, 2020. https://artreview.com/is-this-the -end-of-contemporary-art-as-we-know-it.

Giunta, Andrea. *Avant-Garde, Internationalism, and Politics: Argentine Art in the Sixties*. Durham, NC: Duke University Press, 2007.

González, Jennifer A. "Introduction." In *Chicano and Chicana Art*, edited by Jennifer Gonzalez, C. Ondine Chavoya, Chon Noriega, and Terezita Romo, 1–10. Durham, NC: Duke University Press, 2019.

González, Jorge A. "Cultural Fronts: Towards a Dialogical Understanding of Contemporary Culture." In *Culture in the Communication Age*, edited by James Lull, 106–31. London: Taylor and Francis, 2000.

Gramsci, Antonio. *Selections from the Prison Notebooks*. New York: International, 2012.

Green, Charles, and Anthony Gardner. *Biennials, Triennials, and Documenta: The Exhibitions That Created Contemporary Art*. London: Wiley Blackwell, 2016.

Green, Jonathan, and Nicholas J. Karolides. *The Encyclopedia of Censorship*. New York: Facts on File, 2005.

Greenberg, Clement. "Recentness of Sculpture." In *American Sculpture of the Sixties*, 24–26. Los Angeles: Los Angeles County Museum of Art, 1967.

Greenberg, Clement. "Where Is the Avant-Garde?" *Vogue*, June 1967: 112–23.

Greenberg, Reesa. "The Exhibition as Discursive Event." In *Longing and Belonging: From the Faraway Nearby*, 118–25. Santa Fe, NM: Site Santa Fe, 1995.

Gropius, Walter. "Architecture at Harvard University." *Architectural Record*, March 1956, 9–11.

Gropius, Walter. *Scope of Total Architecture*. New York: Collier, 1970.

Groys, Boris. *The Total Art of Stalinism: Avant-Garde, Aesthetic Dictatorship, and Beyond*. Princeton, NJ: Princeton University Press, 1992.

Guevara, Ernesto. *The Che Guevara Reader: Writings on Guerrilla Strategy, Politics and Revolution*. Translated and edited by David Deutschmann. New York: Ocean, 1977.

Guevara, Ernesto. *La Guerra de Guerrillas*. Havana: Talleres tipográficos del I.N.R.A. Ministerio de Fuerzas Armadas (MINFAR), 1961.

Guevara, Ernesto. "El Socialismo y el Hombre en Cuba." In *Ernesto Guevara: Escritos y Discursos 8*, 253–72. Havana: Editorial de Ciencias Sociales, 1997.

Guilbaut, Serge. *How New York Stole the Idea of Modern Art*. Chicago: University of Chicago Press, 1983.

Guskov, Sergey. "Manifesta 10: A Biennial in Question." *Art21 Magazine*, May 19, 2014. http://magazine.art21.org/2014/05/19/manifesta-10-a-biennial-in -question.

Habermas, Jürgen. "The Public Sphere: An Encyclopedia Article." *New German Critique* 3, 1 (Autumn 1974): 49–55.

Habermas, Jürgen. *The Structural Transformation of the Public Sphere: An Inquiry into a Category of Bourgeois Society*. Cambridge, MA: MIT Press, 1991.

Hall, Stuart. "Marx's Notes on Method: A 'Reading' of the '1857 Introduction.'" *Cultural Studies* 17, no. 2 (2003): 113–49.

Hall, Stuart. "Whose Heritage? Un-settling 'the Heritage,' Re-imagining the Post-nation." In *The Politics of Heritage: The Legacies of Race*, edited by Jo Littler and Roshi Naidoo, 21–31. New York: Routledge, 2004.

Harris, Jonathan. *The Global Contemporary Art World*. London: Routledge, 2017.

Harris, Jonathan. *Globalization and Contemporary Art*. London: Wiley-Blackwell, 2011.

Hart, Armando. "Joseph Stalin." Translated by Ana Portela and Walter Lippman. *Socialist Viewpoint* 4, no. 5 (May–June 2005).

Harvey, David. *Cosmopolitanism and the Geographies of Freedom*. New York: Columbia University Press, 2009.

Harvey, David. "From Managerialism to Entrepreneurialism: The Transformation in Urban Governance in Late Capitalism." In "The Roots of Geographical Change: 1973 to the Present," special issue, *Geografiska Annaler: Series B. Human Geography* 71, no. 1 (1989): 3–17.

Harvey, David. *Spaces of Global Capitalism: Towards a Theory of Uneven Geographical Development*. London: Verso, 2004.

Heidegger, Martin. *Being and Time*. New York: Harper, 1962.

Herrera Ysla, Nelson. "Textil Latinoamericano." In *Tercera Bienal de La Habana, 1989*, 253. Havana: Centro de Arte Wifredo Lam, 1989.

Herzog, Lawrence. "Global Tijuana: The Seven Ecologies of the Border." In *Postborder City: Cultural Spaces of Bajalta California*, edited by Michael Dear and Gustavo Leclerc, 119–42. New York: Routledge, 2001.

Hitters, Erik, and Gregory Richards. "The Creation and Management of Cultural Clusters." *Creativity and Innovation Management* 11 (2002): 234–47.

Hix, Simon. *The Political System of the European Union*. London: Palgrave, 1999.

Hix, Simon. "The Study of the European Community: The Challenge to Comparative Politics." *West European Politics* 17, no. 1 (1994): 1–30.

Hix, Simon. "The Study of the European Union II: The 'New Governance' Agenda and Its Rival." *Journal of European Public Policy* 5, no. (1998): 38–65.

Hlavajová, Mária. "Towards the Normal: Negotiating the 'Former East.'" In *The Manifesta Decade: Debates on Contemporary Art Exhibitions and Biennials in Post-Wall Europe*, edited by Barbara Vanderlinden and Elena Filipovic, 153–66. Cambridge, MA: MIT Press, 2005.

Hobsbawm, Eric. "Introduction: Inventing Traditions." In *The Invention of Tradition*, edited by Eric Hobsbawm and Terence Ranger, 1–14. Cambridge: Cambridge University Press, 2012.

Hollander, Kurt. "Crossover Dreams." *Art in America* (May 1998): 47–50.

John, Rachel S. *Line in the Sand: A History of the U.S.-Mexico Border*. Princeton, NJ: Princeton University Press, 2011.

Johnson, Sonja H. "Thank the Lord for inSITE94." *Arts Monthly*, July 1994.

Jones, Amelia. "Ethnic Envy and Other Aggressions in the Contemporary 'Global' Art Complex." *Nka: Journal of Contemporary African Art* 48 (2021): 96–110.

Jones, Amelia. "The Revolution Is Over." Review of *Art since 1900: Modernism, Antimodernism, Postmodernism*, by Rosalind Krauss, Hal Foster, Benjamin Buchloh, and Yve Alain Bois. *Art Bulletin* 88, no. 2 (2006): 376–79.

Jones, Caroline A. "Form and Formless." In *A Companion to Contemporary Art since 1945*, edited by Amelia Jones, 127–44. Malden, MA: Blackwell, 2006.

Jones, Caroline A. *The Global Work of Art: World's Fairs, Biennials, and the Aesthetics of Experience*. Chicago: University of Chicago Press, 2017.

Jones, Caroline A. "A Longer History." In *The Biennial Reader: An Anthology on Large-Scale Perennial Exhibitions of Contemporary Art*, edited by Elena Filipovic, Marieke van Hal, Solveig Øvstebø, Bergen Kunsthall, and Hatje Cantz Verlag, 66–87. Bergen: Bergen Kunsthall / Hatje Cantz Verlag, 2010.

Jones, Caroline A. *Machine in the Studio: Constructing the Postwar American Artist*. Chicago: University of Chicago Press, 1996.

Joselit, David. *Heritage and Debt: Art in Globalization*. Cambridge, MA: MIT Press, 2020.

Kant, Immanuel. *Critique of the Power of Judgment*. Translated by Paul Guyer and Eric Matthews. Cambridge: Cambridge University Press, 2000.

Kaye, Nick. *Site-Specific Art: Performance, Place, and Documentation*. London: Routledge, 2000.

Kelley, Jeff. *The Border Art Workshop / Taller de Arte Fronterizo* (BAW/TAF: 1984–1989). San Diego: Border Art Workshop Taller de Arte Fronterizo, 1988.

Kester, Grant. *Conversation Pieces: Community and Communication in Modern Art*. 2013; Reprint. Berkeley: University of California Press, 2004.

Kester, Grant. *The One and the Many: Contemporary Collaborative Art in a Global Context*. Durham, NC: Duke University Press, 2011.

Kester, Grant. "Response to Questionnaire on 'The Contemporary.'" *October* 130 (Fall 2009): 7–9.

Kester, Grant. "The Sound of Breaking Glass Part I: Spontaneity and Consciousness in Revolutionary Theory." *e-flux*, no. 30 (December 2011). www.e-flux.com/journal/30/68167/the-sound-of-breaking-glass-part-i-spontaneity-and-consciousness-in-revolutionary-theory.

Kester, Grant. "The Sound of Breaking Glass Part II: Agonism and the Taming of Dissent." *e-flux*, no. 31 (January 2012). www.e-flux.com/journal/31/68221/the-sound-of-breaking-glass-part-ii-agonism-and-the-taming-of-dissent.

Kompatsiaris, Panos. *The Politics of Contemporary Art Biennials: Spectacles of Critique, Theory, and Art*. London: Routledge, 2017.

Kulik, Oleg, and Mila Bredikhina. "Pavlov's Dog." In *Manifesta 1: Rotterdam, the Netherlands 1996*. Rotterdam: Manifesta, 1996.

Kwon, Miwon. "One Place after Another: Notes on Site Specificity." *October* 80 (Spring 1997): 85–110.

Kwon, Miwon. *One Place after Another: Site-Specific Art and Locational Identity*. Cambridge, MA: MIT Press, 2002.

Laşan, Nicoleta. "Article 128 in the Treaty of Maastricht: Harbinger of a New European Cultural Policy?" *Public Administration and Social Policies Review* 6, no. 13 (2014).

Lauer, Mirko. *La Producción Artesanal en América Latina*. Lima: Mosca Azul, 1989.

Lazzarato, Maurizio. "Immaterial Labor." In *Radical Thought in Italy: A Potential Politics*, edited by Paolo Virno and Michael Hardt, 132–46. Minneapolis: University of Minnesota Press, 1996.

Lefebvre, Henri. *Critique of Everyday Life*. London: Verso, 2014.

Lerner, Jesse. "Borderline Architecture." *Cabinet* 13 (Spring 2004): 1–8.

Lippard, Lucy. "Anti-amnesia." In *The Lower Manhattan Sign Project*, 4–7. New York: REPOhistory, 1993.

Llanes Godoy, Llilian. "La Bienal de la Habana." *Third Text* 6, no. 20 (Autumn 1992): 5–12.

Llanes Godoy, Llilian. *Salón de Mayo de París en La Habana, Julio de 1967*. Havana: Artecubano Ediciones, Consejo Nacional Artes Plásticas, 2012.

Loick, Daniel. "The Ethical Life of Counter-Communities." *Critical Times* 4, no. 1 (April 2021): 1–28.

Maclaren Walsh, Jane. "The Dumbarton Oaks Tlazolteotl: Looking beneath the Surface." *Journal de la société des américanistes* 94, no. 1 (2008): 7–43.

Mally, Lynn. *Culture of the Future: The Proletkult Movement in Revolutionary Russia*. Berkeley: University of California Press, 1990.

Manifesta 1 Rotterdam. Rotterdam: European Art Manifestation, 1996.

"Manifesta: The Inaugural Manifesta in Rotterdam." *Frieze*, September–October, 1996.

Marchart, Oliver. *Hegemony Machines: Documenta X to Fifteen and the Politics of Biennalization*. Zurich: OnCurating, 2022.

Martin, Jean-Hubert. "Preface." In *Magiciens de la Terre: Centre Georges Pompidou, Musée national d'art moderne, La Villette, la Grande Halle*, edited by Jean-Hubert Martin and Centre Georges Pompidou, 8–11. Paris: Éditions du Georges Pompidou, 1989.

Marx, Karl. *Capital: A Critique of Political Economy*. Translated by Ben Fowkes. New York: Penguin, 1976.

Marx, Karl. *Early Writings*. London: Penguin, 1992.

Mazars, Pierre. "La peinture se meurt, la peinture est morte." *Le Figaro littéraire*, June 23, 1966, 13.

Mbembe, Achille. "Necropolitics." *Public Culture* 15, no. 1 (2003): 11–40.

McCaughan, Edward J. "'We Didn't Cross the Border, the Border Crossed Us': Artists' Images of the US-Mexico Border and Immigration." *Latin American and Latinx Visual Culture* 2, no. 1 (January 2020): 6–31.

Medina, Cuauhtémoc. "Una línea es un centro que tiene dos lados." In *inSITE94: A Binational Exhibition of Installation and Site-Specific Art*, 54–63. San Diego: Installation Gallery, 1995.

Medina, Cuauhtémoc, Russell Ferguson, and Jean Fisher. *Francis Alÿs*. London: Phaidon, 2007.

Memoria, 1988–1994, Consejo Nacional para la Cultura y las Artes. Mexico City: Dirección General de Publicaciones, 1994.

Mezzandra, Sandro, and Brett Neilson. *Border as Method, or the Multiplication of Labor*. Durham, NC: Duke University Press, 2013.

Mignolo, Walter. *Local Histories / Global Designs: Coloniality, Subaltern Knowledges, and Border Thinking*. Princeton, NJ: Princeton University Press, 2012.

Miller, Jim. "Just Another Day in Paradise? An Episodic History of Rebellion and Repression in America's Finest City." In *Under the Perfect Sun: The San Diego Tourists Never See*, edited by Mike Davis, Kelly Mayhew, and Jim Miller, 159–262. New York: New Press, 2003.

Miller, Partha. "Modern Global Art and Its Discontents." In *Decentering the Avant-Garde*, edited by Per Bäckström and Benedikt Hjartarson, 35–53. Avant-Garde Critical Studies, vol. 30. Leiden, Netherlands: Brill, 2014.

Misiano, Viktor. "Confidential Community vs. the Aesthetics of Interaction." In *East Art Map: Contemporary Art and Eastern Europe*, edited by IRWIN, 456–65. London: Afterall, 2005.

Misiano, Viktor. "The Institutionalization of Friendship." irwin-nsk.org.

Misiano, Viktor. "Interpol: The Apology of Defeat." *Moscow Art Magazine*. http:// moscowartmagazine.com/issue/41/article/799.

Misiano, Viktor. "Response to an Open Letter to the Art World." *SIKSI: The Nordic Art Review*, Summer 1996.

Mize, Ronald L. "Interrogating, Race, Class, Gender and Capitalism along the U.S.-Mexico Border: Neoliberal Nativism and Maquila Modes of Production." *Race, Gender and Class* 15, no. 1/2 (2008): 134–55.

Monsiváis, Carlos. *La cultura de la frontera*. Mexico City: Instituto Nacional de Antropología, 1975.

Montero Fayad, Daniel. *El cubo de Rubik, arte mexicano en los años 90*. Mexico City: Fundación JUMEX, 2013.

Montgomery, Harper. *The Mobility of Modernism: Art and Criticism in 1920s Latin America*. Austin: University of Texas Press, 2017.

Mosquera, Gerardo. *El diseño se generó en octubre*. Havana: Editorial Arte y Literatura, 1989.

Mosquera, Gerardo. "Raíces en acción." *Revolución y Cultura* (February 1988): 32–39.

Muchnic, Suzanne. "Unmasking Mexico's Many Faces: 'Splendors of Thirty Centuries' Arrives in L.A. Next Week; Not Just an Art Show, the Exhibit Is a National Search for Identity." *Los Angeles Times*, September 29, 1991.

Nelson, Adele. *Forming Abstraction: Art and Institutions in Postwar Brazil*. Oakland: University of California Press, 2022.

Nelson Limerick, Patricia. *The Legacy of the Conquest*. New York: Norton, 1987.

Niemojewski, Rafal. *Biennials: The Exhibitions We Love to Hate*. London: Lund Humphries, 2021.

Noriyuki, Duane. "Age of Unarius: El Cajon Group Believes UFOs Are Coming to Them in 2001." *Los Angeles Times*, April 7, 1997. www.latimes.com/archives/la-xpm-1997-04-07-mn-46356-story.html.

Novak, Benjamin, and Marc Santora. "University Backed by George Soros Prepares to Leave Budapest under Duress." *New York Times*, October 25, 2018. www.nytimes.com/2018/10/25/world/europe/hungary-central-european-university-george-soros.html.

Okeke-Agulu, Chika. "Response to 'Questionnaire on the Contemporary.'" *October* 130 (Fall 2009): 44–45.

Ollman, Leah. "'IN/SITE 92' a Comeback for Installation Art: Installation Gallery Makes a New Showing with an Innovative, Multigallery Exhibit Concept." *Los Angeles Times*, September 5, 1992. www.latimes.com/archives/la-xpm-1992-09-05-ca-5612-story.html.

O'Neill, Paul. "The Curatorial Turn: From Practice to Discourse." In *Issues of Curating in Contemporary Art and Performance*, edited by Judith Rugg and Michèle Sedgewick, 13–28. Bristol: Intellect, 2011.

Opinions littéraires, philosophiques et industrielles. Paris: Bossange père, 1825.

Osborne, Peter. *Anywhere or Not at All: Philosophy of Contemporary Art*. New York: Verso, 2013.

Oude Engberink, Gerard, and Frank Miedema. "Governing Urban Regeneration: The Case of Rotterdam." *Geographische Zeitschrift* 2–3, no. 89 (2001): 114–24.

Pagel, David. "ART: A World of Differences; In Presenting Work from 50 Countries, the 'Fourth Biennial of Havana' Proposes That Art Cannot Be Judged by Western Criteria." *Los Angeles Times*, January 12, 1992.

Palau, Marta, and José Luis Barrios. "Dear Marta." In *Marta Palau: naualli*, 213–33. Mexico City: Turner, 2006.

Pejić, Bojana. "The Dialectics of Normality." In *After the Wall: Art and Culture in Post-Communist Europe*, edited by Bojana Pejić and David Elliot, 17–27. Stockholm: Moderna Museet, 1999.

Pejić, Bojana, and David Elliot, eds. *After the Wall: Art and Culture in Post-Communist Europe*. Stockholm: Moderna Museet, 1999.

Pierre, Arnauld. "The Instability of Kinetic Environments." In *The "Do-It-Yourself" Artwork: Participation from Fluxus to New Media*, edited by Anna Dezeuze, 91–114. Manchester: Manchester University Press, 2010.

Piotrowski, Piotr. "Central Europe in the Face of Unification." In *Who if Not We Should at Least Try to Imagine the Future of All This?*, edited by Mária Hlavajová and Jill Winder. Amsterdam: Artimo, 2004.

Plante, Isabel. "Kinetic Multiples: Between Industrial Vocation and Handcrafted Solutions." In *Keep It Moving? Conserving Kinetic Art*, edited by Rachel Rivenc and Reinhart Bek, 104–12. Los Angeles: Getty, 2018.

Pogolotti, Graziella. *Polémicas culturales de los 60*. Havana: Letras Cubanas, 2006.

Povey, John. "Segunda Bienal de La Habana." *African Arts* 20, no. 3 (May 1987): 82–84.

Pratt, Mary Louise. *Imperial Eyes: Travel and Transculturation*. London: Routledge, 1992.

"Questionnaire on 'The Contemporary.'" *October* 130 (Fall 2009): 3–124.

Ravelo Blancas, Patricia. "Protagonismo y poder: Sindicato de Costureras 19 de Septiembre." *Nueva Antropología* 15, no. 49 (1996): 9–30.

Ricci, Clarissa. *Starting from Venice: Studies on the Biennale*. Milan: Et Al, 2010.

Richards, Gregory. *Cultural Tourism in Europe*. Wallingford: CAB International, 1996.

Richards, Gregory, and Julie Wilson. "The Impact of Cultural Events on City Image: Rotterdam, Cultural Capital of Europe 2001." *Urban Studies* 41, no. 10 (2004): 1931–51.

Ring Petersen, Anne. *Migration into Art: Transcultural Identities and Art-Making in a Globalised World*. Manchester: Manchester University Press, 2017.

Robinson, William. "Global Capitalism Theory and the Emergence of Transnational Elites." *Critical Sociology* 38, no. 3 (2012): 349–63.

Rojas-Sotelo, Miguel Leonardo. "Cultural Maps, Networks and Flows: The History and Impact of the Havana Biennale 1984 to the Present." PhD diss., University of Pittsburgh, 2009.

Romero Fernández, Edgar. "La Rectificación de errores en Cuba: Causas e impronta a los 60 años de la Revolución Cubana." *ISLAS* 61, no. 193 (2019): 178–95.

Romero Sotelo, María Eugenia. *Los orígenes del neoliberalismo en México*. Mexico City: Fondo de Cultura Económica, 2016.

Salkowitz-Montoya, Lezlie, and Malaquías Montoya. "A Critical Perspective on the State of Chicano Art." *Metamorfosis*, 3, no. 1 (Spring-Summer 1980): 3–7.

Sánchez, Héctor Antonio. "SEMEFO: La hermosura de cuanto es mortal." *Casa del Tiempo* 5 (2012).

Sánchez Luján, Guilbert. "El Arte del Chicano: 'The Spirit of the Experience.'" *Con/Safos* 7 (1971): 11.

Sánchez Vázquez, Adolfo. *Las ideas estéticas de Marx*. Mexico City: Siglo XXI, 2005.

Sánchez Vázquez, Adolfo. *Invitación a la estética*. Mexico City: Grijalbo, 1992.

Sandell, Richard, Jocelyn Dodd, and Rosemarie Garland-Thomson. *Re-Presenting Disability: Activism and Agency in the Museum*. London: Routledge, 2010.

Sassatelli, Monica. "The Arts, the State, and the EU: Cultural Policy in the Making of Europe." *Social Analysis: The International Journal of Social and Cultural Practice* 51, no. 1 (2007): 28–41.

Schwartz, Ineke. "Manifesta 1." *Metropolis M*, August–September, 1996.

Sekula, Allan. "Between the Net and the Deep Blue Sea (Rethinking the Traffic in Photographs)." *October* 102 (Autumn 2002): 3–34.

Shanks, Rosalie. "The I.W.W. Free Speech Movement: San Diego, 1912." *Journal of San Diego History* 19, no. 1 (1973): 25–33.

Sheren, Ila Nicole. *Portable Borders: Performance Art and Politics in the U.S. Frontera since 1984.* Austin: University of Texas Press, 2015.

Smith, Terry. *Art to Come: Histories of Contemporary Art.* Durham, NC: Duke University Press, 2019.

Smith, Terry. "Biennials: Four Fundamentals, Many Variations." Biennial Foundation, December 2016, www.biennialfoundation.org/2016/12/biennials-four -fundamentals-many-variations.

Smith, Terry. *Thinking Contemporary Curating.* New York: Independent Curators International, 2012.

Sparrow, Glen. "San Diego–Tijuana: Not Quite a Binational City or Region." *Geo-Journal* 54, no. 1 (2001): 73–83.

Spieker, Sven. "SubREAL during the 1990s: Ironic Monuments, Tainted Blood, and Vampiric Realism in a Time of Transition." *ArtMargins Online*, July 10, 2013. https://artmargins.com/subreal-vampire-realism/.

Spivak, Gayatri Chakravorty. *A Critique of Postcolonial Reason: Towards a History of the Vanishing Present.* Cambridge, MA: Harvard University Press, 1996.

Spivak, Gayatri Chakravorty. "Resistance That Cannot Be Recognized as Such." In *Conversations with Gayatri Chakravorty Spivak*, edited by C. Swapan, S. Milevska, and T. E. Barlow, 57–86. Greenford, UK: Seagull, 2006.

Steeds, Lucy. "*Magiciens de la Terre* and the Development of Transnational Project-Based Curating." In *Making Art Global (Part 2): Les Magiciens de La Terre, 1989*, edited by Lucy Steeds, 23–93. London: Afterall, 2013.

Stegeman, Elly. "Manifesta 1." *Metropolis M*, August–September 1996.

Tercera Bienal de La Habana, 1989. Havana: Centro de Arte Wifredo Lam, 1989.

"Toiling Redskins Glad to Labor on Structures in 'Painted Desert.'" *San Diego Union*, May 8, 1914.

Tomlinson, B. R. "What Was the Third World?" *Journal of Contemporary History* 38, no. 2 (2003): 307–21.

Treaty on European Union, February 7, 1992. Luxembourg Office for Official Publications of the European Communities.

Turegano, Preston. "Binational Festival Celebrates the Art of Collaboration." *San Diego Union Tribune*, September 22–28, 1994.

Vega Briones, Germán. "Población Commuter de La Frontera Norte: El Caso de Mexicali-Calexico y Tijuana–San Diego." *Estudios Demográficos y Urbanos* 31, no. 1 (2017): 207–38.

Wallerstein, Immanuel. "The Construction of Peoplehood: Racism, Nationalism, Ethnicity." In *Race, Nation, and Class: Ambiguous Identities*, edited by Étienne Balibar and Immanuel Wallerstein, 71–85. London: Verso, 1991.

Wang, Nina. "Rethinking Authenticity in the Museum Experience." *Annals of Tourism Research* 26, no. 2 (April 1999): 349–70.

Weiss, Rachel. *Making Art Global (Part 1): The Third Havana Biennial, 1989.* London: Afterall, 2011.

Weiss, Rachel. "To Defend the Revolution Is to Defend Culture—but, Which Version?" *Art Margins* 6, no. 1 (2017): 64–82.

Wolff, Larry. *Inventing Eastern Europe: The Map of Civilization in the Mind of the Enlightenment.* Stanford, CA: Stanford University Press, 1994.

Wu, Chin-Tao. "Biennials without Borders." *New Left Review* 57 (May–June 2009): 107–15.

Yard, Sally. *inSITE94.* San Diego: Installation Gallery, 1994.

Yard, Sally. "Tagged Turf in the Public Sphere." In *inSITE94: A Binational Exhibition of Installation and Site-Specific Art,* 34–53. San Diego: Installation Gallery, 1995.

Yúdice, George. *The Expediency of Culture: Uses of Culture in the Global Era.* Durham, NC: Duke University Press, 2003.

Zabel, Igor. "Dialogue East–West: East Is East?" *Art Press* 226, July–August 1997: 37–42.

Zahm, Olivier et al. "An Open Letter to the Art World." *Third Text* 10, no. 34 (1996): 108–9.

Zukin, Sharon. *Loft Living.* New Brunswick: Rutgers University Press, 1989.

art industry, 6, 24, 164, 250, 262n14; biennial conversions and, 241; Border art and, 144; early-boom biennials and, 18, 199; global contemporary art and, 193; globalization of, 25, 71, 139, 249, 263n22; Mexican arts and, 169; trends of, 17
artisanship, 42, 73, 77
artistic innovation, 2, 76, 187
art objects, 8, 10, 14–16, 47, 56, 148, 187, 224
art publics, 9, 101, 192
Asia, 57, 247; artists from, 35; Bienal de La Habana and, 51, 59, 70, 258n10; biennials and, 5, 253n1; Southeast, 34, 72; Southern, 59
audience engagement, 8, 46, 72
authenticity, 10, 65, 147, 161, 253n3; cultural, 90, 110; local, 11, 139; pastiche, 120
autonomy, 179; artistic, 20, 44–45, 162, 209, 211–13, 244; of artist-run spaces, 154; Baja California and, 124, 153; Bienal de La Habana and, 43, 58, 70–71; of Cuban artists, 44–46; of Cuban experts, 53, 57; culture and, 228; of expertise, 57, 136; Manifesta and, 191; spaces of, 31
Avalos, David, 109, 121
avant-garde art, 22; Castro and, 43–44; emancipatory practices of, 246; Lam and, 35; North Atlantic, 94; Third World, 77
avant-gardes, 7, 43, 55, 162, 211–13, 271n6; anticolonial, 249; Castro and, 262n10; Central and Eastern European, 201, 208; Latin American, 31, 70; Mexican, 78, 87, 150, 154, 156–57, 159–60; nationalization of, 155; turn-of-the-century, 244. *See also* neo-avant-gardes; Third World avant-garde

BAD Foundation, 219, 233, 237, 239–40, 282n28; *My House: Your Home*, 233–36
Bakhtin, Mikhail, 237, 259n14
Balibar, Étienne, 17, 182–83
Bauhaus, 76, 157
beauty, 72, 81, 83–84, 88, 93, 251; craft and, 74; judgment of, 77, 249

Belgium, 181, 195–96, 274n2, 275n7, 277n44
belonging, 104, 142, 174, 176; community, 19, 136; myths of, 24, 182
Bennett, Tony, 17, 178. *See also* exhibitionary complex
Benson, Michael, 202, 203*f*
Berelowitz, Jo-Anne, 105, 269n33
Berlin, 15, 283n7; East, 39
Berlin Wall (fall of), 3, 174, 186, 192, 200
Beuys, Joseph, 93, 266n18
Bienal de La Habana, 1–2, 9, 12, 16–17, 22–24, 29–32, 34–43, 46–78, 81, 84–85, 87–93, 127, 157, 196, 199, 224, 243, 245, 249–50, 253n1, 257n44, 258nn9–10; especialistas of, 31, 34–35, 37, 43, 52–63, 70, 72, 77, 81, 84, 89–90, 92; organizers of, 12, 37, 51, 61, 66, 255n15. *See also* curators; Havana
Bienal de São Paulo, 1, 14, 253n1, 256n21
Biennale de la Méditerranée, 14, 70–71, 253n1
Biennale de Paris (Paris Biennial), 15, 38, 187, 253n1
Biennale Grafike, 14, 71, 253n1
biennial conversions, 5–7, 9–11, 23–25, 183, 193, 241, 244–46, 249; at inSITE, 103, 107, 122, 149–50, 163, 169; at Manifesta, 196, 200, 216
Birnbaum, Daniel, 205, 218, 222
Bishop, Claire, 200, 212–13, 238
Block, René, 176, 274n2
Bolivia, 73, 262n13, 263n15
Boltanski, Luc, 10, 223
Border art, 6, 108–10, 117–18, 127, 242, 245; aesthetic conversions and, 22; inSITE and, 12, 24, 110–11, 114, 118, 122, 136–37, 144, 150, 169. *See also* Chicano art
Border Art Workshop/Taller de Arte Fronterizo (BAW/TAF), 4, 109–10, 115–16, 121; *ESL: Tonguetied/Lenguatrabada*, 115*f*, 116–17
borders, 104, 110; Europe without, 183; geopolitical, 197; of liberalism, 2, 4, 10, 17, 20, 22, 24, 26, 243; porosity of, 104, 106. *See also* United States–Mexico border(lands)
Bourdieu, Pierre, 136, 256n31, 265n7, 270n15

contemporary art (continued)
Mexican, 24, 60, 150, 152–53, 266n18;
North Atlantic, 207; Open Society
Foundation and, 190; pan-European,
10; Philip Morris and, 191; production, 9, 12, 94, 151, 206, 241; trends in,
198; worlds, 4, 21, 186, 245. *See also*
global contemporary art
cooperation, 174, 188; Bienal de La Habana and, 62, 70, 86; cultural, 128, 173,
178, 262n11, 275n12; international, 145,
177; NAFTA and, 129; networks of, 35,
258n10; relations of, 55
cosmopolitanism, 19, 100, 138; avant-
garde and, 154; fabricated, 51; global,
9, 245; Marxist, 82
cosmopolitans, 6, 18–19, 23, 135
craft, 22, 24, 73–74, 79, 92; Bienal de
La Habana and, 81, 85–86, 88, 90;
Mosquera on, 84–85, 87; Third World
art and, 77
crafts, 42, 73, 76–77, 85, 90, 93
Craven, David, 155, 272n21
critics, 59–60, 68, 70, 94, 244, 248, 250;
aesthetic conversions and, 8; Bienal
de La Habana and, 258n10; Cuban, 31,
65, 261n39; dialogical aesthetics and,
255n16; discursive labor of, 10; on
Habermas, 215; inSITE and, 137, 144;
Kulik and, 205; Latin American, 65,
260n26; Manifesta and, 188, 195–96,
219, 228; Mexican, 151, 164; modernist,
47; textile art and, 75
Cruzvillegas, Abraham, 164–65, 169,
273n34; *The Grass Is Greener/El pasto
es más verde*, 166–63
Cuba, 36, 67, 243, 260n29, 262n13, 263n15,
265n17; artistic exchanges between
Europe and, 262n10; artistic scenes
in, 159; avant-garde art in, 43–44, 55;
Brigadas José Martí, 49, 63; Columbus's arrival in, 88; cultural policies
in, 261n39; culture and revolutionary
consciousness in, 35, 45; geopolitical
developments outside, 31; foreign
visitors to, 33; Instituto Cubano de
las Artes e Industrias Cinematográficas (ICAIC), 31, 34, 43, 46, 71, 257n3;

Museo Nacional de Bellas Artes, 39,
63, 77, 90; nonorthodox Marxism in,
52, 54, 209; quinqenio gris in, 31–32,
44; relations of production in, 79;
Special Period in Times of Peace, 35,
61–62, 66, 71, 249, 258n12, 263n22,
264n40; Third World and, 40, 51;
threats to, 50; tourism in, 65; US
embargo on, 36, 58, 61–63, 258n12,
262n11, 263n22; visual arts in, 258n10.
See also Casa de las Américas; Castro,
Fidel; foquismo; Guevara, Ernesto;
Santamaría, Haydée
Cuban Communist Party (CCP),
32, 262n11
Cuban Ministry of Culture, 32, 58–59, 61,
71, 74. *See also* Hart, Armando
Cuban Revolution, 11, 33–34, 36, 42, 82
Cuban state, 12, 33, 51, 55, 78
Čufer, Eda, 202, 203*f*
curation, 16, 26, 69–70, 114, 193, 244
curatorial practice, 15–16, 19, 187, 199,
243–44; Bienal de La Habana and,
31, 34; biennial, 22, 25, 102, 244;
independent, 197; Misiano's, 204;
revolutionary, 261n3
curators, 11, 13, 92, 129, 137, 140, 160,
197–200, 211, 216, 222, 244, 246, 248,
250–51; aesthetic conversion and,
7–8, 10; of Bienal de La Habana, 31,
34, 40, 42, 52, 56, 58–59, 65, 71–72,
196 (*see also* Herrera Isla, Nélson;
Mosquera, Gerardo; Noceda, Manuel;
Sánchez, Margarita); Border art
and, 109; expertise of, 21; of inSITE,
111–13, 124, 144 (*see also* Debroise,
Olivier; Yard, Sally); of *Interpol*, 204;
of *Magiciens de la Terre*, 93; of Manifesta, 175, 178, 183, 185–86, 189–91,
194–96, 199, 202, 204, 228, 250, 277n32
(*see also* Martínez, Rosa; Misiano,
Viktor; Néray, Katalin; Obrist, Hans
Ulrich; Renton, Andrew); MCASD, 110;
Mexican, 151, 164; Soros Centers for
Contemporary Art and, 275n2

Dan, Călin, 179–81, 233. *See also* subREAL
Debroise, Olivier, 113, 141, 154, 162, 166